European Yearbook of International Economic Law

More information about this series at http://www.springer.com/series/8165

Marc Bungenberg • Michael Hahn
Christoph Herrmann • Till Müller-Ibold
Editors

The Future of Trade Defence Instruments

Global Policy Trends and Legal Challenges

Editors
Marc Bungenberg
Faculty of Law
Saarland University
Saarbrücken, Germany

Christoph Herrmann
University of Passau
Passau, Germany

Michael Hahn
Institute of European and International
Economic Law
University of Bern
Bern, Switzerland

Till Müller-Ibold
Cleary Gottlieb Steen & Hamilton LLP
Brussels, Belgium

ISSN 2364-8392   ISSN 2364-8406   (electronic)
European Yearbook of International Economic Law
Special Issue
ISBN 978-3-319-95305-2   ISBN 978-3-319-95306-9   (eBook)
https://doi.org/10.1007/978-3-319-95306-9

Library of Congress Control Number: 2018957993

This Springer imprint is published by the registered company Springer Nature Switzerland AG
The registered company address is: Gewerbestrasse 11, 6330 Cham, Switzerland

Editorial

This *EYIEL Special Issue* is devoted to Trade Defence Instruments (TDIs). On 30–31 March 2017, the University of Passau, the Europa-Institut of Saarland University, the Institute of European and International Economic Law and the World Trade Institute of the University of Bern and Cleary Gottlieb Steen & Hamilton LLP jointly organised a conference in Brussels, which was entitled: "The Future of Trade Defence Instruments: Global Policy Trends and Legal Challenges". The event dealt with the most topical issues in the field of trade defence law, notably the expiry of the transitional provisions in China's Accession Protocol to the World Trade Organization (WTO) and its implications for the legal modifications of the European Union's Trade Defence Instruments. To that extent, this *EYIEL Special Issue* does not only contain papers following the presentations made at the conference, but also specially commissioned chapters with a view to providing a more comprehensive overview of the state of play of trade defence law.

Trade Defence Instruments, or Trade Remedies, are first analysed in their legal and political context. Then, the EU rules as they exist today, 8 years after the entry into force of the Lisbon Treaty and after their first thorough modification since the Uruguay Round of the WTO, are analysed and described in the changing international environment, in particular as regards the WTO legal framework. In addition, the European Union (EU) Trade Defence Instruments are compared with other jurisdictions with a view to outlining a national approach towards trade defence as well as competition law or inter alia regional trade agreements. In this context, the implications for the future relationship with the United Kingdom (UK) after Brexit will also be analysed. In doing so, this *EYIEL Special Issue* seeks to provide an up-to-date overview of the state of play of trade defence in the EU and in the world.

The volume is opened by *Michael Hahn's* introduction to "[t]he Multilateral and EU Legal Framework on TDIs", which addresses the EU as well as the WTO legal system on trade defence. The current uncertainties surrounding China in the WTO, the stance of the United States (U.S.) towards the WTO under President Trump and the composition of the Appellate Body lead the author to call the WTO trade regime "a system in crisis". *Brian Petter* and *Reinhard Quick* outline "[t]he Politics of TDI and the Different Views in EU Member States", questioning whether the reform

process evolves as a "[n]ecessary Safety-Valve or Luxurious Rent-Seeking Device?".
In particular, the authors analyse the special case of the chemical industry in their
fight against "the rise of the dragon" China.

The second part of this volume concerns the latest legislative reforms in the field
of trade defence. *Wolfgang Müller* sheds light on the Commission's perspective of
the TDI reform process at the European Union level. In "[t]he EU's New Trade
Defence Laws: A Two Steps Approach", both the new methodology for the calculation of normal value in case of distortions in the exporting country and the modernisation package of the Union's trade defence instruments are described from
within.

Edwin Vermulst's and *Juhi Dion Sud's* contribution concerns "[t]he New Rules
Adopted by the European Union to Address 'Significant Distortions' in the Anti-
Dumping Context". It indicates how the market economy criteria have been dis-
guised as the significant distortions rules. In addition, they discuss and question the
WTO law compatibility of the EU's reformed trade defence rules, inter alia with
regard to a removal of the lesser duty rule. In a similar vein, *Christian Tietje* and
Vinzenz Sacher analyse the EU's reformed Trade Defence Instruments from a WTO
law perspective: "The New Anti-Dumping Methodology of the European Union: A
Breach of WTO Law?". Their contribution examines the consistency of the new
provisions with WTO law. *Dong Fang*, finally, provides a Chinese perspective on
the "[i]nterpretation of Section 15 of China's WTO Accession Protocol" in light of
the recent case "*EU – Price Comparison Methodologies* (DS516)".

Stepping away from anti-dumping law, *Sophia Müller* turns to anti-subsidy law.
In her paper "Anti-Subsidy Investigations against China: The 'Great Leap Forward'
in Reforming EU Trade Defence?", the alternative benchmark methodology, particularly the country-specific benchmarks of China, is discussed and scrutinised
against the WTO legal framework. The latest reforms, she concludes, are a missed
chance to reform properly.

Third, the EU's Trade Defence Instruments are contrasted with substantively
related legal instruments, particularly regional trade agreements and competition
law. As one of the most contentious developments in the EU, Brexit and the uncertainties surrounding the future trade relationship between the EU and the UK must,
of course, be addressed. *Anna Khalfaoui* and *Markus W. Gehring* provide a deeper
analysis of trade defence instruments and competition policy in post-Brexit times in
their paper "What Role for TDIs Between the EU and UK After Brexit: A Trade or
Competition Solution for a Future Problem?". In particular, their contribution evalu-
ates the potential of the EU-Turkey customs union as a model EU27-UK relationship with regard to TDI and competition policy. The authors conclude that this
solution leaves de facto no room for the application of trade defence instruments
between the EU27 and the UK. *Till Müller-Ibold* deals with TDI provisions in the
trade agreements of the EU and draws conclusions on their implications on Brexit
in his contribution "EU Trade Defence Instruments and Free Trade Agreements: Is
Past Experience an Indication for the Future? Implications for Brexit?".

Then, *Bruce Malashevich* and *Mark Love* focus on the United States and its trade
defence policy. "Trade Defence Instruments: The Leading Edge of U.S. Trade

Policy" outlines the relevant U.S. trade policy instruments and concludes that this existing framework can be expansively used by current Trump Administration for its more protectionist trade agenda. Conversely, *Matthias Oesch* and *Tobias Naef* note that trade defence instruments are almost never deployed in Switzerland. In "[t]rade Defence Instruments and Switzerland: The Big Sleep", the authors identify five reasons that explain the inactivity of Switzerland towards trade defence, taking particular account of the Swiss legal framework, the structure of the Swiss industry and its unique characteristics. *Yusong Chen* gives an overview of the Chinese situation in the WTO after 16 years of membership: "Anti-Dumping Laws and Implementation in China: A 16 Years Review after Accession to the WTO". The paper analyses various WTO cases involving China's anti-dumping measures and concludes that China's practices and investigation procedures are improving its position in the world trading system. Finally, *Julien Chaisse* and *Dini Sejko* elaborate on the Trade Remedy provisions in the recently concluded free trade agreement between the EU and Vietnam: "The Latest on the Best? Reflections on Trade Defence Regulation in EU-Vietnam FTA". The analysis assesses the impact of these provisions on the Vietnamese legal system.

The editing of this volume would not have been possible without the help and assistance of *Pieter Van Vaerenbergh*. Last but not least, we thank *Anja Trautmann* from Springer for cooperating once again and ensuring that this volume could be published as scheduled.

Saarbrücken, Germany   Marc Bungenberg
Bern, Switzerland   Michael Hahn
Passau, Germany   Christoph Herrmann
Brussels, Belgium   Till Müller-Ibold
May 2018

Contents

About the Authors

Julien Chaisse is Professor at the Chinese University of Hong Kong (CUHK), Faculty of Law. He is an award-winning scholar of international law with a special focus on the regulation and development of economic globalisation. His teaching and research include international trade/investment law, international taxation, law of natural resources and Internet law. Professor Chaisse's vast publications include *The Regulation of Global Water Services Market* (CUP) and the *International Economic Law and Governance* (OUP). Professor Chaisse is a well-experienced arbitrator and holds leading positions in various research bodies and organisations.

Yusong Chen is counsellor at the Permanent Mission of China to the WTO in Geneva. He holds an LL.B. from Peking University, a Ph.D. from Peking University and an LL.M. from Amsterdam Law School.

Dong Fang is an associate professor of international law, Law School, Xiamen University, China. He earned a doctor of law degree (2003) from Xiamen University, China. His major teaching and research interests cover public international law and international trade law. He publishes extensively in these fields in both Chinese and English. Fang also serves as Deputy Secretary-General of the Chinese Society of International Economic Law. He was a visiting fellow of Law School, Washington University in St. Louis.

Markus W. Gehring is the Arthur Watts Senior Research Fellow in Public International Law at BIICL. He teaches law at the University of Cambridge, is a Fellow in Law of Hughes Hall and serves as Lead Counsel for the Centre for International Sustainable Development Law (CISDL).

He holds an LL.M. from Yale Law School, a Dr. iur. from the Faculty of Law at the University of Hamburg and a second doctorate with his J.S.D. from Yale Law School. He is a barrister and solicitor of the Law Society of Ontario and a Rechtsanwalt (German lawyer) in the Frankfurt/Main Bar in Germany.

Michael Hahn (Dr. iur. Heidelberg, LL.M. Michigan) is the Managing Director of the Institute for European and International Economic Law of the University of Bern Law School and a Director at the University of Bern World Trade Institute. He is on the Faculty of Waikato Law School (Hamilton, New Zealand) and the Europa-Institut of Saarland University (Germany).

Before joining Bern University, Michael was a Full Professor at the University of Lausanne and Waikato and a Senior Lecturer in Germany. He has authored, inter alia, *The World Trade Organization: Law, Practice and Policy* (3rd edition, Oxford University Press, 2015) and is on the editorial board of the *Journal of World Trade*.

Michael advises sovereign and private clients on questions of EU and international economic law.

Anna Khalfaoui is the Satter Fellow at the American Bar Association Rule of Law Initiative and a legal researcher for the Center for Civilians in Conflict and the Columbia Human Rights Institute. She holds an LL.M. from Harvard Law School where she specialises in public international law and international human rights law, prior to which she studied law at the University of Cambridge, Trinity College and European studies at King's College London.

Mark Love currently serves as Senior Vice President of Economic Consulting Services, LLC (ECS). His professional experience includes more than 30 years in international trade litigation, with primary roles in case strategy, economic expert testimony, econometric analysis, trade policy and negotiations. Mr. Love has been a project coordinator for major studies for the U.S. Government on trade barriers affecting high-technology U.S. industries. His current writings focus on the domestic and international forces affecting the evolution of U.S. trade policy. Mr. Love earned his bachelor's degree from Haverford College and his master's degree from the Johns Hopkins University School of Advanced International Studies.

Bruce Malashevich currently serves as President and Chief Executive Officer of Economic Consulting Services, LLC. In a career spanning more than 40 years, Mr. Malashevich has been dedicated to applying the principles of economics to international trade disputes in venues including the United States and various other jurisdictions subject to WTO rules. He frequently testifies as an economic expert and has written and spoken widely. He served as an Associate Member of the "Dispute Settlement in Trade: Training in Law and Economics", a programme established with a grant from the EU, and continues to serve on the U.S. Roster of Experts in disputes arising under NAFTA rules. Mr. Malashevich holds degrees from Princeton University's Woodrow Wilson School of Public and International Affairs and the John Hopkins University School of Advanced International Studies.

Sophia Müller studied law at the University of Passau. She then worked as a Scientific Research Assistant at the University of Passau and several law firms, mainly in the areas of EU economic and foreign trade law and WTO law. She was Visiting Researcher at Beijing Foreign Studies University from September to

December 2016. In November 2017, she completed her Ph.D. thesis on the use of alternative benchmarks in anti-subsidy law with a focus on the relationship between the WTO, the EU and China. She currently prepares for the second state examination at the Higher Regional Court of Frankfurt am Main.

Wolfgang Müller is Head of Unit in DG Trade, European Commission. His unit deals with general policy, WTO relations and relations with industry in the area of trade defence instruments. Before joining the European Commission, he worked with the Daimler Benz group. After the bar exam (2nd "Staatsexamen"), he worked as a research assistant at the University of Constance where he also was awarded a Ph.D. (Dr. jur.). He published extensively on the law of trade defence instruments, at both the EU and WTO level.

Till Müller-Ibold joined Cleary Gottlieb Steen & Hamilton LLP in 1991, became a partner in 2004 and became senior counsel in 2016. Prior to Cleary, he worked for Boesebeck Droste Rechtsanwälte in Düsseldorf where he practised German commercial law and German private international law.

His practice focuses on EU law, where he specialises in certain areas of competition law (such as EU scrutiny of state aid), EU sanctions regulation, public procurement and anti-dumping and trade law, as well as in the representation of private parties and government entities in the European Courts.

Tobias Naef is a visiting researcher at the Lauterpacht Centre for International Law, University of Cambridge. He writes his Ph.D. on the compatibility of EU and WTO law in the area of international data flows at the University of Zurich, where he previously also worked as a research assistant.

Matthias Oesch is Professor of public law, European law and international economic law at the University of Zurich, Switzerland. He is a specialist in Swiss external economic relations, EU law (foundations, institutions, external economic relations), WTO law and regional integration. Previously, he worked as legal counsel in the Federal Department of Economic Affairs and as attorney-at-law in Zurich.

Brian Petter studied in Germany, Sweden and Belgium and holds a master's degree in International Relations. In 2015, he started as a junior trade policy adviser at the European office of the Germany Chemical Industry Association (VCI) in Brussels. Since 2016, he works at the VCI's headquarters in Frankfurt am Main and is responsible for customs, trade controls, excise duties and trade defence law.

Reinhard Quick Following his legal studies at Mannheim University, Reinhard Quick undertook his doctorate at Mannheim University. He completed his education with a Master of Laws (LL.M.) at the University of Michigan. From 1984 until the end of 2016, Reinhard Quick held different positions at the German and European Chemical Industry Associations (VCI, CEFIC). He was a member of the

TTIP Advisory Group of the European Commission (2013–2016). Reinhard Quick was appointed as Honorary Professor for international economic law by Saarland University in 2006. He teaches at the Europa-Institut on the subject of trade and environment. He has published numerous essays on trade policy and European law-related issues.

Vinzenz Sacher is senior researcher and lecturer at the Transnational Economic Law Research Center (TELC) at the Law School of Martin Luther University Halle-Wittenberg.

Dini Sejko is a Ph.D. candidate at the CUHK, Faculty of Law, where he has lectured on International Investment Law. Mr. Sejko is also a Research Affiliate at Tufts University, the Fletcher School, SovereigNET. His research interests include state capitalism and foreign direct investment, and his thesis focuses on the transnational regulatory regime of sovereign wealth funds. Mr. Sejko has been awarded various awards and scholarships and has been invited to present his research at many academic institutions in Hong Kong, Macao, Taiwan, Japan, South Korea, India, Italy, the Netherlands and Cyprus. Mr. Sejko has obtained an LL.M. in International Economic Law (CUHK) and a Combined Bachelor and M.Sc. in Law (Bocconi).

Juhi Dion Sud is a counsel at VVGB Advocaten. Her practice focuses on EU and international trade law and WTO law. Ms. Sud obtained her LL.M. from Vrije Universiteit Brussel (summa cum laude) and LL.B. from the Faculty of Law, Delhi University. She holds a B.A. in History from St. Stephens College, Delhi.

Christian Tietje is Professor of European and International Economic Law and director of the Institute for Economic Law and the Transnational Economic Law Research Center (TELC) at the Law School of Martin Luther University Halle-Wittenberg.

Edwin Vermulst has practised international trade and EU law and policy since 1985 and is a founding partner of VVGB Advocaten. He is a member of the Brussels bar. Mr. Vermulst specialises in the representation of multinationals, governments, trade associations, exporters and importers in WTO, trade remedy and customs cases, and he is, among others, the trade counsel of the World Federation of Sporting Goods Industry (WFSGI). He has co-authored nine books, including landmark comparative analyses of the anti-dumping systems and rules of origin of countries such as Australia, Canada, the EU and the United States. Mr. Vermulst is the Editor-in-Chief of the *Journal of World Trade* and a Faculty member of the World Trade Institute in Bern and the IELPO programme in Barcelona.

Part I
Introduction: TDI in Context

The Multilateral and EU Legal Framework on TDIs: An Introduction

Michael Hahn

Contents

Abstract As a member of the WTO, the EU is obliged to ensure the conformity of its laws, regulations and administrative procedures with its obligations pursuant to WTO law. In turn, these WTO obligations have been strongly shaped by members with significant past experience with TDI use, amongst them the EU. As several contributions analyse and evaluate the new EU regime on TDIs, the purpose of this paper is to highlight the challenges facing the current crisis of the multilateral trade system: in particular, the paper explores the effects the current U.S. blockade of the Appellate Body and the growing pains of the WTO system following the joining of China as a member.

M. Hahn (✉)
University of Bern, School of Law, Institute of European and International Economic Law, Bern, Switzerland

World Trade Institute, Bern, Switzerland
e-mail: michael.hahn@iew.unibe.ch

© Springer International Publishing AG, part of Springer Nature 2018   3
M. Bungenberg et al. (eds.), *The Future of Trade Defence Instruments*,
European Yearbook of International Economic Law,
https://doi.org/10.1007/978-3-319-95306-9_1

1 Introduction

WTO and EU lawyers put three very different bodies of law into the category of "Trade Remedies" (or Trade Defence Instruments, TDIs): the term covers countervailing measures against practices that are characterised as "unfair"—dumping and specific subsidisation—as well as safeguards. WTO law and the jurisprudence of the WTO adjudicative organs treat these three areas quite differently.[1] Being a member of the WTO, the EU is obliged, pursuant to Article XVI:4 WTO Agreement, to ensure the conformity of its *laws, regulations and administrative procedures* with its obligations pursuant to WTO law. Because of this link, and also because the WTO system stands on the shoulder of "prior art", namely the laws and regulations of the frequent users of trade remedies, including, in particular the U.S. and the EU, the international trade remedies environment and the European TDI regime are joined at the hip.

1.1   The Pertinent WTO Agreements

In addition to the GATT addressing trade remedies in its Articles VI, XVI and XIX, each of the three TDIs is the subject of a specific WTO agreement: the Anti-Dumping Agreement (ADA, Agreement on Implementation of Article VI of the General Agreement on Tariffs and Trade 1994) defines both the parameters for dumping and for countervailing measures; in a parallel fashion, the Agreement on Subsidies and Countervailing Measures (ASCM) addresses both the limits for state aid and the pertinent countermeasures; lastly, the Agreement on Safeguards (SG) deals with the undesirable consequences of too much success. All three TDIs have in common that they are a tool to alleviate pain that the domestic industry suffers as a consequence of not being able to successfully compete with imports. However, this is where the communality ends.

Subsidies and dumping are viewed by WTO law as being inherently or at least potentially unfair: even the biggest corporation cannot compete with the French Ministry of Finance, if she chooses help out the local champion; indeed, already the GATT contracting parties "condemned" injurious dumping.[2] Export subsidies are even outlawed altogether—the ASCM uses the word "prohibited", which is almost unheard of elsewhere in WTO legal texts.[3] He who dumps, i.e. selling in export markets below home market price, is doing that under a cloud of ambiguity: is he ripping off his home constituency by asking (only) the foreign consumers for a fair

---

[1] For a first overview, see for safeguards, the excellent overview of Piérola (2014); for subsidies, Coppens (2014); for dumping and anti-dumping, Van den Bossche and Zdouc (2017), pp. 696–768.

[2] Cf. Article VI GATT.

[3] Cf. Article 3 ASCM.

price? Or is he selling below costs, which is almost universally treated as a suspicious act, conducive to creating monopolies or cheating consumers. And if the price abroad is fair, whereas the price at home is way too high—what does that say about the home country's market access regime, if re-imports are for all practical purposes impossible?

Safeguards are a safety valve to undo potential "carnage"[4] in the domestic industry as a consequence of the sharp, sudden and unforeseeable rise of imports.[5] That means that without violating WTO rules, an importing state may (partially) undo the commercial success that was achieved fairly and squarely in the market place due to the overwhelming competitive success of foreign producers. This is in sharp contrast to the normal way things are done in WTO law: as a matter of principle, the WTO system is somewhat pro-competition, pro-choice and against direct (enterprise or industry-specific) state intervention absent a justification other than the competitor's success. It comes as no surprise then, that the Appellate Body has interpreted the safeguard provisions in a restrictive fashion.[6] In fact, the safeguard provisions of the WTO Agreement have become largely unusable by Organisation for Economic Co-operation and Development (OECD) countries, as they would almost certainly not withstand attacks in a WTO Dispute Settlement Understanding (DSU) complaint. It may thus come as no surprise that the EU statistics for 2016 shows zero safeguard investigations.

1.2 The EU Instruments

In the EU, the Basic Anti-Dumping Regulation 2016/1036[7] codifies how protection against dumped imports from countries not members of the European Union works, whereas its sister Regulation 2016/1037[8] codifies how the EU protects itself against subsidised imports from countries not members of the European Union (Basic Anti-Subsidy Regulation). In both areas, litigation is common.[9] Finally, Regulations 2015/478 and 2015/755[10] lay down the ground rules for safeguard measures. The

---

[4] Remarks of President Donald J. Trump, Inaugural Address, Washington, D.C., 20 January 2017, https://www.whitehouse.gov/briefings-statements/the-inaugural-address/ (last accessed 30 April 2018).

[5] The *"language in both Article 2.1 of the Agreement on Safeguards and Article XIX:1(a) of the GATT 1994, (...) requires that the increase in imports must have been recent enough, sudden enough, sharp enough, and significant enough, both quantitatively and qualitatively, to cause or threaten to cause "serious injury".",* Appellate Body Report, *Argentina – Footwear (EC)*, WT/DS121/AB/R, adopted 14 December 1999, DSR 1999:VII, para. 131.

[6] Appellate Body Report, *Argentina – Safeguard Measures on Imports of Footwear*, WT/DS121/AB/R, adopted 14 December 1999, DSR 1999:VII, para. 131.

[7] OJ 2016 L 176/21–54 as amended by OJ 2017 L 228/1–7.

[8] OJ 2016 L 176/55–91 as amended by OJ 2017 L 338/1–7.

[9] Further references see e.g. Van Bael and Bellis (2011), *passim*.

[10] OJ 2015 L 83/16–32; OJ 2015 L 123/33–49. See Müller (2017), pp. 205–226.

recent reform of the EU's TDIs is shaped, inter alia, by the increasing political popularity of trade defence measures (the Parliament has become a *demandeur* for trade remedies), the expiration of the transitional period established by the Chinese Protocol of Accession in December 2017 and the reaction to the *EU – Biodiesel* decisions. This reform will only be touched upon briefly below.[11]

2   The WTO Trade Remedies Regime: A System in Crisis

2.1   *The China Shock*

The most commonly mentioned reason why TDIs have regained prominence everywhere in the world is the success of Chinese exports. Whereas some see the success of a competitive economy that reclaims the position it had prior to the stifling contact with the British Empire, others see an export oriented economy that combines aggressive market forces and strategic coordination from the government and party apparatus.

By joining the WTO in 2001, China undertook to abide by the rules and obligations of the WTO. Knowing that an actual military and geopolitical superpower and a (then potential) economic superpower was joining, China's Western partners insisted that the obligations accepted by China surpassed those of its emerging power peers who had been original members of the WTO.[12] The fact that China had undertaken, in a legally binding fashion, to open its markets and adapt some of its internal rules to the requirements of the WTO agreements contributed in important ways to China's ongoing success story. Not the least, it greatly facilitated internal reform: modification of the status quo was thus not just a function of the wisdom of the leadership, but rather an obligation undertaken to restore China's position as an integral (and important) part of the international economic order. Not the least due to that narrative, internal resistance remained manageable, while at the same time the changes effectuated allowed China to develop as destination for Western investment.

Of course, the Western partners of China knew that they were not admitting just another emerging economy. While the rise of China to the world's biggest producers of goods was even faster than expected, it was abundantly clear in 2001 that China would become the centre of global production for low and medium price products: already then, China was the seventh biggest exporter and eighth biggest importer of merchandise trade.[13]

---

[11] See infra, Sect. 3; for more information on the different perspectives of this reform are addressed in Part II of this book.

[12] Kennedy (2013), pp. 46 et seq.

[13] See World Trade Organization, WTO successfully concludes negotiations on China's entry, 17 September 2001, https://www.wto.org/english/news_e/pres01_e/pr243_e.htm (last accessed 30 April 2018).

The provisions of the protocol of accession[14] are evidence that there was an understanding of short term risks: for example, the prohibition of certain restrictions on the exportation of raw materials[15] was supposed to avoid creating a monopoly for Chinese producers of the products that need that input; the provisions on dumping and subsidies clearly indicate a realisation that for the near future the Chinese political system would use the market economies of its trading partners in ways that they wanted to avoid by inserting special obligations.[16] The same applies to the special

---

[14] World Trade Organization, Ministerial Conference Decision of 10 November 2001 on the Accession of the People's Republic of China, WT/L/432, 23 November 2001.

[15] Espa (2012), pp. 1399–1424.

[16] Cf. Section 15 CAP (Price Comparability in Determining Subsidies and Dumping):

Article VI of the GATT 1994, the Agreement on Implementation of Article VI of the General Agreement on Tariffs and Trade 1994 ("Anti-Dumping Agreement") and the SCM Agreement shall apply in proceedings involving imports of Chinese origin into a WTO Member consistent with the following:

(a) In determining price comparability under Article VI of the GATT 1994 and the Anti-Dumping Agreement, the importing WTO Member shall use either Chinese prices or costs for the industry under investigation or a methodology that is not based on a strict comparison with domestic prices or costs in China based on the following rules:

(i) If the producers under investigation can clearly show that market economy conditions prevail in the industry producing the like product with regard to the manufacture, production and sale of that product, the importing WTO Member shall use Chinese prices or costs for the industry under investigation in determining price comparability;

(ii) The importing WTO Member may use a methodology that is not based on a strict comparison with domestic prices or costs in China if the producers under investigation cannot clearly show that market economy conditions prevail in the industry producing the like product with regard to manufacture, production and sale of that product.

(b) In proceedings under Parts II, III and V of the SCM Agreement, when addressing subsidies described in Articles 14(a), 14(b), 14(c) and 14(d), relevant provisions of the SCM Agreement shall apply; however, if there are special difficulties in that application, the importing WTO Member may then use methodologies for identifying and measuring the subsidy benefit which take into account the possibility that prevailing terms and conditions in China may not always be available as appropriate benchmarks. In applying such methodologies, where practicable, the importing WTO Member should adjust such prevailing terms and conditions before considering the use of terms and conditions prevailing outside China.

(c) The importing WTO Member shall notify methodologies used in accordance with subparagraph (a) to the Committee on Anti-Dumping Practices and shall notify methodologies used in accordance with subparagraph (b) to the Committee on Subsidies and Countervailing Measures.

(d) Once China has established, under the national law of the importing WTO Member, that it is a market economy, the provisions of subparagraph (a) shall be terminated provided that the importing Member's national law contains market economy criteria as of the date of accession. In any event, the provisions of subparagraph (a)(ii) shall expire 15 years after the date of accession. In addition, should China establish, pursuant to the national law of the importing WTO Member, that market economy conditions prevail in a particular industry or sector, the non-market economy provisions of subparagraph (a) shall no longer apply to that industry or sector.

Transitional Safeguard Mechanism[17] to prevent market disruption in importing countries due to the influx of Chinese products. However, with the benefit of hindsight, it seems evident that expectation that the Chinese system would evolve after a prolonged contact with the market economy and become a fully Western economy, despite the maintenance of a Communist one party system, has proven to be not quite correct: Notwithstanding the question whether China is a "market economy",[18] it is clear that the role of the party today is closer to the vision of the founder of the People's Republic than to that of the chief architect of China's economic reforms.[19] Thus, the notion that the central leadership may influence the behaviour of firms and business partners (banks, upstream and downstream associates, but even customers) which have a presence in China and are thus exposed to Chinese measures is far from specious: every private actor has a party cell, every actor will try to act in accordance with wishes of the political leadership. This may render the dividing lines between dumping and subsidies, between private and public somewhat fuzzy.[20] The situation does not become easier in light of the fact, that many strategic actors in China are state-owned. Therefore, it was expected that:

> China's government-owned, or state-operated or owned, enterprises are a big challenge to the system, and it is hard to believe this will not shape some of the thinking about subsidies.… There are … going to be some big problems in those areas and one can predict that in a couple of years some of the definitions in the subsidies code will have to be revised, if that is manageable.[21]

Clearly, the separation of private market and public regulation of state and society—which is an integral part of the concepts underlying WTO law in general and trade remedy laws in particular—will be a helpful distinction in the vast majority of cases. No one doubts that China has used the market to build quickly a very successful economy. However, once a specific determination by the Chinese leadership as to political and economic goals has been determined, it would seem that specific "entrustment or direction"[22] is not required: rather, it would seem the duty of every operator to implement those policy preferences regardless of their specific legal quality. Not doing so may be viewed as opposition to the party line.

In *US – Anti-Dumping and Countervailing Duties,* the Panel seemed to offer an incremental and partial solution to this issue: While state ownership was not *determinative* for assuming that an enterprise (the state-owned enterprise, SOE) would be a tool of the state, it was to be assumed, unless it could be shown that the SOE

---

[17] Paragraph 16 of the Protocol of Accession; see Appellate Body Report, *United States – Measures Affecting Imports of Certain Passenger Vehicle and Light Truck Tyres from China,* WT/DS399/AB/R, adopted 5 September 2011, DSR 2011:IV, paras. 120 and 131 et seq.

[18] Vermulst et al. (2016), pp. 212–228; see also Part II of this book, *passim.*

[19] Illustrative: Phillips T, China told to follow the leader Xi Jinping in thought, word and deed. The Guardian, 5 March 2018, https://www.theguardian.com/world/2018/mar/05/china-told-to-follow-the-leader-xi-jinping-in-thought-word-and-deed (last accessed 30 April 2018).

[20] Wu (2016), pp. 261–324.

[21] Jackson (2003), p. 26.

[22] Cf. Article 1.1(a)(1)(iv) ASCM.

acted pursuant to a business plan independently to party or state guidance. For all practical purposes, this would have created a rebuttable presumption. However, the Appellate Body would have none of that. It refused[23] to follow the Panel's line of reasoning to acknowledge that state-owned enterprises are presumably an instrument of the government; under the conditions of a one-party State, the rebuttal, of course, would not always succeed. Whereas the Panel had accepted "primacy to evidence of majority government ownership",[24] recognising that the assumption of control by the State would be undone by showing that the state-owned enterprise was insulated from State control, the Appellate Body rejected that approach. Rather, it demanded a complainant to show that the Government had vested the operator in question with governmental function or authority and exercised control over its acts ("entrusts and directs").[25] It goes without saying that, under the conditions of a one-party state, it is systemically difficult for foreign operators and even states to show this linkage. The Panel's acceptance of a prima facie rule that state ownership implies government control would have reversed the burden of proof, thus making a review of Chinese practices more realistic.[26]

It is somewhat ironic that the jurisprudence of the Appellate Body does accommodate the lack of specific provision for exempting *research and development* from the regular disciplines of the ASCM (since the fading away of the non-actionable subsidy category) through the recognition of state's right to negate a competitive relationship by creating normatively distinct markets—one for electricity, the other one for energy from renewable sources[27]—but fails to recognise that the paradigm underlying anti-dumping and anti-subsidy law, namely that the normal price is the result of a market mechanism. If it is not, a substitute mechanism is to be applied that leads to "as-if" results.

In a similar vein, the complete ban of "zeroing"[28] is perceived—certainly in the collective U.S. recollection—as a unilateral modification of a foundational political deal. The seriousness of the resistance is made obvious by the unheard opposition of several panels to follow the Appellate Body (not without the contribution of a future Appellate Body member, Mr. David Unterhalter) and by the continuing resistance within the Appellate Body, where, in the *Dishwasher* case, the effort to allow

---

[23] Appellate Body Report, *United States – Definitive Anti-Dumping and Countervailing Duties on Certain Products from China*, WT/DS379/AB/R, adopted 11 March 2011, DSR 2010:III.

[24] Panel Report, *United States – Definitive Anti-Dumping and Countervailing Duties on Certain Products from China*, adopted 22 October 2010, para. 8.136.

[25] Invoking the ILC (International Law Commission) Draft Articles on Responsibility of States for Internationally Wrongful Acts.

[26] Cartland et al. (2012), p. 1001.

[27] Appellate Body Report, *Canada – Measures Relating to the Feed-in Tariff Program*, WT/DS412/AB/R and WT/DS426/AB/R, adopted 6 May 2013, DSR 2013:I, paras. 5.106 et seq.

[28] The practice of the U.S. to put the value of "zero" on any negative dumping, thus leading to dumping whenever there was some dumping (i.e. a positive dumping margin (e.g. with the value "five", i.e. the product is sold "five" below the home market price) during, e.g., 6 months, as it cannot be cancelled out by corresponding (or greater) negative dumping margins during the remainder of the year, because negative dumping is valued at "zero".

zeroing at least in the case of targeted dumping was voted down by a majority.[29] Also, the refusal to read Article 17.6 ADA as a norm granting substantial leeway to investigating authorities and instead insist of full judicial review was perceived as an affront. And lastly, and most currently, the ruling in in *EU – Biodiesel*[30] which rejects the use of costs other than those resulting from the accounts of the exporting producer—thus ultimately referring investigations of alleged Chinese dumping practices back to China and putting in question the common practice to use third-country data—has been perceived, rightly or wrongly, as making it difficult, if not impossible, to cope with certain Chinese practices.

2.2   The Trump Shock

It is fair to say that the jurisprudence of the WTO adjudicative organs, in particular the Appellate Body, had created strong feelings in the United States; this is a somewhat counter-intuitive development: the U.S. was "present at creation" of the GATT/WTO System and had the dual role of midwife and godmother. This is not the place to describe in detail the measures of the United States government to undo the Appellate Body and thereby change the substantive law applicable to countervailing measures relating to dumping and subsidies and, maybe less so, the law relating to safeguard measures. It suffices to remind readers that the U.S., already during the Obama administration, weakened both the Appellate Body and its presence in it by not proposing an American Appellate Body member for renewal in 2011. In 2016, the United States Trade Representative (USTR) chose to escalate its manifestation of disenchantment with the Appellate Body and did not join the otherwise certain consensus for the renewal of a sitting (Korean) Appellate Body member. The 2016 Annual Report of the Appellate Body[31] restates that:

> [O]n 11 May 2016, the DSB Chairman had been informed by one delegation [the US'] that it would be unable to support Mr Chang's reappointment. Shortly thereafter, this delegation publicized its reasons for its opposition to Mr Chang's reappointment. Subsequently, Appellate Body members other than Mr Chang, in a letter signed by the Appellate Body Chair, expressed concerns about the public statement of reasons given for opposition to Mr Chang's reappointment.[32]

In a move that did not win sympathies in Washington D.C., the Appellate Body Members stated in a letter to the Chairman of the DSB that they were "*concerned*

---

[29] Appellate Body Report, *United States – Anti-Dumping and Countervailing Measures on Large Residential Washers from Korea*, WT/DS464/AB/R, adopted 7 September 2016, DSR 2016:II, paras. 5.191 et seq.

[30] Appellate Body Report, *European Union – Anti-Dumping Measures on Biodiesel from Argentina*, WT/DS473/AB/R, adopted 6 October 2016, DSR 2016:IV, paras. 6.37 et seq.

[31] World Trade Organization, Appellate Body Annual Report for 2016, WT/AB/27, 16 May 2017.

[32] World Trade Organization, Appellate Body Annual Report for 2016, WT/AB/27, 16 May 2017, Annex 4.

about the accuracy of some of those reasons and, in particular, about the risks they may carry for the trust that WTO Members place in the independence and impartiality of Appellate Body members, on which the dispute settlement system depends."[33]

With the 45th President of the U.S., the relationship between the institution and its onetime mentor reached a new low: President Trump is on record as describing the WTO as a "disaster"; he has stated that he would leave the WTO, if he considered that it did not serve U.S. purposes.[34] In particular, it has been reported that if the Chinese complaint against the U.S.' and the EU's treatment of China as Non-Market Economy (NME), currently pending at the panel phase (DS 515 and 516) end with a win for China, the U.S. would walk away from the system. Given that the current administration has pulled out of the Trans-Pacific Partnership (TPP), these threats are not perceived as being completely implausible.

As per early 2018, the United States refuses to agree to any appointment to the Appellate Body. It is clear that this is not so much an expression of no-confidence in the Canadian, South American, Asian and EU candidates so far proposed. Rather, the U.S. has expressed in the strongest possible terms criticism of the Appellate Body performance in the last decade: it alleges that the Appellate Body has usurped powers not attributed to it. The implication is that the Appellate Body is operating without proper mandate. The alleged points range include, but are not limited to: "disregard of the 90-day deadline for appeals", "continued service by persons who are not longer AB members", "issuing advisory opinions on issues not necessary to resolve a dispute", "Appellate Body review of fact and review of a Member's law *de novo*" and "the Appellate Body claims its reports are entitled to be treated as precedent".[35] The purpose of this contribution is not to discuss the substantive merit of these reproaches or to evaluate the appropriateness and legality of the U.S. course of action in that context, but rather to highlight the institutional crisis of the WTO dispute settlement mechanism as context and background for the future of TDIs. Not surprisingly, specific criticism is reserved for the Appellate Body's jurisprudence regarding TDIs: The Trump administration voices *"systemic concerns with what it sees as an overly judicially activist Appellate Body that seeks to fill gaps in WTO agreements, which in turn creates new obligations for members and reinterprets what has already been agreed to. Several U.S. administrations have complained that the Appellate Body opines on issues not raised in the appeal and creates jurisprudence with no input from members – largely abandoning deference to*

---

[33] World Trade Organization, Appellate Body Annual Report for 2016, WT/AB/27, 16 May 2017, Annex 4.

[34] See also infra, Malashevich and Love.

[35] All quotes from Office of the United States Trade Representative, 2018 Trade Policy Agenda and 2017 Annual Report of the President of the United States on the Trade Agreements Program Office, March 2018, https://ustr.gov/about-us/policy-offices/press-office/reports-and-publications/2018/2018-trade-policy-agenda-and-2017 (last accessed 30 April 2018), pp. 22–28.

members in the context of trade remedy investigations."[36] It would not seem a far-fetched assumption that the main reason for the U.S. behaviour is indeed the sense that the Appellate Body's interpretation of WTO trade remedies law is flawed. Indeed, the current administration has both not revealed what their desired outcome of its aggressive stand regarding the Appellate Body is and voiced explicit scepticism as to the role of *any* WTO dispute settlement mechanism with regard to trade remedies:

> Congress delegates trade negotiating power to the President, which gives the President considerable control over the outcome of a disagreement with a trading partner. This power can be exercised without relying on a third-party arbiter such as the WTO, which ensures that the United States maintains its sovereignty with respect to economic issues.[37]

As a consequence of the U.S. refusal to appoint new Appellate Body members, the Appellate Body currently consists only of four members. One member's term ends this year (2018); by the end of 2019, there will be one Appellate Body member left, the Chinese citizen Hong Zhao.

2.3   WTO TDI Law Without Appellate Body Monitoring?

Despite the U.S. rhetoric and hostile actions, it continues to use the WTO Dispute Settlement Mechanism actively; the USTR highlights its use in its recent report.[38] Not only *"China is confused by the fact that, on one hand, the U.S. is demanding that the WTO dispute settlement system to continue operating "as normal" as it did in this dispute [China – Anti-Dumping and Countervailing Duty Measures on Broiler Products from the United States], and on the other hand, (...) is actively working to undermine the system by blocking the selection process for vacancies of the Appellate Body."*[39] However, the U.S. declined on 28 February 2018 to support

---

[36] Inside U.S. Trade's World Trade Online, Appellate Body, China NME fights to dominate WTO dispute settlement debate in 2018, 26 December 2017, https://insidetrade.com/daily-news/appellate-body-china-nme-fights-dominate-wto-dispute-settlement-debate-2018 (last accessed 30 April 2018).

[37] Economic Report of the President, Together with The Annual Report of the Council of Economic Advisers, Updating American Trade Policy, February 2018, https://insidetrade.com/sites/insidetrade.com/files/documents/2018/feb/wto2018_0082.pdf (last accessed 30 April 2018), p. 277.

[38] Office of the United States Trade Representative, 2018 Trade Policy Agenda and 2017 Annual Report of the President of the United States on the Trade Agreements Program Office, March 2018, https://ustr.gov/about-us/policy-offices/press-office/reports-and-publications/2018/2018-trade-policy-agenda-and-2017 (last accessed 30 April 2018), pp. 19 et seq.

[39] See Inside U.S. Trade's World Trade Online, China jabs U.S. for using WTO dispute settlement as it complies in poultry fight, 28 February 2018, https://insidetrade.com/daily-news/china-jabs-us-using-wto-dispute-settlement-it-complies-poultry-fight (last accessed 30 April 2018).

a proposal sponsored by 63 WTO members to begin filling three vacancies in the WTO Appellate Body.[40] Where do these developments leave us? It seems quite possible that the current administration will indeed bring the activities of the WTO Appellate Body to an end, at least temporarily. Discussions are taking place that explore the use of the WTO's voting mechanisms (that allow, as ultima ratio to take majority decisions)[41] or, alternatively, a controlled medically-induced *coma* of the Appellate Body by using its members as arbiters pursuant to Article 25 DSU. If this route is taken, it is not impossible that Trump will get back on his campaign promise to leave the WTO.

In light of this highly aggressive approach, the common concerns of many countries, not just OECD members but also developing countries, with regard to the necessity of an adaptation of WTO law to the changed parameters of state involvement in export-oriented economies is taking second and third place, despite the fact that there are significant overlaps in views:[42] After all, it was the EU that suggested in *EU – Biodiesel* that the Appellate Body should move beyond a mechanical application of the ASCM and take the underlying aim of Article VI GATT into account which required, in the EU's view, the necessity to rely on "reasonable" determination the home market value, i.e. a determination that excludes, as much as possible, the state control exercised in a system in which state and economic operators are closely intertwined.

What seems clear, though, is that both the (temporary) incapacitation of the Appellate Body (and, as a consequence, the greater diversity of Panel reports) and the need to reconsider the current rules on subsidies and dumping in light of the surge of state capitalism will merit further attention.

3 The EU Reaction

In the EU, the political pressure to strengthen the TDI toolbox have increased since the first Barroso Commission. Parliament, for obvious reasons particularly receptive to changes in perception, has been at the forefront of the pertinent efforts, whereas Member States have had difficulties to come up with a consolidated

---

[40] See Inside U.S. Trade's World Trade Online, China jabs U.S. for using WTO dispute settlement as it complies in poultry fight, 28 February 2018, https://insidetrade.com/daily-news/china-jabs-us-using-wto-dispute-settlement-it-complies-poultry-fight (last accessed 30 April 2018).

[41] Article IX:1 WTO Agreement.

[42] See for example the shared EU/U.S. Legal Interpretation—Article VI:1 of the General Agreement on Tariffs and Trade 1994, the Second Note Ad GATT 1994 Article VI:1, the Practice of the GATT Contracting Parties in the Application of GATT 1994 Article VI:1, the Accessions of Poland, Romania, and Hungary to the GATT, Article 2 of the Agreement on Implementation of Article VI of the General Agreement on Tariffs and Trade 1994, and Section 15 of the Protocol of Accession of China to the WTO, https://ustr.gov/sites/default/files/enforcement/WTO/US.Legal.Interp.Doc.fin.%28public%29.pdf (last accessed 30 April 2018).

position.[43] The Commission, on the other hand, has tried to reconcile the different views, while simultaneously increasing its pertinent administrative powers, comply with the Appellate Body's view in *EU – Biodiesel* and avoid a scorched earth policy vis-à-vis the Chinese partners.[44]

In December 2017, the EU undertook two important steps to address these concerns. On 12 December 2017, the EU legislator changed its methodology in Regulation 2017/2321[45] to establish the appropriate home market price ("normal value") for exporting countries in which state or other influences may lead to "significant distortions" of market conditions, thus rendering the benchmark for the calculation of dumping margins unreliable. Already on 5 December 2017, based on a Commission initiative originally presented to EU legislators in 2013,[46] the EU institutions also agreed to "modernise" the Union's TDIs.[47]

The proposed regulation sets out to:

- Increase transparency and predictability as concerns the imposition of provisional anti-dumping and anti-subsidy measures. This includes a pre-disclosure period of three weeks after the information is made public in which provisional duties will not yet be applied, as well as additional safety nets addressing the issue of stockpiling.
- Enable investigations to be initiated without an official request from industry, when a threat of retaliation by third countries exists.
- Enable trade unions to submit complaints together with the industry and allow them to become interested parties in the proceedings.
  Shorten the investigation period to a normal period of 7 months, but no later than 8 months. The definitive duties will have to be imposed within 14 months.
- Enable higher duties to be imposed in cases where there are raw material distortions and these raw materials, including energy, account for more than 17% taken individually. This would allow for an adaptation of the level of duties imposed under the "lesser duty rule" if it is in the interest of the EU. The imposition of higher duties will include a target profit set at a minimum of 6%.
- Enable importers to be reimbursed duties collected during an expiry review in the event of trade defence measures not being maintained.
- Take into account social and environmental standards when assessing the acceptability of an undertaking and when establishing the injury elimination margin.[48]

---

[43] Under the Slovak Presidency, the Council finally agreed to a position, Council of the European Union, Trade defence instruments: Council, Council agrees negotiating position, 13 December 2017, http://www.consilium.europa.eu/en/press/press-releases/2016/12/13/trade-defence-instruments-general-approach/pdf (last accessed 30 April 2018).

[44] Overview at Hoffmeister (2015), pp. 365–376.

[45] OJ 2017 L 338/1, pp. 1–7.

[46] European Commission, Communication from the Commission to the Council and the European Parliament on Modernisation of Trade Defence Instruments, Adapting trade defence instruments to the current needs of the European Community, 10 April 2013, COM(2013) 191 final.

[47] See Council, Trade defence instruments: EU ambassadors confirm the outcome of the final political trilogue with European Parliament, 20 December 2017, http://www.consilium.europa.eu/en/press/press-releases/2017/12/20/trade-defence-instruments-eu-ambassadors-confirm-the-outcome-of-the-final-political-trilogue-with-european-parliament/pdf (last accessed 30 April 2018).

[48] Council of the European Union, Trade defence instruments: EU ambassadors confirm the outcome of the final political trilogue with European Parliament, 20 December 2017, http://www.consilium.europa.eu/en/press/press-releases/2017/12/20/trade-defence-instruments-eu-ambassadors-confirm-

Several contributions below tackle in detail the new package.[49] For the purposes of this introductory paper, two aspects merit attention: Firstly, the new rules facilitate to some degree the initiation of investigation and, accordingly, are somewhat more burdensome for third-country-operators. Secondly, while significant doubts remain as to whether the new anti-dumping methodology of Regulation 2017/2321 takes sufficiently on board the findings of the Appellate Body in *EU – Biodiesel* and the law of the ADA, it has been noted by critics and supporters alike that the EU has made an effort to enact legislation that does not single out China. Given China's sensitivity with regard to any measure that is reminiscent of the infamous "uneven treaty" situation prevalent with Western powers in the nineteenth century, this effort by the EU is clearly noted; indeed, one does hear that this is a "Kowtow" to the Middle Kingdom that goes too far. This having said, the Commission has published on 19 December 2017[50] the first and so far only Commission staff working document on significant distortions in the economy of a trading partner that would be thus subject to this methodology: it concerns the People's Republic of China.[51]

4 Conclusion

In contrast to its U.S. partners, the EU tries to advance its trade defence interests in ways that do not endanger the multilateral trading system and its relationship with China. Of course, the devil is detail: there are those who see in the EU TDI reforms defensive measures mainly directed against China that unfairly sanction a very successful emerging country that remains on average poor by OECD standards and has opted for a government system that emphasises less the separation of society and state than Western liberal democracies. Others see a (maybe too) late effort to adapt TDIs to the threat of unfair trade practised by certain trading partners.

The crisis of the WTO dispute settlement mechanism is endangering the relative order that prevails currently with regard to trade remedies. The aggressive uses of trade remedy investigations are well known and so is the unhappiness of the U.S. with some of the Appellate Body jurisprudence and its (somewhat condoned) reluctance to implement some of the pertinent DSB decisions. The possibility, though, that soon the Appellate Body may be a fading memory would endanger the very

---

the-outcome-of-the-final-political-trilogue-with-european-parliament/pdf (last accessed 30 April 2018).

[49] See Part II of this book.

[50] Corrected version on 20 December 2017: see European Commission, Commission staff working document on significant distortions in the economy of the People's Republic of China for the purposes of trade defence investigations, 20 December 2017, SWD(2017) 483 final/2, http://trade.ec.europa.eu/doclib/docs/2017/december/tradoc_156474.pdf (last accessed 30 April 2018).

[51] European Commission, Commission staff working document on significant distortions in the economy of the People's Republic of China for the purposes of trade defence investigations, 20 December 2017, SWD(2017) 483 final/2, http://trade.ec.europa.eu/doclib/docs/2017/december/tradoc_156474.pdf (last accessed 30 April 2018).

basis of the rules-based international trading system: not because the Appellate Body did everything right (it clearly did not), but because it creates a precedent for any big player to walk away from international legal obligations when it suits them. This is a state of international affairs known to Europe and the reason why it embraced more than anyone else the U.S. led post-war effort to have enduring peace coupled with welfare-creating economic stability based on rules.

References

Cartland M, Depayre G, Woznowski J (2012) Is something going wrong in the WTO dispute settlement? J World Trade 46(5):979–1016

Coppens D (2014) WTO disciplines on subsidies and countervailing measures – balancing policy space and legal constraints. Cambridge University Press, Cambridge

Espa I (2012) The Appellate Body approach to the applicability of Article XX GATT in the light of China – raw materials: a missed opportunity? J World Trade 46(6):1399–1424

Hoffmeister F (2015) Modernising the EU's Trade Defence Instruments: mission impossible? In: Herrmann C, Simma B, Streinz R (eds) Trade policy between law, diplomacy and scholarship – Liber amicorum in memoriam Horst G. Krenzler. Springer, New York, pp 365–376

Jackson JH (2003) The impact of China's accession on the WTO. In: Cass DZ, Williams BG, Barker G (eds) China and the world trading system: entering the new millennium. Cambridge University Press, Cambridge, pp 19–30

Kennedy M (2013) The integration of accession protocols into the WTO Agreement. J World Trade 47(1):45–76

Müller W (2017) The EU's Trade Defence Instruments: recent judicial and policy developments. In: Bungenberg M et al (eds) European yearbook of international economic law, vol 8. Springer, Cham, pp 205–226

Piérola F (2014) The challenge of safeguards in the WTO. Cambridge University Press, Cambridge

Van Bael I, Bellis JF (2011) EU anti-dumping and other Trade Defence Instruments. Wolters Kluwer, Alphen aan den Rijn

Van den Bossche P, Zdouc W (2017) The law and policy of the World Trade Organization, 4th edn. Cambridge University Press, Cambridge

Vermulst E, Sud JD, Evenett S (2016) Normal value in anti-dumping proceedings against China post-2016: are some animals less equal than others? Global Trade Customs J 11(5):212–228

Wu M (2016) The "China, Inc." challenge to global trade governance. Harv Int Law J 57(2):261–324

The Politics of TDI and the Different Views in EU Member States: Necessary Safety-Valve or Luxurious Rent-Seeking Device?

Brian Petter and Reinhard Quick

Contents

Abstract The article discusses the tightening of the European Union's Anti-Dumping Regulation as a consequence of the debate on the "Market Economy Status" for China. It gives some facts and figures on the European Union's current anti-dumping activities, in particular those against China. Given China's treatment as a Non-Market Economy, the anti-dumping duties imposed are considerably higher than those imposed against "injurious dumping" from Market Economy countries. The article gives some insights into the chemical industry's thinking on anti-dumping. The industry's export dependency and its quest for further trade liberalisation provides for an interesting case study on how an industrial sector views the politics of anti-dumping. The main part of the article is an analysis of the political discussions and legislative initiatives in the context of China's MES. The European Commission's proposals are discussed as well as the reactions of the European Parliament, the Council of Ministers and those of business stakeholders. With respect to the position of stakeholders, the article elaborates on the difficulties

---

The opinions contained in this article are those of the authors.

B. Petter
German Chemical Industry Association, Frankfurt am Main, Germany
e-mail: petter@vci.de

R. Quick (✉)
Europa-Institut, Saarland University, Saarbrücken, Germany
e-mail: rq@reinhardquick.de

© Springer International Publishing AG, part of Springer Nature 2018   17
M. Bungenberg et al. (eds.), *The Future of Trade Defence Instruments*,
European Yearbook of International Economic Law,
https://doi.org/10.1007/978-3-319-95306-9_2

within German industry to come to an acceptable position on China's MES. The article concludes that the political climate in Europe calls for a tightened and stricter anti-dumping practice. As long as European politicians defend the positions of economic operators who feel threatened by Chinese exports, any discussions on introducing less stringent and more liberal anti-dumping rules will remain an illusion. On the contrary, strict anti-dumping rules are here to stay.

1 Introduction

Already in 1969, the venerable John Jackson wrote in his seminal book about the General Agreement on Tariffs and Trade (GATT): *"perhaps because antidumping duties can so easily be abused and used as a protectionist device [...] the Contracting Parties to GATT have given considerable attention to them over the years."*[1] Nearly 50 years later and after the creation of the World Trade Organization (WTO), it can be easily said that the Members of the WTO give at least as much attention to anti-dumping activities as did their predecessors the GATT Contracting Parties. GATT Article VI sets out the basic rules to prevent misuse of trade defence instruments (TDI). The "Anti-Dumping Agreement" provides for further clarifications on the basic principles and sets forth substantive requirements to be satisfied when imposing an anti-dumping measure. This framework also provides for specific procedural requirements regarding the conduct of anti-dumping investigations and the imposition of anti-dumping measures. WTO Members must respect these rules when deciding to introduce and apply a national anti-dumping policy. Overall, dumping is a legitimate marketing activity in trade aiming e.g. to maintain or increase market shares. However, current rules recognise that WTO Members have under certain conditions the right to correct injurious dumping by imposing additional import duties on the products concerned.

Notwithstanding the WTO's mandatory dispute settlement system and the many clarifications on anti-dumping given by the Appellate Body, the question addressed in the title of our article is more of a rhetorical nature and will not be answered either positively or negatively. We note that WTO Members use anti-dumping measures and more and more challenge the practices of other Members, both legally and politically. Particularly in the "old" industrial world, the use of anti-dumping measures against unfair trade from the "new" industrial world is heavily defended. It seems that the fear of globalisation and the rise of populist/national arguments in the United States (U.S.) and in Europe have silenced the debate on how to further modernise, i.e. liberalise, the Anti-Dumping Agreement. In Europe, the discussions on the granting of the Market Economy Status (MES) to China has led to a hardened position on anti-dumping. The traditional divide between northern more "liberal" and southern more "protectionist" Member States has become blurred due to Brexit

---

[1] Jackson (1969), p. 407.

and what seems a German defection to the southern camp. Although Europe is still far away from applying U.S. anti-dumping practices, some of its liberal positions on anti-dumping (e.g. Lesser Duty Rule) are set to change.

In developing our arguments, we provide an insight into the thinking and experiences of the chemical sector on anti-dumping. The chemical industry provides for an interesting case study. It has a tradition of promoting a "liberal" trade policy calling for the elimination of chemical tariffs both multilaterally and bilaterally, yet at the same time it is one of the main users of the anti-dumping instrument in the European Union (EU).

2 The EU's Anti-Dumping Framework: Some Figures

In the last 5 years, the European Commission's anti-dumping and anti-subsidy department has been quite busy as shown by the 2016 annual report. According to the report, 95 anti-dumping measures and 12 countervailing measures were in force in 2016.[2] Compared to the total amount of anti-dumping and countervailing measures worldwide that were notified to the WTO, these numbers are not excessive: though representing the largest economy in the world, as far as anti-dumping action is concerned, the EU is still far behind other traditional users of anti-dumping measures such as the U.S., Australia, India and Brazil.[3] The gap, however, is closing. In 2016 alone, the European Commission initiated 24 new investigations, almost a 30% increase compared to previous years.

Between 2012 and 2016, not a single safeguard investigation was initiated.[4] Even in times of massive overcapacities in some sectors, the European industry does not seem to consider safeguards as a viable alternative to anti-dumping. Unfortunately, the changes to safeguards agreed upon in the Uruguay Round have not helped to improve the practicability of this instrument which, compared to anti-dumping, is too complicated and burdensome. The differing legal requirements for safeguard and anti-dumping measures appear to incentivise firms to use the latter. Safeguard rules require restrictions on all imports and that might affect a much wider range of exporting nations than the more targeted anti-dumping measures. In the EU, safeguard activities also require a high degree of political support through a qualified rather than a simple majority in the Council of Ministers. Even though the European

---

[2] European Commission, Anti-dumping, anti-subsidy, safeguard statistics covering the 12 months of 2016, 28 February 2017, http://trade.ec.europa.eu/doclib/docs/2017/january/tradoc_155243.pdf (last accessed 30 April 2018), p. 2.

[3] World Trade Organization, Report (2016) of the Committee on Subsidies and Countervailing Measures, G/SCM/148, adopted 25 October 2016, G/L/1157, pp. 17–18; World Trade Organization, Report (2016) of the Committee on Anti-Dumping Practices, G/ADP/23, adopted 27 October 2016, G/L/1158, pp. 13–18.

[4] European Commission, Anti-dumping, anti-subsidy, safeguard statistics covering the 12 months of 2016, 28 February 2017, http://trade.ec.europa.eu/doclib/docs/2017/january/tradoc_155243.pdf (last accessed 30 April 2018), pp. 2–4.

Commission can start a case ex officio—which does not happen very often—the only way for the domestic industry to trigger such an investigation on its own is by mobilising the authorities of one or more EU countries.[5] Besides, one of the main conditions for safeguards is the finding that increased imports have caused or are threatening to cause "serious injury" to the domestic industry instead of only "material injury" as required for anti-dumping action. Furthermore, a safeguard measure goes hand in hand with the expectation of industrial restructuring.[6] Finally and most importantly, if safeguard measures last 5 years, which is the typical duration of anti-dumping duties, the WTO Member imposing them will have to pay compensation to the WTO Members whose trade is affected or face retaliation.[7] Given the fact that safeguards are considered an emergency instrument in trade policy, it is not surprising that WTO Members agreed upon exceptional requirements. In practice, however, even when domestic industries suffer from a general import penetration, the preferred instruments are anti-dumping measures. This is surely an unintended effect.

Although the imports under anti-dumping measures represented less than 1% of the total value of EU-imports between 1995 and 2013, in absolute terms, an annual average of EUR 10 billion of imported goods were subject to anti-dumping restrictions.[8] This is a remarkable figure if one considers that over 10% of the EU's budget is funded by customs duties paid on imported goods. Revenues from customs duties—which include anti-dumping duties—increased to approximately EUR 18 billion in 2016, despite duty suspensions, free trade agreements (FTAs) or unilateral trade preferences for developing countries under the Generalised Scheme of Preferences (GSP).[9] Indeed, academics have referred to anti-dumping measures as a substitute trade policy instrument to protect domestic producers in times when tariff barriers and contingent protection are a priority on the political agenda and are being tackled vigorously.[10] But no one seems to contemplate the possibility that higher or more frequent anti-dumping duties could be a long-term fiscal strategy. Could such duties be the motivation for the European Commission to launch investigations against third countries, instead of restoring in good faith the level playing field for domestic industries in a situation of unfair trade practices? Even though this question cannot be answered due to a lack of data and transparency of the EU public budget, a conflict of interest is evident since the power to take any anti-dumping action relies upon the European Commission.

---

[5] OJ 2009 L 84/1, pp. 7–8.
[6] OJ 2009 L 84/1, pp. 3–4; Agreement on Safeguards, Articles 2–4.
[7] Agreement on Safeguards, Article 8.
[8] Issabekov and Suchecki (2016), pp. 46–59.
[9] OJ 2016 L 48/1, pp. 12 and 22.
[10] Beverelli C, Boffa M and Keck A, Trade policy substitution: theory and evidence from specific trade concerns. WTO Staff Working Papers, ERSD-2014-18, 29 October 2014, https://www.econstor.eu/bitstream/10419/104762/1/799369403.pdf (last accessed 30 April 2018), pp. 32–34; Ketterer (2016), pp. 576–580.

The countries impacted by EU anti-dumping measures are emerging economies in South America and Southeast Asia, such as Indonesia, Thailand, South Korea, Brazil and Argentina, but also India and Russia. Yet, when speaking about the politics of TDI, the country mostly concerned is the People's Republic of China, hereafter referred to as China. Chinese companies appear to be the prime suspect of dumping: with more than 40% of overall anti-dumping initiations launched by the EU between 2012 and 2016, China has been the biggest target.[11] In anti-dumping investigations in the EU, China is treated as a Non-Market Economy (NME). The European Commission uses this derogation to establish the dumping margin by looking at a surrogate or analogue country instead of taking Chinese prices or costs into account, unless the Chinese exporter can clearly demonstrate that market conditions prevail in the industry sector concerned.[12]

The IFO Institute showed in a study in 2016 that the treatment as a Non-Market Economy in anti-dumping investigations and the use of the "analogue country method" leads to high dumping margins. On average, EU anti-dumping duties are at 7% when the European Commission applies the standard methodology. In contrast, this figure rises to 42% for anti-dumping duties imposed against companies originating from Non-Market Economy countries. In this case, the European Commission calculates one dumping margin to apply to all imports on the basis of the price or a constructed value in a Market Economy third country. Under certain conditions, however, single exporters may apply for Market Economy treatment. If their claims are justified the standard methodology applies: "normal value" to calculate dumping will be primarily based on their own prices and costs. Since 2010, the European Commission appears to have adopted a restrictive attitude towards granting Market Economy treatment to Chinese exporters as its application rates have declined to zero.[13] It is interesting to note that quite a few commentators and national authorities acknowledge that the Chinese economy has witnessed a far-reaching shift and that a significant share of all products traded in China is determined by market forces.[14] Yet this assessment does not fit into the actual political context of anti-dumping action against China. After 2012, the situation for exporters based in China improved since the use of an individual treatment for all sampled firms within an anti-dumping case by the European Commission was made manda-

---

[11] European Commission, Anti-dumping, anti-subsidy, safeguard statistics covering the 12 months of 2016, 28 February 2017, http://trade.ec.europa.eu/doclib/docs/2017/january/tradoc_155243.pdf (last accessed 30 April 2018), p. 9; European Commission, Commission Staff Working Document accompanying the document to the 34rd annual report from the Commission to the European Parliament and the Council on the EU's anti-dumping, anti-subsidy and safeguard activities, SWD(2016) 330 final, 18 October 2016, http://eur-lex.europa.eu/legal-content/EN/TXT/PDF/?uri=CELEX:52016SC0330&from=EN (last accessed 30 April 2018), pp. 15–19.

[12] OJ 2016 L 176/21, p. 26.

[13] Yalcin et al. (2016), pp. 13–14; Melin (2012), pp. 505–506.

[14] Johnson (2013), p. 61; United States Trade Representative, 2016 report to Congress on China's WTO Compliance, January 2017, https://ustr.gov/sites/default/files/2016-China-Report-to-Congress.pdf (last accessed 30 April 2018), pp. 2–8.

tory, reducing the average duties up to 30%.[15] Despite the possibility of individual treatment, Chinese exporters are in a disadvantageous position compared to the companies based in other WTO Member States.

Apart from the unfavourable treatment mentioned above, the criteria by which the European Commission chooses the analogue or surrogate country and the data on which the calculation of "normal value" relies are vague. The International Bar Association argued in its 2010 report that the analogue country selection method seems "arbitrary or inappropriate" since the European Commission prefers to use data from companies in the United States or in Turkey where production costs tend to be considerably higher than in China. The U.S. instead focuses on analogue countries with a similar level of economic development (e.g. India, Pakistan and Indonesia).[16] Even within interim reviews, Chinese companies seem to be treated harshly by the European Commission. In 2013, Nita and Zanardi found "robust evidence that when Chinese firms are reviewed, which occurs less frequently than for firms of other nationalities, their anti-dumping measures are reduced much less in comparison with other cases. On average, their duties are actually increased."[17] It is therefore not surprising that China insists on receiving Market Economy Status not only in the EU but also in all other jurisdictions in which this status affects the choice of methods to calculate "normal value" within anti-dumping investigations. For many policy makers and stakeholders it might be disappointing to realise that China's main interest is to improve the entrance into third countries' markets using legal WTO channels and not necessarily getting the highly appreciated Western label of a de facto Market Economy.

3 The Special Case of Chemicals and the Rise of the Dragon

In the EU, the European Commission mostly opens an investigation after receiving a complaint from producers located in EU Member States. Of all anti-dumping measures in force against Chinese exporters in 2014, mostly companies from Germany, France, Italy and Spain were involved and most of those cases were brought by the metal and the chemical industries.[18] Do these industries suffer from a lack of comparative advantage vis-à-vis their competitors in China? Based on the analysis of 523 CN8 commodity codes covered by EU anti-dumping proceedings

---

[15]Yalcin et al. (2016), p. 13; European Parliamentary Research Service, Calculation of dumping margins. EU and US rules and practices in light of the debate on China's market economy status—in-depth analysis, May 2016, http://www.europarl.europa.eu/RegData/etudes/IDAN/2016/583794/EPRS_IDA(2016)583794_EN.pdf (last accessed 30 April 2018), pp. 15–16.

[16]International Bar Association (IBA), Anti-dumping investigations against China in Latin America, 2010, https://www.ibanet.org/ENews_Archive/IBA_Jan_2010_ENews_AntiDumping_investigations_against_China.aspx (last accessed 30 April 2018), pp. 5–14.

[17]Nita and Zanardi (2013), p. 1477.

[18]Yalcin et al. (2016), pp. 31–37.

between 2000 and 2013, Issabekov and Suchecki determined in 2016 that in over 75% of all cases the EU did not hold a comparative advantage.[19] Yet, does a lack of comparative advantage also exist with respect to chemicals?

In the past, the U.S. was the largest chemical producing nation followed by Japan and Germany. Recent developments have completely changed this picture. In a short time, China has become the chemical manufacturer *par excellence*. In 2016, the Chinese chemical industry closed in on EUR 1.7 trillion annual turnover and today, it is even larger than the EU and the U.S. chemical industry combined. The U.S. takes second place, followed by Germany and Japan. Between 2011 and 2016, the production average annual growth rate increased by 10.5%, this development is shown within all segments of the chemical industry. China not only produces commodity chemicals but is also increasing its market share in fine and specialty chemicals as well as in pharmaceuticals. China's chemical industry currently shows the highest growth potential in international comparison.[20]

Asia as a whole has become the largest chemical producing and consuming region in the world. Since 2009, China is the number one market for chemicals. Only 3 years before this turning point, the picture was completely different. Asia consumed only 34% of the world's chemicals, the other two thirds were shared between Europe and the Contracting Parties of the North American Free Trade Agreement (NAFTA). In 2016, Asia increased its consumption to impressive 57%, while Europe's and NAFTA's share on the world consumption of chemicals decreased in both cases to nearly 18%.[21] Notwithstanding its leading position, currently, the Chinese chemical industry cannot cover its own demand. In 2016, China was the second largest chemical importer, with only the U.S. consuming higher amounts of chemical imports. As a matter of fact, China depends on imports of chemicals.[22] The beneficiaries of this situation are European and U.S. companies. Nevertheless, the Chinese chemical industry is a serious competitor, who is raising the pressure on the world market. Even if it is still a net importer of chemicals, the

---

[19] Issabekov and Suchecki (2016), pp. 58–59.

[20] Verband der Chemischen Industrie e.V., Länderbericht China. Daten und Fakten zur Chemieindustrie, July 2017, https://www.vci.de/ergaenzende-downloads/laenderbericht-china-chemie-kurz.pdf (last accessed 30 April 2018), p. 1; Verband der Chemischen Industrie e.V., Prognos AG, The German Chemical Industry 2030. VCI-Prognos study—Update 2015/2016, 31 May 2017, https://www.vci.de/vci-online/services/publikationen/broschueren-faltblaetter/vci-prognos-study-the-german-chemical-industry-2030-update-2015-2016.jsp (last accessed 30 April 2018), p. 20.

[21] Verband der Chemischen Industrie e.V., Chemiemärkte weltweit (Teil I). Umsatz, Handel, Verbrauch von Chemikalien und Investitionen in der Chemie, July 2017, https://www.vci.de/ergaenzende-downloads/chemiemaerkte-weltweit-folien-teil-1.pdf (last accessed 30 April 2018), p. 22.

[22] Verband der Chemischen Industrie e.V., Chemiemärkte weltweit (Teil I). Umsatz, Handel, Verbrauch von Chemikalien und Investitionen in der Chemie, July 2017, https://www.vci.de/ergaenzende-downloads/chemiemaerkte-weltweit-folien-teil-1.pdf (last accessed 30 April 2018), p. 36.

industry is also actively exporting chemicals. In the last years, China's chemical exports increased to over EUR 100 billion, closely following the U.S. and Germany.[23]

According to a recent study commissioned by the German Chemical Industry Association (VCI) on the future of the chemical industry in Germany, Germany and Japan will defend their positions on the global market as top producers following the Chinese and U.S. chemical industries. It is expected that both the Chinese and the U.S. chemical industries will become stronger, in the case of the U.S. driven by a comparative advantage due to an affordable and abundant supply of shale gas and shale oil. In contrast, Germany's but also Europe's comfortable position will change, in particular with regard to basic chemicals. The authors of the report expect that Germany will focus on the production of high-value specialty chemicals. Resource-intensive basic chemicals will continue being produced and Germany's chemical industry will remain integrated, but they will play a less important role due to a decline in competitiveness, whereas imports of preliminary products will grow in order to cover demand. By 2030, the foreign trade balance regarding basic chemicals could hence be negative and the domestic industry will have to deal with this new development.[24] A sharp rise in imports could possibly intensify the pressure on the European market for basic chemicals and result in an increase of complaints by EU-producers and therefore of anti-dumping investigations.

The study's prediction across all chemical segments is positive. In the long-term, Germany's chemical industry is expected to grow faster than the overall economy and by 2030, its production volume is estimated to exceed EUR 245 billion. Exports are also forecast to rise strongly. It is expected that in 2030, Germany will continue to have a trade surplus in most chemical sectors.[25] One key issue that distinguishes the chemical industry from other industry sectors is its long tradition of internationalisation. It seizes the opportunities and benefits from economic globalisation and has successfully adapted to major challenges over the years. The chemical industry is highly integrated in global value chains and has heavily invested all over the world. In fact, the gigantic increase in capacity of chemical production in China is largely financed by direct investments from foreign business partners. In the past years, Asia has gradually become the second largest recipient of foreign investments from the German chemical and pharmaceutical industry and is today a region which

---

[23] Verband der Chemischen Industrie e.V., Chemiemärkte weltweit (Teil I). Umsatz, Handel, Verbrauch von Chemikalien und Investitionen in der Chemie, July 2017, https://www.vci.de/ergaenzende-downloads/chemiemaerkte-weltweit-folien-teil-1.pdf (last accessed 30 April 2018), p. 35.

[24] Verband der Chemischen Industrie e.V., Prognos AG, The German Chemical Industry 2030. VCI-Prognos study—Update 2015/2016, 31 May 2017, https://www.vci.de/vci-online/services/publikationen/broschueren-faltblaetter/vci-prognos-study-the-german-chemical-industry-2030-update-2015-2016.jsp (last accessed 30 April 2018), pp. 19–30.

[25] Verband der Chemischen Industrie e.V., Prognos AG, The German Chemical Industry 2030. VCI-Prognos study—Update 2015/2016, 31 May 2017, https://www.vci.de/vci-online/services/publikationen/broschueren-faltblaetter/vci-prognos-study-the-german-chemical-industry-2030-update-2015-2016.jsp (last accessed 30 April 2018), pp. 26 and 45.

has the best prospects for future growth.[26] Internationalisation firstly assures that this industry sector profits from the growth in more dynamic markets worldwide and secondly maintains its global competitiveness.

Internationalisation explains the industry's position on trade defence instruments. The German chemical industry is decidedly interested in further trade liberalisation improving market access, removing investment restrictions and eliminating trade barriers in third countries. Given its export intensity, the industry is subject to anti-dumping investigations and measures from third countries.[27] Therefore, it has an interest in a well-balanced application of domestic anti-dumping laws and is rather reticent to support a tightening of the instrument since such a tightening could also be legally applied by other countries and could consequently negatively affect its exports. To sum up, the chemical industry defends the use of the anti-dumping instrument to survive in a highly competitive world but is critical towards a unilateral strengthening of the instrument.

4 The European Union Has Its Eye on China

Today, trade defence policy is going through a major scrutiny and adjustment process. Because of left-wing criticism of and outright right-wing opposition to further trade liberalisation, even moderate politicians, such as European Commission President Jean-Claude Juncker and French President Emmanuel Macron, insist on tightening the rules against "unfair" trade.[28] Although it is not evident that European politicians are reflecting public opinion on this issue, the institutions of the European Union have put forth two initiatives during the last lustrum to change the trade defence legislation.[29]

---

[26] Verband der Chemischen Industrie e.V., VCI-Investitionsbericht 2017. Analyse der Investitionstrends der chemisch-pharmazeutischen Industrie im In- und Ausland, 17 July 2017, https://www.vci.de/ergaenzende-downloads/investitionsbericht-2017-1.pdf (last accessed 30 April 2018), p. 5.

[27] European Commission, Report from the Commission to the Council and the European Parliament—13th report overview of third country trade defence actions against the European Union for the year 2015, 15 June 2016, COM(2016) 392 final, https://ec.europa.eu/transparency/regdoc/rep/1/2016/EN/1-2016-392-EN-F1-1.PDF (last accessed 30 April 2018), pp. 3–5.

[28] European Political Strategy Centre, Two visions, one direction. Plans for the future of Europe as laid out in President Juncker's State of the Union and President Macron's Initiative for Europe, 15 July 2014, https://ec.europa.eu/epsc/sites/epsc/files/epsc_-_two_visions_one_direction_-_plans_for_the_future_of_europe.pdf (last accessed 30 April 2018), p. 3.

[29] European Commission, Proposal for a Regulation of the European Parliament and of the Council amending Council Regulation (EC) No 1225/2009 on protection against dumped imports from countries not members of the European Community and Council Regulation (EC) No 597/2009 on protection against subsidised imports from countries not members of the European Community, 10 April 2013, COM(2013) 192 final, http://eur-lex.europa.eu/legal-content/EN/TXT/?uri=COM:2013:0192:FIN (last accessed 30 April 2018); European Commission, Proposal for a Regulation of the European Parliament and of the Council amending Regulation (EU) 2016/1036

Already in 2013 and after intensive discussions, the European Commission adopted a first proposal to modernise the EU's trade defence instruments. Its goal was to streamline and expedite procedures, to improve transparency and ultimately to impose higher duties by removing the so-called Lesser Duty Rule (LDR) in cases of circumvention, subsidisation or when structural raw material distortions prevail.[30] By systematically applying the LDR, the EU is more lenient than the WTO obligations, guaranteeing that the anti-dumping duty is fixed at the strict minimum necessary to restore a level playing field for the EU industry concerned and avoiding a punitive nature. Under the contemporary circumstances, the European Commission seems to be forced to give up its position as a role model and to adapt to the practice in the U.S.—a step, which was called for by several industry associations, including steel, metal and chemicals.

The tightening of the regulation is also shown by the proposal that the European Commission would be able to take things in its own hands by initiating investigations without an official request from industry (ex officio) when a third country is threatening with retaliation. Even though the Commission's proposal to gear up was certainly tempting, it has been a red line for several EU Member States for quite a while. A group of 14 traditionally pro-free trade countries—among them the United Kingdom, Austria, Belgium, the Netherlands and Finland—joined forces and formed a blocking minority in the Council against the changes to the LDR. As shown by a 2014 study from Moore and Dunoff: *"EU members' positions on trade remedy actions can depend importantly on national production patterns and firms' responses to economic pressures from globalisation and the further development of global supply chains."*[31] Nearly 3 years later, the ministers in the Council reached a spectacular breakthrough understanding in December 2016. The motivation behind the political agreement on a negotiation position for the "trilogue" with the European Commission and the European Parliament was not quite the pure expression of Rousseau's *volonté générale* but rather a forced reaction to a deadline set in China's WTO Accession Protocol that ventured into a fully overheated—and sometimes misleading—public debate in the EU about whether a Market Economy per se exists in China.

On 11 December 2001, after several years of negotiations, China became an official Member of the WTO following a decision which had been taken only one

---

on protection against dumped imports from countries not members of the European Union and Regulation (EU) 2016/1037 on protection against subsidised imports from countries not members of the European Union, 9 November 2016, COM(2016) 721 final, http://eur-lex.europa.eu/legal-content/EN/TXT/?uri=COM:2016:0721:FIN (last accessed 30 April 2018).

[30] European Commission, Proposal for a Regulation of the European Parliament and of the Council amending Council Regulation (EC) No 1225/2009 on protection against dumped imports from countries not members of the European Community and Council Regulation (EC) No 597/2009 on protection against subsidised imports from countries not members of the European Community, 10 April 2013, COM(2013) 192 final, http://eur-lex.europa.eu/legal-content/EN/TXT/?uri=COM:2013:0192:FIN (last accessed 30 April 2018), pp. 2–3.

[31] Dunoff and Moore (2014), p. 149.

month earlier at the fourth WTO Ministerial Meeting held in Doha.[32] Section 15 of the Chinese WTO Accession Protocol includes provisions that derogate from the general non-discrimination principle and allow WTO Members to use a different anti-dumping methodology in cases against imports from China. This provision allows a deviation from calculating "normal value" based on a strict comparison with domestic prices or costs in China if the producers under investigation cannot clearly show that Market Economy conditions prevail.[33]

The protocol also stipulates that "in any event" this provision expires on 11 December 2016 or before in case China demonstrates under the national law of the importing WTO Member that it is a Market Economy.[34] In view of China's entry into the WTO as well as its inevitable rise and unstoppable integration into the world economy, Western industrialised economies took preparatory measures. In the late 1990s, the former European Community and its Member States decided to explicitly adjust their anti-dumping instrument. Back in 1979, the Basic Anti-Dumping Regulation was significantly amended introducing the analogue country method in reference to a new category of countries referred to as Non-Market Economies.[35] Through this adjustment, the European Community mirrored the global political division at that time assuming that in the neighbouring centrally planned economies domestic prices and costs were artificially low since they were set by the state and not by market forces. Almost two decades later, China became a Member of the WTO. In addition, the European Communities recognised the Chinese government's progress on liberalisation by reclassifying it from a Non-Market Economy to a Transition Economy. In 1998, the European Commission proposed an exception to the general assumption for Non-Market Economies. This exception applies when one or more Chinese based companies subject to investigation prove that in their sector competition and market conditions for manufacture and sale prevail. In that case, the European Commission should use Chinese prices and costs instead of data from an analogue country to calculate "normal value" using the so-called standard methodology and treating China equally to other WTO Members in anti-dumping cases.[36] In practice though, as mentioned above, the European Commission does not use this method very often.

It is important to highlight that all Member States of the former European Community accepted the new terms and were aware of the deadline set in the Chinese Accession Protocol to the WTO. But most underestimated China's predicted

[32] World Trade Organization, Report on the Working Party on the Accession of China, WT/ACC/CHN/49, adopted 1 October 2001, p. 65; World Trade Organization, Accession of China. Invocation by El Salvador of Article XIII of the Marrakesh Agreement establishing the World Trade Organization with respect to China, WT/L/429, adopted 7 November 2001, p. 1.

[33] World Trade Organization, Ministerial Conference Decision of 10 November 2001 on the Accession of the People's Republic of China, WT/L/432, 23 November 2001, pp. 8–9.

[34] World Trade Organization, Ministerial Conference Decision of 10 November 2001 on the Accession of the People's Republic of China, WT/L/432, 23 November 2001, p. 9.

[35] OJ 1979 L 339/1, pp. 1–3.

[36] OJ 1998 L 128/18, pp. 18–19.

exceptional economic development. Many academics and policy makers in the early 2000s did not—or did not want to—believe in China's potential and its hard-working, ambitious population which by the beginning of the Millennium had already crossed the 1.2 billion-mark.[37] Over the years, the Chinese central government set incentives by implementing reforms and creating a stable framework for foreign investments and growth in the country. Western corporations realised their opportunities and did not hesitate to go Asian.

With the Chinese accession to the WTO, the European Commission set up an MES Working Group for a deep assessment of China's progress towards Market Economy. For this purpose, the European Commission established a formal consultation mechanism, as well as criteria to evaluate the progress.[38] One might expect that for such an extremely sensitive diplomatic issue, the European Union would define an appropriate legal framework, but since the Russian Federation had already been evaluated with the same MES criteria, perhaps it was not politically correct for the European Commission to choose a less arbitrary procedure. Unlike the Russian Federation to which Market Economy Status was granted in 2002, China had, and still has, to walk a rocky road.

After several unsuccessful consultations, both parties decided to set the issue aside. Even though the 2008 Commission report indicated a general recognition of China's "considerable progress" towards achieving Market Economy Status and of its economy as a *"modern and increasingly market-based system,"* merely one of the five criteria had been fulfilled by eliminating state intervention in the area of privatisation and by removing non-market forms of exchange or compensation.[39] Since 2012, both parties have chosen to let time decide. During the following years, only a few academic commentators and lawyers paid attention to the fact that the European Union was running out of time to take any preventive measures to adjust the trade relations with China. The language of some parts of the Chinese WTO Accession Protocol led to intensive legal arguments of both supporters and opponents of MES for China.[40]

As the December 2016 deadline came closer, voices got louder and the discussions about the meaning and the implications of the rules and the deadline set in the Chinese WTO Accession Protocol became increasingly controversial. The European Commission held two orientation debates (January and July 2016) and organised intensive stakeholder contacts and a public consultation. In October 2016, the

---

[37] See https://data.worldbank.org/indicator/SP.POP.TOTL?locations=CN (last accessed 30 April 2018).

[38] European Commission, Commission Staff Working Document on the progress by the People's Republic of China towards graduation to market economy status in trade defence investigations, 19 September 2008, SEC(2008) 2503 final, http://trade.ec.europa.eu/doclib/docs/2009/june/tradoc_143599.pdf (last accessed 30 April 2018), p. 5.

[39] European Commission, Commission Staff Working Document on the progress by the People's Republic of China towards graduation to market economy status in trade defence investigations, 19 September 2008, SEC(2008) 2503 final, http://trade.ec.europa.eu/doclib/docs/2009/june/tradoc_143599.pdf (last accessed 30 April 2018), pp. 4 and 26.

[40] Rosentahl and Beckington (2014), pp. 254–355; Ruessmann and Beck (2014), p. 463; Noel (2016), pp. 299–305; Yu and Guan (2017), pp. 23–24; Vermulst et al. (2016), pp. 212–228.

European Council considered that *"unfair trade practices need to be tackled efficiently and robustly"* and requested adequate provisions to address situations in which market conditions do not prevail.[41] Industry opponents to Market Economy Status for China were also very active. AEGIS Europe, an industry alliance representing over 25 industries, started a well-organised political campaign across the European Union to impede greater penetration of the EU market by Chinese exporters.[42] Their lobbying intensified and concentrated on the European Parliament. In fact, following the entry into force of the Lisbon Treaty in 2009, the European Parliament has acquired extended law-making powers becoming a focal point for interest groups. The influence of AEGIS Europe's political campaign and media response on the Members of the European Parliament (MEPs) was such that the Parliament felt motivated to adopt a resolution which states that China is not a Market Economy.[43] Despite this statement, the political families in the European Parliament had quite different views on anti-dumping and the MES issue. The Group of European Conservatives and Reformists (ECR) as well as the Alliance of Liberals and Democrats for Europe (ALDE) focused on the need for the EU to fully comply with WTO rules,[44] whilst the European People's Party (EPP), the Progressive Alliance of Socialists and Democrats (S&D) and the Green-European Free Alliance (Greens-EFA) emphasised that China was not a Market Economy unless the five MES-criteria established by the EU had been fulfilled.[45] Only far right groups

---

[41] European Council, European Council meeting (20 and 21 October 2016)—Conclusions, 21 October 2016, EUCO 31/16, http://data.consilium.europa.eu/doc/document/ST-31-2016-INIT/en/pdf (last accessed 30 April 2018), pp. 4–5.

[42] AEGIS EUROPE, Statement on fair trade rules, https://static1.squarespace.com/static/5537b2fbe4b0e49a1e30c01c/t/55896e07e4b024895ff23f2d/1435069959931/15+06+23+AEGIS+Europe+-+Statement+on+fair+trade+rules.pdf (last accessed 30 April 2018), p. 1.

[43] European Parliament, European Parliament resolution of 12 May 2016 on China's market economy status, 12 May 2016, P8_TA(2016)0223, http://www.europarl.europa.eu/sides/getDoc.do?pubRef=-//EP//NONSGML+TA+P8-TA-2016-0223+0+DOC+PDF+V0//EN (last accessed 30 April 2018), p. 2.

[44] European Parliament, Motion for a Resolution on China's market economy status (2016/2667(RSP)) ECR Group, 10 May 2016, B8-0611/2016, http://www.europarl.europa.eu/sides/getDoc.do?pubRef=-//EP//NONSGML+MOTION+B8-2016-0611+0+DOC+PDF+V0//EN (last accessed 30 April 2018), pp. 2–3; European Parliament, Motion for a Resolution on China's market economy status (2016/2667(RSP)) ALDE Group, 10 May 2016, B8-0607/2016, http://www.europarl.europa.eu/sides/getDoc.do?pubRef=-//EP//NONSGML+MOTION+B8-2016-0607+0+DOC+PDF+V0//EN (last accessed 30 April 2018), pp. 2–3.

[45] European Parliament, Motion for a Resolution on China's market economy status (2016/2667(RSP)) PPE Group, 10 May 2016, B8-0608/2016, http://www.europarl.europa.eu/sides/getDoc.do?pubRef=-//EP//NONSGML+MOTION+B8-2016-0608+0+DOC+PDF+V0//EN (last accessed 30 April 2018), pp. 2–3; European Parliament, Motion for a Resolution on China's market economy status (2016/2667(RSP)) S&D Group, 10 May 2016, B8-0609/2016, http://www.europarl.europa.eu/sides/getDoc.do?pubRef=-//EP//NONSGML+MOTION+B8-2016-0609+0+DOC+PDF+V0//EN (last accessed 30 April 2018), pp. 2–3; European Parliament, Motion for a Resolution on China's market economy status (2016/2667(RSP)) Verts/ALE Group, 10 May 2016, B8-0612/2016, http://www.europarl.europa.eu/sides/getDoc.do?pubRef=-//EP//NONSGML+MOTION+B8-2016-0612+0+DOC+PDF+V0//EN (last accessed 30 April 2018), pp. 2–3.

Europe of Nations and Freedom (ENF) and Europe of Freedom and Direct Democracy (EFDD) as well as far left European United Left-Nordic Green Left (GUE-NGL) adopted a confrontational rhetoric by refusing a unilateral de facto recognition of China's Market Economy Status.[46] VoteWatch Europe analysed the debate and the voting behaviour in the European Parliament. Italian and French MEPs led the opposition to granting MES whilst mainly Dutch, Polish and Swedish MEPs were more in favour. The split also went through political families. For example, some of the French socialists had more extreme positions than German S&D MEPs. German EPP MEPs only stated that China was not a Market Economy, but they did not vote in favour of more stringent rules.[47] The hesitation of the German politicians can be explained by the different socio-economic interests: while Germany's labour force seems to be among the most exposed if commercial ties with China are upgraded, Germany-based importers are among the beneficiaries of reduced customs duties, considering that the port of Hamburg is the second biggest point of entry in the EU for Chinese goods.

As the EU's largest economy and one of the main users of anti-dumping measures, the situation in Germany is obviously quite interesting. Since 2005, the successive Governments led by Chancellor Angela Merkel have been well aware of Germany's competitive position in the global economy. Perhaps it is no surprise that Chancellor Merkel even considered concessions to China. She repeatedly indicated her support for China's Market Economy Status on the condition that the Chinese Government implements reforms and sensitive German industries are properly safeguarded. In contrast, at the debate's most heated point in March 2016 during a parliamentary session in the German Bundestag on the challenges faced by the steel industry, the then Vice-Chancellor and Minister for Economic Affairs as well as leader of the Social Democratic Party Sigmar Gabriel adopted quite a strong and defensive position which seemed to be in contrast to Chancellor Merkel's past statements: *"China cannot be granted Market Economy Status if China does not abide by the rules of market economies […]. We need to enforce the rules of trade and fair competition, and we cannot give Market Economy Status to countries that are obviously not market economies […]. When there is fair competition the best prevail, not*

---

[46] European Parliament, Motion for a Resolution on China's market economy status (2016/2667(RSP)) EFDD Group, 10 May 2016, B8-0604/2016, http://www.europarl.europa.eu/sides/getDoc.do?pubRef=-//EP//NONSGML+MOTION+B8-2016-0604+0+DOC+PDF+V0//EN (last accessed 30 April 2018), pp. 2–4; European Parliament, Motion for a Resolution on China's market economy status (2016/2667(RSP)) ENF Group, 10 May 2015, B8-0605/2016, http://www.europarl.europa.eu/sides/getDoc.do?pubRef=-//EP//NONSGML+MOTION+B8-2016-0605+0+DOC+PDF+V0//EN (last accessed 30 April 2018) pp. 2–3; European Parliament, Motion for a Resolution on China's market economy status (2016/2667(RSP)) GUE/NGL Group, 10 May 2016, B8-0610/2016, http://www.europarl.europa.eu/sides/getDoc.do?pubRef=-//EP//NONSGML+MOTION+B8-2016-0610+0+DOC+PDF+V0//EN (last accessed 30 April 2018), pp. 2–5.

[47] Frantescu DP (2016) The European and national politics behind China's market economy status. VoteWatch Europe, 18 May 2016, http://www.votewatch.eu/blog/the-european-and-national-politics-behind-chinas-market-economy-status/ (last accessed 30 April 2018).

those with abysmal wages, the worst environmental standards and those who are receiving support from the state to flood the market."[48]

Minister Gabriel emphasised the importance of "fairness". Fairness, as seen by some politicians, has little in common with the concept of dumping as a form of price discrimination between markets. Although anti-dumping instruments are applied to react to "unfair trade", they are by no means an instrument to equalise or harmonise legislative differences with respect to domestic environment, labour, employment or other social regulations. Unfortunately, the determination of "normal value" is increasingly overshadowed by this new narrative to the detriment of the traditional concept of comparative advantage of cost or production. Almost no one in the political debate mentioned that the application of non-MES in anti-dumping proceedings always leads to high anti-dumping duties. And certainly no one questioned the fact that the European Commission automatically compares Chinese export prices with third party prices or costs, rather than with Chinese prices. This is quite surprising considering that China is in an advanced stage of a transitional process, shifting from a centrally planned to a market-based economy, where prices in several industrial sectors are set by market conditions and competition. The heated debate on the Market Economy Status shows that the approach to TDI has considerably changed over the last years and is quite different from the situation 16 years ago when China became the 143rd WTO Member.

In November 2016, the European Commission adopted another legislative proposal to amend the Basic Anti-Dumping Regulation. The Commission suggests applying a new method of assessing market distortions in third countries when calculating anti-dumping duties. Instead of a specific reference to Non-Market Economy, the Commission solely distinguishes between WTO Members and non-WTO Members when establishing "normal value". For WTO Members, "normal value" shall, in principle, be determined on the basis of domestic prices of the like product or the costs of the product in the exporting country. This standard methodology will be complemented by a mandatory methodology which applies in case the European Commission identifies significant market distortions in the course of an investigation. Such market distortions exist if domestic prices and costs do not reflect market conditions due to state intervention. In such situations, "normal value" would be constructed on the basis of costs of production and sale reflecting undistorted prices.[49] In its impact assessment accompanying the legislative proposal, the Commission mentions on the one hand that legislative changes were necessary due to the unclear language contained in the Chinese WTO Accession Protocol and, on the other hand, that "*since the distortions in the Chinese economy*

---

[48] Deutscher Bundestag, Stenografischer Bericht—167. Sitzung. Sigmar Gabriel, Bundesminister BMWi—16357 D, 16358 D, 28 April 2016, Plenarprotokoll 18/167, http://dipbt.bundestag.de/doc/btp/18/18167.pdf (last accessed 30 April 2018) translated by AEGIS EUROPE, Press Release: Industry welcomes German Minister's statement about China's Market Economy Status: "China must abide by the rules", 29 April 2016, http://www.aegiseurope.eu/news/press-release-industry-welcomes-german-ministers-statement-about-chinas-market-economy-status-china-must-abide-by-the-rules (last accessed 30 April 2018).

[49] European Commission, COM(2016) 721 final.

continue to exist, using Chinese prices and costs for calculating dumping would in many cases significantly understate the actual level of dumping and many measures imposed on that basis would not be effective in remedying the injury caused by the dumped imports."[50] In another assessment of the proposal, the European Commission finds that if it were to apply Market Economy Status in anti-dumping investigations against China this would reduce anti-dumping duties by about 30%. Lower anti-dumping duties would result in lower Chinese prices on the EU market with the consequence of a considerable increase in Chinese exports (18–28%) to the disadvantage of the domestic industry. Such an approach would also result in considerable job losses in the EU.[51]

During the legislative procedure, the EU institutions widely recognised the value of the proposed approach in order to address dumping in regards to products produced in China by maintaining the effectiveness of the anti-dumping instrument and guarantying compliance with the EU's international obligations. After comparatively short "trilogue" negotiations, the Commission, the European Parliament and the Council of Ministers reached a compromise[52] and the new methodology for determining "normal value" entered into force on 20 December 2017.[53] The amended anti-dumping legislation is "country-neutral" and "non-discriminatory" on its face. If market distortions exist, the new methodology is mandatory and will apply to all WTO Members in order to establish an undistorted "normal value" and hence a determination to grant Market Economy Status to a specific country becomes superfluous. For non-WTO Members "normal value" will continue to be determined on the basis of the "analogue country" methodology.

In order to identify such market distortions, the legislation provides an extensive but not exhaustive list of state induced distortions, e.g. public policies or measures

---

[50] European Commission, Commission Staff Working Document—executive summary of the impact assessment accompanying the document Proposal for a Regulation of the European Parliament and of the Council amending Regulation (EU) 2016/1036 on protection against dumped imports from countries not members of the European Union and Regulation (EU) 2016/1037 on protection against subsidised imports from countries not members of the European Union, 9 November 2016, SWD(2016) 371 final, http://eur-lex.europa.eu/LexUriServ/LexUriServ.do?uri= SWD:2016:0371:FIN:EN:PDF (last accessed 30 April 2018), p. 2.

[51] European Commission, Commission Staff Working Document—Assessment of the economic impact of changing the methodology for calculating normal value in trade defense investigations against China accompanying the document Proposal for a Regulation of the European Parliament and of the Council amending Regulation (EU) 2016/1036 on protection against dumped imports from countries not members of the European Union and Regulation (EU) 2016/1037 on protection against subsidised imports from countries not members of the European Union, 9 November 2016, SWD(2016) 372 final, http://eur-lex.europa.eu/LexUriServ/LexUriServ.do?uri=SWD:2016:0372: FIN:EN:PDF (last accessed 30 April 2018), p. 5.

[52] Lange B (2017) Hart erkämpftes Ergebnis. Besserer Anti-Dumping-Schutz für Arbeitsplätze und Wachstum in Europa durchgesetzt. SPD-Gruppe im Europäischen Parlament, 3 October 2017, https://www.spd-europa.de/pressemeldungen/hart-erkaempftes-ergebnis-3179 (last accessed 30 April 2018).

[53] OJ 2017 L 338/1, Article 11(4).

discriminating in favour of domestic suppliers.[54] The evidence for distortions has to be delivered by the Commission Services. Therefore, the EU legislator obliges the Commission to *"prepare and issue reports describing the specific circumstances of the market in any given sector, and point out if prices and costs in the exporting country are unsuitable to be compared to the export price to calculate dumping."*[55] The domestic industry will be able to rely on these reports or on any other type of evidence when introducing an anti-dumping complaint.[56] During the anti-dumping investigation, the Commission must justify the use of the new methodology by assessing all verifiable evidence available, including evidence presented by the exporting producers under investigation claiming that their costs are undistorted.[57] Consequently, the EU legislator took into account the concerns of some EU industries and shifted the burden of proof in a complaint on the Commission. The same day on which the new legislation entered into force, the Commission published its first country report on state-induced distortions. The country selected was obviously China.[58] At the time of writing, the Commission is preparing the country report on Russia.

In case significant distortions are identified in the course of an investigation, the Commission will disregard the costs which are generated in a third country based on the assumption that these costs do not represent the costs reflecting normal market conditions. Moreover, distorted costs are deemed to reflect public policy decisions that a state has legitimately and at its own discretion decided to set, but which affect a fair comparison between the export price to the EU and "normal value" for the product required to determine the dumping margin. In conclusion, the aim of the Commission is to compare two factors which are based on the same underlying principles.

To adjust a situation in which one or several production costs are significantly distorted and therefore not appropriate for calculating "normal value", the legislation recognises three different sources which the Commission may use to collect the necessary data for its calculations. Such sources include: undistorted domestic costs, undistorted international prices, costs, or benchmarks or the costs of production and sale in an appropriate representative country. For the selection of this appropriate representative third country the new methodology prescribes two criteria that shall be applied subsequently. Firstly, the representative country should have a similar level of economic development according to the country income

---

[54] OJ 2017 L 338/1, Article 2(6a)(b).

[55] European Commission, Commission proposes changes to the EU's anti-dumping and anti-subsidy legislation, 9 November 2016, MEMO/16/3605, http://europa.eu/rapid/press-release_MEMO-16-3605_en.htm (last accessed 30 April 2018); OJ 2017 L 338/1, Article 2(6a)(c).

[56] OJ 2017 L 338/1, Article 2(6a)(d).

[57] OJ 2017 L 338/1, Article 11(9).

[58] European Commission, Commission Staff Working Document on significant distortions in the economy of the People's Republic of China for the purposes of trade defence investigations, 20 December 2017, SWD(2017) 483 final/2, http://trade.ec.europa.eu/doclib/docs/2017/december/tradoc_156474.pdf (last accessed 30 April 2018).

classifications by the World Bank. Secondly, if more than one country should be appropriate, the Commission shall give preference to the country with the highest level of social and environmental protection with reference to the record on signing, ratifying and complying with core conventions.[59] The Commission pointed out that if it *"has a choice between a number of appropriate representative countries with a similar level of economic development as the exporting country under investigation, the level of social and environmental protection in the representative source country will be taken into account in the selection."*[60] It is clear that the Commission, also in the future, will not rely on Chinese prices but will construct "normal value" by reference of an adequate analogue country. This is worrying since it extends the notion of "fairness" by taking social and environmental protection into account. The intended consequence of the new methodology will be high anti-dumping duties.

It is interesting to note that in the course of legislative discussion, the European Parliament in particular strongly advocated to allow compensation for social and environmental dumping which goes beyond economic dumping and is inadmissible under WTO-rules. The European Parliament's legislative document for the plenary session of July 2017 contains many amendments with respect to domestic environment, labour, employment and other social regulations and is hence a reflection of the above mentioned new "fairness"-narrative concerning anti-dumping.[61] Is the European Parliament trying to misuse the anti-dumping instrument to address legitimate comparative advantages in third countries? It seems that also the found compromise reflects this rather protectionist narrative. Although the compromise designed was incorporated in the new methodology in a subtle manner, it might become subject of WTO-disputes soon.

Chinese officials repeatedly complained about the discriminatory treatment of Chinese exports in anti-dumping cases. Just one day after the expiry date, after requesting consultations under the WTO's dispute-settlement mechanism over the U.S. and EU's practices of anti-dumping, Chinese Minister of Commerce Gao Hucheng pointed out in an article published by the People's Daily and by MOFCOM: *"Article 15 of the Protocol on the Accession of the People's Republic of China to the WTO stipulates [...] that starting from December 11, 2016, any future anti-dumping cases against China should make comparison with prices or costs in China. Since*

---

[59] OJ 2017 L 338/1, Article 2(6a)(a).

[60] European Commission, The EU is changing its anti-dumping and anti-subsidy legislation to address state induced market distortions, 4 October 2017, http://europa.eu/rapid/press-release_MEMO-17-3703_en.htm (last accessed 30 April 2018).

[61] European Parliament, Report on the proposal for a regulation of the European Parliament and of the Council amending Regulation (EU) 2016/1036 on protection against dumped imports from countries not members of the European Union and Regulation (EU) 2016/1037 on protection against subsidised imports from countries not members of the European Union (COM(2016)0721—C8-0456/2016—2016/0351(COD)) Committee on International Trade—Salvatore Cicu, 27 June 2017, A8-0236/2017, http://www.europarl.europa.eu/sides/getDoc.do?pubRef=-//EP//NONSGML+REPORT+A8-2017-0236+0+DOC+PDF+V0//EN (last accessed 30 April 2018), pp. 6–7, 13–14 and 30–34.

this obligation has been written into the international treaty, each WTO member should fulfil it without doubt [...]. Most of the WTO Members have fulfilled their obligations stipulated under the Article 15 in the protocol ahead or on schedule by terminating the "surrogate country system" against China. But a few have refused to do so. They even tried to obscure the term "market economy" with their domestic logic, or cite overcapacity in some industries as an excuse for delay. The WTO rules, as a matter of fact, did not provide detailed definition of "market economy" [...]. As for those who refuse to keep their promises, China will adamantly protect its legitimate interests and reserve the right to take further measures."[62]

It is worth mentioning that over half of all WTO Members, including Argentina, Russia, Brazil, Australia, South Korea, South Africa and Switzerland, already recognised China's Market Economy Status. Many of those countries are commodity suppliers and some of them have brought fewer anti-dumping cases against China in the last years than the EU and the U.S. In many cases, China has secured its Market Economy Status negotiating free trade agreements or promoting Chinese foreign direct investment. But still, of all 32 WTO Members ever having initiated anti-dumping proceedings against China, only 14 intensive anti-dumping users have been convinced to grant MES under domestic law.[63]

To sum up, when speaking about the politics of TDI today, we speak about the politics vis-à-vis China. Although China has become the EU's second biggest trading partner after the U.S., political cooperation between the EU and China is a cumbersome issue. The negotiations on a bilateral investment agreement launched in 2013 are difficult, not only because of European political opposition to investment agreements as such, but also because of Chinese barriers to investment and strong government intervention in the overall economy. In 2016, the European Commission adopted a new strategy on China which includes a trade agenda to improve market access opportunities. The strategy refers to European values and insists on *"reciprocity, a level playing field and fair competition across all areas of co-operation"*.[64] Furthermore, President Juncker has also proposed a framework for screening foreign direct investment which will affect the EU's relations with China.[65] It remains to be seen whether the EU and China will achieve a common understanding on rules-based bilateral trade ties. In the meantime, both sides will

---

[62] Ministry of Commerce People's Republic of China, Minister Gao Hucheng's signed article on People's Daily on 12 December: China will firmly protect its legitimate interests and multilateral trade system, 12 December 2016, http://english.mofcom.gov.cn/article/newsrelease/significantnews/201612/20161202196164.shtml (last accessed 30 April 2018).

[63] Yalcin et al. (2016), p. 21.

[64] European Commission, High Representative of the Union for Foreign Affairs and Security Policy, Joint Communication to the European Parliament and the Council. Elements for a new EU Strategy on China, 22 June 2016, JOIN(2016) 30 final, http://eeas.europa.eu/archives/docs/china/docs/joint_communication_to_the_european_parliament_and_the_council_-_elements_for_a_new_eu_strategy_on_china.pdf (last accessed 30 April 2018), p. 2.

[65] European Commission, State of the Union 2017—Trade Package: European Commission proposes framework for screening of foreign direct investments, 14 September 2017, IP/17/3183, http://europa.eu/rapid/press-release_IP-17-3183_en.htm (last accessed 30 April 2018).

continue to apply their rules according to which companies and investors must operate within their borders.

5   The Debate on China's MES Within Industry

MES was, and still is, a difficult subject for German industry. Whilst no sector of industry questions the necessity of an efficient and effective anti-dumping instrument, the views on MES are quite varied. Within the Federation of German Industries (Bundesverband der Deutschen Industrie e.V., BDI), industry tried hard to reach a compromise on the issue. In order not be "voiceless", the BDI eventually adopted in 2016 and 2017 several position papers which constitute the lowest common denominator of the two opposing positions: the general disagreement of the export-oriented sectors and the "alliance for fair trade" led by the steel industry.

Initially, it seemed premature for the German industry to take a definitive position on China's Market Economy Status. The industry considered that it was up to the EU institutions to decide and recommended that policy makers should align with the U.S. government. It also indicated that the Chinese Government still had homework to do, as the Commission's conditions for MES had not been met.[66] As mentioned above, the European Commission did not decide on whether to grant MES or not but launched a public consultation. Meanwhile, the "alliance for fair trade" and its European counterpart AEGIS Europe mobilised workers and trade unions to protest on the streets against granting Market Economy Status to China. The protesters were concerned about negative impacts in terms of job loss and reduced growth, as the decision to grant MES would have severely hit some industrial sectors such as steel, metal and solar industry, which are already suffering from Chinese overcapacities and fierce competition. Since these protests had a rather positive response, one could have had the impression that industry in general opposed the granting of MES to China.

Some resistance within German industry emerged, however, when three highly internationalised key sectors, chemicals, electronics and mechanical engineering, joined forces and acted as a counterbalance during the negotiations of a BDI strategy paper.[67] This time, the strategy agreed upon in the BDI resembled a more nuanced and balanced understanding that represented the view of both sides of the German industrial environment. It recognised the indispensable economic partnership between the EU and China on an equal footing despite existing differences and

---

[66] Bundesverband der Deutschen Industrie e.V., China's market economy status, 7 January 2016, https://bdi.eu/media/themenfelder/internationale_maerkte/downloads/BDI_MES_Final_Englisch. pdf (last accessed 30 April 2018), p. 1.

[67] Verband der Chemischen Industrie e.V. and Verband Deutscher Maschinen- und Anlagenbau e.V., Zentralverband Elektrotechnik- und Elektronikindustrie, Joint position of the chemical, electrical and mechanical engineering industry on China's market economy status, 19 October 2016, https://www.vci.de/langfassungen/langfassungen-pdf/2016-10-19-eu-and-china-must-find-common-solution-vci-vdma-zvei.pdf (last accessed 30 April 2018), pp. 1–2.

barriers on trade and investment matters. The BDI also clarified specific concerns the opposing sectors were having in case the European Commission would treat China as a Market Economy. Some industries feared a change of the rules concerning the burden of proof. How should European companies demonstrate that market conditions do not prevail in China? Their main concern was that industry's anti-dumping requests would not contain sufficient evidence to establish a prima facie case due to lack of transparency of the Chinese market in several industry sectors.[68]

Unlike the fundamental and dogmatic issues of the public MES debate, this relatively technical explanation did not attract much attention. After the European Commission's proposal to change the methodology in anti-dumping investigations was made public—without explicitly granting Market Economy Status to China— the reaction by AEGIS Europe and some key MEPs seemed excessive notwithstanding the fact that the European Commission offered to help affected industries with sectoral studies and assessments on whether market conditions in the specific sector prevailed in China or not. In contrast, BDI's assessment of the proposal had been neutral: *"From the perspective of German industry, the reform proposal is a first step in the right direction but leaves room for improvement in several areas."*[69]

The discussion in Germany was in sharp contrast to the discussions within the Confederation of European Business (BusinessEurope). BusinessEurope's position paper was far more legal in scope than BDI's position, concluding that Market Economy Status should not be granted to China.[70] The BDI did not reach such a conclusion and several industry sectors, not solely from Germany, firmly opposed BusinessEurope's position. They considered that business should not answer such a highly complicated legal question but rather let the WTO's dispute settlement system take the final decision.[71] Nevertheless, the opinion in Brussels was more radical due to the influence of voices from Italy, Spain, France, Portugal and Poland that clearly opposed granting Market Economy Status. This is not surprising, as according to the European Commission nearly 80% of all EU job losses would occur in

---

[68] Bundesverband der Deutschen Industrie e.V., BDI position on the issue of China's market economy status, 27 July 2016, https://bdi.eu/media/user_upload/20160727_BDI-Position_MES_China_English.pdf (last accessed 30 April 2018), pp. 1–2.

[69] Bundesverband der Deutschen Industrie e.V., BDI Assessment of the European Commission's Proposal on Reforming the EU Basic Anti-Dumping Regulation, 19 April 2017, https://bdi.eu/media/themenfelder/internationale_maerkte/BDI_Assessment_of_the_European_Commission_s_Proposal_on_Reforming_the_EU_Basic_Anti-Dumping_Regulation_April_2017.pdf (last accessed 30 April 2018), p. 1.

[70] BusinessEurope, Position Paper—China's Market Economy Status, 11 December 2015, https://www.businesseurope.eu/sites/buseur/files/media/position_papers/rex/2015-12-11_chinas_market_economy_status.pdf (last accessed 30 April 2018), p. 2.

[71] European Chemical Industry Council, Cefic views on Market Economy Status (MES) for China, 16 April 2015, http://www.cefic.org/Documents/RESOURCES/PositionPapers/Cefic-views-on-market-economy-status-MES-for-China.pdf (last accessed 30 April 2018), pp. 2–3; Foreign Trade Association, To ME or not to ME: China's status after 11 December 2016, 19 November 2015, http://itp.fta-intl.org/resource/me-or-not-me-chinas-status-after-11-december-2016 (last accessed 30 April 2018), pp. 9–10.

those countries along with Germany.[72] In comparison to Germany, however, those Member States have been more severely affected by the financial crisis as well as the subsequent recessions and depend mostly on the impacted industries. Germany on the other hand benefits from diverse economic structures and a large industry base that accounts for approximately 25% of the GDP.[73]

Several reasons can be mentioned why the German industry had difficulties in agreeing on a substantive position on the MES issue. The traditional response is the clash between the export-oriented sectors and the import-suffering sectors. In Germany, industries that internationalised and kept integrated into the world economy established themselves as leading sectors. German cars, electronics, chemicals and mechanical engineering are highly competitive in the expanded global marketplace and are the roots of Germany's successful export-led growth model. Whilst recognising the difficult situation of the import-suffering sectors, these industries did not want to put their export and foreign investment successes in jeopardy when adopting their position on China's MES and they were adamant to avoid Chinese retaliatory action.

More importantly, however, the discussion showed an important change of attitude related to global value chains. In the past, companies accepted dumping as unfair and, hence, accepted the consequence, i.e. paying higher duties on dumped imports or change sources. Nowadays, as far as inputs are concerned, companies involved in global value chains question the reason behind anti-dumping duties on inputs and occasionally would prefer to import "dumped" inputs. Thus, some companies no longer view dumped inputs as "unfair" and do question the methodologies used by governments to calculate anti-dumping duties.

To sum up, the difficulty in reaching a position within the BDI does not indicate a complete change of attitude vis-à-vis anti-dumping, but it confirms, however, an interesting development, i.e. that in a world of global value chains the traditional concept of anti-dumping might no longer be valid.[74] It will therefore be interesting to observe whether domestic policies take such views on the effects of globalisation into account when deciding in the future on "market distortions" in anti-dumping investigations.

---

[72] Directorate General for Trade of the European Commission, Change in the methodology for antidumping investigations concerning China, 3 February 2016, http://trade.ec.europa.eu/doclib/docs/2016/february/tradoc_154241.pdf (last accessed 30 April 2018), p. 2.

[73] Statistisches Bundesamt, Bruttoinlandsprodukt 2016 für Deutschland. Begleitmaterial zur Pressekonferenz am 12. Januar 2017 in Berlin, 12 January 2017, https://www.destatis.de/DE/PresseService/Presse/Pressekonferenzen/2017/BIP2016/Pressebroschuere_BIP2016.pdf?__blob=publicationFile (last accessed 30 April 2018), p. 11.

[74] Ahamad (2013), p. 88.

6 Conclusions: Rethinking TDI in a Globalised Interconnected World—An Illusion

Rethinking trade defence instruments is not a new idea. After the successful liberalisation package decided in the Uruguay Round, it was felt that states would increasingly resort to anti-dumping action to avoid the necessary domestic adjustment processes. Hence, suggestions have been put forward on how to discipline the use of this instrument by resorting to competition policy concepts.[75] The fundamental question of the debate was whether price discrimination between markets should be considered actionable or whether it should be regarded as a "normal competitive market expanding behaviour" and only be acted against in case of "predatory" or "strategic" dumping?[76] Under such a concept, the trigger for a defensive measure would be an anti-competitive behaviour, such as the pricing below cost in order to drive all other suppliers out of the market. The substitution of anti-dumping with competition policy would reduce anti-dumping action considerably. An OECD study finds that over 90% of all anti-dumping actions in several OECD countries would not have been successful under competition law.[77] It is unfortunate that the rich academic debate does not find a corollary in politics.

At the multilateral level, changes to existing rules cannot be expected. At the beginning of the Doha Round, many hoped that the WTO would agree on a competition policy chapter. Such new rules could have influenced the anti-dumping concept. Yet, the negotiations on competition (one of the four so-called Singapore issues) in the Doha Round never took off. At the Ministerial Conference in Cancún in 2003, ministers failed to find a consensus on the issue with the consequence that the subject was taken off the negotiating agenda.[78] The Doha-"Rules Negotiations" which deal, inter alia, with anti-dumping will also not lead to fundamental changes since the mandate requires that the negotiators preserve the basic concepts and principles of the Anti-Dumping Agreement,[79] notwithstanding the activities of the "friends of anti-dumping negotiations" which have made *"many proposals for*

---

[75] Hoekman and Mavroidis (1996), p. 36.

[76] World Trade Organization, Intervention of Allan Fels during the WTO Public Forum 2010, Session 36: Antidumping regime: A view from the competition policy perspective, 17 September 2010, https://www.wto.org/english/forums_e/public_forum10_e/programme_e.htm#session36 (last accessed 30 April 2018).

[77] Organisation for Economic Co-operation and Development, Trade and Competition. Frictions after the Uruguay Round, International Trade and Investment Division. Economic Department Working Papers No. 165, OCDE/GD(96)105, 1996, http://www.oecd.org/regreform/reform/1863507.pdf (last accessed 30 April 2018), pp. 8 and 17.

[78] Woolcock S, The Singapore Issues in Cancun: a failed negotiation ploy or a litmus test for global governance. London School of Economics, http://www.lse.ac.uk/internationalRelations/centresandunits/ITPU/docs/woolcocksingaporeissues.pdf (last accessed 30 April 2018), pp. 5–8.

[79] See https://www.wto.org/english/tratop_e/dda_e/dohaexplained_e.htm#antidumping (last accessed 30 April 2018).

tightening disciplines on the conduct of anti-dumping investigations."[80] Lately, even the WTO's crown jewel, its dispute settlement system, has come under attack, in particular by the U.S., because of the Appellate Body's interpretations of the rules of the Anti-Dumping Agreement.[81] The U.S. now even opposes the reappointment of WTO Appellate Body Members because of these rulings—another very disturbing policy development.[82]

At the bilateral or plurilateral level, the situation is slightly different. Whilst the vast majority of existing free trade agreements provide for action against dumping, there are some exceptions, namely the FTAs between Australia and New-Zealand, Canada and Chile, the European Free Trade Association (EFTA) and Singapore, EFTA and Chile, EFTA and the EU. These agreements aim for a deep integration and link, to a certain extent, the abolition of anti-dumping to the application of competition rules.[83] The European Union is a prime example for such deep integration. By monitoring the behaviour of companies to prevent anti-competitive practices, the European Commission secures a fair Single Market so that the availability of trade defence instruments is no longer necessary.[84] A study conducted by the Kommerskollegium analyses the effects of the abolition of anti-dumping measures after the 2004 enlargement of the EU. It notes that the abolition of 16 anti-dumping measures against Eastern European countries as a consequence of their accession to the EU in 2004 *"did not cause injury to EU15 industry in terms of price undercutting and lost market share."*[85] It also shows that competition rules would not have been applicable to the former dumping practices due to the relatively small market share the accession countries had with respect to the dumped products.[86] The study

---

[80] See https://www.wto.org/english/tratop_e/dda_e/meet08_brief04_e.htm (last accessed 30 April 2018).

[81] Behsudi A (2017) Lighthizer's WTO crusade. Politico, 1 October 2017, http://www.politico.com/tipsheets/morning-trade/2017/01/lighthizers-wto-crusade-218162 (last accessed 30 April 2018).

[82] Permanent Mission of the United States of America to the United Nations and Other International Organizations in Geneva, Statement by the United States at the Meeting of the WTO Dispute Settlement Body, 23 May 2016, https://geneva.usmission.gov/wp-content/uploads/2016/05/May23.DSB_.pdf (last accessed 30 April 2018), pp. 11–19.

[83] Kasteng J and Prawitz C, Eliminating Anti-Dumping measures in regional trade agreements. The European Union example. Kommerskollegium 23 November 2013, https://www.kommers.se/Documents/dokumentarkiv/publikationer/2013/rapporter/report-eliminating-anti-dumping-measures_webb.pdf (last accessed 30 September 2017), p. 5.

[84] European Parliamentary Research Service, EU competition policy: key to a fair Single Market, 2 June 2014, 140814REV1, http://www.europarl.europa.eu/EPRS/140814REV1-EU-Competition-Policy-FINAL.pdf (last accessed 30 April 2018), pp. 1–16.

[85] Kasteng J and Prawitz C, Eliminating Anti-Dumping measures in regional trade agreements. The European Union example. Kommerskollegium 23 November 2013, https://www.kommers.se/Documents/dokumentarkiv/publikationer/2013/rapporter/report-eliminating-anti-dumping-measures_webb.pdf (last accessed 30 April 2018), p. 15.

[86] Kasteng J and Prawitz C, Eliminating Anti-Dumping measures in regional trade agreements. The European Union example. Kommerskollegium 23 November 2013, https://www.kommers.se/Documents/dokumentarkiv/publikationer/2013/rapporter/report-eliminating-anti-dumping-measures_webb.pdf (last accessed 30 April 2018), pp. 13–14.

concludes: *"What were once considered as third country imports that caused injury to the EU's domestic industry, as well as triggering the use of anti-dumping measures, have, subsequent to the enlargement, been considered normal business practices in-line with the requirements for "fair competition".*"[87] Upon accession to the European Union, dumping miraculously disappears.

Switzerland is another noticeable example: it is the "pacifist" in a world of "anti-dumping warriors", in so far as it does not have an anti-dumping law nor does it apply anti-dumping measures against foreign products.[88] Such "unilateral disarmament" has had the effect that *"the Swiss export economy has also been largely spared any anti-dumping tariffs in recent years."*[89]

Although the new generation of trade agreements might offer the potential for deeper economic and political cooperation, anti-dumping regulations will not undergo significant liberalising steps over the next years and Switzerland will most likely remain an "island". Even the negotiations of "deeper" agreements, such as the Transatlantic Trade and Investment Partnership (TTIP) and the Trans-Pacific Partnership (TPP) provided for anti-dumping. The political reality of today seems to call for a tightening of the anti-dumping instrument by changing the narrative of "dumping" insofar as, in some cases, price comparison will take societal considerations into account. The suggestions to reconsider the concept of dumping or to tighten the disciplines on the conduct of anti-dumping investigations seem far away. As long as economic operators do not raise their voices against stricter rules anti-dumping measures are here to stay and the rethinking of TDI remains an illusion.

References

Ahamad N (2013) Estimating trade in value-added: why and how? In: Elms DK, Low P (eds) Global value chains in a changing world. WTO Publications, Geneva, pp 85–108
Dunoff LJ, Moore OM (2014) Footloose and duty-free? Reflections on European Union anti-dumping measures on certain footwear from China. World Trade Rev 13(2):149–178
Hoekman BM, Mavroidis PC (1996) Dumping, antidumping and antitrust. J World Trade 30(1):27–52
Issabekov N, Suchecki AM (2016) Analysis of the EU anti-dumping policy in terms of the revealed comparative advantages. Comp Econ Res 19(5):43–61
Jackson JH (1969) World trade and the law of GATT. The Michie Company, Charlottesville

---

[87] Kasteng J and Prawitz C, Eliminating Anti-Dumping measures in regional trade agreements. The European Union example. Kommerskollegium 23 November 2013, https://www.kommers.se/Documents/dokumentarkiv/publikationer/2013/rapporter/report-eliminating-anti-dumping-measures_webb.pdf (last accessed 30 April 2018), p. 1.

[88] WTO Trade Policy Review Body, Report by the Secretariat on Switzerland and Liechtenstein, WT/TPR/S/355/Rev.1, 22 September 2017, pp. 10 and 58.

[89] Stern M, Conquering the Swiss market: marketing, import regulations, distribution networks, import promotion services, 15 July 2009, http://www.sacu.int/docs/efta_fta/switzerland.pdf (last accessed 30 April 2018), p. 9.

Johnson V (2013) Market economy treatment of Chinese producers under the Indian antidumping regime. Global Trade Customs J 8(2):53–61

Ketterer TD (2016) EU anti-dumping and tariff cuts: trade policy substitution? World Econ 39(5):576–596

Melin Y (2012) Market economy treatment in EU anti-dumping investigations following the judgement of the Court of Justice of the EU in Xinanchem. Global Trade Customs J 7(11/12):504–506

Nita AC, Zanardi M (2013) The first review of European Union antidumping reviews. World Econ 36(12):1455–1477

Noel S (2016) Why the European Union must dump so-called non-market economy methodologies and adjustments in its antidumping investigations. Global Trade Customs J 11(7/8):296–305

Rosentahl P, Beckington J (2014) The People's Republic of China, a market economy or a non-market-economy in anti-dumping proceedings starting on December 12, 2016? Global Trade Customs J 9(7/8):352–355

Ruessmann L, Beck J (2014) 2016 and the application of NME methodology to Chinese producers in anti-dumping investigations. Global Trade Customs J 9(10):457–463

Vermulst E, Sud JD, Evenett SJ (2016) Normal value in anti-dumping proceedings against China post 2016: are some animals less equal than others? Global Trade Customs J 11(5):212–228

Yalcin E, Felbermayr G, Sandkamp A (2016) New trade rules for China? Opportunities and threats for the EU. Requested by the European Parliament's Committee on International Trade. Publications Office [of the EU], Luxembourg

Yu M, Guan J (2017) The non-market economy methodology shall be terminated after 2016. Global Trade Customs J 12(1):16–24

Part II
TDI in a Changing Global Framework

The EU's New Trade Defence Laws: A Two Steps Approach

Wolfgang Müller

In memoriam Neil Macdonald

This article is dedicated to the memory of my former colleague Neil Macdonald who passed away in March 2018. He was a friend and a mentor. His knowledge, his sense of humour and his energy have inspired generations of officials in the EU's trade defence services.

Contents

Abstract The article describes in detail the far-reaching changes to the EU's trade defence instruments (the Basic Anti-Dumping Regulation and the Basic Anti-Subsidy Regulation). For the first time since the WTO Uruguay Round, these laws have been subject to a major overhaul. This major overhaul has been achieved in two

Any views expressed in this article are personal and cannot be attributed to the European Commission.

W. Müller (✉)
European Commission, DG Trade, Brussels, Belgium
e-mail: wolfgang.mueller@ec.europa.eu

© Springer International Publishing AG, part of Springer Nature 2018
M. Bungenberg et al. (eds.), *The Future of Trade Defence Instruments*,
European Yearbook of International Economic Law,
https://doi.org/10.1007/978-3-319-95306-9_3

steps. In December 2017, a new methodology for the calculation of normal values in case of state-induced distortions in the exporting country was introduced. In a second step, in May 2018, a large number of other changes to the two Basic Regulations will enter into force. The most important of these changes cover a revision of the rules on the calculation of the injury margin and a pre-notification of interested parties 3 weeks prior to the imposition of provisional measures. Moreover, the new rules accept trade unions as interested parties and they recognise—in well-defined circumstances—the importance of multilateral labour and environmental agreements.

1 Introduction

The years 2017 and 2018 mark an important move forward in the development of the Union's trade defence instruments.[1] These instruments remained almost unchanged since the end of 1994, i.e. when the results of the Uruguay Round were transposed into Union law. In 2017, one major legislative proposal was signed into law, i.e. the new methodology for the calculation of normal value in case of distortions in the exporting country. The second major change was agreed between the co-legislators in a trilogue on 5 December 2017 and will enter into force in the course of 2018. This second change is about the modernisation of the Union's trade defence instruments which covers mostly procedural issues and the lesser-duty rule.

2 Modernisation Package

2.1 Legislative History

The Commission proposed, back in spring 2013, a package to modernise the Union's trade defence instruments. That package pursued six different objectives, i.e. to improve transparency and predictability, to address problems of retaliation by third countries against Union producers wishing to avail themselves of trade defence instruments, strengthening enforcement of trade defence measures, facilitating cooperation, optimisation of review practice and codification of some changes to the Commission's practice which became necessary because of jurisprudence.[2] The

---

[1] Basic Anti-Dumping Regulation, OJ 2016 L 176/21; Basic Anti-Subsidy Regulation, OJ 2016 L 176/55. There is a third trade defence instrument, i.e. the safeguard instrument that is not, however, affected by any of the legislative changes discussed in this contribution.

[2] European Commission, Communication from the Commission to the Council and the European Parliament on Modernisation of Trade Defence Instruments: Adapting trade defence instruments to the current needs of the European economy, COM(2013) 191 final, 10 April 2013, http://trade. ec.europa.eu/doclib/docs/2013/april/tradoc_150837.pdf (last accessed 30 April 2018).

European Parliament adopted its first reading position 1 year later.[3] While the guiding principle of the Commission proposal was to bring benefits for all economic actors affected by the operation of trade defence instruments, the Parliament's ideas would—if implemented—have changed this balance considerably in favour of the Union industry. The Parliament rejected all Commission proposals in favour of importing interests, notably the reimbursement of anti-dumping and anti-subsidy duties in case of expiry reviews that did not result in a renewal of measures and pre-disclosure, i.e. that all interested parties would receive a notification about the Commission's intention about any action at provisional stage of an investigation. The Council remained for a long time divided about the proposal and only the Slovak presidency finally managed to unblock the situation on 13 December 2016.[4] The Council compromise remained closer to the original Commission proposal than the Parliament's position but was slightly tilted towards importing interests, for instance by providing a 4 weeks pre-disclosure and showing considerable reticence against any changes to the application of the lesser-duty rule. The final compromise that the Institutions reached in a trilogue on 5 December 2017[5] and that is scheduled to be signed into law before summer 2018 has in a pragmatic way re-established the original balance between importing and producing interests in the Union, but has introduced many new elements.

2.2 Key Features of the December Trilogue Compromise

2.2.1 Improved Calculation of the Injury Margin

The WTO Anti-Dumping and Anti-Subsidy Agreements fix the maximum level of the duty at the dumping and the subsidy margin respectively.[6] They also stipulate that a lower duty would be "desirable" if that duty is adequate to remove the injury

---

[3] European Parliament, Protection against dumped and subsidised imports from countries not members of the EU, Resolution of 16 April 2014, P7_TA(2014)0420. The modernisation file itself as well as its discussion in the European Parliament is described in detail in: Hoffmeister (2015), pp. 365–376.

[4] See Council, Trade defence instruments: Council agrees negotiating position, 13 December 2017, http://www.consilium.europa.eu/en/press/press-releases/2016/12/13-trade-defence-instruments-general-approach/ (last accessed 30 April 2018). The text of the provisional agreement resulting from the inter-institutional negotiations was released by the European Parliament on the occasion of the endorsement of the agreement by INTA on 28 January 2018: see http://www.emeeting.europarl.europa.eu/committees/agenda/201801/INTA/INTA(2018)0122_1P/sitt-7666743 (last accessed 30 April 2018). The compromise has now been signed into entered into the force of law, see Regulation (EU) 2018/825, OJ 2018 L 143/1.

[5] The Commission's press release can be found here: European Commission, Commission welcomes landmark deal modernising the EU's trade defence, 5 December 2017, http://europa.eu/rapid/press-release_IP-17-5136_en.htm (last accessed 30 April 2018).

[6] Article 9.1 *in fine* of the Agreement on Implementation of Article VI of GATT 1994 (WTO Anti-Dumping Agreement) provides: "*It is desirable (…) that the duty be less than the margin [of dumping] if such lesser duty would be adequate to remove the injury to the domestic industry.*" Articles

to the domestic industry. This is the so-called lesser-duty rule. The injury margin is calculated by comparing the price of the dumped/subsidised imports with the target price of the Union industry, if the former is lower than the latter. The difference is expressed as a percentage of the Cost, Insurance and Freight (CIF) import price. A synonym for target price is the term "non-injurious price". The Union applies this lesser-duty rule in all cases by using a well-developed set of rules which over time became more and more sophisticated. The guiding principle was expressed by the Court in *EFMA*:

> It follows that the profit margin to be used by the Council when calculating the target price that will remove the injury in question must be limited to the profit margin which the Community industry could reasonably count on under normal conditions of competition, in the absence of the dumped imports. It would not be consistent with Articles 4(1) and 13(3) of the basic regulation to allow the Community industry a profit margin that it could not have expected if there were no dumping.[7]

It was generally felt that these rules no longer fully reflect what is needed to adequately remove injury caused to the Union industry by the dumped/subsidised imports. In particular, they do not track fully the underlying economic reality. Therefore, the modernisation package as finally agreed establishes a set of additional rules that will henceforth be applied when determining the injury margin:

– The new rules make sure that the counterfactual approach accepted by the Court in order to establish the injury margin is no longer the only guiding principle. When calculating the target price, instead of only examining what profit the industry could earn in the absence of dumped imports as required by *EFMA*, i.e. under normal conditions of competition, further considerations can now be taken into account. The new rules provide a non-exhaustive list of such conditions *"such as the level of profitability before the increase of imports from the country under investigation, the level of profitability needed to cover the full costs and investments, R&D and innovation"*; moreover, the profit margin shall in any case be higher than 6%.[8]

– In line with the importance that the European Parliament attaches to the respect of Multilateral Environmental Agreements and core International Labour Organisation (ILO) conventions, the modernisation package clarifies that the target price shall duly reflect the Union industry's costs resulting from these agreements. More importantly, the new text stipulates that the target price shall also take account of the future costs that the Union industry will incur during the

---

7.5 and 8.1 contain similar provisions in relation to price undertakings and provisional measures. The corresponding provisions in the Agreement on Subsidies and Countervailing Measures (ASCM or WTO Anti-Subsidy Agreement) can be found in its Articles 17.5, 18.1(b) and 19.2.

[7] GC, Case T-210/95, *EFMA v Council*, ECLI:EU:T:2005:455, para. 60. This aspect was not appealed.

[8] See the new paragraph 2c to Article 7 of the Basic Anti-Dumping Regulation and the new paragraph 1a of the Basic Anti-Subsidy Regulation.

usual 5-year period of measures.[9] This new provision can in particular be relevant in the context of additional costs resulting from emission trading schemes.
– While the above two topics were hardly controversial, the adaptation of the lesser-duty rule in cases of raw material distortions operated by the exporting country was a matter of considerable debate. The discussion focussed on (a) whether it was appropriate to cater for this type of distortion, (b) the relevant level of exporters' costs that should be affected in order for such a distortion being relevant, and (c) whether there should be a closed or an open list of relevant distortions. The original Commission proposal neither contained a list of relevant distortions nor did it specify a minimum threshold of costs of production of the exporter that need to be affected by such a distortion. The European Parliament compromise proposal did not contain thresholds and lists either. While the European Parliament proposal essentially aimed at the disapplication of the lesser-duty rule, the Council compromise wanted to narrowly circumscribe a more focused application of the lesser-duty rule in case of such raw material distortions. The final compromise found in December 2017 is a pragmatic and pertinent one. First, it clarified that only such raw material distortions are relevant if they are contained in a list kept by the Organisation for Economic Cooperation and Development (OECD). If the OECD adds further distortions to the current list, these will become relevant once the Commission has endorsed them in a delegated act. Second, the new methodology in relation to raw material distortions can only be applied, if the distorted raw material accounts for at least 17% of the costs of manufacturing of exporters. This ensures that only raw materials that strongly influence the competitiveness of economic operators can trigger the application of the new rules.
– Last but not least, the co-legislators saw the risk that the new rules could result in duty levels that were not sustainable, in particular, for the downstream industry. Therefore, a specific Union interest test was designed: Paragraph 2a to Article 7 stipulates, when examining whether a duty lower than the margin of dumping would be sufficient to remove injury, that the Commission shall take into account whether there are raw material distortions with regard to the product concerned. Paragraph 2b in turn provides that when carrying out the Union interest test in accordance with Article 21, special consideration shall be given to the matter of raw material distortions and the duty level to remove injury: *"Where the Commission, on the basis of all information submitted, can clearly conclude that it is in the Union's interest to determine the amount of the provisional measures in accordance with paragraph 2a of this Article, paragraph 2 shall not apply."* Paragraph 2 sets out that the default approach to applying the lesser duty rule as quoted elsewhere, i.e. *"[t]he amount of the provisional anti-dumping duty shall not exceed the margin of dumping as provisionally established, but it should be less than the margin if such lesser duty would be adequate to remove injury to the*

---

[9] See the new paragraph 2d to Article 7 of the Basic Anti-Dumping Regulation and the new paragraph 1b of the Basic Anti-Subsidy Regulation.

Union industry." Note that the Union interest test as set out in Article 21 of the Basic Anti-Dumping Regulation is designed as a negative test, i.e. in case of dumping and resulting injury measures are deemed to be in the interest of the Union unless it is established that there are overriding interests against the imposition of duties. By contrast, the test in paragraph 2b requires a positive Union interest finding in order to determine the duty level pursuant to paragraph 2a.[10]

The rules described above apply in relation to provisional and definitive duties as well for price undertakings.

2.2.2 Pre-Disclosure Prior to Provisional Anti-Dumping and Anti-Subsidy Measures

One of the most thorny topics was whether or not parties should be informed prior to the imposition of provisional anti-dumping and anti-subsidy measures and if so, how much time this should be done before the adoption of such measures. The Commission argued in its 2013 proposal that this should happen 2 weeks prior to such measures. Pre-disclosure was appropriate in order to avoid an information asymmetry notably between interested parties that follow closely the investigation and are generally reasonably well aware of the sequence of events, while provisional measures often come as a surprise to SMEs that are not necessarily interested parties but are potentially affected by such measures. The European Parliament in its position adopted in 2014 rejected this idea altogether while the Council wanted to have a pre-disclosure of 4 weeks.

The compromise finally reached is perhaps typical for the Union. Given that pre-disclosure is an entirely new concept (it appears that up to now no trade remedy law of any WTO Member contains such a mechanism) and that nobody has any practical experience in this field the co-legislators agreed to a pre-disclosure of 3 weeks. They also underlined that pre-disclosure does not prejudice any subsequent Commission decision in particular about provisional measures. Two years after the entry into force of the modernisation package, the Commission shall review whether the new practice has led to an undermining of provisional measures. This undermining is defined as a substantial rise in imports that occurred during the pre-disclosure period and causes additional injury to the Union industry, despite the precautionary measures provided for in Articles 14(5)(a) and 9(4). The Commission shall adopt a delegated act either reducing the pre-disclosure period from 3 to 2 weeks if such undermining has happened or increasing it to 4 weeks in case the 2 year trial period did not show such undermining.

Two additional points need mentioning. First, in line with the underlying idea of pre-disclosure to eliminate information asymmetries, the new Basic Regulations stipulate that the Commission shall make public on its website the information of its intention to impose provisional duties including the possible duty rates at the same time when it provides interested parties with the relevant information. Second, the

---

[10] See the new paragraphs 2a and 2b to Article 7 of the Basic Anti-Dumping Regulation.

co-legislators were worried that the period of pre-disclosure could be abused by exporters and importers to stockpile dumped or subsidised merchandise before the imposition of provisional duties. Therefore, the rules on pre-disclosure provide for a precautionary measure, i.e. that whenever possible, pre-disclosure should be accompanied by registration of imports (this would allow to collect duties retroactively if the conditions set out in Article 10(4) of the Basic Anti-Dumping Regulation are met) or, if there was no registration but stockpiling occurred against all expectations, to adjust the injury margin for the purposes of establishing the definitive duty levels.[11]

2.2.3 Price Undertakings

The modernisation package has considerably clarified the rules concerning the acceptance of undertakings. Price undertakings offered by exporters are an alternative to anti-dumping or anti-subsidy duties. The current text of the Basic Regulations made the acceptance of such undertakings conditional upon whether the Commission *"is satisfied that the injurious effect of the dumping is thereby eliminated"* (see Article 8(1) of the Basic Anti-Dumping Regulation and—*mutatis mutandis*—Article 13(1)(b) of the Basic Anti-Subsidy Regulation). In addition to the updated rules on the determination of the injury margin as described supra, the modernisation package has introduced three changes with regard to undertakings. First, procedural rules have been changed in order to better safeguard transparency. Save in exceptional circumstances, undertakings may not be offered later than 5 days prior to the period during which comments on definitive disclosure can be made, so as to ensure that other parties have a possibility to comment on the undertaking. Furthermore, before the Commission accepts an undertaking offer, the Union industry shall be given an opportunity to comment with regard to the main features of the undertaking.[12] Second, both the WTO Anti-Dumping Agreement and the current Basic Regulation make it clear that undertaking offered need not to be accepted inter alia for reasons of general policy. The new rules clarify that the reasons of general policy comprise in particular the principles and obligations set out in Multilateral Environmental Agreements and protocols thereunder, to which the Union is a party, and those ILO conventions which are listed in an Annex. Third, the European Parliament was keen in highlighting the need that undertakings really eliminate the injurious effects of dumping. This is the reason why a new recital to the Basic Regulations will specify that the Commission shall only accept an offer for an undertaking where it is satisfied, based on a prospective analysis, that it

---

[11] See the new paragraph 1 of Article 7 in conjunction with paragraph 4 of Article 9 and a new Article 19a of the Basic Anti-Dumping Regulation. The corresponding provisions in the Basic Anti-Subsidy Regulation can be found in paragraph 1 of Article 12 in conjunction with paragraph 1 of Article 15 and 29a of the Basic Anti-Subsidy Regulation.

[12] See the new paragraph 7 of Article 6 of the Basic Anti-Dumping Regulation and the new paragraphs 1 to 4 of Article 13 of the Basic Anti-Subsidy Regulation.

effectively eliminates the injurious effect of dumping. Article 8(1) of the Basic Anti-Dumping Regulation and Article 13(1) of the Basic Anti-Subsidy Regulation have also been changed to reflect this standard.[13]

2.2.4 Recognition of the Role of Trade Unions

For the first time, the Basic Regulations will recognise the role of trade unions in anti-dumping and anti-subsidy investigations. Trade unions have now the right, but only jointly with the Union industry, to lodge an application for the initiation of an anti-dumping or anti-subsidy investigation. They may also support such an application.[14] By contrast, in the U.S., trade unions can lodge such cases independently. It would appear to be appropriate that the legislator did not copy the U.S. approach as the relevant "sufficient evidence"[15] for lodging a complaint, notably as far as injury is concerned will rarely be in the possession of trade unions and normally emanates from the Union industry. The new rules clarify however that even in the case of a joint application, the Union industry can withdraw the case on their own volition, without the consent of the trade union in case the latter was a co-sponsor of the application. Finally, the list of interested parties of anti-dumping and anti-subsidy investigations now also includes trade unions.[16]

2.2.5 Extension of Anti-Dumping and Anti-Subsidy Duties to the Exclusive Economic Zone (EEZ) and the Continental Shelf

Up to now, anti-dumping and anti-subsidy duties only apply to the customs territory of the EU. Consequently, such duties cannot be levied on imports for instance of steel and tubes and pipes that are consumed on oil rigs or in wind turbines located outside the zone of nautical 12 miles. In other words, Union law contained a gap that does not exist in some other jurisdictions like the U.S., Canada or India. The modernisation package closes this gap in two steps. First, Article 14(3) as amended and a new Article 14a of the Basic Anti-Dumping Regulation provide for the possibility to apply such duties to the EEZ/Continental Shelf.[17] However, this does not apply to all products subject to duties but only to those that are consumed in significant

---

[13] See Recital 18.

[14] See the new subparagraph added to paragraph 1 of Article 5 of the Basic Anti-Dumping Regulation and the new subparagraph added to paragraph 1 of Article 9 of the Basic Anti-Subsidy Regulation.

[15] See Article 5(3) of the Basic Anti-Dumping Regulation and Article 10(3) of the Basic Anti-Subsidy Regulation.

[16] See the new paragraph 7 of Article 6 of the Basic Anti-Dumping Regulation and new paragraph 7 of Article 11 of the Basic Anti-Subsidy Regulation.

[17] The Basic Anti-Subsidy Regulation contains the corresponding provisions in its new paragraph 3 to Article 24 and the new Article 24a.

quantities in the EEZ/Continental Shelf. Whether or not a duty applies to these two offshore destinations will be specified in the regulation imposing an anti-dumping or anti-subsidy duty. Note that the reference to "*where this [i.e. the delivery of the dumped/subsidised imports] would cause injury to the Union industry*" does not appear to be a special condition that needs to be met. This follows from the fact that originally the European Parliament proposed to insert the corresponding text into Article 1(1) of the Basic Anti-Dumping Regulation. In that provision, the reference to the causation of injury is only generic while the substantive rules are contained in Article 3. However, the rules on the EEZ/Continental Shelf did not sit well in Article 1(1). In the course of the trilogues, it was therefore decided for ease of reference to concentrate most of the rules on this issue in a separate article. In other words, by operating this move, the reference to injury was also copied but it does not appear that the co-legislators wanted to introduce an additional injury test beyond the condition that the product must be consumed offshore in significant quantities. Second, the technical modalities of applying anti-dumping and anti-subsidy duties to the EEZ/Continental Shelf are not specified yet, notably because it was not possible to make a wholesale reference to the Union's Customs Code to this effect. Therefore, the legislators decided that these details should be worked out and embodied in a so-called "customs tool". This will be an implementing act to be adopted in accordance with the Examination Procedure pursuant to Article 15(3) of the Basic Anti-Dumping Regulation/Article 25(3) of the Basic Anti-Subsidy Regulation.

2.2.6 Strengthening the Role of Small and Medium Sized Enterprises (SMEs)

It was a particular concern of the European Parliament to ensure that trade remedy instruments are also accessible to SMEs. Hence, it proposed in its 2014 first reading position numerous new rules that were designed to facilitate the "life" of SMEs in such investigations. However, some of these proposals were very difficult if not impossible to apply in practice. The Council shared the European Parliament's wish to support SMEs but went for a more realistic list of possible support measures. The co-legislators decided to stipulate that the Commission shall maintain an SME help desk in order to facilitate access to the trade remedy instruments for diverse and fragmented industry sectors, largely composed of SMEs. The new provision also provides a non-exhaustive list of tasks/functions of this help desk:

- to raise awareness of the instrument;
- to provide general information and explanations on procedures, how to file a complaint, to release standard questionnaires in all languages of the Union and to reply to general, not case specific queries;
- to make available standard forms for statistics to be submitted for standing purposes and questionnaires.

Moreover, in anti-dumping and anti-subsidy investigations, respondents to the Commission's questionnaire usually have to provide company specific cost and sales data for a certain period, usually 1 year prior to initiation. This period is called the investigation period but must not be confused with the duration of the investigation itself. The investigation period usually has a duration of 12 months but shorter or longer periods are on rare occasions chosen. Pulling together the relevant information is not always easy in particular when the investigation period is across two financial years. The Modernisation Package now stipulates that investigation periods shall, whenever possible, especially in the case of diverse and fragmented sectors largely composed of SMEs, coincide with the financial year.[18]

2.2.7 Procedural Rules

Last but not least, the Modernisation Package contains a number of new procedural rules:

- Provisional anti-dumping measures shall normally be adopted within 7 months but not later than 8 months from initiation.[19] Currently, provisional measures must be adopted within 9 months. Moreover, the overall duration of investigations will be reduced from a maximum of 15 months to a maximum of 14 months.[20] The duration of anti-subsidy investigations remains unchanged.
- Anti-dumping and countervailing duties collected during any expiry review that results in a repeal of the measures shall be reimbursed. The repayment is without any interest.[21]
- The rules on ex officio initiation of investigations have been strengthened in case of threats of retaliation to the Union industry from a third country. The new rules clarify that while there is no obligation of the Union industry to cooperate in cases of ex officio initiations, as the original Commission proposal has provided for, the Commission can send a request for cooperation to the Union industry.[22]
- Up to now, the Basic Regulations did not contain any explicit rules on the adoption of guidelines or interpretative notes by the Commission although on rare occasions such notes and guidelines have been released in the past. The Commission's intention to release four guidelines as part of the Modernisation Package has brought to the fore the question as to what rules should be followed exactly before adopting such guidelines. The question was also to what extent

---

[18] See the new paragraphs 1a and 9 of Article 6 of the Basic Anti-Dumping Regulation and the new paragraphs 1a and 9 of Article 10 of the Basic Anti-Subsidy Regulation.
[19] See the new paragraph 1 of Article 7 of the Basic Anti-Dumping Regulation.
[20] See the revised paragraph 9 of Article 6 of the Basic Anti-Dumping Regulation.
[21] See the new paragraph 5 of Article 11 of the Basic Anti-Dumping Regulation and the new subparagraph in Article 18(1) of the Basic Anti-Subsidy Regulation.
[22] See Recital 7 as well as the new paragraph 10 of Article 6 of the Basic Anti-Dumping Regulation and the new paragraph 11 of Article 11 of the Basic Anti-Subsidy Regulation.

the European Parliament and Council should have a say when it comes to the adoption. The compromise found was the following: Before adopting such guidelines and interpretative notes, a public consultation needs to be carried out in line with Article 11(3) of the Treaty of the European Union. Parliament and Council may express their views as well.[23]

2.2.8 "Housekeeping"

The Modernisation Package also contains a number of changes to the Basic Regulations that were mostly necessary because WTO jurisprudence has made some provisions irrelevant. Example: According to the second sentence of the current Article 9(3) of the Basic Anti-Dumping Regulation, exporters with a dumping margin below 2% (de minimis dumping) shall not be subject to duties but they may be reinvestigated in any review carried out pursuant to Article 11. However, the Appellate Body, in *Mexico – Anti-Dumping Measures on Rice*,[24] has excluded the possibility of a reinvestigation of de minimis exporters. Therefore, the Modernisation Package has removed this sentence that refers to the possibility of a reinvestigation.[25] Note that the aforementioned WTO jurisprudence does not exclude to conduct an entirely new investigation pursuant to Article 5 of the Basic Anti-Dumping Regulation against such de minimis exporters.[26]

2.2.9   Changes to the Basic Anti-Subsidy Regulation

As described above, most of the changes described apply to the anti-dumping and the anti-subsidy instrument. However, there are some noteworthy exceptions which are summarised in more detail in this section.

First, in principle the co-legislators accepted the Commission proposal to abolish the lesser-duty rule altogether with regard to countervailing measures. However, they have built in one emergency break, i.e. a special Union interest test: Where the Commission, on the basis of all information submitted, can clearly conclude that it is not in the Union's interest to impose provisional measures on the higher subsidy amount (as opposed to the lower injury margin), the provisional countervailing duty shall be the amount adequate to remove injury to the Union industry. Similar provisions apply with regard to definitive duties and price undertakings. Contrary to the

---

[23] See the new paragraph 8 of Article 14 of the Basic Anti-Dumping Regulation and the new paragraph 8 of Article 24 of the Basic Anti-Subsidy Regulation.

[24] Appellate Body Report, *Mexico – Definitive anti-dumping measures on beef and rice (complaint with respect to rice)*, WT/DS295/AB/R, adopted 29 November 2005, DSR 2005:VI, paras. 207–211.

[25] See the new paragraph 3 of Article 9 of the Basic Anti-Dumping Regulation as well as the new paragraph 3 of Article 15 of the Basic Anti-Subsidy Regulation.

[26] GC, Case T-156/11, *Since Hardware (Guangzhou) v Council*, ECLI:EU:T:2012:431.

anti-dumping instrument, the design of this test is a "negative" one. In other words, there is no need to positively establish that the level of the measures should correspond to the higher subsidy margin as this level would remove injury. Rather, the higher subsidy margin is the default level of the measure, unless there is clear evidence on the file pointing to the need for a lower duty-level at the level of the injury margin. Therefore, while the additional union interest test with regard to the lesser-duty rule is a "positive" one for the anti-dumping instrument it is a negative one for the anti-subsidy instrument. The latter is in line with the usual Union interest rules.[27]

Second, the duration of the investigation as well as the period within which provisional countervailing measures need to be adopted has not been changed, contrary to the anti-dumping instrument.

3 New Calculation Methodology

Dumping is a comparison of normal value and export price and occurs if the latter is lower than the former. On 20 December 2017, Regulation (EU) 2017/2321 entered into force which contains an entirely new methodology for the calculation of the normal value.[28] The key condition for applying this methodology is the existence of distortions in the economy of the exporting country. This section describes the "mechanics" of the new methodology, i.e. the conditions and the modalities of its application. Note that the topics that were most intensively discussed in the legislative process were the notion of distortions, the question of the burden of proof for the existence of distortions and how reports could be used in the context of establishing distortions.

The same legislative act also changed the Basic Anti-Subsidy Regulation but these changes are not set out here for reasons of brevity.

The Commission made the proposal leading to this Regulation on 9 November 2016. In doing so, it referred to the circumstances prevailing in certain countries that are Members of the WTO and the experience gathered from the case-law. Both made it appropriate to amend the methodology used to determine the normal value and the dumping margin for the countries concerned, in particular those currently subject to the provisions of Article 2(7)(b) and (c) of the Basic Anti-Dumping Regulation.[29]

---

[27] See the new paragraph 1 of Article 12 of the as well as the new paragraph 1 of Article 13 and the new subparagraph 3 in paragraph 1 of Article 15 of the Basic Anti-Subsidy Regulation.

[28] OJ 2017 L 338/3.

[29] European Commission, Proposal for a Regulation of the European Parliament and of the Council amending Regulation (EU) 2016/1036 on protection against dumped imports from countries not members of the European Union and Regulation (EU) 2016/1037 on protection against subsidised imports from countries not members of the European Union, COM(2016) 721 final, http://www.europarl.europa.eu/RegData/docs_autres_institutions/commission_europeenne/com/2016/0721/COM_COM(2016)0721_EN.pdf (last accessed 30 April 2018). See also European Commission,

3.1   When Does the New Calculation Methodology Apply?

The normal value is by default calculated by using the costs and prices of exporters in their home market. However, the use of such costs and prices is not appropriate if the exporting country interferes in its economy in a way which goes significantly beyond the regulatory function of the State. The new rules first define the contours of the new methodology:

> In case it is determined, when applying this or any other relevant provision of this Regulation, that it is not appropriate to use domestic prices and costs in the exporting country due to the existence in that country of significant distortions within the meaning of point (b), the normal value shall be constructed exclusively on the basis of costs of production and sale reflecting undistorted prices or benchmarks, subject to the following rules.[30]

The concept of distortions is further elaborated in Article 2(6a)(b) but note that this provision does not contain an exhaustive description of what amounts to a relevant distortion:

> Significant distortions are those distortions which occur when reported prices or costs, including the costs of raw materials and energy, are not the result of free market forces because they are affected by substantial government intervention. In assessing the existence of significant distortions regard shall be had, inter alia, to the potential impact of one or more of the following elements:
>
> – the market in question being served to a significant extent by enterprises which operate under the ownership, control or policy supervision or guidance of the authorities of the exporting country;
> – state presence in firms allowing the state to interfere with respect to prices or costs;
> – public policies or measures discriminating in favour of domestic suppliers or otherwise influencing free market forces;
> – the lack, discriminatory application or inadequate enforcement of bankruptcy, corporate or property laws;
> – wage costs being distorted; and
> – access to finance granted by institutions which implement public policy objectives or otherwise not acting independently of the state.[31]

Recital 4 *in fine* of Regulation (EU) 2017/2321 provides that when "*assessing the existence of significant distortions, relevant international standards, including core conventions of the International Labour Organisation (ILO) and relevant multilateral environmental conventions, should be taken into account, where appropriate.*" It remains to be seen how this will be translated into practice. Note that the text makes it clear that this cannot apply to each and every case but only "when appropriate".

Commission proposes changes to the EU's anti-dumping and anti-subsidy legislation, 9 November 2016,   http://trade.ec.europa.eu/doclib/press/index.cfm?id=1573&title=Commission-proposes-changes-to-the-EUs-anti-dumping-and-anti-subsidy-legislation (last accessed 30 April 2018). See also Müller (2017), pp. 205–225.

[30] See 1st sentence of Article 2(6a)(a).

[31] See Article 2(6a)(b).

3.2   How Is the Normal Value To Be Calculated in Case of Distortions?

As described above, in case of relevant distortions, the normal value must be constructed on the basis of non-distorted costs and prices. Article 2(6a)(a), second and third sentence, lists a number of options, without however creating a strict hierarchy between them:

> The sources the Commission may use include:
>
> – corresponding costs of production and sale in an appropriate representative country with a similar level of economic development as the exporting country, provided the relevant data are readily available; where there is more than one such country, preference shall be given, where appropriate, to countries with an adequate level of social and environmental protection;
> – if it considers appropriate, undistorted international prices, costs, or benchmarks; or
> – domestic costs, but only to the extent that they are positively established not to be distorted, on the basis of accurate and appropriate evidence, including in the framework of the provisions on interested parties in point (c).
>
> Without prejudice to Article 17, that assessment shall be done for each exporter and producer separately. The constructed normal value shall include an undistorted and reasonable amount for administrative, selling and general costs and for profits.

Recital 6 of Regulation (EU) 2017/2321 clarifies further the concept of adequate social and environmental protection: "*When data are sourced in representative countries and the Commission has to establish whether the level of social and environmental protection in such countries is adequate, it is necessary for the Commission to examine whether those countries comply with core ILO and relevant multilateral environmental conventions.*"

3.3   Procedural Aspects

3.3.1   Use of Reports

It is obvious that the research and documentation of distortions in an exporting country can be a challenging and time-consuming task. At the same time, and as we have seen above in the section on the Modernisation Package, provisional anti-dumping measures will be imposed more expeditiously and the overall duration of investigations will be shortened. Indeed, one important parameter to measure the effectiveness of trade defence instruments is to check how quickly they bring relief to the Union industry against dumped or subsidised, i.e. unfairly traded imports. The Commission has anticipated this problem when making its proposal by providing for the possibility of writing a report that describes distortions in a given exporting country or sector.

Where the Commission has well-founded indications of the possible existence of significant distortions as referred to in point (b) in a certain country or a certain sector in that
country, and where appropriate for the effective application of this Regulation, the
Commission shall produce, make public and regularly update a report describing the market
circumstances referred to in point (b) in that country or sector.[32]

The amendment also stipulates how such a report shall be used in any given
investigation:

Such reports and the evidence on which they are based shall be placed on the file of any
investigation relating to that country or sector. Interested parties shall have ample opportunity to rebut, supplement, comment or rely on the report and the evidence on which it is
based in each investigation in which such report or evidence is used. In assessing the existence of significant distortions, the Commission shall take into account all the relevant
evidence that is on the investigation file.[33]

The aforementioned provision shows clearly that the report does not contain as
such a conclusion whether an exporting country maintains relevant distortions.
Rather, it is for the Commission as investigating authority to establish in an anti-
dumping investigation itself whether such distortions exist. In order to do so, the
Commission has to follow the general quasi-judicial procedure. The new Article
2(6a)(c) echoes the generally applicable procedures, i.e. that the investigating
authority can only draw the necessary conclusions once all parties have had the possibility to express their views on the report and—if they so wish—to submit evidence that they consider relevant in this context.

The new rules not only elucidate the function of the report during an anti-
dumping investigation but they also clarify the relationship between the report and
the application by the Union industry for the launch of an investigation.

When filing a complaint in accordance with Article 5, or a request for a review in accordance with Article 11, Union industry may rely on the evidence in the report referred to in
point (c) of this paragraph, where meeting the standard of evidence in view of Article 5(9),
in order to justify the calculation of the normal value.[34]

In other words, the existence of a report entitles the Union industry to construct
the normal value by using one of the options in the second sentence of Article 2(6a)(a)
instead of using home market data relating to the exporting country subject to the
industry application. However, the report does not dispense the Union industry from
furnishing information about the actual calculation of the normal value by using this
methodology.

Up to now, the Commission has released one such report that describes the situation in China. Its title is "Commission staff working document on significant distortions in the economy of the People's Republic of China for the purpose of trade

---

[32] See first sentence of Article 2(6a)(c).
[33] See second and third sentence of Article 2(6a)(c).
[34] See Article 2(6a)(d).

defence investigations."[35] The report is a technical document which will be used only in the context of trade defence investigations. It does not express any political views, preferences or judgements and is purely descriptive.[36] China was selected because the majority of trade defence investigations concerns imports from China. The Commission has made it clear in its press release of 20 December 2017 that other reports will be prepared on the basis of the same criteria: their relative importance in the EU's anti-dumping activity, as well as indications that there may be distortions related to government interventions in the economy. The next country report will concern Russia.[37]

Note finally that the use of the new calculation methodology does not depend on the existence of a report about distortions in the exporting country. In other words, the new calculation methodology can also be applied if the application filed by the industry for the initiation of an investigation contains sufficient evidence pointing to the existence of relevant distortions in the exporting country.

3.3.2 The Investigation

Subparagraph (e) of Article 2(6a) describes the procedural steps from the beginning until the end of the investigation.

Where the Commission finds that there is sufficient evidence, pursuant to Article 5(9), of significant distortions within the meaning of point (b) of this paragraph and decides to initiate an investigation on that basis, the notice of initiation shall specify that fact. The Commission shall collect the data necessary to allow the construction of the normal value in accordance with point (a) of this paragraph.

The parties to the investigation shall be informed promptly after initiation about the relevant sources that the Commission intends to use for the purpose of determining normal value pursuant to point (a) of this paragraph and shall be given 10 days to comment. For that purpose, interested parties shall be given access to the file, which shall include any evidence on which the investigating authority relies, without prejudice to Article 19. Any evidence regarding the existence of significant distortions may only be taken into account if it can be verified in a timely manner within the investigation, in accordance with Article 6(8).[38]

---

[35] The report can be found here: European Commission, Commission Staff Working Document on significant distortions in the economy of the People's Republic of China for the purposes of trade defence investigations, SWD(2017) 483 final/2, http://trade.ec.europa.eu/doclib/docs/2017/december/tradoc_156474.pdf (last accessed 30 April 2018).

[36] See fact sheet released by the Commission on 20 December 2017: European Commission, The EU's new trade defence rules and first country report, 20 December 2017, http://europa.eu/rapid/press-release_MEMO-17-5377_en.htm (last accessed 30 April 2018).

[37] See European Commission, EU puts in place new trade defence rules, 20 December 2017, http://europa.eu/rapid/press-release_IP-17-5346_en.htm (last accessed 30 April 2018).

[38] See Article 2(6a)(e).

3.4   Changed Scope of Article 2(7) of the Basic Anti-Dumping Regulation

Article 2(7) covered up to the legislative change also a number of non-market economy countries that are WTO Members, such as Armenia, China and Vietnam. In fact, this provision contained a non-exhaustive list of countries falling under this provision. This has changed as WTO Members no longer fall within the scope of Article 2(7). The fact that WTO Members have been removed from the scope of Article 2(7) does not, however, mean that they have been graduated to market economy status.[39] The scope of Article 2(7) is now defined by Annex I of Regulation (EU) 2015/755 of the European Parliament and of the Council of 29 April 2015 on common rules for imports from certain third countries.[40] Article 2(7) reads now as follows:

> In the case of imports from countries which are, at the date of initiation of the investigation, not members of the WTO and listed in Annex I to Regulation (EU) 2015/755 of the European Parliament and of the Council (*), normal value shall be determined on the basis of the price or constructed value in an appropriate representative country, or the price from such a third country to other countries, including the Union, or where those are not possible, on any other reasonable basis, including the price actually paid or payable in the Union for the like product, duly adjusted if necessary to include a reasonable profit margin. The appropriate representative country shall be selected in a reasonable manner, due account being taken of any reliable information made available at the time of selection, and in particular of cooperation by at least one exporter and producer in that country. Where there is more than one such country, preference shall be given, where appropriate, to countries with an adequate level of social and environmental protection. Account shall also be taken of time limits. Where appropriate, an appropriate representative country which is subject to the same investigation shall be used. The parties to the investigation shall be informed promptly after its initiation of the country envisaged and shall be given 10 days to comment.
>
> (*) Regulation (EU) 2015/755 of the European Parliament and of the Council of 29 April 2015 on common rules for imports from certain third countries (OJ L 123, 19.5.2015, p. 33).

4   Conclusion

The successful conclusion of the two legislative proposals in the area of the EU's trade defence instruments is important in two respects. First, it demonstrates that the Union is capable of adapting its trade defence instruments to changing economic and political circumstances. The references to social and environmental protection as expressed in international labour conventions and multilateral environmental agreements as well as the recognition of the role of trade unions adds a further perspective to the Union's trade defence instruments and underline the importance that

---

[39] See Recital 2 of Regulation (EU) 2017/2321.
[40] OJ 2015 L 123, p. 33.

the institutions (and the general public) attach to fairness of international trade. Second, the totality of the new rules shows that this is a major overhaul of the existing rules. The challenge ahead shifts from law making to implementing the new rules.

References

Hoffmeister F (2015) Modernising the EU's trade defence instruments: mission impossible? In: Herrmann C, Simma B, Streinz R (eds) Trade policy between law, diplomacy and scholarship – liber amicorum in memoriam Horst G. Krenzler. Springer, New York, pp 365–376

Müller W (2017) The EU's trade defence instruments: recent judicial and policy developments. In: Bungenberg M et al (eds) European yearbook of international economic law. Springer, Cham, pp 205–225

The New Rules Adopted by the European Union to Address "Significant Distortions" in the Anti-Dumping Context

Edwin Vermulst and Juhi Dion Sud

> *You can fool some people some time, but you can't fool all the people all the time.*
> Bob Marley, Get Up, Stand Up (1973)

Contents

Abstract On 9 November 2016, the European Commission (Commission) finally presented its long-awaited proposal on how to calculate normal value in anti-dumping proceedings involving Chinese producers post-11 December 2016. Although projected as supposedly "neutral" in terms of its application ratione territoriae, the text, context and its expected implementation indicate that the claimed neutrality is just a fig leaf. As was of course perfectly foreseeable, the proposal did not make it through the co-decision procedure (Article 294 Treaty on the Functioning

E. Vermulst (✉) · J. D. Sud
VVGB Advocaten, Brussels, Belgium
e-mail: eve@vvgb-law.com; jsu@vvgb-law.com

© Springer International Publishing AG, part of Springer Nature 2018
M. Bungenberg et al. (eds.), *The Future of Trade Defence Instruments*,
European Yearbook of International Economic Law,
https://doi.org/10.1007/978-3-319-95306-9_4

63

of the EU) in time and, equally foreseeable, China initiated a World Trade Organization (WTO) dispute settlement proceeding against the European Union (EU) on 12 December 2016 (Request for consultations by China, European Union— Measures related to price comparison methodologies, G/ADP/D116/1, G/L/1170, WT/DS516/1, 12 December 2016.). After protracted negotiations, on 3 October 2017, the Council and the European Parliament agreed on a compromise proposal which was eventually adopted by both the institutions and will shape the EU's new approach in anti-dumping cases against China, and possibly other countries, in the years to come. However, the WTO-compatibility of the new provisions is questionable as discussed in this article.

1 Introduction

The new provisions for assessing and addressing "significant distortions" in the context of EU anti-dumping investigations as agreed upon by the Council and European Parliament (significant distortions provisions)[1] will enter into force on 20 December 2017. This paper analyses the significant distortions provisions and comments on their WTO-compatibility. It will also briefly address the Commission's parallel proposal to abolish the lesser duty rule (LDR) in certain cases in the framework of the EU's trade defence instruments' modernisation exercise (TDI modernisation proposal). The paper will, however, not discuss the legality of the EU's current "non-market economy"/analogue country methodology as this subject has been extensively discussed in prior literature.[2]

2 Background

When China joined the WTO in 2001, the EU reserved the right to continue to use its analogue country methodology[3] to determine normal value in anti-dumping proceedings against imports from China as long as China at the macro-economic level did not meet the five (cumulative) EU criteria[4] for being treated as a market economy.

---

[1] For the text of the significant distortions rules, see http://eur-lex.europa.eu/legal-content/EN/TXT/PDF/?uri=CELEX:32017R2321&from=EN (last accessed 30 April 2018).

[2] See e.g. Vermulst et al. (2016), pp. 212–228, and all the articles on the subject referred to in footnote 4.

[3] See, for more detail, Vermulst (2010) pp. 299–307.

[4] See Commission staff working document, Impact assessment, Possible change in the calculation methodology of dumping regarding the People's Republic of China (and other non-market economies) accompanying the document Proposal for a Regulation of the European Parliament and of the Council amending Regulation (EU) 2016/1036 on protection against dumped imports from

In the view of the EU, as of today, most[5] of these criteria have not been met by China which is not surprising in light of their vagueness:

1. A low degree of government influence over the allocation of resources and decisions of enterprises, whether directly or indirectly (e.g. through public bodies), for example through the use of state-fixed prices or discrimination in the tax, trade or currency regimes;
2. An absence of state-inducted distortions in the operation of enterprises linked to privatisation and the use of non-market trading or compensation system;
3. The existence and implementation of a transparent and non-discriminatory company law which ensures adequate corporate governance (application of international accounting standards, protection of shareholders, public availability of accurate company information);
4. The existence and implementation of a coherent, effective and transparent set of laws which ensure the respect of property rights and the operation of a functioning bankruptcy regime; and
5. The existence of a genuine financial sector which operates independently from the state and which in law and practice is subject to sufficient guarantee provisions and adequate supervision.[6]

---

countries not members of the European Union and Regulation (EU) 2016/1037 on protection against subsidised imports from countries not members of the European Union, SWD(2016) 370 final, 9 November 2016, http://eur-lex.europa.eu/LexUriServ/LexUriServ.do?uri=SWD:2016:037 1:FIN:EN:PDF (last accessed 30 April 2018), p. 13. Compare Commission Staff Document on progress by the People's Republic of China towards graduation to Market Economy Status in Trade Defence Investigations, SEC(2008) 2503 final, 19 September 2008, http://trade.ec.europa.eu/doclib/docs/2009/june/tradoc_143599.pdf (last accessed 30 April 2018), p. 4.

[5] The EU found in 2004 that China met the second criterion, Vermulst et al. (2016), p. 223. The last assessment by the EU took place in 2008.

[6] The five country-wide criteria are very similar to the five criteria that individual NME producers must satisfy in order to qualify for market economy treatment (MET) under Article 2(7)(c) of the EU's Basic Anti-Dumping Regulation, OJ 2016 L 176/21:

– decisions of firms regarding prices, costs and inputs, including for instance raw materials, cost of technology and labour, output, sales and investment are made in response to market signals reflecting supply and demand, and without significant State interference in that regard and costs of major inputs substantially reflect market values;
– firms have one clear set of basic accounting records which are independently audited in line with international accounting standards and are applied for all purposes;
– the production costs and financial situation of firms are not subject to significant distortions carried over from the former non-market economy system, in particular in relation to deprecation of assets, other write-offs, barter trade and payment via compensation of debts;
– the firms concerned are subject to bankruptcy and property laws which guarantee legal certainty and stability for the operation of firms; and
– exchange rate conversions are carried out at the market rate.

According to Commission data, in the 5-year period 2006–2010, 173 MET applications were received and 37 were granted; in the 5-year period 2011–2015, 75 applications were received and four were granted (see Commission staff working document, Impact assessment, Possible change

Indeed, the fact that the EU granted Russia market economy status (MES) in 2002 and Ukraine in 2005—even before they joined the WTO—strongly indicates that the criteria are subject to arbitrary application and that the decision to treat a country as a market economy for anti-dumping purposes is not so much an economic, but rather a political decision.

While it seemed widely accepted that the EU would terminate its analogue country methodology vis-à-vis China on December 2016[7] and the Commission as well as the European Parliament's legal teams endorsed this approach in the beginning of 2015, some 25 EU industry associations with a strong interest in the EU's continued use of such methodology against Chinese (and Vietnamese) producers formed AEGIS Europe[8] and started lobbying intensively against the EU granting MES to China.

In February 2016, the Commission then issued an "inception impact assessment"[9] in which it outlined three options to address the issue:

---

in the calculation methodology of dumping regarding the People's Republic of China (and other non-market economies) accompanying the document Proposal for a Regulation of the European Parliament and of the Council amending Regulation (EU) 2016/1036 on protection against dumped imports from countries not members of the European Union and Regulation (EU) 2016/1037 on protection against subsidised imports from countries not members of the European Union, SWD(2016) 370 final, 9 November 2016, http://eur-lex.europa.eu/LexUriServ/LexUriServ.do?uri =SWD:2016:0371:FIN:EN:PDF (last accessed 30 April 2018), p. 6). This shows the wide discretion that the Commission has in assessing the MET criteria and the arguably arbitrary application.

[7] See Karel De Gucht (then EU trade Commissioner) (2013) Modernisation of trade Defence— Getting the Job Done, Brussels, 7 November 2013, http://trade.ec.europa.eu/doclib/docs/2013/ november/tradoc_151873.pdf (last accessed 30 April 2018): "...in 2016 China will get market economy status."

Moreover, the EU itself argued in the WTO dispute, *EC – Fasteners (China)*, that section 15 of China's Accession Protocol "entitles" it to treat China as a NME, until 2016. Appellate Body Report, *European Communities – Definitive Anti-Dumping Measures on Certain Iron or Steel Fasteners from China*, WT/DS397/AB/R, adopted 15 July 2011, DSR 2011:II, paras. 25, 361.

Additionally, in the proposal for the EU's position on the accession of China to the WTO, the Commission stated as follows: "*The EU's present legislation which provides specific procedures for dealing with cases of alleged dumping by Chinese exporters, which may not yet be operating in normal market economy conditions, will remain available for up to fifteen years after China enters the WTO...*", European Council, Proposal for a Council Decision establishing the Community position within the Ministerial Conference set up by the Agreement establishing the World Trade Organization on the accession of the People's Republic of China to the World Trade Organization, COM(2001) 517 final—2001/0218(CNS), http://trade.ec.europa.eu/doclib/docs/2016/november/ tradoc_155079.pdf (last accessed 30 April 2018), Recital 54. See Suse A (2017) Old wine in a new bottle: the EU's response to the expiry of section 15(a)(ii) of China's WTO protocol of accession, 3 April 2017, https://ssrn.com/abstract=2952015 (last accessed 30 April 2018).

[8] See http://www.aegiseurope.eu (last accessed 30 April 2018). AEGIS Europe groups industry associations in various sectors such as steel (Eurofer), bicycles (EBMA), solar panels and cells (EU ProSun), metals (Eurometaux), metal alloys (Euroalliages) and ceramics (Cerame-Unie).

[9] See European Commission, DG Trade, Inception impact assessment, January 2016, http:// ec.europa.eu/smart-regulation/roadmaps/docs/2016_trade_002_dumping_investigations_china_ en.pdf (last accessed 30 April 2018).

- Maintain the status quo, in other words "do nothing", which however was made clear by the Commission may not be the ideal option;[10]
- Modify the EU's Basic Anti-Dumping Regulation by excluding China from the list of NMEs, effectively resulting in the application of the standard normal value calculation method to Chinese producers; or
- Compromise solution consisting of (a) new provisions to address "cost distortions", (b) grandfathering of existing measures, (c) investigating and countervailing new subsidy schemes found in the course of an investigation, and (d) abolition of the LDR in certain cases.

At the same time, the Commission started a public consultation which eventually led to more than 5000 responses, of which 80% reportedly opposed granting MES to China.

Furthermore, on 12 May 2016, the European Parliament overwhelmingly adopted a resolution (546-28, with 77 abstentions) to not grant China MES as long as it did not meet the five EU criteria.

On 20 July 2016, an orientation debate[11] took place in the College of Commissioners which—unsurprisingly—focused on the modalities of the compromise solution mentioned above with the clear message that the grant of MES to China was not foreseen and was not the subject of discussion any more. Banking on the overcapacity issue, the outcome of the debate focused on a highly protectionist orientation of the anticipated changes. In fact, the EU Trade Commissioner Cecilia Malmström bizarrely claimed on the one hand that the EU would abide by its WTO obligations post-11 December 2016,[12] but on the other hand assured that the proposed compromise solution would result in the same level of duties as the analogue country method.[13]

---

[10] The inception impact assessment report states as follows: "*Certain provisions in the Protocol on the accession of China to the WTO expire in 2016, and this may affect the ability of other WTO Members, such as the EU, to use the Non-Market-Economy methodology automatically.*" See European Commission, DG Trade, Inception impact assessment, January 2016, http://ec.europa.eu/smart-regulation/roadmaps/docs/2016_trade_002_dumping_investigations_china_en.pdf (last accessed 30 April 2018), p. 4.

[11] See European Commission, College orientation debate on the treatment of China in anti-dumping investigations, 20 July 2016, http://europa.eu/rapid/press-release_IP-16-2567_en.htm (last accessed 30 April 2018).

[12] See European Commission, Commission urges Member States to support proposals to strengthen European defences against unfair trade, 19 October 2016, http://europa.eu/rapid/press-release_IP-16-3475_en.htm (last accessed 30 April 2018); European Commission, Commission proposes changes to the EU's anti-dumping and anti-subsidy legislation, 9 November 2016, http://europa.eu/rapid/press-release_MEMO-16-3605_en.htm, (last accessed 30 April 2018): "*The purpose is to make sure that Europe has trade defence instruments that are able to deal with current realities – notably overcapacities – in the international trading environment, while fully respecting the EU's international obligations in the legal framework of the World Trade Organization (WTO)... The proposal is important because it means that the EU is living up to its WTO commitments.*"

[13] See also, Cecilia Malmström, Hard nut to crack—between openness and trade defence, 9 November 2016, https://ec.europa.eu/commission/commissioners/2014-2019/malmstrom/blog/hard-nut-crack-between-openness-and-trade-defence_en (last accessed 30 April 2018): "*The pro-*

On 9 November 2016, the Commission then made its proposal publicly available.[14] Needless to say, while the proposal was not in time for adoption prior to the 11 December 2016 deadline and China brought the EU to the WTO on 12 December 2016 challenging the EU's analogue country methodology,[15] the herculean task before the EU institutions was to reach a compromise on the future approach. Following persistent Commission efforts, on 3 May 2017, the EU Ambassadors adopted a position for negotiating with the European Parliament[16]— that was endorsed by the Council on 11 May 2017[17]—for "a new, country-neutral methodology for assessing market distortions in third countries." The Council's position largely reflected the main elements of the Commission's proposal with certain additions particularly as regards the situations indicative of significant distortions.

The European Parliament's International Trade Committee also drafted amendments to the Commission's proposal, which were approved (33-3 with 2 abstentions) on 20 June 2017.[18] The European Parliament, while demanding an increased role for itself, further contributed to the expansion of circumstances for determining significant distortions to include lack of compliance with social, environmental and fiscal standards, and potential discriminatory measures against foreign investments among others.

---

posal that the Commission is presenting brings together these views; maintaining a similar level of anti-dumping duties as today, while introducing more flexibility to counter distortions that were not properly captured before."

See also European Commission, Commission proposes changes to the EU's anti-dumping and anti-subsidy legislation, 9 November 2016, http://europa.eu/rapid/press-release_MEMO-16-3605_en.htm (1 last accessed 30 April 2018): *"The Commission's Impact Assessment demonstrates that the new methodology will result in a broadly equivalent level of anti-dumping duties as is currently the case."*

[14] See European Commission, Commission proposes changes to the EU's anti-dumping and anti-subsidy legislation, 9 November 2016, http://europa.eu/rapid/press-release_MEMO-16-3605_en.htm (last accessed 30 April 2018).

[15] Request for consultations by China, *European Union – Measures related to price comparison methodologies*, WT/DS516/1, G/L/1170, WT/DS516/1, 12 December 2016.

[16] See Council, Anti-dumping methodology: Council agrees negotiating position, 3 May 2017, http://www.consilium.europa.eu/en/press/press-releases/2017/05/03-anti-dumping/ (last accessed 30 April 2018).

[17] See Foreign Affairs Council, Main results: New anti-dumping methodology, 11 May 2017, http://www.consilium.europa.eu/en/meetings/fac/2017/05/11/ (last accessed 30 April 2018).

[18] See European Parliament, More robust anti-dumping rules to defend EU industry and jobs, 20 June 2017, http://www.europarl.europa.eu/news/en/press-room/20170620IPR77802/more-robust-anti-dumping-rules-to-defend-eu-industry-and-jobs (last accessed 30 April 2018).

Finally, on 3 October 2017, the European Parliament and the Council reached an agreement[19] on the significant distortions provisions[20] which was endorsed by the Council on 11 October 2017[21] and the International Trade Committee of the European Parliament on 12 October 2017.[22] The European Parliament adopted the text of the significant distortions provisions on 15 November 2017[23] and the Council on 4 December 2017.[24]

3 The Significant Distortions Provisions

In terms of the overall approach, the new provisions in the Basic Anti-Dumping Regulations[25] have two fundamental aspects:

1. *Erasing the perceived cause of the problem*: The list of NMEs has been scrapped and the issue of China's recognition as a market economy has been side-stepped. In other words, as a matter of law, the non-standard/analogue country methodology currently applied to WTO members that are considered to be NMEs by the EU—such as China, Vietnam and Kazakhstan—will no longer be applied to

---

[19] See European Commission, Commission welcomes agreement on new anti-dumping methodology, 3 October 2017, http://trade.ec.europa.eu/doclib/press/index.cfm?id=1735 (last accessed 30 April 2018).
See also European Parliament, EU anti-dumping measures that protect jobs: MEPs and ministers strike deal, 3 October 2017, http://www.europarl.europa.eu/news/en/press-room/20171003IPR85229/eu-anti-dumping-measures-that-protect-jobs-meps-and-ministers-strike-deal (last accessed 30 April 2018).

[20] See European Commission, The EU is changing its anti-dumping and anti-subsidy legislation to address state induced market distortions, 5 October 2017, http://trade.ec.europa.eu/doclib/press/index.cfm?id=1736 (last accessed 30 April 2018).

[21] See Council, Anti-dumping: EU agrees on new rules for protecting its producers against unfair trade practices, 11 October 2017, http://www.consilium.europa.eu/en/press/press-releases/2017/10/11-anti-dumping-unfair-practices/ (last accessed 30 April 2018).

[22] See European Parliament, Trade MEPs back informal deal on EU anti-dumping measures, 12 October 2017, http://www.europarl.europa.eu/news/en/press-room/20171012IPR85905/trade-meps-back-informal-deal-on-eu-anti-dumping-measures (last accessed 30 April 2018).

[23] See European Parliament, Parliament passes new anti-dumping rules to protect EU jobs and industry, 15 November 2017, http://www.europarl.europa.eu/news/en/press-room/20171110IPR87817/parliament-passes-new-anti-dumping-rules-to-protect-eu-jobs-and-industry (last accessed 30 April 2018).

[24] See Council, Anti-dumping: Council adopts new rules against unfair trade practices, 4 December 2017, http://www.consilium.europa.eu/en/press/press-releases/2017/12/04/anti-dumping-council-adopts-new-rules-against-unfair-trade-practices/pdf (last accessed 30 April 2018).

[25] The EU Basic Anti-Subsidy Regulation 2016/1037 has also been amended to include a provision that the Commission can investigate and countervail subsidies discovered in the course of an investigation, provided that the exporting country is duly notified and consulted. This provision added in a sub-paragraph to Article 10(7) of the EU Basic Anti-Subsidy Regulation essentially covers existing practice and will not be discussed further.

those WTO members.[26] Instead, a new Article 2(6a) has been inserted in the Basic Anti-Dumping Regulation which introduces the de jure country-neutral concept of "significant distortions"; and

2. *Addressing "significant distortions"*: A thorny issue for the EU, as far as China is concerned, is government intervention supposedly precluding the independent operation of market forces. The new provisions address this through the introduction of a non-exhaustive list of factors—expanded by the Council and the European Parliament—for assessing the existence of "significant distortions". In case of a finding of "significant distortions", the new provisions provide for the use of third country prices/costs or international prices/benchmarks to establish normal value.

The significant distortions provisions also include amendments to Articles 11(3) and 11(4) of the Basic Anti-Dumping Regulation for grandfathering the anti-dumping measures at the current level. This is intended to preclude interested parties from asking for interim or newcomer reviews on the basis of the new approach. A new sub-paragraph has been added to Article 11(3) and Article 11(4) which stipulates that the new methodology for normal value establishment shall not replace the original methodology used for the determination of normal value until the date of initiation of the first expiry review following the entry into force of the significant distortions provisions.

Furthermore, an additional sub-paragraph has been added to Article 11(9) providing that in relation to the circumstances relevant for the determination of the normal value pursuant to Article 2, due account shall be taken of all relevant evidence, including relevant reports regarding the circumstances prevailing on the domestic market of the exporters and producers and the evidence on which they are based, which has been placed on the file, and upon which interested parties have had an opportunity to comment.

3.1   Assessing "Significant Distortions"

First, according to the new Article 2(6a)(b) "significant distortions" are defined as distortions which occur "...*when reported prices or costs, including the costs of raw materials and energy, are not the result of free market forces because they are affected by substantial government intervention.*"

Second, relevant factors for this assessment shall include the potential impact of one or more of the following elements:

---

[26] Non-WTO NMEs will continue to be subject to the application of the analogue country methodology. Such countries would be covered by the new Article 2(7) which basically replicates the thus far applicable Article 2(7)(a).

- Whether the market in question is to a significant extent served by enterprises which operate under the ownership, control or policy supervision or guidance of the authorities of the exporting country;
- State presence in firms allowing the state to interfere with respect to prices or costs;
- Public policies or measures discriminating in favour of domestic suppliers or otherwise influencing free market forces;
- The lack of or discriminatory application or inadequate enforcement of bankruptcy, corporate or property laws;
- Distortion of wage costs; and
- Access to finance granted by institutions implementing public policy objectives or otherwise not acting independently from the state.

Third, in terms of the evidence of "significant distortions", per the new Article 2(6a)(c), *"where the Commission has well-founded indications of the possible existence of significant distortions ... in a certain country or a sector thereof"*, it *"... shall produce, make public and regularly update a report..."* describing the market circumstances referred to in Article 2(6a)(b).

Article 2(6a)(c) further provides that the Commission's country/sector-specific report and the evidence on which it is based "shall" be placed on the file of any investigation pertaining to that country or sector and interested parties "shall" have ample opportunity to rebut, supplement, comment or rely on the report and the underlying evidence in each anti-dumping case in which such report or evidence is used. The Commission, in making its assessment of significant distortions, shall take into account all the relevant evidence on the investigation record.

Additionally, according to the new Article 2(6a)(d), EU complainants may rely on the evidence in the Commission's reports when they lodge complaints or request reviews to justify the calculation of the normal value. The possible reversal of the burden of proof such that the EU complainants would have to provide evidence of the existence of "significant distortions" in a complaint was a sticky issue in the negotiations due to intense opposition from and lobbying by the EU domestic industry. The fact sheet issued by the Commission following the compromise between the EU institutions clarifies that the proposed amendments do not impose any additional burden on the EU industry and in fact, *"[i]t is the Commission who [sic] will have the additional work to establish that significant distortions exist in a particular country. When lodging a request for the initiation of an anti-dumping investigation EU industry will be able to rely on the Commission's detailed country and sector level reports as evidence that distortions exist."*[27]

---

[27] See European Commission, The EU is changing its anti-dumping and anti-subsidy legislation to address state induced market distortions, 5 October 2017, http://trade.ec.europa.eu/doclib/press/index.cfm?id=1736 (last accessed 30 April 2018).

Fourth, Article 2(6a)(e) provides that when the Commission finds that there is sufficient evidence pursuant to Article 5(9) of the Basic Anti-Dumping Regulation that "significant distortions" exist and it decides to initiate an investigation on that basis, the notice of initiation shall specify this. Additionally, the Commission "shall" collect the data required for the construction of the "undistorted" normal value and evidence regarding the existence of "significant distortions" "...*may only be taken into account if it can be verified in a timely manner within the investigation.*"

Article 2(6a)(e) further provides that interested parties in an anti-dumping investigation shall be informed promptly after initiation about the relevant sources that the Commission intends to use for the purpose of determining the "undistorted" normal value and would be given 10 days to comment. In order to make their comments, interested parties would be granted access to the investigation file and all evidence relied upon by the Commission subject of course to confidentiality provisions.

3.2   Addressing "Significant Distortions"

Per Article 2(6a)(a), if the Commission considers that "...*it is not appropriate to use domestic prices and costs in the exporting country due to the existence of significant distortions ... the normal value shall be constructed exclusively on the basis of costs of production and sale reflecting undistorted prices or benchmarks...*"; the sources that the Commission "may" use to arrive at such an "undistorted" constructed normal value include the following:

1. "*corresponding costs of production and sale in an appropriate representative country with a similar level of economic development as the exporting country, provided the relevant data are readily available.*" In this context, if there is more than one analogue country available, preference "shall" be given to countries with an adequate level of social and environmental protection; or
2. if considered appropriate, "...*undistorted international prices, costs, or benchmarks*"; or
3. domestic costs, only to the extent that they are positively established not to be distorted, on the basis of accurate and appropriate evidence. The appropriateness of using domestic costs would be assessed on an exporter/producer-specific basis.

Additionally, "...*an undistorted and reasonable amount for administrative, selling and general costs and for profits*" shall be used for the purpose of the constructed normal value.

4 The TDI Modernisation Proposal and Possible Removal of the LDR

In the context of its 2013 trade defence instruments' modernisation exercise, on 10 April 2013, the Commission disclosed its legislative proposal.[28] Apart from other protectionist elements such as the initiation of ex officio investigations in case of a perceived threat of retaliation, the Commission proposed to remove the LDR in case of "structural raw material distortions" and subsidies.

The European Parliament, during its first reading in 2014, then proposed to also remove the LDR in cases involving countries with insufficient social or environmental standards[29] or where the complainants are SMEs.

However, the EU Member States were unable to agree on this proposal,[30] as a result of which various alternatives were proposed. For example, in May 2016, France and Germany, pressured by their steel industries, jointly proposed to remove the LDR in cases of structural raw material distortions (including export taxes/restrictions, subsidies and dual pricing) and "massive over-capacities".

In June 2016, the Commission then followed up with a non-paper, suggesting that massive over-capacity in a country would exist if it equals or surpasses EU consumption of the product concerned during the investigation period.

On 13 December 2016, during the Slovak Presidency, the Committee of Permanent Representatives (Coreper) agreed on a TDI modernisation package that includes a relatively modest LDR component.[31] Under the Coreper-agreed proposal, the LDR would be removed in cases involving raw material distortions where such raw materials, including energy, account for more than 27% of the cost of production in total and more than 7% taken individually.

---

[28] European Commission, Proposal for a Regulation of the European Parliament and of the Council amending Council Regulation (EC) No 1225/2009 on protection against dumped imports from countries not members of the European Community and Council Regulation (EC) No 597/2009 on protection against subsidised imports from countries not members of the European Community, COM(2013) 192 final, 10 April 2013, http://trade.ec.europa.eu/doclib/docs/2013/april/tradoc_150838.pdf (last accessed 30 April 2018).

[29] Defined as countries that have not ratified core ILO conventions or environmental agreements to which the EU is a party.

[30] It would seem that Austria, Belgium, Cyprus, Czech Republic, Denmark, Estonia, Finland, Ireland, Latvia, Malta, Slovenia, Sweden and the UK were against the proposal.

[31] See Council, Trade defence instruments: Council agrees negotiating position, 13 December 2016, http://www.consilium.europa.eu/en/press/press-releases/2016/12/13/trade-defence-instruments-general-approach/ (last accessed 30 April 2018).

Finally, the trilogue between the EU institutions led to a compromise agreement on 5 December 2017.[32] Reportedly,[33] the compromise agreement entails the following:

1. *LDR*: The LDR will not be applied in cases of structural raw material distortions where such raw materials individually account for 17% of the cost of production of the investigated product, and in case of subsidisation;
2. *Social and environmental standards*: The actual and future costs of compliance with social and environmental standards by EU producers would be taken into account in the calculation of the injury margin. Additionally, non-compliance of social and environmental standards could be a basis to refuse an undertaking. Moreover, higher costs for complying with social and environmental standards could be a basis for an interim review;
3. *Target profit for injury margin calculation*: A minimum 6% target profit will be applied for the calculation on the non-injurious price for injury margin calculation;
4. *Notice period*[34]: A notice period of 3 weeks—from the public disclosure of provisional measures—during which the provisional duty would not be applied has been agreed upon. The notice period is intended to be reviewed after 2 years to assess if there was stockpiling. In case of the latter, the notice period would be reduced to 2 weeks and in case of absence of stockpiling the period would be increased to 4 weeks.

The compromise proposal of 5 December 2017 was confirmed by the Member States on 19 December 2017,[35] and endorsed by the International Trade Committee

---

[32] See European Commission, Commission welcomes landmark deal modernising the EU's trade defence, 5 December 2017, http://europa.eu/rapid/press-release_IP-17-5136_en.htm (last accessed 30 April 2018); see also European Parliament, Tougher defence tools against unfair imports, MEPs strike deal with ministers, 6 December 2017, http://www.europarl.europa.eu/news/en/press-room/20171205IPR89528/tougher-defence-tools-against-unfair-imports-meps-strike-deal-with-ministers (last accessed 30 April 2018).

[33] See e.g. Mlex report, EU negotiators strike deal on overhaul of trade defense rules, 6 December 2017.

[34] The Commission initially proposed to provide interested parties with a limited pre-disclosure—including a summary of the dumping and injury margin calculations—of 2 weeks in advance of the imposition of provisional measures, and proposed the non-imposition of provisional measures for a period of 2 weeks pursuant to the pre-disclosure. See proposed amendments to Articles 7 and 19 in the Proposal for a Regulation of the European Parliament and of the Council amending Council Regulation (EC) No 1225/2009 on protection against dumped imports from countries not members of the European Community and Council Regulation (EC) No 597/2009 on protection against subsidised imports from countries not members of the European Community, COM(2013) 192 final, 10 April 2017.

[35] See Council, Trade defence instruments: EU ambassadors confirm the outcome of the final political trilogue with European Parliament, 19 December 2017, http://www.consilium.europa.eu/en/press/press-releases/2017/12/20/trade-defence-instruments-eu-ambassadors-confirm-the-outcome-of-the-final-political-trilogue-with-european-parliament/ (last accessed 30 April 2018).

of the European Parliament on 23 January 2018.[36] After formal adoption, the new rules are expected to come into force in 2018.

5 Assessment

5.1 Assessment of the Significant Distortions Provisions

Overall, the significant distortions provisions are imprecise and unclear as far as the key concepts and details are concerned. This is perhaps on purpose to complicate WTO challenges. A natural consequence of the ambiguity of the legal provisions will be a significant increase in the Commission's already excessive discretion in anti-dumping investigations. Moreover, although ostensibly country neutral, the text, context and timing of the provisions as well as the follow-up actions of the Commission leave no doubt that China is going to be the main target at least in the initial period of application.

To elaborate, first, the significant distortions provisions are marred by severe unclarity as far as the main elements are concerned.

The new provisions conflate domestic sales prices and costs of production and no distinction regarding the criteria for finding "significant distortions" with respect to the two has been made. It remains unclear whether for instance sales prices would first be tested for distortion, whether distorted costs would be the cause of rejection of domestic sales prices or whether simply on account of country-wide/sector-specific reports all domestic sales prices and costs would be deemed to be significantly distorted.

Furthermore, it is unclear as to how the provisions of Article 2(6a) would be applied in conjunction with Articles 2(3) to 2(5) of the Basic Anti-Dumping Regulation which deal with the establishment of normal value.

Additionally, the criteria for assessing the existence of "significant distortions"—apart from being non-exhaustive—lack a proper definition or threshold. To give a few examples, as regards wage cost distortion, it is not clear under what circumstances can wage costs be deemed to be distorted. Similarly, it is not clear as to what is implied by "public policies or measures... otherwise influencing free market forces" and under what circumstances "public policies or measures discriminating in favor of domestic suppliers..." are indicative of significant distortion. Indeed, almost every country in the world—including EU Member States—has policies to promote its domestic industries for example in the form of subsidy schemes involving funding, tax breaks, duty drawback, local content policies or non-tariff trade barriers. Similarly, the extent of state presence in firms allowing interference with prices or costs that would amount to "significant distortion" is questionable, e.g.

---

[36] See European Commission, Commission welcomes progress in approval of the modernised EU's trade defence rules, 23 January 2018, http://trade.ec.europa.eu/doclib/press/index.cfm?id=1788 (last accessed 30 April 2018).

whether the mere presence of government appointed officials on a company's board will be sufficient or more is required.

Moreover, in addition to the fact that the significant distortions criteria on account of their ambiguous wording will be subject to discriminatory as well as expansive interpretation and application by the Commission on a case-specific basis as seen in the context of the MET assessments, a plain reading of these criteria indicates that they subsume the current MET criteria in Article 2(7)(c) of the Basic Anti-Dumping Regulation.[37] Put bluntly, the "significant distortion" criteria are simply the repackaged MET criteria.

Second, while the significant distortions provisions refer to horizontal country-wide reports, the criteria for assessing significant distortions are mostly company-specific[38] and otherwise sector-specific.[39] Therefore, while the nature and content of the reports is only known to the Commission thus far, to what extent the country or sector-specific reports would serve as "evidence" of significant distortions at a company-specific level is questionable. Indeed, it is quite commonly seen in anti-subsidy investigations that subsidy schemes available to a particular industry or sector are not availed of by specific exporting producers.

Third, the provisions indicate that once there is a country or sector-specific report, a determination of significant distortions would likely be a foregone conclusion in anti-dumping cases concerning that country/sector of that country. This follows from the fact that the Commission has assured that there will be no increase in the evidentiary burden on EU complainants and that they can simply rely on the country/sector-specific reports to meet the standard of evidence required under Article 5(9) of the Basic Anti-Dumping Regulation.[40] A finding of distortion will then undoubtedly become a self-fulfilling prophecy.

Following from the above, once the investigation is initiated, the establishment of normal value for exporting producers on the basis of undistorted costs will be a given as it would be unlikely that the Commission would find its own report/evidence therein insufficient evidentiary proof of significant distortions. In addition to the fact that there is no provision pursuant to which interested parties would have the opportunity to rebut the significant distortions claim, individual exporting producers would find it difficult to provide evidence for a sector or the economy as a whole.

In this regard it is relevant to note that the new provisions do provide a possibility of using individual exporting producers' "undistorted" costs if they can be positively

---

[37] See Article 2(7)(c) of the EU's Basic Anti-Dumping Regulation.

[38] See for instance the following criteria in Article 2(6a)(b): state presence in firms allowing the state to interfere with prices or costs; wage cost distortion; access to finance from institutions implementing public policy objectives; lack of/discriminatory application of bankruptcy, corporate or property laws.

[39] See for instance the following criteria in Article 2(6a)(b): market in question is to a significant extent served by state-owned/controlled firms; public policies discriminating in favour of domestic suppliers.

[40] See Article 2(6a)(e).

established to be undistorted on the basis of appropriate and accurate evidence. However, it would likely be extremely difficult, if not impossible, for a company that is determined to be a part of a distorted sector to prove that its costs are undistorted, as the Commission's current MET practice evidences. This assessment is supported by the sentence in Article 2(6a)(e) that promptly after initiation interested parties would be informed of the sources that the Commission intends to use to establish the undistorted normal value. Exporting producer-specific undistorted prices is one of the sources listed in proposed Article 2(6a)(a) but filing information on the absence of distortion by exporting producers and its verification could hardly be expected to be completed so shortly or promptly after the initiation of the investigation.

Fourth, once the investigation is initiated including with regard to "significant distortions", normal value would be established on the basis of undistorted costs in a representative country or using international benchmarks. While the excessive discretion available to the Commission in selecting benchmarks and supposedly representative third countries is evident, nothing else about the application of these sources is. Particularly, it is not clear whose factors of production will be used and how. Further complicating the establishment of the undistorted costs is the fact that, on the one hand, Article 2(6a)(a) states that undistorted costs would need to be used and, on the other hand, that a representative country with a similar level of economic development would need to be selected. The criteria, if any, that the Commission would consider for determining that a particular country is "representative" and that the costs in the representative country are undistorted, have not been outlined. To conflate things further, if social and environmental standards are to be taken into account, then it is unlikely that any country with a similar level of economic development would be found for the commonly investigated countries by the EU.

Based on the above, it can be safely concluded that inflated dumping margins can be expected to result from the use of the new methodology to establish normal value.

The above having been said, it is clear that China is the main target of the Commission's ostensibly country neutral provisions. Several factors evidence this. To begin with, the significant distortions provisions are the outcome of the discussion that was started to address the expiry of a specific provision in China's accession protocol. Moreover, the various criteria for assessing the existence of "significant distortions"—apart from replicating the MET criteria—reflect key Commission determinations in anti-subsidy cases against China. Thus, the context and timing of their adoption evidence that China will be the key target. This seems to be confirmed by recent press reports that the Commission has issued a country report only for China and no other such reports are envisaged at least in the short to medium term.[41] Apparently, the Commission, in anticipation of the entry in force of

---

[41] See Blenkinsop P, EU to single out Chinese imports in report on market distortions. Reuters, 5 October 2017, https://in.reuters.com/article/us-eu-china-trade/eu-to-single-out-chinese-imports-in-report-on-market-distortions-idINKBN1CA1N2 (last accessed 30 April 2018).

the new rules has already prepared a 400+ page report on macro-economic distortions in the Chinese economy.

5.2 Questionable WTO-Compatibility of the Significant Distortions Provisions

The Commission and the Council have claimed the significant distortions provisions to be non-discriminatory, WTO-compliant and based on the rules of the Anti-Dumping Agreement.[42] All these assertions however are questionable.

First, from an overall perspective, the rejection of exporting producers' prices or costs due to a finding of country-wide or sector-wide distortions seems inconsistent with the concept of "dumping" which as noted by the Appellate Body concerns the pricing behaviour of individual exporters/foreign producers. In *US – Zeroing (Japan)*, for example, the Appellate Body stated as follows:

> …the Anti-Dumping Agreement prescribes that dumping determinations be made in respect of each exporter or foreign producer examined. This is because dumping is the result of the pricing behaviour of individual exporters or foreign producers. Margins of dumping are established accordingly for each exporter or foreign producer on the basis of a comparison between normal value and export prices, both of which relate to the pricing behaviour of that exporter or foreign producer.[43]

Similarly, in *US – Stainless Steel (Mexico)*, the Appellate Body held that "… *Article VI:1 of the GATT 1994 and Article 2.1 of the Anti-Dumping Agreement address the pricing practice of an exporter.*"[44]

In fact, in *US – Continued Zeroing*, the EU itself argued that "… *it is clear from Articles VI:1 and VI:2 of the GATT 1994 and various provisions of the Anti-Dumping Agreement that…*"*dumping" and "margin of dumping" are exporter-specific concepts…*"[45]

Second, the new provisions treat the existence of significant distortions as a circumstance permitting (1) the automatic rejection of domestic sales prices of inves-

---

[42] See Council, Anti-dumping methodology: Council agrees negotiating position, 3 May 2017, http://www.consilium.europa.eu/en/press/press-releases/2017/05/03-anti-dumping/ (last accessed 30 April 2018): "*The new methodology for calculating dumping is based on rules established by the WTO anti-dumping agreement.*"

Also European Commission, Commission welcomes agreement on new anti-dumping methodology, 3 October 2017, http://europa.eu/rapid/press-release_IP-17-3668_en.htm (last accessed 30 April 2018): "*The rules are formulated in a country-neutral way and in full compliance with the EU's WTO obligations.*"

[43] Appellate Body Report, *United States – Measures Relating to Zeroing and Sunset Reviews*, WT/DS322/AB/R, adopted 9 January 2007, DSR 2006:V, para. 111.

[44] Appellate Body Report, *United States – Final Anti-Dumping Measures on Stainless Steel from Mexico*, WT/DS344/AB/R, adopted 30 April 2008, DSR 2006:VI, para. 86.

[45] Appellate Body Report, *United States – Continued Existence and Application of Zeroing Methodology*, WT/DS350/AB/R, adopted 4 February 2009, DSR 2008:XI, para. 101.

tigated exporting producers and the construction of normal value, and (2) the rejection of the costs of investigated exporting producers while constructing the normal value.[46] Such an interpretation is however at odds with the Anti-Dumping Agreement as it blurs the methodical approach of the different provisions of the Anti-Dumping Agreement as well as the difference between domestic sales prices and exporting producers' cost of production.

More specifically, Article 2.2 of the Anti-Dumping Agreement[47] permits the construction of normal value in three situations, namely in case of no domestic sales of the like product in the ordinary course of trade, insufficient (less than 5%) domestic sales of the like product or when a particular market situation exists in the domestic market. The list of the three situations is exhaustive[48] and does not permit any additions such as the one envisaged by the EU, i.e. significant distortion of the domestic prices or costs.

Additionally, whether for the purpose of the sales below cost test or the construction of the normal value, the establishment of the cost of production is subject to the rules set out in Article 2.2.1.1 of the Anti-Dumping Agreement.[49] The first sentence of Article 2.2.1.1 identifies the records of the investigated exporter or producer as the exclusive source for establishing the cost of production[50] unless the records are inconsistent with the exporting country's Generally Accepted Accounting Principles (GAAP) or do not reasonably reflect the costs associated with the production and sale of the product under consideration.[51] Thus, the rejection of exporting producers' costs is permitted only if either of the two conditions in Article 2.2.1.1 is not met. Seen in this light, the rejection of the recorded production costs

---

[46] Article 2(6a)(a).

[47] Article 2.2 of the Anti-Dumping Agreement states as follows: *"When there are no sales of the like product in the ordinary course of trade in the domestic market of the exporting country or when, because of the particular market situation or the low volume of the sales in the domestic market of the exporting country, such sales do not permit a proper comparison, the margin of dumping shall be determined by comparison with a comparable price of the like product when exported to an appropriate third country, provided that this price is representative, or with the cost of production in the country of origin plus a reasonable amount for administrative, selling and general costs and for profits."*

[48] The use of facts available to establish the normal value is a separate matter.

[49] The Appellate Body noted in *EU – Biodiesel* (Argentina) that *"...Article 2.2.1.1 includes rules pertaining to the calculation of the "cost of production" for purposes of determining the normal value under Article 2.2."* See Appellate Body Report, *European Union – Anti-Dumping Measures on Biodiesel from Argentina*, WT/DS473/AB/R, adopted 6 October 2016, DSR 2016:IV, para. 6.17.

[50] Appellate Body Report, *European Union – Anti-Dumping Measures on Biodiesel from Argentina*, WT/DS473/AB/R, adopted 6 October 2016, DSR 2016:IV, para. 6.18.

[51] The first sentence of Article 2.2.1.1 of the Anti-Dumping Agreement states as follows: *"For the purpose of paragraph 2, costs shall normally be calculated on the basis of records kept by the exporter or producer under investigation, provided that such records are in accordance with the generally accepted accounting principles of the exporting country and [the recorded costs] reasonably reflect the costs associated with the production and sale of the product under consideration."*

of investigated exporting producers on account of a finding of significant distortion of costs as envisaged in the new provisions would be inconsistent with Article 2.2.1.1 of the Anti-Dumping Agreement because it would be tantamount to introducing an additional criterion not provided for in the Anti-Dumping Agreement.

Additionally, the Appellate Body ruling in *EU – Biodiesel (Argentina)* does not support the Commission's proposed approach.[52] The latter report establishes that if an investigating authority considers that the actual and accurately recorded costs of an exporting producer are distorted or unreasonable, it cannot simply reject those costs and use international benchmarks or third country producers' costs by relying on the second condition in the first sentence of Article 2.2.1.1 of the Anti-Dumping Agreement. In the underlying administrative investigation concerning the *EU – Biodiesel (Argentina)* dispute, the Commission had rejected the Argentine producers' actual and verified costs of soya beans—the main raw material to make biodiesel—on the ground that the domestic prices of soya beans were lower than the international prices due to the distortion created by the Argentine export tax system. The Commission instead used the average of the reference prices of soya beans published by the Argentine Ministry of Agriculture for export FOB Argentina (minus the fobbing costs)—which the Commission considered reflected international prices—for the construction of the normal value.[53]

Following Argentina's challenge of the above methodology, the Appellate Body held that the condition that the records reasonably reflect the costs associated with the production and sale of the product under consideration refers to "... *whether the records kept by the exporter or producer suitably and sufficiently correspond to or reproduce those costs incurred by the investigated exporter or producer that have a genuine relationship with the production and sale of the specific product under consideration.*"[54] On this basis, it held that, contrary to the EU's arguments:

1. This condition did not permit the EU to consider costs which would pertain to the production and sale of biodiesel in normal circumstances, i.e. in the absence of the alleged distortion caused by Argentina's export tax system, for the construction of the normal value[55]; and
2. To the extent costs are genuinely related to the production and sale of the product under consideration, there is no additional or abstract standard of "reasonableness" governing the meaning of "costs"[56] in the above condition that permits an

---

[52] Appellate Body Report, *European Union – Anti-Dumping Measures on Biodiesel from Argentina*, WT/DS473/AB/R, adopted 6 October 2016, DSR 2016:IV.

[53] Council Implementing Regulation (EU) No 1194/2013 of 19 November 2013 imposing a definitive anti-dumping duty and collecting definitively the provisional duty imposed on imports of biodiesel originating in Argentina and Indonesia, OJ 2013 L 315/2, Recitals 35–40.

[54] Appellate Body Report, *European Union – Anti-Dumping Measures on Biodiesel from Argentina*, WT/DS473/AB/R, adopted 6 October 2016, DSR 2016:IV, para. 6.26.

[55] Appellate Body Report, *European Union – Anti-Dumping Measures on Biodiesel from Argentina*, WT/DS473/AB/R, adopted 6 October 2016, DSR 2016:IV, para. 6.30.

[56] Appellate Body Report, *European Union – Anti-Dumping Measures on Biodiesel from Argentina*, WT/DS473/AB/R, adopted 6 October 2016, DSR 2016:IV, para. 6.37.

investigating authority to disregard the records kept by the exporter or producer if the authority determines that the costs in such records are not reasonable. On this basis, the Appellate Body endorsed the Panel finding that the EU acted inconsistently with Article 2.2.1.1 because:

> ... the EU authorities' determination that domestic prices of soybeans in Argentina were lower than international prices due to the Argentine export tax system was not, in itself, a sufficient basis under Article 2.2.1.1 for concluding that the producers' records do not reasonably reflect the costs of soybeans associated with the production and sale of biodiesel, or for disregarding those costs when constructing the normal value of biodiesel.[57]

In order to implement the above-mentioned Appellate Body ruling, the Commission opened an interim review[58] and recently issued a Regulation amending the anti-dumping duty rates for the Argentine exporting producers. In the said Regulation, the Commission categorically ruled out that the Argentine export tax system could form the basis for a cost adjustment. The Commission interpreted the Appellate Body ruling above to imply that "... *the operation of the export tax system in Argentina cannot 'as such' trigger a cost adjustment under Article 2.2.1.1 ADA however well-reasoned or documented its distortive effects may be...*"[59] and that "... *the EU could not disregard the costs actually incurred and accurately recorded when constructing the normal value of biodiesel in Argentina on the basis of distortions stemming from the mere existence of the Argentina export tax system.*"[60]

Although much will depend on the practical application, the significant distortions provisions seem to be incoherent with the above stance of the Commission. The text of Article 2(6a)(a) mandates the rejection of the actual production costs of investigated exporting producers if "significant distortions" at the country-wide or sector-specific levels—due to state policies and intervention—are found and further obliges the construction of the normal value on the basis of international benchmarks or third country costs. Thus, significant distortions stemming from government intervention or policies are a basis for cost adjustment under the new provisions.

Third, the sources in Article 2(6a)(a) for establishing the cost of production and sale include undistorted international prices, costs or benchmarks and costs of

---

[57] Appellate Body Report, *European Union – Anti-Dumping Measures on Biodiesel from Argentina*, WT/DS473/AB/R, adopted 6 October 2016, DSR 2016:IV, para. 6.55.

[58] Commission Notice of initiation regarding the anti-dumping measures in force on imports of biodiesel originating in Argentina and Indonesia, following the recommendations and rulings adopted by the Dispute Settlement Body of the World Trade Organisation in the EU—Anti-Dumping Measures on Biodiesel dispute (DS473), OJ 2016 C 476/3.

[59] Commission Implementing Regulation (EU) 2017/1578 of 18 September 2017 amending Implementing Regulation (EU) No 1194/2013 imposing a definitive anti-dumping duty and collecting definitively the provisional duty imposed on imports of biodiesel originating in Argentina and Indonesia, OJ 2017 L 239/9, Recital 68. See also Recitals 51–55.

[60] Commission Implementing Regulation (EU) 2017/1578 of 18 September 2017 amending Implementing Regulation (EU) No 1194/2013 imposing a definitive anti-dumping duty and collecting definitively the provisional duty imposed on imports of biodiesel originating in Argentina and Indonesia, OJ 2017L 239/9, Recital 73.

production and sale in a representative third country. Prima facie, the use of these sources will likely not result in a cost of production in the country of origin as required by Article 2.2 of the Anti-Dumping Agreement and interpreted by the Appellate Body as "... *the price paid or to be paid to produce something within the country of origin.*"[61] In *EU – Biodiesel (Argentina)*, the Appellate Body explained that "... *Article 2.2 of the Anti-Dumping Agreement refers to "the cost of production in the country of origin"...*" *and "... given the fact that Article 2.2.1.1 starts with the phrase "[f]or the purpose of paragraph 2", the interpretation of the term "costs" in Article 2.2.1.1, for purposes of calculating the costs of production, must be consistent with how the term "cost" is understood in Article 2.2. Thus, insofar as the cost of production is concerned, the costs "calculated on the basis of records kept by the exporter or producer" under Article 2.2.1.1 must lead to a cost "in the country of origin"...*"[62]

In the same dispute, the Appellate Body held that Article 2.2 of the Anti-Dumping Agreement and Article VI:1(b)(ii) of the GATT 1994 "...*do not limit the sources of information or evidence that may be used in establishing the cost of production in the country of origin to sources inside the country of origin*"[63] and do not preclude under certain circumstances (e.g. when the obligation to rely on costs does not apply or the information in the exporting producers' records cannot be used), an investigating authority from relying on other in-country and out-of-country evidence to establish the costs. However, the Appellate Body also underlined that in such case, an investigating authority cannot substitute the cost(s) from outside the country of origin for the "*cost of production in the country of origin*" and the investigating authority has to ensure that the out-of-country of origin information is used to arrive at the "*cost of production in the country of origin*" and the costs of production established need to reflect conditions prevailing in the country of origin.[64]

However, if third country costs or international benchmarks were to be used to establish the cost of production, it would be done to remove the perceived cost

---

[61] Appellate Body Report, *European Union – Anti-Dumping Measures on Biodiesel from Argentina*, WT/DS473/AB/R, adopted 6 October 2016, DSR 2016:IV, para. 6.69.

[62] Appellate Body Report, *European Union – Anti-Dumping Measures on Biodiesel from Argentina*, WT/DS473/AB/R, adopted 6 October 2016, DSR 2016:IV, para. 6.23. In para. 6.24, the Appellate Body further noted as follows: "... *in our view, Article 2.2 of the Anti-Dumping Agreement concerns the establishment of the normal value through an appropriate proxy for the price of the like product in the ordinary course of trade in the domestic market of the exporting country when the normal value cannot be determined on the basis of domestic sales.*[129]*The costs calculated pursuant to Article 2.2.1.1 of the Anti-Dumping Agreement must be capable of generating such a proxy. This supports the view that the "costs associated with the production and sale of the product under consideration" in Article 2.2.1.1 are those costs that have a genuine relationship with the production and sale of the product under consideration. This is because these are the costs that, together with other elements, would otherwise form the basis for the price of the like product if it were sold in the ordinary course of trade in the domestic market.*"

[63] Appellate Body Report, *European Union – Anti-Dumping Measures on Biodiesel from Argentina*, WT/DS473/AB/R, adopted 6 October 2016, DSR 2016:IV, para. 6.74.

[64] Appellate Body Report, *European Union – Anti-Dumping Measures on Biodiesel from Argentina*, WT/DS473/AB/R, adopted 6 October 2016, DSR 2016:IV, para. 6.73.

distortion found and precisely because such costs would not be influenced by country-wide/sectoral distortions. Therefore, adapting the out-of-country of origin costs to the conditions prevailing in the investigated country market would imply re-introducing the effect of the very factors that are perceived to be distortive and this would run counter to the whole aim of the new provisions. The above having been said, as the practical application of the Appellate Body's statements is yet to be tested and the extent and type of adaptation required to the out-of-country information is unclear, it is likely to lead to another WTO case in the future should the EU take this road.

Furthermore, that the EU industry will not need to provide additional evidence to support the claim of "significant distortions" but can simply rely on the Commission report(s) seems to blur the lines between a complaint-based and ex officio investigation. The Commission would be discharging the burden of proof which however is on the EU producers pursuant to Article 5.3 of the Anti-Dumping Agreement. Furthermore, the adequacy and accuracy assessment as required by Article 5.4 of the Anti-Dumping Agreement for the admissibility of a complaint will also not be objectively applied by the Commission as it would not discredit its own reports.

Finally, the grandfathering provisions added to Articles 11(3) and 11(4) of the EU Basic Anti-Dumping Regulation seem to be inconsistent with Article 18.3 of the Anti-Dumping Agreement[65] and can likely be challenged on an "as such" basis.

While it remains to be seen how the Commission will implement the significant distortions provisions, clearly these provisions are not as WTO-compliant as the Commission would have stakeholders believe and their application is likely to result in more WTO-inconsistent practices in EU anti-dumping investigations.

5.3 Possible WTO-Inconsistency Due to the Concurrent Application of the "Significant Distortions" Provisions and the Removal of the LDR

The proposed removal of the LDR in case of structural raw material distortions and subsidisation is probably difficult to challenge in the WTO in light of the *EU – Footwear* panel report which basically held that WTO members have wide discretion in the application of the LDR as the rule is not mandatory under the Anti-Dumping Agreement.[66] This also applies in the context of the WTO Agreement on Subsidies and Countervailing Measures.

---

[65] Article 18.3 of the Anti-Dumping Agreement states as follows: "*Subject to subparagraphs 3.1 and 3.2, the provisions of this Agreement shall apply to investigations, and reviews of existing measures, initiated pursuant to applications which have been made on or after the date of entry into force for a Member of the WTO Agreement.*"

[66] Panel Report, *European Union – Anti-Dumping Measures on Certain Footwear from China*, WT/DS405/R, adopted 28 October 2011, paras. VII.920–VII.935, especially paras. 924 and 927: "*While the term "lesser duty" is not defined in the AD Agreement, it is clear that this term refers*

However, that does not make it good policy. The rationale for the EU's adoption of the LDR arguably is to strike a balance between the interests of EU producers to be protected against injurious dumping and the interests of EU users,[67] consumers and importers to have access to imported products at low prices. However, the removal of the rule in case of structural raw material distortions and subsidies seems designed to punish third country producers that benefit from such distortions and subsidies.

From a legal perspective, normal value construction in case of "significant distortions" and the concurrent non-application of the LDR may potentially result in a problem of "double remedies"—also referred to as "double counting"—in case of parallel anti-dumping and anti-subsidy investigations against the same product on account of the common element of subsidies. "Double remedies" was defined in *US – Anti-Dumping and Countervailing Duties (China)* by the Appellate Body as a circumstance *"… in which the simultaneous application of anti-dumping and countervailing duties on the same imported products results, at least to some extent, in the offsetting of the same subsidization twice"*[68] and was found to be WTO-inconsistent.[69] The Appellate Body in that case clearly warned that the issue of "double remedies" is not limited to NME cases but may also arise in the context of market economies:

---

to the concept of an anti-dumping duty less than the full amount of the margin of dumping, as described in Article 9.1. It is also clear from the text of Article 9.1, and China does not dispute, that the imposition of a lesser duty is "desirable", but is not an obligation for WTO Members. Beyond stating that a lesser duty is desirable, if such lesser duty would be "adequate to remove the injury to the domestic industry", Article 9.1 says nothing about how the amount of a lesser duty should be established. … In our view it is clear, and indeed, China does not contend otherwise, that Article 9.1 does not prescribe any methodology or criteria for the determination of the amount of a lesser duty, should a Member choose to apply one.

(…)

We…consider that while the imposition of a duty at a level adequate to remove the injury is clearly contemplated by Article 9.1, this does not limit the basis on which an investigating authority may choose to apply a duty less than the full amount of the margin of dumping. Even assuming that, as in this case, an investigating authority's stated basis for application of a lesser duty is to impose a duty at a level adequate to "eliminate the material injury to the…industry caused by the dumped imports without exceeding the dumping margins", this does not, in our view, establish that Article 3.1 is relevant to the establishment of the level of lesser duty to be applied. There is, in our view, no basis in the text of Article 3.1 for the conclusion that it requires any particular approach to the calculation of a level of duty that will be sufficient to remove the injury determined to exist." (Footnotes omitted)

[67] DG Growth of the EU has spent significant time on developing a policy ensuring better access to raw materials for US producers, see, e.g. https://ec.europa.eu/growth/sectors/raw-materials/policy-strategy_en (last accessed 30 April 2018).

[68] Appellate Body Report, *United States – Definitive Anti-Dumping and Countervailing Duties on Certain Products from China*, WT/DS379/AB/R, adopted 11 March 2011, DSR 2010:III, para. 541.

[69] Appellate Body Report, *United States – Definitive Anti-Dumping and Countervailing Duties on Certain Products from China*, WT/DS379/AB/R, adopted 11 March 2011, DSR 2010:III, para. 583. See also Vermulst and Gatta (2012), pp. 143–158.

Double remedies may also arise in the context of domestic subsidies granted within market economies when anti-dumping and countervailing duties are concurrently imposed on the same products and an unsubsidized, constructed, or third country normal value is used in the anti-dumping investigation.[70]

The problem of double remedies could arise because the alleged subsidisation would be addressed once via the dumping margin—as subsidies are one of the key elements considered in assessing "significant distortion"—and to a certain extent again via the subsidy margin.

More specifically, if significant distortions are found in the anti-dumping case on account of subsidies, then automatically the LDR would not be applied in the same anti-dumping case and in the parallel anti-subsidy case.[71] In such a situation, in the anti-dumping case, the alleged significant distortions affecting prices and costs would be addressed by using a constructed normal value on the basis of undistorted international prices, costs, or benchmarks, or costs of production and sale in an appropriate representative country. While it is not clear to what extent the actual costs of the investigated exporting producers would be disregarded and replaced, even from a conservative viewpoint, if some production cost elements are based on international benchmarks or representative country data, the resulting dumping margin—which would be higher than in the absence of the cost adjustment—would not only address price discrimination or dumping but equally the alleged subsidies that distorted the exporting producer's cost of production.

In parallel, the anti-subsidy duty would likely also partially cover production-related domestic subsidies (whether direct or indirect) or "access to finance granted by institutions implementing public policy objectives" or the effects of "public policies or measures discriminating in favour of domestic suppliers or otherwise influencing free market forces". The latter two are criteria to assess the existence not only of significant distortions but also of key "subsidies" countervailed by the Commission at least in cases concerning China.

6 Conclusions

While Bob Marley noted that "*[y]ou can fool some people some time, but you can't fool all the people all the time*", it would appear that the significant distortions provisions have fooled no one. On the one hand, the EU has re-instituted the MET criteria with enhanced discretion for itself thereby inducing legal uncertainty in EU anti-dumping practice and, on the other hand, it is simply not possible for the EU to maintain the same level of anti-dumping duties as under the analogue country

---

[70] Appellate Body Report, *United States – Definitive Anti-Dumping and Countervailing Duties on Certain Products from China*, WT/DS379/AB/R, adopted 11 March 2011, DSR 2010:III, para. 543.

[71] Due to the existence of subsidies and possibly the satisfaction of the structural raw material distortion threshold.

methodology and to be WTO-compliant, just as one cannot have one's cake and eat it too. This explains both the vigorous opposition[72] of EU producers' lobbying groups such as AEGIS Europe to the new provisions addressing significant distortions and China's intention to not limit its WTO MES dispute with the EU to the relevant provisions of the current EU Basic Anti-Dumping Regulation, but to also include both the significant distortions provisions and the TDI modernisation rules.[73]

In fact, at the time of writing, the significant distortions provisions, although they have not entered into force, have already met criticism from—in addition to China— Russia, Kazakhstan, Egypt, Kuwait, Oman, Qatar, the United Arab Emirates and Colombia.[74] While the EU has thus far ducked a formal response to questions on the significant distortions provisions from countries such as Russia[75] on the ground that these provisions are yet to be formally adopted as law,[76] now that these provisions will soon enter into force and applied, WTO litigation is inevitable.

Additionally, it would seem that—blinded by its intention to pacify certain EU industries' complaints against Chinese government policies and exports from China to the EU—the Commission has overlooked the likely mirror effects of its significant distortions provisions: The new methodology is likely to backfire on EU exporting producers because countries such as India, Brazil and Argentina which

---

[72] AEGIS Europe, New Commission proposal undermines legal certainty in EU trade defence policy, 9 November 2016, http://www.aegiseurope.eu/news/press-release-new-commission-anti-dumping-proposal-undermines-legal-certainty-in-eu-trade-defence-policy (last accessed 30 April 2018). More recently, see O'Connor B, A short primer on China, anti-dumping and the Commission's proposal on significant distortions. Italy Europe 24, 10 April 2017, http://www.italy24.ilsole24ore.com/art/laws-and-taxes/2017-04-10/a-short-primer-on-china-anti-dumping-and-the-commission-s-proposal-on-significant-distortions--184706.php?uuid=AEGnKy2 (last accessed 30 April 2018).

[73] Request for the establishment of a Panel, *European Union – Measures related to price comparison methodologies,* G/ADP/D116/1, G/L/1170, WT/DS516/1, 12 December 2016, fn. 2: *"At present, China is aware of two legislative processes implicating potential changes to relevant provisions of the Basic Regulation: (i) the legislative process initiated by the European Commission's Proposal for a Regulation of the European Parliament and of the Council amending Regulation (EU) 2016/1036 on protection against dumped imports from countries not members of the European Union and Regulation (EU) 2016/1037 on protection against subsidised imports from countries not members of the European Union, dated 9 November 2016 (COM(2016) 721 final); and, (ii) the legislative process initiated by the European Commission's Proposal for a Regulation of the European Parliament and of the Council amending Council Regulation (EC) No 1225/2009 on protection against dumped imports from countries not members of the European Community and Council Regulation (EC) No 597/2009 on protection against subsidised imports from countries not members of the European Community (COM(2013) 192 final). This request includes any changes made to the Basic Regulation pursuant to the legislative processes initiated by these proposals."*

[74] Meeting of the Committee on Anti-Dumping Practices of 25 October 2017.

[75] Questions posed by the Russian Federation regarding the proposal for the EU Basic Anti-Dumping Regulation concerning determination of normal value, G/ADP/W/497, 27 April 2017.

[76] European Union's reply to questions posed by the Russian Federation regarding the proposal for the EU Basic Anti-Dumping Regulation concerning determination of normal value, G/ADP/W/499, 23 October 2017.

are also leading users of trade defence instruments emulate EU law and practice. Moreover, countries against which this methodology is used in the future are likely to retaliate as well. With EU companies being major targets of trade remedy cases in third countries, it is only a question of time before the EU's significant distortions methodology will be used against them.[77]

References

Vermulst E (2010) EU Anti-dumping law and practice. Sweet & Maxwell, London, pp 299–307
Vermulst E, Gatta B (2012) Disciplining the use of TDI against China through WTO dispute settlement. Global Trade Customs J 7(4):143–158
Vermulst E, Sud J, Evenett S (2016) Normal value in anti-dumping proceedings against China post-2016: are some animals less equal than others. Global Trade Customs J 11(5):212–228

---

[77] In fact, in the Australian anti-dumping investigation against prepared or preserved tomatoes from Italy, the Australian Anti-Dumping Commission determined that the recorded cost of raw tomatoes of two Italian companies did not reasonably reflect competitive market costs associated with the production or manufacture of the investigated product because subsidies in the form of direct income support payments made to growers of raw tomatoes in Italy—under the Single Payment Scheme which is a part of the EU's Common Agricultural Policy—significantly affected the prevailing market prices in Italy for raw tomatoes. The Anti-Dumping Commission adjusted—to calculate the "true cost of production"—the verified recorded costs of the producers by adding an amount reflecting the direct income support payments in EURO per kg of raw tomatoes produced during the investigation period. See Australian Government Anti-Dumping Commission, Final report No. 276, Dumping of prepared or preserved tomatoes exported from Italy by Feger Di Gerardo Ferraioli S.P.A. and La Doria S.P.A., 18 January 2016, section 6.4. While the Anti-Dumping Review Panel (ADRP) later overturned this determination on the narrow ground that the advantage conferred to the tomato growers by the subsidies was not transferred to the processors/producers of the product concerned, it seems only a question of time before similar or other EU subsidy programs will become a basis for cost adjustments by third country investigating authorities.

The New Anti-Dumping Methodology of the European Union: A Breach of WTO Law?

Christian Tietje and Vinzenz Sacher

Contents

Abstract Following the expiry of Article 15(a)(ii) of China's Accession Protocol to the WTO, the European Union faced the substantive challenge to rework its Basic Anti-Dumping Regulation. This paper seeks to provide an overview over the legislative process of the new Anti-Dumping methodology of the European Union and to analyse the new provisions on their consistency with WTO law. We hereby argue that the remaining parts of Article 15 of China's Accession Protocol do not allow for the continuous application of the pre-existing EU approach and that also the new approach of the European Union is in violation of Articles 2.2.1.1 and 2.2 of the

C. Tietje (✉)
Institute for Economic Law, Halle-Wittenberg, Germany

Transnational Economic Law Research Center (TELC), Law School of Martin Luther University, Halle-Wittenberg, Germany
e-mail: christian.tietje@jura.uni-halle.de

V. Sacher
Transnational Economic Law Research Center (TELC), Law School of Martin Luther University, Halle-Wittenberg, Germany
e-mail: vinzenz.sacher@jura.uni-halle.de

© Springer International Publishing AG, part of Springer Nature 2018
M. Bungenberg et al. (eds.), *The Future of Trade Defence Instruments*,
European Yearbook of International Economic Law,
https://doi.org/10.1007/978-3-319-95306-9_5

89

Anti-Dumping Agreement as well as Article VI:1(b)(ii) of the GATT, especially in the light of the recent Appellate Body decision in *EU – Biodiesel*.

1 Introduction

Recent trade relations between China and the European Union are stressed by continuing disputes over the European Union's treatment of dumped imports originating in China.[1] In the past, the Commission treated China as a non-market economy, based on the famous Article 15 of China's Accession Protocol (CAP) to the WTO, which previously allowed for an alternative approach to determining normal value in anti-dumping investigations.[2] In the wake of Article 15(a)(ii) CAP's expiration in December 2016, China expected the European Union to change its treatment of Chinese imports and to turn to the standard procedures of determining normal value under the WTO's Anti-Dumping Agreement (ADA). The European Union, on the other hand, persistently refuses to acknowledge China as a market-economy for political reasons.[3] Due to dramatic worldwide overcapacities in steel production, predominantly but not exclusively caused by subsidised Chinese producers, the pressure of the domestic European steel industry on the Commission is very strong.[4] Consequently, the Commission faced the substantive challenge to rework the EU's Basic Anti-Dumping Regulation, giving weight to the expiry of Article 15(a)(ii) CAP on the one hand and the remaining thread for the domestic industry due to unfair trade practices on the other.

---

[1] Euractiv, China frets over new EU anti-dumping duties on steel. Euractiv.com with Reuters, 28 February 2017, https://www.euractiv.com/section/economy-jobs/news/china-frets-over-new-eu-anti-dumping-duties-on-steel (last accessed 30 April 2018).

[2] In detail on China's Accession Protocol: Qin (2003), pp. 487 et seq.; concerning the legal status of WTO Accession Protocols: Kennedy (2013), pp. 58 et seq.; Liu (2014), p. 751.

[3] The European Parliament explicitly opposed to a recognition of China as a market economy in May 2016 and requested the Commission to handle possible anti-dumping duties strictly, see: European Parliament, Resolution on China's market economy status, 2016/2667(RSP), 12 May 2016, http://www.europarl.europa.eu/sides/getDoc.do?pubRef=-//EP//TEXT+TA+P8-TA-2016-0223+0+DOC+XML+V0//EN (last accessed 30 April 2018); the Council on the other hand published a more careful statement: *"In this context the European Council believes that unfair trade practices need to be tackled efficiently and robustly. (…) This requires a (…) modernisation of all trade defence instruments by the end of 2016."*, European Council, Conclusions on meeting 20–21 October 2016, EUCO 31/16, 21 October 2016, http://www.consilium.europa.eu/media/24257/20-21-euco-conclusions-final.pdf (last accessed 30 April 2018), p. 5; EU-Commissioner for Trade, Cecilia Malmström even said: *"Yet China is far from being a market economy"*, Cecilia Malmström, The future of EU trade policy, Brussels, 24 January 2017, http://trade.ec.europa.eu/doclib/docs/2017/january/tradoc_155261.pdf (last accessed 30 April 2018).

[4] World Steel Production has doubled in the last 20 years, whereas China's market share grew from 15 to nearly 50%: World Steel Association, World Steel in Figures 2017, https://www.worldsteel.org/en/dam/jcr:0474d208-9108-4927-ace8-4ac5445c5df8/World+Steel+in+Figures+2017.pdf (last accessed 30 April 2018), p. 6.

Finally, the Commission published a long-awaited proposal for reworking the respective Regulation in November 2016. After intensive discussions with representatives of the Parliament and the Council, the legislative organs of the European Union agreed on a final text by end of 2017, which entered into force on 20 December 2017.[5] This final text abolishes the traditional distinction between "market" and "non-market economies" in EU law and stipulates a new country-neutral approach in determining normal value based on "significant distortions" of the price of the product, similar to the methodology of Australia and the U.S.[6]

After giving a brief insight in the problems, occurring in wake of the expiry of Article 15(a)(ii) CAP (Sect. 2), this paper seeks to provide an analysis of the new provisions of the EU's Basic Anti-Dumping Regulation (Sect. 3) and assesses its conformity with WTO-law, especially in the light of the recent *EU – Biodiesel* decision of the Appellate Body (Sect. 4).

2 The Expiry of Article 15(a)(ii) of China's Accession Protocol

In the context of WTO law, a product is considered to be "dumped" if it is "*introduced into the commerce of another country at less than its normal value*" (Article 2.1 ADA; Article VI:1 GATT). Consequently, a finding of dumping requires a comparison between the actual import price of a product and its normal value. Whereas the actual price is usually a matter of fact, the determination of the normal value comes along with several difficulties.

WTO law stipulates that "normal value" shall principally be based on the price of the product when destined for consumption in the exporting country (Article 2.1 ADA), but also recognises for certain situations where this approach might not be appropriate (Article 2.2 ADA). In the case of non-market economies, WTO law provides an exemption clause which allows for an alternative approach in determining normal value—the so called "analogue" or "third-country method" (Second Ad Note to Article VI GATT).[7] Hereby, a WTO Member may simply refer to the price of the product in question in a third country as "normal value" instead of the price in the respective non-market economy. This method is obviously open to abuse, since a deliberate selection of the third country might result in a very high normal

---

[5] OJ 2017 L 338/1.
[6] In detail on the Australian Approach: Zhou (2015), p. 980; Australia did recognise China formally as a Market Economy in the wake of the negotiations on a Free Trade Agreement, though: Memorandum of Understanding between the Department of Foreign Affairs and Trade of Australia and the Ministry of Commerce of the People's Republic of China on the Recognition of China's Full Market Economy Status and the Commencement of Negotiation of A Free Trade Agreement between Australia and the People's Republic of China, 18 April 2005, http://dfat.gov.au/trade/agreements/in-force/chafta/Pages/australia-china-fta.aspx (last accessed 30 April 2018).
[7] In detail on this provision: Snyder (2001), pp. 380 et seq.; Polouektov (2002), pp. 6 et seq.

value and thereby in a very high dumping margin.[8] Thus, the requirements of these provisions are so narrow that, presently, not a single WTO Member would qualify as a non-market economy anymore.[9]

Nevertheless, the "analogue method" could still be used in relation to a WTO Member if the Accession Protocol of this member explicitly provides for it.[10] In the case of China, Article 15 of its Accession Protocol inter alia stated the following:

(a) In determining price comparability (…), the importing WTO Member **shall** use either Chinese prices or costs for the industry under investigation or a methodology that is not based on a strict comparison with domestic prices or costs in China **based on the following rules**:

(i) *If the producers under investigation can clearly show that market economy conditions prevail (…), the importing WTO Member shall use Chinese prices or costs (…);*
(ii) *The importing WTO Member may use a methodology that is not based on a strict comparison with domestic prices or costs in China if the producers under investigation cannot clearly show that market economy conditions prevail (…).* (emphasis added)

The second subparagraph of Article 15(a) hence provided the possibility for the application of the "analogue method". However, this exact subparagraph expired 15 years after China's accession to the WTO on 11 December 2016. Nevertheless, there has been a frequent and longstanding discussion regarding the effect of the remaining chapeau of Article 15(a) CAP.[11]

---

[8] BKP Development Research & Consulting, Evaluation of the European Union's Trade Defence Instruments, Final Evaluation Study Volume 1, 27 February 2012, http://trade.ec.europa.eu/doclib/docs/2012/march/tradoc_149236.pdf (last accessed 30 April 2018), p. 292; Cliff Stevenson, Mayer, Brown, Row & Maw LLP, Evaluation of EC Trade Defence Instruments, December 2005, Final Report, http://trade.ec.europa.eu/doclib/docs/2006/february/tradoc_127382.pdf (last accessed 30 April 2018); De Kok (2016), p. 519.

[9] Adamantopoulos (2010) para. 24; Tietje C and Nowroth K, Myth or Reality? China's Market Economy Status under WTO Anti-Dumping Law after 2016. Policy Papers on Transnational Economic Law No. 34, December 2011, http://telc.jura.uni-halle.de/sites/default/files/telc/PolicyPaper34.pdf (last accessed 30 April 2018), p. 10; Yan (2010), p. 162; also see the obiter dictum of the Appellate Body in the *EC – Fasteners* decision: *"We observe that the second Ad Note to Article VI:1 refers to a "country which has a* **complete** *or substantially complete* **monopoly of its trade**" *and* "where all domestic prices are fixed *by the State"*" (emphasis added), Appellate Body Report, *European Communities – Definitive Anti-Dumping Measures on Certain Iron or Steel Fasteners from China*, WT/DS397/AB/R, adopted 15 July 2011, DSR 2011:II, para. 285 and fn. 460.

[10] Tietje C and Nowroth K, Myth or Reality? China's Market Economy Status under WTO Anti-Dumping Law after 2016. Policy Papers on Transnational Economic Law No. 34, December 2011, http://telc.jura.uni-halle.de/sites/default/files/telc/PolicyPaper34.pdf (last accessed 30 April 2018), p. 4; Appellate Body Report, *China – Measures Related to the Exportation of Various Raw Materials*, WT/DS394/AB/R, adopted 30 January 2012, DSR 2011:V, para. 278; Appellate Body Report, *European Communities – Definitive Anti-Dumping Measures on Certain Iron or Steel Fasteners from China*, WT/DS397/AB/R, adopted 15 July 2011, DSR 2011:II, para. 289.

[11] Recently among others: Zhou and Peng (2018), p. 7; Sacher (2017), pp. 20 et seq.; Yu and Guan (2017), pp. 16 et seq.; Depayre (2016), pp. 42 et seq.; Miranda (2016a), pp. 244 et seq.; Miranda (2014), pp. 94 et seq.; Miranda (2016c), pp. 447 et seq.; Miranda (2016b), pp. 306 et seq.; Gatta (2014a), pp. 144 et seq.; Gatta (2014b), p. 165; Graafsma and Kumashova (2014), pp. 154 et seq.; Stewart et al. (2014), pp. 272 et seq.; Vermulst et al. (2016), pp. 212 et seq.; Zhenghao (2016),

Whereas several authors hold the opinion that Article 15(a) still provides for the "analogue method" because its chapeau still mentions the possibility to use a methodology that is not based on a strict comparison with domestic prices or costs in China,[12] the majority of commentators are sceptical about the possibility of the analogue method's continuous use.[13] Especially in light of Article 15 CAP's systematic structure, the interplay of both its subparagraphs and its drafting history, it can be concluded that the use of the analogue method is not applicable in relation to China any more.[14]

This exact question is now also in the centre of an ongoing dispute between China and the EU. China initiated a dispute settlement proceeding the day after the expiry of Article 15(a)(ii) and claims that the continuous application of the "analogue method" by the European Union violates its obligations under the WTO-Agreements.[15]

3 The New Methodology of the European Union

3.1 Overview of the Legislative Procedure

In the run-up to the expiry of Article 15(a)(ii) CAP, increasing attention has been paid to the potential reaction of the European Commission; indeed, there has been much speculation regarding how exactly the new EU anti-dumping law could be

---

pp. 229 et seq.; Noel (2016), pp. 296 et seq.; Searles (2016), pp. 430 et seq.; O'Connor (2015), p. 176; O'Connor B, The EU Does Not Have to Make China a Market Economy in 2016, March 2015, https://www.lexology.com/library/document.ashx?g=e68313f5-db9d-445b-879a-bfd6a03e9fd6 (last accessed 30 April 2018); O'Connor B, The Myth of China and Market Economy Status in 2016, http://worldtradelaw.typepad.com/files/oconnorresponse.pdf (last accessed 30 April 2018); O'Connor B, Market-economy status for China is not automatic, CEPR's policy portal, 27 November 2011, http://voxeu.org/article/china-market-economy (last accessed 30 April 2018).

[12] Miranda (2014), pp. 100 et seq.; O'Connor B, The EU Does Not Have to Make China a Market Economy in 2016, March 2015, http://www.lexology.com/library/document.ashx?g=e68313f5-db9d-445b-879a-bfd6a03e9fd6 (last accessed 30 April 2018); O'Connor B, The Myth of China and Market Economy Status in 2016, http://worldtradelaw.typepad.com/files/oconnorresponse.pdf (last accessed 30 April 2018); Posner (2014), p. 149.

[13] Graafsma and Kumashova (2014), pp. 154 et seq.; Tietje C and Nowroth K, Myth or Reality? China's Market Economy Status under WTO Anti-Dumping Law after 2016, Policy Papers on Transnational Economic Law No. 34, December 2011, http://telc.jura.uni-halle.de/sites/default/files/telc/PolicyPaper34.pdf (last accessed 30 April 2018), p. 7; De Kok (2016), p. 527; Gatta (2014b), p. 165; Vermulst et al. (2016), pp. 212 et seq.; Zhou and Peng (2018).

[14] For a detailed analysis of the bilateral drafting history of Article 15 CAP between China and the United States, Zhou and Peng (2018), p. 13. With respect to an analysis of the wording of Article 15 see, Zhou and Peng (2018), p. 6; Sacher (2017), pp. 20 et seq.

[15] Panel Report, *European Union – Measures Related to Price Comparison Methodologies*, WT/DS516/9, adopted 10 March 2017.

composed.[16] After several benchmark-tests, internal discussions and public consultations, the EU Commission launched its long-expected proposal for a new approach in dealing with potentially dumped imports from China in November 2016.[17] This so-called "November-proposal" basically abolished the "market-economy" doctrine in EU anti-dumping law and replaced it with a new approach, giving weight to the actual price-distortions in each respective country.[18] Hereby, normal value was supposed to be constructed on the basis of undistorted prices. Unsurprisingly, this proposal was immediately criticised by China and was subject to heated discussions.[19]

The European Economic and Social Committee took a stand on the proposal, suggesting not to limit the distortion-analysis to economic factors, but rather to extend it by also considering compliance with international labour standards and Multilateral Environment Agreements.[20] This point of view also carried through to the legislative process in the European Parliament. Its Committee on International Trade (INTA) worked out several far-reaching amendments and stuck to the proposal of the European Economic and Social Committee. Consequently, it stipulated that, in determining whether a price is distorted, a distinguishing factor shall be whether the country in question complies with core labour standards under the International Labour

---

[16] Among others: Nicely (2014), p. 160; De Kok (2016), p. 515; Gatta (2014a), p. 144; Searles (2016), p. 430; Noel and Zhou (2016), p. 559; Rao (2013), p. 152; Noel (2016), p. 296.

[17] European Commission, Commission opens a public consultation on future measures to prevent dumped imports from China, 10 February 2016, http://trade.ec.europa.eu/doclib/press/index. cfm?id=1455 (last accessed 30 April 2018); European Commission, Commission Staff Working Document, Impact Assessment, Possible change in the calculation methodology of dumping regarding the People's Republic of China (and other non-market economies) accompanying the document Proposal for a Regulation of the European Parliament and the Council amending Regulation (EU) 2016/1036 on protection against dumped imports from countries not members of the European Union and Regulation (EU) 2016/1037 on protection against subsidised imports from countries not members of the European Union, SWD(2016) 370 final, 9 November 2016, http://trade.ec.europa.eu/doclib/docs/2016/november/tradoc_155080.pdf (last accessed 30 April 2018).

[18] Proposal for a regulation of the European Parliament and the Council amending Regulation (EU) 2016/1036 on protection against dumped imports from countries not members of the European Union and Regulation (EU) 2016/1037 on protection against subsidised imports from countries not members of the European Union, COM(2016) 721 final, 9 November 2016, http://eur-lex.europa. eu/legal-content/EN/TXT/PDF/?uri=CELEX:52016PC0721&from=EN (last accessed 30 April 2018).

[19] Global Times, China says EU's proposed anti-dumping rules disappointing. Global Times, 10 November 2016, http://www.globaltimes.cn/content/1017190.shtml (last accessed 30 April 2018); China also refers to the proposal of the Commission in its Request for the Establishment of a Panel: Panel Report, *European Union – Measures Related to Price Comparison Methodologies*, WT/ DS516/9, adopted 10 March 2017, para. 12.

[20] European Economic and Social Committee, Opinion on the Proposal for a Regulation amending Regulation (EU) 2016/1036 on protection against dumped imports from countries not members of the European Union and Regulation (EU) 2016/1037 on protection against subsidised imports from countries not members of the European Union, REX/483-EESC-2017, 29 March 2017, http:// www.eesc.europa.eu/our-work/opinions-information-reports/opinions/rex483-trade-defence-instruments-methodology (last accessed 30 April 2018).

Organization (ILO) Convention, environmental agreements to which the EU is a party or even relevant Organisation for Economic Co-operation and Development (OECD) conventions pertaining to the field of taxation.[21] Hence, it was the first proposal for a legal text to directly counteract so-called social- or eco-dumping.

As might be expected, this strict approach did not gain the acceptance of the Commission and the Council. In a complicated trilogue between the three organs, an informal agreement was reached which still gave weight to the points of the Parliament, albeit in a different way.[22] This agreement later resulted in the final text, published in the Official Journal of the European Union on 19 December 2017.

3.2 Analysis of the New Provisions of the EU's Basic Anti-Dumping Regulation

Under the new provisions of the EU's Basic Anti-Dumping Regulation, the pre-existing Article 2(7)—which previously stipulated the EU's market-economy doctrine—is drastically narrowed. In relation to any WTO Member, the "analogue method" is no longer applicable. Instead, a new Article 2(6a) applies; it stipulates the following:

> (a) In the case it is determined (...) that it is not appropriate to use domestic prices and costs in the exporting country due to the existence (...) of significant distortions (...) normal value shall be constructed (...)

Consequently, once it is established that "significant distortions" exist in the country in question, the Commission must construct normal value, irrespective of whether the requirements of Article 2(3) of the Regulation would be fulfilled. In Article 2(6a)(b), the new provision establishes which circumstances qualify for "significant distortions":

> Significant distortions are those distortions which occur when reported prices or costs, including the costs of raw materials and energy, are not the result of free market forces because they are affected by substantial government intervention.

---

[21] Report on the proposal for a regulation of the European Parliament and of the Council amending Regulation (EU) 2016/1036 on protection against dumped imports from countries not members of the European Union and Regulation (EU) 2016/1037 on protection against subsidised imports from countries not members of the European Union (COM(2016)0721—C8-0456/2016—2016/0351(COD)), 27 June 2017, http://www.europarl.europa.eu/sides/getDoc.do?pubRef=//EP//NONSGML+REPORT+A8-2017-0236+0+DOC+PDF+V0//EN (last accessed 30 April 2018), pp. 13 et seq.

[22] European Parliament, EU anti-dumping measures that protect jobs: MEPs and ministers strike deal, http://www.europarl.europa.eu/news/en/press-room/20171003IPR85229/eu-anti-dumping-measures-that-protect-jobs-meps-and-ministers-strike-deal (last accessed 30 April 2018); Provisional Agreement resulting from interinstitutional negotiations, European Commission, Proposal for a regulation of the European Parliament and of the Council amending Regulation (EU) 2016/1036 on protection against dumped imports from countries not members of the European Union and Regulation (EU) 2016/1037 on protection against subsidised imports from countries not members of the European Union, COM(2016) 721 final, 9 November 2016.

The explicit listing of costs of raw materials and energy is supposed to cover the cases of so called "input-dumping", a constellation where the state has a strong influence on the energy- or raw-materials-market and, as a consequence, domestic producers are able to produce at much more competitive prices.[23]

The provision then sets up an illustrative list of criteria that indicate the existence of "significant distortions", which includes, inter alia, state presence in firms, allowing for price interference of authorities; dominant position of state-owned or -controlled enterprises; public policies influencing free market forces; and distorted wage costs or access to finance by public bodies. Still, several other criteria could indicate "significant distortions", since the list in subparagraph (b) is non-exhaustive.

To ensure that European producers are not troubled by a high burden of proof regarding the situation in the country in question, subparagraph (c) stipulates that the Commission is obliged to provide detailed information. For this purpose, it shall prepare and publish a comprehensive report describing the specific market circumstances in a given country once it has well-founded indications of the possible existence of significant distortions in that country. When filing in a complaint to initiate anti-dumping proceedings, the respective Union industry may rely on the evidence in the aforementioned report of the Commission.

Once it is established that the respective country suffers from "significant distortions" and it is therefore not appropriate to use domestic prices and costs, normal value is to be constructed

> (...) exclusively on the basis of costs of production and sale reflecting undistorted prices or benchmarks (...)[24]

The information the Commission may refer to when constructing undistorted prices is provided in a non-exhaustive list. Besides undistorted international reference prices, the list also provides for the costs of production in an appropriate representative country, with a similar level of economic development as a possible source. With respect to the latter, the provision requires that:

> (...) where there is more than one such country, preference shall be given, where appropriate to countries with an adequate level of social and environmental protection; (...)[25]

This phrasing is a direct consequence of the negotiating process between the Commission, the Council, and Parliament. It represents the remains of the strict social- and eco-dumping provisions the European Parliament suggested in their amendment-proposal. Still, the chosen wording leaves much room for interpretation. First, the provision requires more than one potential country with a similar level of economic development to be qualified for price-comparison. Second, the

---

[23] In detail on the issues relating to "input-dumping", see: Tietje et al. (2011), pp. 1071 et seq.; Pogoretskyy (2009), pp. 313 et seq.; Shadikhodjaev (2016), pp. 705 et seq.

[24] See the new Article 2(6a)(a) Regulation (EU) 2016/1036.

[25] See the new Article 2(6a)(a) Regulation (EU) 2016/1036.

wording of "appropriate" and "adequate" provides a high flexibility for the Commission in its decision-process during anti-dumping investigations.

Finally, the new anti-dumping provisions also entail certain transitional provisions laid down in Article 11 of the Basic Anti-Dumping Regulation. Pursuant to these provisions, the new methodology in Article 2(6a) shall only apply to future investigations. Pre-existing anti-dumping measures enacted under the old Article 2(7) by the use of the "analogue-method" shall explicitly stay in force until the first expiry review.

4 Conformity with WTO Law

WTO law allows for the initiation of a dispute settlement proceeding also against an abstract legal provision. According to the Appellate Body, the provision itself (*"as such"*) as well as a certain measure applying the provision (*"as applied"*) may be subject to a legal proceeding.[26] Further, the discretionary nature of a measure is no barrier to an "as such" challenge.[27] Even though the Appellate Body has not yet established a clear and universal legal framework for a discretionary provision to be WTO-consistent, with respect to Article 2.2 of the ADA, it stated that the provision in question must at least leave room to be applied in a manner consistent with WTO law.[28] Hence, a discretionary provision can only violate Article 2.2 of the ADA *"as such"* if it leaves no room for a WTO law-consistent application.

---

[26]Appellate Body Report, *United States – Sunset Reviews of Anti-Dumping Measures on Oil Country Tubular Goods from Argentina*, WT/DS268/AB/R, adopted 29 November 2004, DSR 2004:IV, para. 172; Appellate Body Report, *United States – Anti-Dumping Act of 1916*, WT/DS136/AB/R, adopted 28 August 2000, DSR 2000:V and VI, paras. 60 et seq. and 92 et seq.; Appellate Body Report, *United States – Continued Existence and Application of Zeroing Methodology*, WT/DS350/AB/R, adopted 4 February 2009, DSR 2008:XI, paras. 179 et seq.; Appellate Body Report, *United States – Sunset Review of Anti-Dumping Duties on Corrosion-Resistant Carbon Steel Flat Products from Japan*, WT/DS244/AB/R, adopted 15 December 2003, DSR 2003:V, para. 81; Appellate Body Report, *Argentina – Measures Affecting the Importation of Goods*, WT/DS438/AB/R, adopted 15 January 2015, DSR 2014:IX, para. 5.103.

[27]Appellate Body Report, *United States – Anti-Dumping Act of 1916*, WT/DS136/AB/R, adopted 24 August 2000, DSR 2000:V and VI, fn. 59; Appellate Body Report, *United States – Sunset Review of Anti-Dumping Duties on Corrosion-Resistant Carbon Steel Flat Products from Japan*, WT/DS244/AB/R, adopted 15 December 2003, DSR2003:V, para. 89; Appellate Body Report, *European Union – Anti-Dumping Measures on Biodiesel from Argentina*, WT/473/AB/R, adopted 6 October 2016, DSR 2016:IV, paras. 6.229, 7.271; in detail on this issue also: Kang (2012), p. 879; Lockhart and Sheargold (2010), p. 379; Naiki (2004), p. 52; Howse and Staiger (2006), p. 254; Lester (2011), p. 372; Bhuiyan (2002), p. 571.

[28]Appellate Body Report, *European Union – Anti-Dumping Measures on Biodiesel from Argentina*, WT/473/AB/R, adopted 6 October 2016, DSR 2016:IV, paras. 6.281 et seq.

4.1   The "Significant Distortions"-Approach

According to the new approach of the EU's Basic Anti-Dumping Regulation, normal value shall be constructed if it is not appropriate to use domestic prices and costs due to significant distortions. Article 2.2 of the WTO Anti-Dumping Agreement, on the other hand, allows for the construction of normal value only in these cases:

> When there are **no sales** of the like product **in the ordinary course of trade** (1.) in the domestic market of the exporting country or when, because of the **particular market situation** (2.) (…) sales do not permit a proper comparison (…) (emphasis added)

Hence, the European Union's approach is only WTO-consistent if it is in line with at least one of these Article 2.2 ADA requirements.

4.1.1   Ordinary Course of Trade

Even though the ADA does not contain a comprehensive definition of "ordinary course of trade", by applying the Articles 31 et seq. of the Vienna Convention on the Law of Treaties, Article 2.2 of the ADA must be interpreted in good faith in accordance with the ordinary meaning to be given to it in its context and in light of the object and purpose of the ADA.[29]

Turning to its ordinary meaning, the wording of "ordinary course" means "*belonging to the regular or usual order or course of things.*"[30] The regular or usual course of trade is, by transactions of sale and purchase, characterised by the seller's intent to realise a profit. Consequently, whenever a product is transferred outside of this regular course, i.e. in the case of transfers within segmentations of a global enterprise, it shall be regarded outside the "ordinary course of trade". This interpretation can also be based on the more accurate French version of the legal text which translates "ordinary course of trade" as "*au cours d'opération commerciales normales*".[31]

---

[29] According to Article 3.2 DSU WTO-law shall be interpreted "*(...) in accordance with customary rules of interpretation of public international law.*" The Appellate Body clarified that this provision allows for the Articles 31 et seq. of the Vienna Convention on the Law of Treaties to be used for interpreting WTO-law: Appellate Body Report, *United States – Standards for Reformulated and Conventional Gasoline*, WT/DS2/AB/R, adopted 20 May 1996, DSR 1996:I, para. 17.

[30] See http://www.oed.com/view/Entry/132361 (last accessed 30 April 2018).

[31] According to Article 33(1) of the Vienna Convention on the Law of Treaties, the text of a treaty is equally authoritative in each language. The Appellate Body consistently refers to the Spanish or the French version in interpreting the WTO-Agreements, see i.e.: Appellate Body Report, *European Communities – Measures Affecting Asbestos and Products Containing Asbestos*, WT/DS135/AB/R, adopted 12 March 2001, DSR 2000:XI, para. 91; Appellate Body Report, *United States – Final Anti-Dumping Measures on Stainless Steel from Mexico*, WT/DS344/AB/R, adopted 30 April 2008, DSR 2008:I, fn. 200.

The wording of "*opération commerciales*" implies a stronger connection to the commercial interests of the parties of the transaction.[32] Turning to its context, Article 2.2.1 gives a certain guidance to the meaning of this requirement. Even though this provision does not constitute a comprehensive legal definition,[33] it states that sales of a product may be treated as not being in the ordinary course of trade and disregarded

> only if (...) such sales are made within an extended period of time in substantial quantities and are at prices which do not provide for the recovery of all costs (...)[34]

Consequently, since uneconomic transactions shall be regarded outside the ordinary course of trade, the intent to make profit with a transaction is indeed a decisive criterion when handling the requirement of "ordinary course of trade". Pursuant to Article 2.2 ADA, there *must not be any sales* in the ordinary course of trade in the respective country in question to allow for the construction of normal value. Therefore, due to a certain set of circumstances, any transaction of a given product must not be economic transactions of sale and purchase. According to the EU's approach, normal value may already be constructed once it is established that it is not appropriate to use domestic prices and costs due to significant distortions. Such distortions shall exist, i.e. when reported prices or costs are not the result of free market forces because they are affected by government intervention. However, lower prices due to government intervention do not necessitate the conclusion that all transactions of the product itself are affected in a way that they are not traded in an economic transaction of sale and purchase. To the contrary, the lower price results in a higher competitiveness of the product in question, which is actually the overall goal of its producer *due to* the producer's intent to make a profit with the transaction. In other words: A price resulting from circumstances other than free market forces does not mean that the actual transaction no longer follows economic procedures. Consequently, the EU's approach to construct normal value in the case of significant distortions cannot be based on the "ordinary course of trade" requirement in Article 2.2 ADA.[35]

4.1.2 Particular Market Situation

The only remaining possibility to construct normal value under WTO law is in the case of a "particular market situation" that results in sales not permitting a proper comparison. The WTO Anti-Dumping Agreement does not provide any guidance on how to interpret this broad wording in Article 2.2, but there has been increasing

---

[32] Noel (2016), p. 303.

[33] Appellate Body Report, *United States – Anti-Dumping Measures on Certain Hot-Rolled Steel Products from Japan*, WT/DS184/AB/R, adopted 24 July 2001, DSR 2001:II, para. 139.

[34] Article 2.2.1 ADA.

[35] For a detailed analysis on this requirement, see: Sacher (2017), pp. 25 et seq.

100 C. Tietje and V. Sacher

discussion regarding the meaning of Article 2.2 among academic authors in recent times.[36]

A "situation" is a *"condition or state of something".*[37] Related to a market, it refers to the state of the market itself and not to the circumstances leading to the situation. "Particular" means *"belonging or relating to one (...) thing as distinguished from another; special."*[38] Hence, the specific condition of the market must differ from the normal state of a market. A market is normally balanced by the interplay of free market forces of supply and demand. However, whenever a market situation is particular, pricing is not determined by these market forces but rather influenced by external factors.

Still, the use of the word "situation" narrows this determination down to the actual circumstances of the market itself. A finding of a particular market situation thus cannot be based on the mere existence of government interference alone. Rather, the interference must lead to a dysfunction of free market forces of supply and demand.

This interpretation is also supported by an overarching contextual analysis of the Anti-Dumping Agreement one the one hand and the Agreement on Subsidies and Countervailing Measures on the other. The Anti-Dumping Agreement seeks to provide the possibility to counteract injurious dumping by private actors.[39] The Agreement on Subsidies and Countervailing Measures, however, provides for the challenging or counteracting of state subsidies. Hence, the latter explicitly links to the action of a state, whereas the former ties in with economic actions of individuals. Consequently, it would be contrary to the plain idea of WTO anti-dumping law to base the finding of a particular market situation solely on the behaviour of the state.

The EU's new approach, however, requires construction of normal value *"when reported prices or costs (...) are not the result of free market forces because they are affected by substantial government intervention."*[40] Thus, it does simply limit the cases of normal value construction to the situation of substantial government intervention. The intervention itself does not trigger normal value construction though. Rather, there must be a positive finding that pricing is no longer the result of free market forces. This approach can therefore basically find its support in the requirement of "particular market situation" under Article 2.2 ADA. Whether the specific chosen construction method is in line with WTO-law is a distinct question.

---

[36] Zhou and Percival (2016), p. 863; Gatta and Nicely (2016), p. 239; Gatta (2014b), p. 170; Noel (2016), p. 303.

[37] See http://www.oed.com/view/Entry/180520 (last accessed 30 April 2018).

[38] See http://www.oed.com/view/Entry/138260 (last accessed 30 April 2018).

[39] Appellate Body Report, *United States – Anti-Dumping and Countervailing Measures on Large Residential Washers from Korea*, WT/DS464/AB/R, adopted 7 September 2016, DSR 2016:II, para. 5.52; Appellate Body Report, *European Union – Anti-Dumping Measures on Biodiesel from Argentina*, WT/473/AB/R, adopted 6 October 2016, DSR 2016:IV, para. 6.25.

[40] Article 2(6a)(b) Regulation (EU) 2016/1036.

4.2   Normal Value Construction Method

The Anti-Dumping Agreement contains specific provisions on the procedure of constructing normal value. According to Article 2.2 ADA:

(...) the margin of dumping shall be determined by comparison (...) with the **cost of production in the country of origin** plus a reasonable amount for administrative, selling and general costs and for profits. (emphasis added)

Even though Article 2.2.1.1 stipulates that costs shall normally be calculated on the basis of records kept by the exporter or producer under investigation, it still leaves room for other sources to be regarded in constructing normal value. The Appellate Body recently highlighted that investigating authorities are not limited in the sources of information used for the determination of normal value in the *EU – Biodiesel* decision:

We do not see, however, that the first sentence of Article 2.2.1.1 precludes information or evidence from other sources from being used in certain circumstances. Indeed, it is clear to us that, in some circumstances, the information in the records kept by the exporter (...) may need to be analysed (...) including (...) sources outside the "country of origin."[41]

Whereas this might at first glimpse seem like an investigating authority is free in determining normal value, the Appellate Body later pointed out correctly that the wording of Article 2.2 ADA marks a strict boundary for constructing normal value:

This, however, does not mean that an investigating authority may simply substitute the costs from outside the country of origin for the "cost of production in the country of origin". Indeed, Article 2.2 of the Anti-Dumping Agreement and Article VI:1(b)(ii) of the GATT 1994 make clear that the determination is of the "cost of production [...] in the country of origin". Thus, whatever the information that it uses, **an investigating authority has to ensure that such information is used to arrive at the "cost of production in the country of origin"**. Compliance with this obligation may require the investigating authority to **adapt** the information that it collects.[42] (emphasis added)

Consequently, in constructing normal value, an investigating authority must never simply substitute the costs of producers by reference to international prices or other information. Any information the authorities refer to must instead be used to arrive at the cost of production in the country of origin. This reading of the Appellate Bodies decision was also identically applied by the Panel in the more recent *EU – Biodiesel (Indonesia)* case.[43]

In consequence, an investigation authority needs to "adapt" any collected information from external sources. It is not yet finally clear how far reaching this obligation to "adapt" actually is. Does this require that prevailing distortions in a market

---

[41] Appellate Body Report, *European Union – Anti-Dumping Measures on Biodiesel from Argentina*, WT/473/AB/R, adopted 6 October 2016, DSR 2016:IV, para. 6.71.

[42] Appellate Body Report, *European Union – Anti-Dumping Measures on Biodiesel from Argentina*, WT/473/AB/R, adopted 6 October 2016, DSR 2016:IV, para. 6.73.

[43] Report of the Panel, European Union – Anti-Dumping Measures on Biodiesel from Indonesia, WT/480/P/R, adopted 25 January 2018, para. 7.3.

must be included in order to "adapt" an information to arrive at the "cost of production in the country of origin" or can the distortions simply be ignored? In a more optimistic reading of the Appellate Body decision, one might argue that it is sufficient to weight the respective production factors value in the exact amount as they proportionally take in the domestic producers production process. However, this runs afoul the requirement of Article 2.2 ADA because any distortion in the market at issue is a circumstance in the country of origin that needs to be regarded. If normal value construction must be based on the cost of production in the country of origin, this means that prevailing distortions must be included rather than excluded. A simple weighting of production factors still gives no meaning to prevailing distortions in the respective market. As shown above, the Anti-Dumping Agreement—other than the SCM-Agreement—links to actions of individuals and does not sanction state intervention in markets. If there is a distortion in the market at issue, the individual producer can—as a fact—produce cheaper and at a more competitive price. Hence, to arrive at "cost of production in the country of origin" this very distortion needs to be taken into account. In short: if an authority collects data from external sources (i.e. third countries or international reference prices) these data have to be adapted in a way that they reflect the prevailing distortions in the market at issue.

However, the new approach of the European Union is composed exactly to the contrary. It governs that, in case of significant distortions, normal value shall be constructed.

> **exclusively** on the basis of costs of production and sale reflecting **undistorted** prices or benchmarks (...)[44] (emphasis added).

Hence, as a result, the constructed normal value must not be distorted any more after it is constructed. The whole purpose of the normal value construction under the EU's approach is to subtract out the distortion in the market at issue. As a consequence, the new methodology of Article 2(6a) of the EU's Basic Anti-Dumping Regulation leaves no room for a WTO-consistent application and therefore "as such" violates Article 2.2 ADA as interpreted by the Appellate Body in the *EU – Biodiesel (Argentina)* decision.

4.3   Transitional Provisions

Finally, the encompassed transitional provisions of the new EU approach stipulate that pre-existing measures shall stay into force, irrespective of the change of law, at least until their first expiry review. This also and especially applies to the imposed anti-dumping duties on Chinese products, based on the application of the analogue-method under Article 15(a) of China's Accession Protocol. After the expiry of subparagraph (ii) as shown above, this method is no longer applicable. Even under the

---

[44] Article 2(6a)(a) Regulation (EU) 2016/1036.

most optimistic reading of Article 2.2 ADA, the method only allows for a construction of normal value and never—as conducted under the analogue-method—a substitution of domestic with third country prices. Furthermore, Article 18.4 ADA requires WTO Members to permanently ensure the conformity of domestic laws, regulations and administrative procedures with the provisions of the ADA. Therefore, the continuous application or maintenance of a measure, imposed on the basis of the analogue-method in relation to China has violated WTO law since 11 December 2016.

5   Conclusion

Ultimately, it must be concluded that the new approach of the European Union violates WTO Anti-Dumping law. Whereas the general approach of constructing normal value in the case of significant distortions is eligible under WTO law, the chosen construction method violates Articles 2.2.1.1 and 2.2 of the Anti-Dumping Agreement as well as Article VI:1(b)(ii) of the GATT, especially in the light of the recent Appellate Body decision in *EU – Biodiesel*. From a political point of view, it seems that the EU attempted to find a similar way of essentially continuing its previous practice under the analogue-method.

However, WTO law leaves no room for normal value construction irrespective of the cost of production in the country of origin. Hence, the European Union's approach to subtract out any potential price distortions in constructing normal value cannot be brought in line with WTO law. Consequently, it is highly likely that China will succeed in the current WTO dispute settlement proceedings initiated against the continuous application of the analogue-method since December 2016 and the new provisions of the EU's Basic Anti-Dumping Regulation.

References

Adamantopoulos K (2010) Article VI GATT. In: Wolfrum R, Stoll PT, Hestermeyer H (eds) WTO – trade in goods. Max Planck Commentary on World Trade Law. Martinus Nijhoff, Leiden

Bhuiyan S (2002) Mandatory and discretionary legislation: the continued relevance of the distinction under the WTO. J Int Econ Law 5(3):571–604

De Kok J (2016) The future of EU trade defence investigations against imports from China. J Int Econ Law 19(2):515–547

Depayre G (2016) Why the EU anti-dumping practice to adjust inputs costs in situations where such costs are "artificially low" is legitimate and justified. Global Trade Customs J 11(2):42–45

Gatta B (2014a) Special focus issue, China's market economy status after 2016. Global Trade Customs J 9(4):144–145

Gatta B (2014b) Between "automatic market economy status" and "status quo": a commentary on "interpreting paragraph 15 of China's Protocol of Accession". Global Trade Customs J 9(4):165–172

Gatta B, Nicely M (2016) U.S. Trade Preferences Extension Act (TPEA) of 2015 could lead to increased use of "particular market situation" in calculating normal value in anti-dumping cases. Global Trade Customs J 11(5):238–243

Graafsma F, Kumashova E (2014) In re China's protocol of accession and the Anti-Dumping Agreement: temporary derogation or permanent modification? Global Trade Customs J 9(4):154–159

Howse R, Staiger R (2006) United States – Anti-Dumping Act of 1916 (original complaint by the European Communities) – recourse to arbitration by the United States under 22.6 of the DSU, WT/DS136/ARB, 24 February 2004: a legal and economic analysis. World Trade Rev 5(1):254–279

Kang J (2012) The presumption of good faith in the WTO "as such" cases: a reformulation of the mandatory/discretionary distinction as an analytical tool. J World Trade 46(4):879–912

Kennedy M (2013) The integration of accession protocols into the WTO Agreement. J World Trade 47(1):45–76

Lester S (2011) A framework for thinking about the "discretion" in the mandatory/discretionary distinction. J Int Econ Law 14(2):369–402

Liu J (2014) Accession protocols: legal status in the WTO legal system. J World Trade 48(4):751–722

Lockhart N, Sheargold E (2010) In search of relevant discretion: the role of the mandatory/discretionary distinction in WTO law. J Int Econ Law 13(2):379–421

Miranda J (2014) Interpreting paragraph 15 of China's protocol of accession. Global Trade Customs J 9(3):94–103

Miranda J (2016a) More on why granting China market economy status after December 2016 is contingent upon whether China has in fact transitioned into a market economy. Global Trade Customs J 11(5):244–250

Miranda J (2016b) A comment on Vermulst's article on China in anti-dumping proceedings after December 2016. Global Trade Customs J 11(7/8):306–313

Miranda J (2016c) Implementation of the "shift in burden of proof" approach to interpreting paragraph 15 of China's Protocol of Accession. Global Trade Customs J 11(10):447–453

Naiki Y (2004) The mandatory/discretionary distinction in WTO law: the US – Section 301 case and its aftermath. J Int Econ Law 7(1):23–72

Nicely M (2014) Time to eliminate outdated non-market economy methodologies. Global Trade Customs J 9(4):160–164

Noel S (2016) Why the European Union must dump so-called "non-market economy" methodologies and adjustments in its anti-dumping investigations. Global Trade Customs J 11(7/8):296–305

Noel S, Zhou W (2016) Replacing the non-market economy methodology: is the European Union's alternative approach justified under the World Trade Organization Anti-Dumping Agreement? Global Trade Customs J 11(11/12):559–567

O'Connor B (2015) Much ado about "nothing": 2016, China and market economy status. Global Trade Customs J 10(2015):176–180

Pogoretskyy V (2009) The system of energy dual pricing in Russia and Ukraine: the consistency of the energy dual pricing system with the WTO Agreement on Anti-Dumping. Global Trade Customs J 4(10):313–323

Polouektov A (2002) Non-market economy issues in the WTO anti-dumping law and accession negotiations – revival of a two-tier membership? J World Trade 36(1):1–37

Posner T (2014) A comment on interpreting paragraph 15 of China's protocol of accession by Jorge Miranda. Global Trade Customs J 9(4):146–153

Qin J (2003) "WTO-plus" obligations and their implications for the World Trade Organization system. J World Trade 37(3):483–522

Rao W (2013) China's market economy status under WTO antidumping laws after 2016. Tsinghua China Law Rev 5:151–168

Sacher V (2017) Neuer Kurs im Umgang mit China? Die Reformvorschläge zum EU-Antidumpingrecht und ihre Vereinbarkeit mit WTO-Recht. Institut für Wirtschaftsrecht, Juristische und Wirtschaftswissenschaftliche Fakultät, Martin-Luther-Universität Halle-Wittenberg, Halle (Saale)

Searles J (2016) The European Union's options for China dumping methodology after 11 December 2016. Global Trade Customs J 11(10):430–439

Shadikhodjaev S (2016) Russia and energy issues under the WTO system. J World Trade 50(4):705–732

Snyder F (2001) The origins of the "nonmarket economy": ideas, pluralism and power in EC anti-dumping law about China. Eur Law J 7(4):369–434

Stewart T, Fennell W, Bell S, Birch N (2014) The special case of China: why the use of a special methodology remains applicable to China after 2016. Global Trade Customs J 9(6):272–279

Tietje C, Kluttig B, Franke M (2011) Cost of production adjustments in anti-dumping proceedings: challenging raw material inputs dual pricing systems in EU anti-dumping law and practice. J World Trade 45(5):1071–1102

Vermulst E, Sud J, Evenett S (2016) Normal value in anti-dumping proceedings against China post-2016: are some animals less equal than others? Global Trade Customs J 11(5):212–228

Yan L (2010) Anti-dumping in the WTO, the EU and China, the rise of legalization in the trade regime and its consequences. Wolters Kluwer, Alphen aan den Rijn

Yu M, Guan J (2017) The non-market economy methodology shall be terminated after 2016. Global Trade Customs J 12(1):16–24

Zhenghao L (2016) Interpreting paragraph 15 of China's accession protocol in light of the Working Party Report. Global Trade Customs J 11(5):229–237

Zhou W (2015) Australia's anti-dumping and countervailing law and practice: an analysis of current issues incompatible with free trade with China. J World Trade 49(5):975–1010

Zhou W, Peng D (2018) EU – Price Comparison Challenging Methodology (DS516): the non-market economy methodology in light of the negotiating history of Article 15 of China's WTO accession protocol. J World Trade 52(3):505–533

Zhou W, Percival A (2016) Debunking the myth of "particular market situation" in WTO anti-dumping law. J Int Econ Law 19(4):863–892

EU – Price Comparison Methodologies (DS516): Interpretation of Section 15 of China's WTO Accession Protocol

Dong Fang

Contents

Abstract The article elaborates the issue regarding the interpretation of Section 15 of China's WTO Accession Protocol and dismisses the legal opinions of the European Union and the United States in *European Union – Price Comparison Methodologies* (DS516). The so-called "shifting in burden of proof" approach held by the European Union and the United States actually only terminates part of Section 15(a)(ii), and it also self-contradictory with the other two claims held by the European Union and the United States at the same time in the same case, i.e., the chapeau and (i) of Section 15(a) are still valid and Section 15 is not an exception clause. Based on the structure of Section 15 and the Interpretation of Section 15 by the Appellate Body in *EC – Fasteners*, which are not necessarily dicta, the article concludes that Section 15(a) as a whole has expired. In addition, China may try to claim that its Accession Protocol which is a contractual agreement deserves a different more flexible interpretation method, which is not rare in the practice of general international law.

D. Fang (✉)
Law School, Xiamen University, Xiamen, Fujian Province, P.R. China
e-mail: fangdong@xmu.edu.cn

© Springer International Publishing AG, part of Springer Nature 2018   107
M. Bungenberg et al. (eds.), *The Future of Trade Defence Instruments*,
European Yearbook of International Economic Law,
https://doi.org/10.1007/978-3-319-95306-9_6

1 Introduction

In recent years, the issue of the interpretation of Section 15 of the Protocol on the Accession of the People's Republic of China (China's Accession Protocol, CAP) has caused a lot of controversy.[1] On 12 December 2016, China requested the European Union to enter into consultations pursuant to Article 4 of the Understanding on Rules and Procedures Governing the Settlement of Disputes (DSU). According to China, *"under Paragraph 15(a)(ii) of the Accession Protocol, importing WTO Members were, subject to certain conditions, exceptionally permitted to use a methodology not based on a strict comparison with domestic prices or costs in China. But Paragraph 15(d) provides that "[i]n any event, the provisions of subparagraph (a)(ii) shall expire 15 years after the date of accession," namely, on 11 December 2016. Accordingly, from that date, the WTO rules that govern the determination by WTO Members of all elements of price comparability now apply to imports from China. However, the European Union continues to determine normal value on the basis of a special calculation methodology unless the producer establishes that it meets certain criteria, as set forth below. Thus, the European Union is in violation of its international obligations."*[2]

A focus issue in this case is the interpretation of Section 15(a) and (d) of China's Accession Protocol. Section 15 of China's Accession Protocol, entitled "Price Comparability in Determining Subsidies and Dumping", reads in relevant part:

Article VI of the GATT 1994, the Agreement on Implementation of Article VI of the General Agreement on Tariffs and Trade 1994 ("Anti-Dumping Agreement") and the SCM Agreement shall apply in proceedings involving imports of Chinese origin into a WTO Member consistent with the following:

(a) In determining price comparability under Article VI of the GATT 1994 and the Anti Dumping Agreement, the importing WTO Member shall use either Chinese prices or costs for the industry under investigation or a methodology that is not based on a strict comparison with domestic prices or costs in China based on the following rules:

(i) If the producers under investigation can clearly show that market economy conditions prevail in the industry producing the like product with regard to the manufacture, production and sale of that product, the importing WTO Member shall use Chinese prices or costs for the industry under investigation in determining price comparability;

(ii) The importing WTO Member may use a methodology that is not based on a strict comparison with domestic prices or costs in China if the producers under investigation cannot clearly show that market economy conditions prevail in the industry producing the like product with regard to manufacture, production and sale of that product.

(…)

---

[1] Miranda (2014, 2016a, b, c), Gatta (2014a, b), Posner (2014), Graafsma and Kumashova (2014), Nicely (2014), Stewart et al. (2014), Rosenthal and Beckington (2014), Ruessmann and Beck (2014), O'Connor (2015), Vermulst et al. (2016), Zhenghao (2016), Noel (2016), and Searles (2016).

[2] Request for Consultations by China, *European Union – Measures Related to Price Comparison Methodologies*, WT/DS516/1, 15 December 2016.

(d) Once China has established, under the national law of the importing WTO Member, that it is a market economy, the provisions of subparagraph (a) shall be terminated provided that the importing Member's national law contains market economy criteria as of the date of accession. In any event, the provisions of subparagraph (a)(ii) shall expire 15 years after the date of accession. In addition, should China establish, pursuant to the national law of the importing WTO Member, that market economy conditions prevail in a particular industry or sector, the non-market economy provisions of subparagraph (a) shall no longer apply to that industry or sector.

2 Interpretation of Section 15 CAP: Rebuttal to the Legal Opinions of the European Union and United States

2.1 *Interpretation of Section 15 CAP by the Appellate Body in* EC – Fasteners

It should be noted that the Appellate Body has made some statements related to the Interpretation of Section 15 in the *EC – Fasteners* case. For example, the Appellate Body has pointed out that *"Paragraph 15(d) of China's Accession Protocol establishes that the provisions of Paragraph 15(a) expire 15 years after the date of China's accession (that is, 11 December 2016)."*[3] It is oblivious that the Appellate Body referred to "Paragraph 15(a)", not "Paragraph 15(a)(ii)". But a popular view is that such statement is only a obiter dictum,[4] which held by both the European Union and United States.

According to European Union, in the *EC – Fasteners* case, the Appellate Body was not called upon to rule on the issue whether Section 15(a)(ii) or Section 15(a) would be terminated on 11 December 2016. Such issue was not the subject of any exchange of argument between the parties or the third parties. As common sense, the Appellate Body would have intended to resolve such an important issue *en passant*.[5]

The United States advocated that the Appellate Body did not consider the textural difference in Section 15(d), the first sentence of which refers to "the provisions of subparagraph (a)", the second sentence of which refers to "the provisions of

---

[3] Appellate Body Report, *European Union – Anti-Dumping Measures on Biodiesel from Argentina*, WT/DS473/AB/R, adopted 15 July 2011, DSR 2016:IV, para. 289.

[4] Miranda (2014), p. 101, fn. 24; Posner (2014), p. 151, O'Connor (2015), p. 179; Miranda (2016b), p. 309.

[5] In this case, the EU's first written submission and the US' third party submission and legal interpretation to the panel have been made public, while China has only released its opening statement at the Panel's meeting. First Written Submission by the European Union, *European Union – Measures Related to Price Comparison Methodologies*, WT/DS516/1, 14 November 2017, para. 117.

subparagraph (a)(ii)" and the third sentence refers to "non-market economy provisions of subparagraph (a)". The interpretation of Section 15, and subparagraph (d) in particular, was not at issue in the appeal in *EC – Fasteners*. Therefore, the statement by Appellate Body did not reflect a considered interpretive effort on this point.[6]

A widely-quoted classical definition of a dictum is *"an expression of opinion in regard to some point or rule of law, made by a judge in the course of a judicial opinion, but not necessary to the determination of the case before the court."*[7] Because dicta *"are not the judicial determinations of the court, they are never entitled to the force and effect of precedents, in the same or other courts, and do not preclude the rendering of a subsequent contrary decision."*[8]

Till now, the Appellate Body mentioned dicta in three cases. In the *Canada – Periodicals* case, the Appellate Body held that the statement by the panel in *EEC – Oilseeds* is regarded as dicta because it is about a moot issue.[9] In the *US – Shrimp (Article 21.5 – Malaysia)* case, the Appellate Body pointed out that the reasoning by themselves in *United States – Shrimp* was not dicta since it was essential to their ruling.[10] In the *US – Gambling* case, the Appellate Body clarified that, as the complainant was not challenging a practice as such, the Panel's statement on whether "practice" as such may be challenged as a "measure" was a mere obiter dictum.[11]

Based on these statements, it seems that the Appellate Body's main criteria for distinguishing dicta from holding are whether the legal opinions are relevant or essential to the decision.[12] One must notice that the Appellate Body never said any legal opinion by themselves are dicta.

More importantly, even if one can accept that the above-mentioned statement by the Appellate Body related to the expiry of Section 15(a) is a dictum in *EC – Fasteners*, one must bear in mind that the interpretation by Appellate Body in that case also related some other aspect of Section 15, which are not necessarily dicta.[13]

---

[6]Legal Interpretation Submitted by the United States, *European Union – Measures Related to Price Comparison Methodologies*, WT/DS516/1, para. 8.7.

[7]Black (2010), p. 166.

[8]Black (2010), p. 176.

[9]Appellate Body Report, *Canada – Certain Measures Concerning Periodicals*, WT/DS31/AB/R, adopted 30 July 1997, DSR 1997:II.

[10]Appellate Body Report, *United States – Import Prohibition of Certain Shrimp and Shrimp Products*, Recourse to Article 21.5 of the DSU by Malaysia, WT/DS58/AB/RW, adopted 21 November 2001, DSR 2001:IV, para. 107.

[11]Appellate Body Report, *United States – Measures Affecting the Cross-Border Supply of Gambling and Betting Services*, WT/DS285/AB/R, adopted 20 April 2005, DSR 2005:V. para. 131.

[12]Gao (2018), p. 22.

[13]See the relevant analysis below.

2.2   The Legal Consequence of the "Expiry" of Section 15(a)(ii) CAP

Since the second sentence in Section 15(d) provides that "*[i]n any event, the provisions of subparagraph (a)(ii) shall expire 15 years after the date of accession,*" it is an uncontroversial issue that Section 15(a)(ii) has expired. But what is the legal consequence of "expiry"?

According to China, the "expiry" of Section 15(a)(ii) means there is no longer any basis under the Accession Protocol for WTO Members to abandon Chinese prices and costs in anti-dumping proceedings involving China. They shall apply general rules regarding the determination of normal value under the WTO covered agreements.[14]

But the responding party European Union and third-party United States all disagreed with such opinion. They contended that the termination of Section 15(a)(ii) only means a change in the rule of burden of proof.

According to the United States, "*[w]hat changed on 11 December 2016, was that the China-specific rule on standard of evidence expired.*"[15] The rule of "burden of proof" under the Anti-Dumping Agreement is contained in the final sentence of Article 2.4 of such Agreement, "*the authorities shall indicate to the parties in question what information is necessary to ensure a fair comparison and shall not impose an unreasonable burden of proof on those parties.*" But Section 15 introduced a "particular standard of evidence" before 11 December 2016 such that if the Chinese producers cannot clearly show that market economy conditions prevail in the industry producing the like product, the importing WTO Member can make an unrebutted presumption regarding the non-existence of market economy conditions and adopt a methodology that was not based on a strict comparison with domestic prices or costs in China. The importing WTO Member need not to impose any kind of burden of proof on other parties, i.e., the domestic industry. After 11 December 2016, the so called China-specific rule on standard of evidence has expired and the importing WTO Member shall follow the rule of "burden of proof" under the last sentence of Article 2.4 of the Anti-Dumping Agreement, which means that the investigating authority must have an adequate evidentiary basis for its determinations, including any determination to accept or reject Chinese prices and costs, and must not impose an unreasonable burden of proof on any sub-set of interested parties, e.g. the Chinese producers.[16]

---

[14] Opening Statement by Ambassador Zhang Xiangchen as a part of the Oral Statement of China at the First Substantive Meeting of the Panel in the dispute: *European Union – Measures Related to Price Comparison Methodologies,* WT/DS516/1, 6 December 2017, para. 7.

[15] Legal Interpretation Submitted by the United States, *European Union – Measures Related to Price Comparison Methodologies,* WT/DS516/1, para. 8.5.1.

[16] Legal Interpretation Submitted by the United States, *European Union – Measures Related to Price Comparison Methodologies,* WT/DS516/1, para. 8.5.

The European Union also advocated since the expiry of Section 15(a)(ii), that the legal position with respect to the burden of proof under Section 15 changed significantly. There is now no China-specific rule regarding the burden of proof on Chinese producers and the rule in the Anti-Dumping Agreement concerning burden of proof shall be applied.[17]

This kind of so-called "shifting in burden of proof" approach is not new. Bernard O'Connor first proposed this idea in 2011[18] and subsequently obtained the agreement of some European trade law lawyers.[19] Opponents are mainly questioned it from two aspects: First, Section 15 does not contain any provisions on the burden of proof. This explanation is only a fiction. Second, Paragraph 151 of the Report of the Working Party on China's Accession to WTO stipulates the criteria that must be followed by WTO members in the application of non-market methodologies in order to "execute Section 15(a) (ii)". This in turn proves that the scope of regulation in Section 15(a)(ii) is by no means limited to the burden of proof.[20]

The author believes that there are two problems with the "shifting in burden of proof" approach.

First, this understanding actually only terminates part of subparagraph (a)(ii), which is a direct violation of the explicit requirement of the second sentence of Section 15(d), that is, "the provisions of subparagraph (a)(ii) shall expire". It is evident that the subparagraph (a)(ii) contains a conditional clause and a main clause. The conditional clause is: "*[t]he producer under investigation cannot clearly prove that the industry that produces the same kind of product has market economy conditions in the manufacture, production and sale of the product.*" The main sentence reads: "*[t]he WTO's importing members may use methods that are not based on strict comparisons with Chinese domestic prices or costs.*" The purpose of the second sentence of Section 15(d) is, of course, the termination of both the conditional clause and the main clause. The main point of the "shifting in burden of proof" approach is that only the conditional clause is terminated and the main clause is still valid. That is, after the conditional clause which stipulates so-called China-specific rule of burden of proof has been terminated, the WTO Members may resort to the last sentence of Article 2.4 of the Anti-Dumping Agreement to invoke the general rule of burden of proof, which will be introduced as a new conditional clause associated with the main clause. So the main sentence in subparagraph (a)(ii) never lose its effectiveness from beginning to end.

Secondly, the "shifting in burden of proof" approach conflicts with the other two claims of the European Union and the United States.[21]

---

[17] European Union First Written Submission, *European Union – Measures Related to Price Comparison Methodologies,* WT/DS516/1, para. 110.

[18] Bernard O'Connor, Market-economy status for China is not automatic, November 2011, http://www.voxeu.org/article/china-market-economy (last accessed 30 April 2018).

[19] Miranda (2014), p. 99; Stewart et al. (2014), p. 276.

[20] Graafsma and Kumashova (2014), pp. 156–157.

[21] See the relevant analysis below.

2.3   Are the Chapeau and Paragraph (i) of Section 15(a) of the Protocol Expired?

Judging from the provisions of Section 15(d) of the Protocol, there are differences in the so-called "termination" objects. The first sentence stipulates that *"the provisions of subparagraph (a) shall be terminated"* once China has confirmed that it is a market economy based on the domestic law of the WTO's importing members; the second sentence stipulates that *"the provisions of subparagraph (a)(ii) shall expire 15 years after the date of accession"*; the third sentence stipulates that *"the non-market economy provisions of subparagraph (a) shall no longer apply"* if China can that market economy conditions prevail in a particular industry or sector.[22]

Both the European Union and the United States believe that this textual difference has important legal significance. On 11 December 2016, only subparagraph (a)(ii) expired and the chapeau of Section 15(a) and (a)(i) are still valid.

The European Union believes that the differences in the provisions of Section 15(d) of the Protocol are intentional. Comparing the similar provisions of the China-US bilateral agreement on accession to the WTO and China's Protocol to Access the WTO, *"the negotiators specifically procured that the text be amended so that the second sentence no longer refers to Section 15(a) as a whole, but instead refers only to Section 15(a)(ii). Negotiators need to ensure that the rest of Section 15 is still applicable before China becomes a market economy country."*[23]

The author believes that it is self-contradictory between this assertion and the so-called "shifting in burden of proof" approach advocated by the European Union and United States at the same time in the same case. As mentioned earlier, both the European Union and the United States believe that the legal effect of the termination of subparagraph (a)(ii) merely implies a change in the rule of burden of proof. That is, before 11 December 2016, as long as the Chinese producers under investigation "cannot clearly show" that market economy conditions prevail in the industry producing the like product, the importing WTO Member may abandon Chinese prices or costs. However, after 11 December 2016, even if the Chinese producers "cannot clearly show" that market economy conditions, the importing member cannot directly resort to "methods not based on a strict comparison with Chinese domestic prices or costs". Instead, it shall resort to the relevant provisions of Article 2.4 of the Anti-Dumping Agreement and allocate the burden of proof between the interested parties fairly. Based on this view, whether the Chinese producers "can clearly show" or "cannot clearly show" is no longer a legal element related to the burden of proof. But the European Union and United States try to claim that Section 15(a)(i) is still valid, which clearly stipulates that if the Chinese producers under investigation "can clearly show" market economy conditions, the importing WTO Member must use Chinese prices or costs in determining price comparability. It is beyond dispute that

---

[22] Emphasis added by the author.

[23] European Union First Written Submission, *European Union – Measures Related to Price Comparison Methodologies*, WT/DS516/1, para. 113.

main effect of Section 15(a)(i) is the establishment of "clearly show" standard and the so-called "shifting in burden of proof" approach makes it invalid.[24] As the Appellate Body has emphasised, *"one of the corollaries of the "general rule of interpretation" in the Vienna Convention is that interpretation must give meaning and effect to all the terms of a treaty. An interpreter is not free to adopt a reading that would result in reducing whole clauses or paragraphs of a treaty to redundancy or inutility."*[25]

More importantly, the Appellate Body has indirectly answered this question in the *EC – Fasteners* case, when it clarified the issue of interpretation of Section 15(d).

2.4 Interpretation of Section 15(d) CAP

The first sentence of Section 15(d) provides that, once China has established, under the national law of the importing WTO Member, that it is a market economy, the provisions of subparagraph (a) shall be terminated provided that the importing Member's national law contains market economy criteria as of the date of accession. In the opinion of the European Union, *"[t]his is a **country-wide** provision. The reference to the national law of the importing Member specifically embeds the rule in the municipal law of the WTO Members other than China. This reflects a legitimate concern on the part of other Members that, unless and until China becomes a market economy, Section 15(a) **as a whole** should not be terminated."*[26]

The second sentence of Section 15(d) provides that, in any event, the provisions of subparagraph (a)(ii) shall expire 15 years after the date of accession. The United States pointed out that "in any event" in the second sentence means that even after 11 December 2016, China may not have become a "market economy", the situation contemplated in the first sentence.[27]

The third sentence of Section 15(d) provides that, in addition, should China establish, pursuant to the national law of the importing WTO Member, that market economy conditions prevail in a particular industry or sector, the non-market economy provisions of subparagraph (a) shall no longer apply to that industry or sector. According to the United States, the introductory phrase establishes that the subject matter of this sentence is "in addition" to the subject matter of the first and second

[24] Graafsma and Kumashova (2014), p. 156.

[25] Appellate Body Report, *United States – Standards for Reformulated and Conventional Gasoline*, WT/DS2/AB/R, adopted 29 April 1996, DSR 1996:I, para. 23.

[26] European Union First Written Submission, *European Union – Measures Related to Price Comparison Methodologies*, WT/DS516/1, para. 103 (emphasis added).

[27] Legal Interpretation Submitted by the United States, *European Union – Measures Related to Price Comparison Methodologies*, WT/DS516/1, para. 8.3.3.

sentence. This suggests the third sentence remains applicable after the expiry of subparagraph (a)(ii).[28]

According to the author, the Appellate Body has answered this question clearly in *EC – Fasteners*. In that case, the European Union claimed that Section 15 allows it to treat China as an non-market economy country for the purpose of applying anti-dumping rules and, in particular, Article 9.5 of the Anti-Dumping Agreement, which is related to the review carried out by the investigating authorities for the purpose of determining individual margins of dumping for any exporters or producers in the exporting country in question who have not exported the product to the importing Member during the period of investigation.[29] According to the European Union, the scope of Section 15 is not limited to the determination of the normal value in antidumping investigations. China responded that Section 15 does not contain an official recognition by China that it is an NME, but only a temporary and limited derogation from the rules in the Anti-Dumping Agreement on the determination of the normal value with respect to imports from China.[30] The Appellate Body supported the view held by China:

> Paragraph 15(d) of China's Accession Protocol establishes that the provisions of Paragraph 15(a) expire 15 years after the date of China's accession (that is, 11 December 2016). It also provides that other WTO Members shall grant before that date the early termination of Paragraph 15(a) with respect to China's entire economy or specific sectors or industries if China demonstrates under the law of the importing WTO Member "that it is a market economy" or that "market economy conditions prevail in a particular industry or sector". Since Paragraph 15(d) provides for rules on the termination of Paragraph 15(a), its scope of application cannot be wider than that of Paragraph 15(a). Both paragraphs concern exclusively the determination of normal value. In other words, Paragraph 15(a) contains special rules for the determination of normal value in antidumping investigations involving China. Paragraph 15(d) in turn establishes that these special rules will expire in 2016 and sets out certain conditions that may lead to the early termination of these special rules before 2016.[31]

In any case, this statement is not a obiter dicta, since it is a direct answer to the issue of the scope of Section 15. This issue was raised by the European Union in the appellate process and went through the exchange of argument between the parties or the third parties.

It is indisputable that the Appellate Body clarified that the scope of application of Section 15(d) cannot be wider than that of Section 15(a) and both paragraphs concern exclusively the determination of normal value. This statement directly

---

[28] Legal Interpretation Submitted by the United States, *European Union – Measures Related to Price Comparison Methodologies,* WT/DS516/1, paras. 8.3.3 and 8.3.6.

[29] European Union First Written Submission, *European Union – Measures Related to Price Comparison Methodologies,* WT/DS516/1, para. 49.

[30] Appellee Submission of China, *European Communities – Definitive Anti-Dumping Measures on Certain Iron or Steel Fasteners from China,* WT/DS397/AB/8, para. 49.

[31] Appellate Body Report, *European Communities – Definitive Anti-Dumping Measures on Certain Iron or Steel Fasteners from China,* WT/DS397/AB/R, adopted 15 July 2011, DSR 2011:II, para. 289.

overturned the foregoing point held by the European Union that the first sentence of Section 15(d) reflects a legitimate concern that Section 15(a) as a whole should not be terminated unless and until China becomes a market economy. It also dismissed the view of the United States that some parts of Section 15(d) remains applicable after the expiry of Section 15(a)(ii). In addition, the Appellate Body analysed two possibilities regarding the termination of Section 15(a). Such special rules will expire in 2016, or they will be terminated early before 2016 as long as certain conditions are met.

According to the points of view of the Appellate Body, the author believes that Section 15(a) and 15(d) have a crossover and deferred relationship.

First, according to the first sentence and the third sentence of paragraph (d), before 11 December 2016, once China meets the market economy standards of other members at the national or industrial level, Section 15(a) will be terminated. There is no need for the Chinese producers to bear the burden of proof and to distinguish between the two possibilities: success (subparagraph (a)(i)) or failure (subparagraph (a)(ii)).

Second, before 11 December 2016, if China is unable to meet the market economy standards of other members at national or industrial level, subparagraph (a) will be applied in two circumstances: subparagraph (a)(i) or (a)(ii).

Third, according to the second sentence of Paragraph (d), "in any event", after 11 December 2016, Paragraph (a)(ii) is terminated. Even if the Chinese producers under investigation cannot clearly show that market economy conditions prevail in the industry, the importing WTO Member may not use a methodology which is not based on a strict comparison with domestic prices or costs in China. The reason why the second sentence of Section 15(d) only refers to subparagraph (a)(ii) is that there is no need for the Chinese producers to bear the burden of proof at all after 11 December 2016. Subparagraph (a)(ii) actually implies an expiry date, therefore the whole Section 15(a) is actually terminated.

Fourth, after 11 December 2016, China no longer needs to establish the market economy status at the national or industrial level, because this is an obligation that China can choose to perform in order to enjoy the right of "the early termination of these special rules" before 11 December 2016. After 11 December 2016, these special rules must be terminated, so there is no need for China to bear the burden of proof.

2.5   Is Section 15 CAP an Exception Clause?

The European Union stressed that in past cases the Appellate Body was particularly careful in addressing the relationship between a particular provision of China's Accession Protocol and other provisions of WTO Agreements. *"Where such provisions contain differences, even subtle differences, such differences must be respected, particularly where significant legal consequences result therefrom. In this case, the relevant terms that govern the relationship between China's Accession Protocol and the other cited provisions of WTO law are "apply" and "consistent with", and those terms must be respected and given their proper meaning.*"[32] *"In light of this rela-tionship of consistent application, Section 15 does not constitute an "exception" to Article VI of the GATT 1994 or the Anti-Dumping Agreement and is not in the nature of an "affirmative defence".*"[33] *"It also means that Section 15 must be understood as interpreting and applying the terms of Article VI of the GATT 1994 and the Anti-Dumping Agreement and the SCM Agreement.*"[34]

The United States also claimed that the introductory Paragraph to Section 15 states that the GATT 1994 and the Anti-Dumping Agreement "shall apply... consistent with the following", referring to the remainder of Section 15. Use of the phrase "consistent with" suggests Section 15 is not to be viewed as an exception or in contradiction to the named agreements. The text is not "subject to", "provided that", "in the event of conflict" or other similar wording which are always used in the exception provisions within the WTO Agreement. For other agreements to apply "consistent with" Section 15, they should be read as compatible or in agreement with each other. Section 15 is not an exception to the GATT 1994 or the Anti-Dumping Agreement but confirms that in determining price comparability under those agreements, an importing Member may in certain circumstances reject an industry's prices or costs. Section 15 provides that Article VI:1 of the GATT 1994 and the Anti-Dumping Agreement continue to apply consistent with the terms of Section 15.[35]

From another perspective, the United States has actually recognised that the exception provisions within the WTO Agreement do not have uniform labels and wording. The author believes that the main legal function of the exception clause is to provide the legitimacy for violating other general obligations. Therefore, what is important is not the wording of the clause, but the actual content.

In fact, in the *EC – Fasteners* case, the Appellate Body has implicated acknowl-edged that Section 15 is an exception clause:

> Like the second Ad Note to Article VI:1 of the GATT 1994, Paragraph 15(a) of China's Accession Protocol permits importing Members to **derogate from** a strict comparison with domestic prices or costs in China, that is, in respect of the determination of the normal value......We consider that, while Section 15 of China's Accession Protocol establishes **special rules** regarding the domestic price aspect of price comparability, it does not contain **an open-ended exception** that allows WTO Members to treat China differently for other purposes under the Anti-Dumping Agreement and the GATT 1994, such as the determina-tion of export prices or individual versus country-wide margins and duties.[36]

---

[32] First Written Submission by the European Union, *European Union – Measures Related to Price Comparison Methodologies*, WT/DS516/1, 14 November 2017, para. 76.

[33] First Written Submission by the European Union, *European Union – Measures Related to Price Comparison Methodologies*, WT/DS516/1, 14 November 2017, para. 77.

[34] First Written Submission by the European Union, *European Union – Measures Related to Price Comparison Methodologies*, WT/DS516/1, 14 November 2017, para. 80.

[35] Legal Interpretation Submitted by the United States, *European Union – Measures Related to Price Comparison Methodologies*, WT/DS516/1, para. 8.6.

[36] Appellate Body Report, *European Communities – Definitive Anti-Dumping Measures on Certain Iron or Steel Fasteners from China*, WT/DS397/AB/R, adopted 15 July 2011, DSR 2011:II, para. 290 (emphasis added).

One should pay attention to the terms used by the Appellate Body, "derogate from", "special rules" and "an open-ended exception". It is evident that Section 15 is not "an open-ended exception", but indeed an exception.

It should also be emphasised that the argument to deny the "exceptional" nature of Section 15 and the view that the termination of Section 15(a)(ii) only means the change of the burden of proof are also contradictory, which are advocated by the European Union and the United States at the same time in the same case.

As mentioned earlier, both the European Union and the United States believe that after 11 December 2016, with the termination of Section 15(a)(ii), the "China-specific" burden of proof rule expired and the evidence rules of the Anti-Dumping Agreement would be applied instead. In other words, the core point of view of the United States and the European Union is that the main legal value of the "Old Section 15" is to design specific evidence rules for China, which is clearly different from the counterpart rules in the Article 2.4 of the Anti-Dumping Agreement.

The European Union further pointed out that despite the adoption of this "China-specific" burden of proof rule, "*Section 15 remained consistent with the Anti-Dumping Agreement because it did not conflict with the Anti-Dumping Agreement, which only requires that the investigating authority of an importing Member must not impose an unreasonable burden of proof on a particular interested party or on either sub-set of interested parties. In other words, Section 15 confirmed that, with respect to China and Chinese industries or exporters, in all the circumstances, it was reasonable to place the burden of proof on the Chinese exporters.*"[37]

The mistake of this view is that if we consider the "China-specific" rule of burden of proof is still "reasonable" and does not belong to the "unreasonable" burden of proof prohibited by Article 2.4 of the Anti-Dumping Agreement, such "Chinese-specific" rule is already integrated with the burden of proof rule under Article 2.4 of the Anti-Dumping Agreement. This is tantamount to negating the value of Section 15(a), i.e. setting "Chinese-specific" evidence rule, which is emphasised by the European Union and the United States. In addition, in the anti-dumping investigation procedure, is it "reasonable" if the alleged burden of proof is unilaterally imposed on Chinese producers?

It is worth noting that the Appellate Body once asserted that Article 2.4 of the Anti-Dumping Agreement proscribes some general obligation. "*Article 2.4 sets forth a general obligation to make a 'fair comparison' between export price and normal value. This is a general obligation that, in our view, informs all of Article 2...*"[38]

The author believes that the requirement of subparagraph (a)(ii) that the burden of proof shall be unilaterally imposed on Chinese producers is clearly in violation of Article 2.4 of the Anti-Dumping Agreement, which provides "*the authorities shall indicate to the parties in question what information is necessary to ensure a*

---

[37] First Written Submission by the European Union, *European Union – Measures Related to Price Comparison Methodologies*, WT/DS516/1, 14 November 2017, para. 98 (footnotes omitted).

[38] Appellate Body Report, *European Communities – Anti-Dumping Duties on Imports of Cotton-type Bed Linen from India*, WT/DS141/AB/R, adopted 1 March 2001, DSR 2000:XIII, para. 59.

fair comparison and shall not impose an unreasonable burden of proof on those parties." There is a clear conflict between these two provisions. Therefore, if the European Union and the United States insist on the so-called "Chinese-specific" rule of burden of proof, they must acknowledge that subparagraph (a)(ii) is an exception to the general evidence rules in Article 2.4 of the Anti-Dumping Agreement. Since the main legal value of the "Old Section 15" lies in setting the so-called "China-specific" rule of burden of proof, it can only be regarded as an exception clause of the Anti-Dumping Agreement. Therefore, the EU and the United States cannot claim either Section 15 is not an "exceptional" clause, or the legal value of (a)(ii) is limited to the "China-specific" burden of proof at the same time.

3 General Methodological Issues Concerning the Interpretation of China's Accession Protocol

An undeniable fact is that although China's Accession Protocol is an integral part of the WTO Agreement,[39] it is different from the multilateral trade agreements in the WTO system that aims to create a general code of conduct for all WTO members. In concluding the Accession Protocol, China and other members had no intention to create general rules, but to make certain special arrangements in dealing with the trade relations between China and other members and to achieve the exchange and balance of certain rights and obligations. Section 15 is a typical example of an "entry fee". China's Accession Protocol therefore has a strong "contractual colour."[40] The problem is that, in interpreting China's Accession Protocol, the Appellate Body has never considered the specificity of the Protocol and still upholds a strict (even more rigorous) textualism position. The typical manifestation is the repeated scrutiny of the structure of words, sentences and clauses by the Appellate Body in response to the question of whether Article XX of GATT 1994 can be applied to the specific provisions of the Protocol.[41]

---

[39] Section 3.1 of China's Accession Protocol: *"This Protocol, which shall include the commitments referred to in paragraph 342 of the Working Party Report, shall be an integral part of the WTO Agreement."*

[40] Qin (2003), pp. 509–518.

[41] In *China – Publications and Audiovisual Products*, the Appellate Body found that, by virtue of the introductory clause of Section 5.1 of China's Accession Protocol, China could, in that dispute, invoke Article XX(a) of GATT 1994 to justify provisions found to be inconsistent with China's trading rights commitments under its Accession Protocol. (Appellate Body Report, *China – Measures Affecting Trading Rights and Distribution Services for Certain Publications and Audiovisual Entertainment Products*, WT/DS363/AB/R, adopted 21 December 2009, DSR 2009:III, paras. 216–230). However, in *China – Raw Materials*, the Appellate Body pointed out that paragraph 11.3 of China's Accession Protocol *"does not include any express reference to Article XX of the GATT 1994, or to provisions of the GATT 1994 more generally"*. They drew a contrast between the text of paragraph 11.3 and the language contained in paragraph 5.1, paragraph 11.1, paragraph 11.2, which include such general references. Such "omission" in paragraph 11.3 suggest that WTO Members did not intend to incorporate the defences available under Article

It may be precisely because of this methodological orientation that China, the European Union, and the United States are also trying to start with the word, sentence and syntax of Section 15, in order to find out favourable explanations. Is it possible for China to claim that the "contractual nature" of the "Protocol" is different from other multilateral trade agreements in the WTO system, so that there should be differences in interpretation methods?

Let us see the opening statement by Ambassador Zhang Xiangchen as a part of the Oral Statement of China at the first substantive meeting of the Panel in DS516:

> As a third party in this dispute, the United States contends that long before China acceded to the WTO there had been "longstanding rights in the GATT and WTO to reject prices or costs that are not determined under market economy conditions". I was dumbfounded by this proposition. Section 15 of China's Accession Protocol was, for the most part, negotiated bilaterally between the United States and China, and it was one of the toughest and most contentious issues between the two sides. I myself participated in almost every round of those bilateral negotiations, including the final round in Beijing when the bilateral Agreement on Market Access was signed. The United States' contention is beyond the imagination of those, including myself, who actually participated in the negotiations.
>
> In the early rounds of the negotiations, the United States insisted that China's accession would require special rules so that the United States would be able to maintain its then-current antidumping methodology (treating China as a non-market economy). China disagreed initially, but relented in later rounds on the premise that such special rules must end five years after accession. The United States counter-offered with a "review clause" proposal that entitles importing Members to review whether the methodologies would continue to be appropriate. The standoff persisted for several rounds, until the United States accepted that the "non-market economy provision" would have a definitive end-point, proposing that "[i]n any event the non-market economy provision will expire twenty years after the date of accession". Ultimately, the two sides arrived at a "middle ground" of 15 years, as eventually adopted in Section 15 of China's Accession Protocol. In the negotiations, China also sought and obtained provisions requiring "early termination" of the special rules under some circumstances, i.e., under the condition that China has established under the national law of the importing WTO Members that it is a market economy or that market economy conditions prevail in a particular industry or sector. After the negotiations were concluded, numerous public statements by WTO Members including the United States and the European Union confirmed the deal they struck with China.[42]

It seems that China tries to argue that the real intentions of China and the United States in concluding the related article of the bilateral agreement are that the special rules must be terminated after some years. Is it possible for the Appellate Body to take such intentions into consideration seriously? Unfortunately, the answer may be negative if the Appellate Body still adheres to the strict textualism interpretation method. China may try to claim that its Accession Protocol deserves a different

---

XX GATT 1994 of into paragraph 11.3. (Appellate Body Report, *China – Measures Related to the Exportation of Various Raw Materials*, WT/DS394/ABR, adopted 30 January 2012, DSR 2011:V, paras. 278–304).

[42] Opening Statement by Ambassador Zhang Xiangchen as a part of the Oral Statement of China at the First Substantive Meeting of the Panel in the dispute: *European Union – Measures Related to Price Comparison Methodologies*, WT/DS516/1, 6 December 2017, paras. 10–11 (footnotes omitted).

more flexible interpretation method, which is not rare in the practice of general international law.

There was a traditional treaty classification in international law, that is, contractual treaties and law-making treaties. In the years before the 1969 Vienna Convention on the Law of Treaties was promulgated, international treaties were often compared with domestic legislation and contracts. The contractual treaties corresponded to contracts in domestic law and law-making treaties corresponded to domestic legislation.[43] Correspondingly, in the process of interpreting these two types of treaties, the factors considered and emphasised are also different. The interpretation of contractual treaties focuses on exploring the subjective intentions of parties through inspections of preparatory works; while the interpretation of constructive treaties emphasises more on the objective exploration of the true meaning of treaty terms.[44]

The International Court of Justice expressed some related opinions in the case *Reservations to the Convention on the Prevention and Punishment of the Crime of Genocide* (1951): *"In such a convention the contracting States do not have any interests of their own; they merely have, one and all, a common interest, namely, the accomplishment of those high purposes which are the raison d'être of the convention. Consequently, in a convention of this type one cannot speak of individual advantages or disadvantages to States, or of the maintenance of a perfect contractual balance between rights and duties."*[45] From these statements, it can be seen that although the International Court of Justice did not expressly categorise the contractual treaties and the law-making treaties, it implicitly recognised this classification.[46]

In the process of drafting Articles 31 and 32 of the Vienna Convention on the Law of Treaties of 1969, whether or not to distinguish between the interpretation rules based on the classification of the treaties had also led to discussions. The final result is no distinction. But the International Law Commission pointed out that although for the purpose of formulating the general rules of interpretation, the Commission did not consider it necessary to make such a distinction between law-making and other treaties, it is true that the character of a treaty may affect the question whether the application of a particular principle, maxim or method of interpretation is suitable in a particular case.[47]

With the conclusion and entry into force of the Vienna Convention on the Law of Treaties of 1969, the absolute dominance of Articles 31 and 32 in the interpretation of international treaties (including the WTO Agreement) has been widely recognised. The different types of treaties and the different emphasis on interpretation

---

[43] Lauterpacht (1927), pp. 155–202.

[44] Wright (1929), pp. 102–104.

[45] ICJ Reports, *Reservations to the Convention on the Prevention and Punishment of the Crime of Genocide, Advisory Opinion of May 28th, 1951*, para. 23, p. 12.

[46] Pauwelyn (2003), pp. 909–910.

[47] Draft Articles on the Law of Treaties with Commentaries, 1966, Yearbook of the International Law Commission, 1966, Vol. II, para. 219.

factors seem to be gradually forgotten, but it cannot be denied that this classification still has its reasonable value.

One can find some new developments of this issue. At its 64th session, in 2012, the International Law Commission decided to appoint Mr. Georg Nolte as Special Rapporteur for the topic "Subsequent agreements and subsequent practice in relation to interpretation of treaties". In 2013, Mr. Georg Nolte presented the first report to the International Law Commission, which contained draft conclusion 1: "*The interpretation of a treaty in a specific case may result in a different emphasis on the various means of interpretation contained in articles 31 and 32 of the Vienna Convention, in particular on the text of the treaty or on its object and purpose, depending on the treaty or on the treaty provisions concerned.*"[48]

In order to support this draft conclusion, the Special Rapporteur cited many examples. In the WTO, Panels and the Appellate Body typically concentrate on the text of the respective agreement. So far the Appellate Body has not put a particular emphasis on the object and purpose as a means of interpretation.[49] In the International Center for the Settlement of Investment Disputes (ICSID), although the jurisprudence of Tribunals is far from following a uniform approach, they have, so far, neither put a conspicuous emphasis on the object and purpose as a means of interpretation nor on the presumed intentions of the parties to the Convention when they concluded it.[50] In the Inter-American Court's jurisprudence the "object and purpose" appears to play the most important role among the different means of interpretation.[51]

In the consideration of this issue, the International Law Commission debated whether it would be appropriate to refer, in draft conclusion 1, to the "nature" of the treaty as a factor which would typically be relevant to determining whether more or less weight should be given to certain means of interpretation. Some members considered that the subject-matter of a treaty (e.g. whether provisions concern purely economic matters or rather address the human rights of individuals and whether the rules of a treaty are more technical or more value-oriented) as well as its basic structure and function (e.g. whether provisions are more reciprocal in nature or more intended to protect a common good) may affect its interpretation. They indicated that the jurisprudence of different international courts and tribunals suggested that this is the case. It was also mentioned that the concept of the "nature" of a treaty is not alien to the Vienna Convention (see e.g. Article 56(1)(a)) and that the concept of the "nature" of the treaty and/or of treaty provisions had been included in other work of the Commission, in particular on the topic of the Effects of Armed Conflicts

---

[48] First report on subsequent agreements and subsequent practice in relation to treaty interpretation by Georg Nolte, Special Rapporteur, UN Doc. A/CN.4/660, 19 March 2013, para. 28.

[49] First report on subsequent agreements and subsequent practice in relation to treaty interpretation by Georg Nolte, Special Rapporteur, UN Doc. A/CN.4/660, 19 March 2013, para. 11.

[50] First report on subsequent agreements and subsequent practice in relation to treaty interpretation by Georg Nolte, Special Rapporteur, UN Doc. A/CN.4/660, 19 March 2013, para. 13.

[51] First report on subsequent agreements and subsequent practice in relation to treaty interpretation by Georg Nolte, Special Rapporteur, UN Doc. A/CN.4/660, 19 March 2013, paras. 19–20.

on Treaties. Other Members, however, considered that the draft conclusion should not refer to the "nature" of the Treaty in order to preserve the unity of the interpretation process and to avoid any categorisation of treaties. The point was also made that the notion of the "nature of the treaty" was unclear and that it would be difficult to distinguish it from the object and purpose of the treaty. The International Law Commission ultimately decided to leave the question open and to make no reference in draft conclusion 1 to the nature of the treaty for the time being.[52]

But the International Law Commission stressed that the obligation to place "appropriate emphasis on the various means of interpretation" may, in the course of the interpretation of a treaty in specific cases, result in a different emphasis on the various means of interpretation depending on the treaty or on the treaty provisions concerned.[53]

The author believes that in accordance with this view of the International Law Commission, China can advocate special considerations in the interpretation of its Accession Protocol, i.e. taking the real intentions of China into consideration seriously.

4 Conclusion

The interpretation of Section 15 of China's WTO Accession is now a hot issue in the practices of WTO Law. In DS516, the European Union and the United States try to argue that the legal consequence of "expiry" of Section 15(a)(ii) is only "shifting in burden of proof", and the chapeau and (i) of Section 15(a) are still valid and Section 15 is not an exception clause. But these claims are self-contradictory and inconsistent with the views of the Appellate Body in *EC – Fasteners* Case, that is, Section 15 is an exception clause and Section 15(a) has expired. In addition, China may try to claim that its Accession Protocol which is a contractual agreement deserves a different more flexible interpretation method, which is not rare in the practice of general international law.

Acknowledgements The article is supported by the National Social Science Fund of China (Grant No. 13CFX115) and the Chinese Ministry of education of Humanities and Social Science Project (Grant No. 12YJC820023).

---

[52] Report of the International Law Commission, 65th session, 2013, UN Doc. A/68/10, paras. 19–20.
[53] Report of the International Law Commission, 65th session, 2013, UN Doc. A/68/10, para. 18.

References

Black HC (2010) Handbook on the law of judicial precedents, or, the science of case law. Gale, Making of Modern Law, Michigan

Gao H (2018) Dictum on dicta: Obiter dicta in WTO disputes. World Trade Rev 17(2):1–25

Gatta B (2014a) China's market economy status after 2016. Global Trade Customs J 9(4):144–145

Gatta B (2014b) Between 'automatic market economy status' and 'status quo': a commentary on 'Interpreting paragraph 15 of China's protocol of accession'. Global Trade Customs J 9(4):165–172

Graafsma F, Kumashova E (2014) In re China's protocol of accession and the anti-dumping agreement: temporary derogation or permanent modification. Global Trade Customs J 9(4):154–159

Lauterpacht H (1927) Private law sources and analogies of international law: with special reference to international arbitration. Longmans, Green and Co. Ltd., Bombay

Miranda J (2014) Interpreting paragraph 15 of China's protocol of accession. Global Trade Customs J 9(3):94–103

Miranda J (2016a) More on why granting China market economy status after December 2016 is contingent upon whether China has in fact transitioned into a market economy. Global Trade Customs J 11(5):244–250

Miranda J (2016b) A comment on Vermulst's article on China in anti-dumping proceedings after December 2016. Global Trade Customs J 11(7/8):306–313

Miranda J (2016c) Implementation of the 'shift in burden of proof' approach to interpreting paragraph 15 of China's protocol of accession. Global Trade Customs J 11(10):447–453

Nicely MR (2014) Time to eliminate outdated non-market economy methodologies. Global Trade Customs J 9(4):160–164

Noel S (2016) Why the European Union must dump so-called 'non-market economy' methodologies and adjustments in its anti-dumping investigations. Global Trade Customs J 11(7/8):296–305

O'Connor B (2015) Much ado about 'nothing': 2016, China and market economy status. Global Trade Customs J 10(5):176–180

Pauwelyn J (2003) A typology of multilateral treaty obligations: are WTO obligations bilateral or collective in nature? Eur J Int Law 14(5):909–910

Posner TR (2014) A comment on interpreting paragraph 15 of China's protocol of accession by Jorge Miranda. Global Trade Customs J 9(4):146–153

Qin JY (2003) "WTO-plus" obligations and their implications for the World Trade Organization legal system: an appraisal of the China accession protocol. J World Trade 37(3):509–518

Rosenthal PC, Beckington JS (2014) The People's Republic of China: a market economy or a non-market economy in anti-dumping proceedings starting on December 12, 2016? Global Trade Customs J 9(7/8):352–355

Ruessmann L, Beck J (2014) 2016 and the application of an NME methodology to Chinese producers in anti-dumping investigations. Global Trade Customs J 9(10):457–463

Searles J (2016) The European Union's options for China dumping methodology after 11 December 2016. Global Trade Customs J 11(10):430–439

Stewart TP, Fennell WA, Bell SM, Birch NJ (2014) The special case of China: why the use of a special methodology remains applicable to China after 2016. Global Trade Customs J 9(6):272–279

Vermulst E, Sud JD, Evenett SJ (2016) Normal value in anti-dumping proceedings against China post-2016: are some animals less equal than others. Global Trade Customs J 11(5):212–228

Wright Q (1929) The interpretation of multilateral treaties. Am J Int Law 23:102–104

Zhenghao L (2016) Interpreting paragraph 15 of China's accession protocol in light of the working party report. Global Trade Customs J 11(5):229–237

Anti-Subsidy Investigations Against China: The "Great Leap Forward" in Reforming EU Trade Defence?

Sophia Müller

Contents

Abstract This paper examines the use of alternative benchmarks in anti-subsidy law. Whereas alternative benchmarking in the determination of normal value is common practice in anti-dumping law, it only recently established itself in often-neglected anti-subsidy law. During the last score of years, the WTO Appellate Body has not only developed general legal rules for the use of alternative benchmarks in anti-subsidy law by interpretation of Article 14 ASCM, but WTO accession

S. Müller (✉)
Frankfurt, Germany

© Springer International Publishing AG, part of Springer Nature 2018
M. Bungenberg et al. (eds.), *The Future of Trade Defence Instruments*,
European Yearbook of International Economic Law,
https://doi.org/10.1007/978-3-319-95306-9_7

procedures have even spawned country-specific alternative benchmark regimes. The most illustrious example is certainly the People's Republic of China. Taking the example of EU investigations against China, this paper analyses both normative deficits and practical consequences of alternative benchmarking in WTO anti-subsidy law. Reconsidering function and principles of the WTO as major institution for international trade regulation, it argues that the introduction of country-specific alternative benchmark provisions in anti-subsidy law has left the legal boundaries of the WTO and is hence in violation of WTO law. Thus, reform is due—and despite recent efforts on EU level, still remains an open issue.

1 Introduction

In 1958, the Chairman of the Chinese Communist Party, Mao Zedong, initiated several reform policies that were to take the young People's Republic a "great leap forward" towards an industrialised economy.[1]

Almost 60 years later, China has accomplished its transformation into a major player on the global market. In 2001, the "Middle Kingdom" also became the 143rd member of the WTO.[2] To mitigate the effects of the transformation of the former socialist country into a modern market economy, however, the Chinese government still extensively grants support to Chinese enterprises, mostly former state-owned enterprises (SOEs) in core industries, which are consequently able to offer their products on the world market at prices far below actual production costs—and far below the prices of their competitors.

By now, it is thus China's trading partners like the EU that are aiming at a "great leap forward" in tackling the detrimental effects of this subsidy-induced dumping on their domestic markets. Of the three trade defence instruments, anti-dumping (AD), anti-subsidy (AS) and safeguards, it has always been AD that has served as the cornerstone of trade defence. In the EU, for instance, out of 827 AD and AS investigations in total, 732 constituted AD cases (89%), whereas only 89 AS proceedings have been conducted (11%).[3] Although structurally similar, the inhibition of endangering bilateral relations through directly investigating fellow states instead of private entities seemed to prove too high a threshold to overcome the reluctance of national investigating authorities to resort to the AS instrument.

In the quest for alternative strategies, however, such concerns have been set aside. During the last 15 years, the AS remedy has re-entered the stage of global trade defence and been increasingly applied in cases of subsidy-induced dumping. In particular in the U.S., it had even become common practice to combine an AD and an AS investigation in countering allegedly lowly-priced imports. From 2007 to

---

[1] For a detailed account on Mao's reforms, see Walder (2015), pp. 152 et seq.
[2] See www.wto.org/english/thewto_e/countries_e/china_e.htm (last accessed 30 April 2018).
[3] See http://trade.ec.europa.eu/doclib/html/113191.htm (last accessed 30 April 2018).

2014, of a total of 603 U.S. anti-subsidy investigations, 347, i.e. 58%, have been doubled with respective anti-dumping proceedings.[4]

Due to the special economic character of China, where not all sectors of economy are fully market-driven yet, one feature is deemed indispensable to effectively tackle trade distortions by Chinese imports: the use of alternative benchmark methodologies.

In non-market economy (NME) situations, domestic prices and costs of a country are for instance either non-existing or cannot be relied on because they are too heavily distorted.[5] This impairs the identification of realistic in-country market prices, which in consequence makes it per se impossible to determine the dumping margin or the amount of benefit respectively. To enable a meaningful duty calculation, nevertheless, domestic market prices or costs are replaced by alternative values, e.g. costs of production or market prices from comparable third-countries. This practice also has a welcome side effect for investigating authorities. With price surrogates very likely being considerably higher than original domestic values, the amount of duty is consequently inflated.[6]

The use of alternative benchmarks constitutes a long-standing practice in AD law and contributes much to the success of the AD instrument—especially as regards investigations against China. Here, Section 15(a)(ii) of the Protocol of Accession of China to the WTO (CAP)[7] explicitly permitted all other WTO members to use alternative benchmark methodologies in AD investigations against Chinese producers unless the producers could positively demonstrate that their sectors of economy were market-driven and, thus, domestic prices and costs reliable. As the producers were, however, hardly ever able to meet the necessary requirements,[8] the provision left investigating authorities in a comfortable position.

Section 15(a)(ii) CAP, however, expired on 12 December 2016. Today, it is heavily discussed whether the use of alternative benchmarks in AD investigations against

---

[4] Figures from Bown C, Global Countervailing Duties Database. The World Bank, www.econ. worldbank.org/ttbd/gcvd (last accessed 30 April 2018). By now, the WTO Appellate Body has interdicted this practice because of the double remedy issue. Subsides were offset twice through the imposition of both anti-dumping and countervailing duties. For extensive discussion of the origin of the double remedy issue see Kelly (2014), p. 6, fn. 26; regarding legal implications following the WTO AB's ruling in Appellate Body Reports, *United States – Definitive Anti-Dumping and Countervailing Duties on Certain Products from China*, WT/DS379/AB/R, adopted 11 March 2011, DSR 2010:III, see Prusa and Vermulst (2013), pp. 220–224; Ahn (2001), pp. 761 et seq.

[5] The WTO Appellate Body has positively identified these two NMES situations in its jurisprudence, e.g. Appellate Body Report, *United States – Final Countervailing Duty Determination with Respect to Certain Softwood Lumber from Canada*, WT/DS257/AB/R, adopted 17 February 2004, DSR 2003:VI, paras. 98 et seq. The Tribunal has, however, not excluded that beyond, other NMES exist.

[6] MacLean (2012), p. 191.

[7] World Trade Organization, Ministerial Conference Decision of 10 November 2001 on the Accession of the People's Republic of China, WT/L/432, 23 November 2001.

[8] Grieger (2017), p. 3.

China is still permitted by WTO law.[9] This situation of legal insecurity in AD law brings the AS instrument as alternative in trade defence to the fore.

Unlike AD law, the introduction of alternative benchmark methodologies into AS law constituted only a recent development. Rather, AS law had been deemed generally inapplicable in NME situations.[10] The paramount element in calculating the amount of countervailing duty (CVD) constitutes the determination of the benefit received by a producer through the financial contribution of the government. The amount of benefit is determined by comparing the conditions of the governmental contribution to the general conditions on the domestic market in the country investigated—which, in NME situations, constitutes a nonsensical comparison of two identical values, rendering no benefit.[11]

By today, however, the use of alternative benchmarks for a meaningful benefit calculation has established itself in AS law and is even stipulated in Section 15(b) CAP—which, unlike its sibling AD provision Section 15(a)(ii) CAP, is permanent. The often presumed "less evil brother to anti-dumping"[12] seems to offer investigating authorities a real alternative to AD proceedings after 12 December 2016.

The current application of alternative benchmark methodologies in AS law is, however, highly problematic. Its exact legal prerequisites as well as the process of selecting the price surrogate still remain largely in the dark and present countries investigated as well as the investigating authorities themselves with difficulties. Would a policy switch to AS law really secure the future effectiveness of the system and constitute the desired "great leap forward" in EU trade defence?

In addressing this question, this contribution first retraces the genesis of the alternative benchmark regime in WTO AS law. Then, it analyses the practical implications of this framework using an example of EU AS investigations against China. After addressing legality issues of both the current EU approach and the underlying WTO legal framework, this article concludes with a look on the status quo of present AS law reforms.

---

[9] Just see Yalcin et al. (2016), pp. 16 et seq.

[10] One famous example as regards the inapplicability of AS law in NMES is the U.S. Georgetown Steel case (U.S. Court of Appeals, Judgment of 18 September 1986, 801 F.2d 1308). In its reasoning, the court held that in NMES, subsidies could not be positively identified as there was no determinable difference between the government conditions and those in the market, because a true market did not exist. The same problem of economic logic of course also exists in AD law. There, it was, however, never really conceived as impediment in the application of AD law against NME countries. See Hoyt (1988), p. 1671.

[11] Van Bael and Bellis (2011), p. 140.

[12] Zhao L and Wang Y (2008) Trade remedies and non-market economies: Economic implications of the first U.S. countervailing duty case on China. Policy Research Working Paper No. 4560, https://openknowledge.worldbank.org/bitstream/handle/10986/6319/wps4560.pdf?sequence=1&isAllowed=y (last accessed 30 April 2018), p. 36.

2 The Use of Alternative Benchmarks in WTO Anti-Subsidy Law

WTO AS law comprises two distinct legal regimes for the use of alternative benchmark methodologies: a general regime that is applicable to the great majority of WTO members and country-specific regimes for both China and Viet Nam.

2.1 The General WTO Legal Framework on Alternative Benchmark Methodologies

Unlike in case of AD law, the alternative benchmark regime of AS law is not explicitly laid down in the WTO agreements. Rather, the rules have been derived by the WTO Appellate Body through interpretation of Article 14 of the Agreement on Subsidies and Countervailing Measures (ASCM). Besides general formal requirements regarding the benefit calculation, the provision contains exemplary guidelines for the calculation of the amount of subsidy for four different types of subsidies. In a negative list, it gives indications as to which practices shall not be considered as conferring a benefit and, as such, not constitute a countervailable subsidy. Article 14(a) ASCM addresses the government provision of equity capital, Article 14(b) and (c) ASCM government loans and loan guarantees and Article 14(d) ASCM concerns the provision of goods or services or purchase of goods by a government.

Not all of the four types of subsidies have yet been equipped with an alternative benchmark regime. Article 14(a) and (c) ASCM have never been subject to respective WTO jurisprudence, although it seems likely that the Appellate Body will recognise the applicability of alternative benchmarks also in these cases.[13]

The use of surrogate prices has first been permitted by the WTO Appellate Body in *US – Softwood Lumber IV*[14] in connection with Article 14(d) ASCM in the year 2004. In the longstanding dispute between Canada and the U.S. on Canadian stumpage fees for timber, the WTO Appellate Body held that Article 14(d) ASCM, despite its wording that "*the adequacy of remuneration shall be determined in relation to prevailing market conditions for the good or service in question in the country of provision or purchase,*" contained enough flexibility to allow for the use of price surrogates, mainly because the term "in relation to" was not to be understood as mandating a strict price comparison.[15] Thus, whenever in-country prices did not

---

[13] Panel Report, *United States – Final Countervailing Duty Determination with Respect to Certain Softwood Lumber from Canada*, WT/DS257/R, adopted 17 February 2004, para. 10.122.

[14] Appellate Body Report, *United States – Final Countervailing Duty Determination with Respect to Certain Softwood Lumber from Canada*, WT/DS257/AB/R, adopted 17 February 2004, DSR 2003:VI.

[15] Appellate Body Report, *United States – Final Countervailing Duty Determination with Respect to Certain Softwood Lumber from Canada*, WT/DS257/AB/R, adopted 17 February 2004, DSR 2003:VI, para. 89.

exist or were too distorted to constitute meaningful benchmarks, the application of price surrogates was allowed. Notably, the Appellate Body referred to government predominance as such a situation of market distortion, which it understood as the ability of the government to substantially influence or effectively determine the price building mechanisms on the market.[16] Market shares and market power were named as indicators for the assessment of the respective market situation in the country investigated.[17] The exact concepts of both indicators, however, were not elaborated on further. Finally, as regards the selection of the alternative benchmark, the Appellate Body named world market prices and the costs of production as potential surrogates but stressed that no restrictions existed in the choice of surrogate if only the surrogate *"relates or refers to, or is connected with"*[18] the original domestic market conditions in the country investigated.

In *US – Anti-Dumping and Countervailing Duties (China)*[19] in the year 2011, the Appellate Body transferred its jurisprudence on the use of alternative benchmark methodologies to Article 14(b) ASCM. As the wording of Article 14(b) ASCM did not contain any explicit reference to the use of in-country market conditions, the applicability of surrogates in cases where government actions distorted domestic interest rates was not in doubt.[20] For the selection of the alternative benchmark, no other prerequisite than comparability to existing domestic interest rates was required.[21]

The Appellate Body has thus step-by-step developed alternative benchmark regimes for both Articles 14(b) and (d) ASCM. Both regimes, however, still suffer from several severe "birth defects". Whereas, in line with the reasoning of the Appellate Body, there are indeed convincing arguments for opening the benefit calculation to the use of alternative benchmarks, the legal prerequisites for their application largely remain undefined. Neither "government market distortion" nor "government predominance" are concepts that make apparent for both countries

---

[16]Appellate Body Report, *United States – Final Countervailing Duty Determination with Respect to Certain Softwood Lumber from Canada,* WT/DS257/AB/R, adopted 17 February 2004, DSR 2003:VI, para. 102; Appellate Body Report, *United States – Definitive Anti-Dumping and Countervailing Duties on Certain Products from China,* WT/DS379/AB/R, adopted 25 March 2011, DSR 2010:III, para. 441.

[17]Appellate Body Report, *United States – Definitive Anti-Dumping and Countervailing Duties on Certain Products from China,* WT/DS379/AB/R, adopted 25 March 2011, DSR 2010:III, para. 441.

[18]Appellate Body Report, *United States – Final Countervailing Duty Determination with Respect to Certain Softwood Lumber from Canada,* WT/DS257/AB/R, adopted 17 February 2004, DSR 2003:VI, para. 106.

[19]Appellate Body Report, *United States – Definitive Anti-Dumping and Countervailing Duties on Certain Products from China,* WT/DS379/AB/R, adopted 25 March 2011, DSR 2010:III.

[20]Appellate Body Report, *United States – Final Countervailing Duty Determination with Respect to Certain Softwood Lumber from Canada,* WT/DS257/AB/R, adopted 17 February 2004, DSR 2003:VI, paras. 479, 484, 487.

[21]Appellate Body Report, *United States – Final Countervailing Duty Determination with Respect to Certain Softwood Lumber from Canada,* WT/DS257/AB/R, adopted 17 February 2004, DSR 2003:VI, para. 484.

investigated and investigating authorities whether or not the application of alternative benchmarks is warranted. Despite a certain degree of comparability with existing in-country conditions, the selection of the surrogate value also depends entirely on the discretion of the investigating authorities. Altogether, the general WTO AS law regime on the use of alternative benchmark methodologies has so far remained a loose and obscure framework—with a clear advantage for investigating authorities.

2.2 The Country-Specific WTO Legal Frameworks

Besides the general alternative benchmark regime in WTO AS law, country-specific regimes exist. In the light of the core WTO principle of non-discrimination, this comes rather unexpected. Whereas WTO AD law—in Article VI GATT, Ad Note 2 Article VI:1 GATT and Articles 2.2, 2.3 and 2.7 ADA—indeed contains provisions that enable a country-specific treatment in the determination of normal value, such regulations do not apply in WTO AS law. The possibility of deviation from in-country market prices in AS investigations against *"a country which has a complete or substantially complete monopoly of its trade and where all domestic prices are fixed by the State,"* which existed under former GATT AS law in Article 15 of the Tokyo Round Subsidies Code,[22] ceased to apply after the foundation of the WTO in 1995.

2.2.1 The Rationale for the Introduction of Country-Specific Alternative Benchmark Regimes

The recent integration of country-specific alternative benchmark regimes into AS law is a product of accession negotiations. For the first time, such a regime has been agreed upon in the course of China's accession to the WTO. Incumbent WTO members feared that AS law would otherwise be virtually inapplicable to China because of the persistent government influence on its domestic market.[23] The legal framework for the integration of the country-specific provisions into WTO law was set by Article XII:1 WTO Agreement. As only provision loosely regulating the WTO accession process,[24] the so-called "loophole in the system"[25] granted to the

---

[22] Agreement on Interpretation and Application of Articles VI, XVI and XXIII of the General Agreement on Tariffs and Trade, 12 April 1979.

[23] Wu (2011), pp. 233 et seq.

[24] Cattaneo O and Primo Braga CA, Everything You Always Wanted to Know about WTO Accession (But Were Afraid to Ask). World Bank, Policy Research Working Paper 5116, November 2009, http://documents.worldbank.org/curated/en/440471468331183983/pdf/WPS5116.pdf (last accessed 30 April 2018), pp. 12 et seq.

[25] Qin (2015), p. 389.

negotiating parties enormous leeway with respect to the nature of the accession commitments.[26] Thus, both China, and in its suit, Viet Nam,[27] had to accept special alternative benchmark regimes upon accession to the WTO.

2.2.2 The China- and Viet Nam-Specific Alternative Benchmark Regimes

Substantively, the Chinese and the Vietnamese special frameworks are identical. Section 15(b) CAP, for instance, provides that in AS proceedings that concern the types of subsidies listed in Article 14 ASCM, principally the general provisions of the ASCM shall apply; but

> if there are special difficulties in that application, the importing WTO Member may then use methodologies for identifying and measuring the subsidy benefit which take into account the possibility that prevailing terms and conditions in China may not always be available as appropriate benchmarks. In applying such methodologies, where practicable, the importing WTO Member should adjust such prevailing terms and conditions before considering the use of terms and conditions prevailing outside China.

At first glance, the special alternative benchmark regime appears well-drafted. But further scrutiny reveals that its legal prerequisites are far from clear. Several terms are referred to that are either entirely novel to WTO AS law or that have been transferred from other provisions and now cannot sensibly be applied any more in their original understandings.

The core prerequisite of "special difficulties", for instance, can historically be traced back to early GATT AD law. In the GATT Review Session of 1954–1955, Czechoslovakia proposed an amendment to Article VI:1(b) GATT 1947 to enable the application of alternative methodologies for the determination of normal value in AD investigations against state-trading countries.[28] This should protect such countries from unfair findings of dumping, which would invariably result from the use of the state-determined domestic "market" price.[29] The transfer of this term to country-specific special provisions of WTO AS law entails several questions. Does the use of "special difficulties" also automatically confer to China and Viet Nam the status of state-trading economies? Or does the transfer of the respective terminology set up an additional prerequisite for the applicability of the special alternative benchmark regimes in the sense that the character of China and Viet Nam as state-trading countries in the meaning of Ad Note 2 Article VI:1 GATT has to be positively proven before the special regimes may be resorted to? Or has the term been

---

[26] Regarding the traditional distinction of the different accession commitments, see Qin (2015), p. 389; and Qin (2003), p. 485.

[27] World Trade Organisation, Report on the Working Party on the Accession of Viet Nam, WT/ACC/VNM/48, 27 October 2006, para. 255.

[28] Proposals by the Czechoslovak Delegation, see World Trade Organization, Proposals by the Czechoslovak Delegation, Review Working Party II on Tariffs, Schedules and Customs Administration, W.9/86, 9 December 1954.

[29] Polouektov (2002), pp. 6 et seq.; Thorstensen et al. (2013), p. 778.

transferred in an adapted meaning and is thus no longer connected to the context of the Ad Note 2 Article VI:1 GATT?[30] In addition, when is the use of Chinese prices and costs no longer "appropriate" or adjustments of domestic values no longer "practicable"? The results of such considerations depend entirely on the reasoning of the investigating authorities—which will then hardly be justiciable.

3 Applying the Alternative Benchmark Methodologies: EU Anti-Subsidy Investigation Practice Against China

The consequences of the imprecise and obscure legal frameworks for the use of alternative benchmark methodologies in WTO AS law show clearly in their implementation and practical application, e.g. in EU AS cases against China.

3.1 The EU Anti-Subsidy Legal Framework on the Use of Alternative Benchmarks

EU AS law on the use of alternative benchmarks is closely aligned to its WTO role model. Article 6 of the Basic Anti-Subsidy Regulation (BASR)[31] in its paragraphs (a) to (d)(i) corresponds to Article 14 ASCM. Article 6(a) BASR covers the government provision of equity capital, Article 6(b) deals with loans, Article 6(c) with loan guarantees and Article 6(d) finally addresses the provision of goods or services and the purchase of goods by a government.

In addition, however, since the year 2002, EU AS law does indeed contain a special provision on the use of alternative benchmarks for the provision of goods or services or purchase of goods by a government in Article 6(d)(ii) BASR:

If there are no such prevailing market terms and conditions for the product or service in question in the country of provision or purchase which can be used as appropriate benchmarks, the following rules shall apply:

(i) the terms and conditions prevailing in the country concerned shall be adjusted, on the basis of actual costs, prices and other factors available in that country, by an appropriate amount which reflects normal market terms and conditions; or

(ii) when appropriate, the terms and conditions prevailing in the market of another country or on the world market which are available to the recipient shall be used.

In cases where domestic prices and costs in a country do not constitute appropriate benchmarks, these in-country prices shall first be tried to adjust to reflect market

---

[30] On the possible interpretations of special difficulties and their respective consequences for the applicability of Section 15(b) CAP, see Mueller (2016), p. 882.
[31] OJ 2016 L 176/55.

economy conditions. "When appropriate", third-country or world market prices may be employed.

Two issues are particularly noteworthy about this legal amendment. First, the timing of the amendment strikes as remarkable. When the EU enacted Article 6(d)(ii) BASR in 2002, WTO AS law had not yet been interpreted by the Appellate Body to generally allow for the application of alternative benchmark methodologies in NME situations. Rather, the sole WTO role model at this time proved to be Section 15(b) CAP. Nevertheless, the Council regarded such provisions *"prudent [...] in cases where a market benchmark does not exist in the country concerned."*[32] This and the fact that the wordings of both provisions strongly resemble each other, makes it seem very probable that the EU relied on at that time genuine China-specific WTO law and transformed it into general EU AS law. Second, considering that Section 15(b) CAP did not limit the deviation from in-county prices to certain types of subsidies, it makes one wonder why the EU considered a restriction to only type (d)-subsidies necessary.

Today, in accordance with the WTO Appellate Body's reasoning in *US – Anti-Dumping and Countervailing Duties (China)*, the EU also applies alternative benchmark methodologies on loan subsidies although this is not reflected in the wording of Article 6(b) BASR.

3.2   Indications from EU Anti-Subsidy Investigation Practice Against China

Despite the open-termed legal framework and the large of amount of discretion which this bestowed upon the EU Commission as investigating authority, the use of alternative benchmark methodologies in EU investigation practice against China has already become rather predictable.

The EU only started leading AS investigations against China in the year 2010. Since then, the EU has launched ten cases altogether (11% of total investigations), which makes China the EU's number two AS target—after India, against which the EU has so far initiated 26 investigations (19%).[33]

Already the opening case of EU anti-subsidy investigations against China, *Coated Fine Paper (China)*,[34] set important standards for future case practice. In *Coated Fine Paper (China)*, the Commission identified three different types of subsidies to the papermaking industry: tax, tariff and grant programmes (Article 6(a)

---

[32] Regulation (EC) No. 1973/2002, OJ 2002 L 305/4, Recital 1.

[33] As of 31 December 2016, see http://trade.ec.europa.eu/doclib/docs/2006/december/tradoc_113191.12.2015.xls (last accessed 30 April 2018) and http://trade.ec.europa.eu/doclib/docs/2017/january/tradoc_155243.pdf (last accessed 30 April 2018).

[34] Council Implementing Regulation (EU) No. 452/2011 of 6 May 2011 imposing a definitive anti-subsidy duty on imports of coated fine paper originating in the People's Republic of China, OJ 2011 L 128/18.

BASR), preferential lending (Article 6(b) BASR) and undue provision of goods by the government in the form of land-use rights (LURs) (Article 6(d) BASR). Regarding the two latter types of subsidies, the Commission rejected the use of existing Chinese values and employed alternative benchmarks.

3.2.1 The Use of Alternative Benchmarks in Cases of Loan Subsidies (Article 6(b) BASR)

In its investigation into market conditions in the Chinese banking sector, the Commission first examined the influence of policy plans and guidelines, notably the 2007 Papermaking Plan, and concluded that the government of China exerted undue influence on the market through these instruments.[35] The Commission in particular rejected the argument that policy plans did not constitute formally binding legislation in China—in fact, "guideline" would be a more accurate translation from the Chinese than "plan".[36] Second, the investigation yielded that Chinese banks did not adjust the risk premium when acquiring loans of Chinese companies with foreign banks.[37] Third, the high amount of SOEs in the banking sector induced the Commission to conclude that the state majorly influenced the conditions on the lending market, e.g. via the People's Bank of China as principal setter of lending rates.[38] Thus, the Commission held that the lending market in China was distorted.

In selecting the alternative benchmark, the Commission adjusted Chinese interest rates "to reflect normal market risk."[39] For assessing the market risk that adhered to loans to Chinese companies, it referred to a Bloomberg rating and "deemed [it] appropriate"[40] to award to companies of the Chinese papermaking industry grade BB, which constituted the highest "non-investment grade" available.[41] Besides, the

---

[35] Council Implementing Regulation (EU) No. 452/2011 of 6 May 2011 imposing a definitive anti-subsidy duty on imports of coated fine paper originating in the People's Republic of China, OJ 2011 L 128/18, para. 97.

[36] Qian (2012), p. 962.

[37] Council Implementing Regulation (EU) No. 452/2011 of 6 May 2011 imposing a definitive anti-subsidy duty on imports of coated fine paper originating in the People's Republic of China, OJ 2011 L 128/18, para. 83.

[38] Council Implementing Regulation (EU) No. 452/2011 of 6 May 2011 imposing a definitive anti-subsidy duty on imports of coated fine paper originating in the People's Republic of China, OJ 2011 L 128/18, paras. 84 et seq.

[39] Council Implementing Regulation (EU) No. 452/2011 of 6 May 2011 imposing a definitive anti-subsidy duty on imports of coated fine paper originating in the People's Republic of China, OJ 2011 L 128/18, para. 98.

[40] Council Implementing Regulation (EU) No. 452/2011 of 6 May 2011 imposing a definitive anti-subsidy duty on imports of coated fine paper originating in the People's Republic of China, OJ 2011 L 128/18, para. 99.

[41] Council Implementing Regulation (EU) No. 452/2011 of 6 May 2011 imposing a definitive anti-subsidy duty on imports of coated fine paper originating in the People's Republic of China, OJ 2011 L 128/18, para. 99.

Commission added an "appropriate"[42] risk premium. Upon the objection of one producer that it had actually received a more favourable A1 rating from Moody's, the Commission argued that this rating had only been awarded due to the undue advantages from the subsidisation and rejected it as "fruit of the poisonous tree".[43]

3.2.2 The Use of Alternative Benchmarks in Cases of Undue Government Provision of Goods (Article 6(d) BASR)

In its scrutiny of the land law system in China, the Commission started from the Chinese legal framework. Therein, Article 2 of the Land Administration Law stated that all land was in the ownership of the state—which let the Commission conclude that "there appear to be no available private benchmarks at all in China".[44] Only land-use rights (LURs) could be obtained through public bidding, quotation or auction. Moreover, all transfers of LURs between private individuals depended on governmental approval.[45] As a result, the government monopolised the primary and predominantly influenced the secondary market for land. In addition, the huge Chinese price deficit in comparison to Taiwan, which the Commission later chose as appropriate third country for the selection of the alternative benchmark, "demonstrates that the amount paid for land-use rights by the cooperating exporters is well below the normal market rate."[46]

In the light of the heavy state character of the land market, a price adjustment was not deemed possible. Rather, after extensive analysis of nine different factors, the Commission concluded that Taiwan constituted the appropriate analogue country for the benefit calculation. Altogether, the Commission took into account the similar level of economic development and structure of Taiwan and the respective Chinese provinces, physical proximity, the high level of infrastructure on both sides, strong economic cross-border connections, population density, the similarity

---

[42] Council Implementing Regulation (EU) No. 452/2011 of 6 May 2011 imposing a definitive anti-subsidy duty on imports of coated fine paper originating in the People's Republic of China, OJ 2011 L 128/18, para. 99.

[43] Council Implementing Regulation (EU) No. 452/2011 of 6 May 2011 imposing a definitive anti-subsidy duty on imports of coated fine paper originating in the People's Republic of China, OJ 2011 L 128/18, para. 326; see also Vermulst and Gatta (2012), pp. 549 et seq.

[44] Council Implementing Regulation (EU) No. 452/2011 of 6 May 2011 imposing a definitive anti-subsidy duty on imports of coated fine paper originating in the People's Republic of China, OJ 2011 L 128/18, para. 260.

[45] Council Implementing Regulation (EU) No. 452/2011 of 6 May 2011 imposing a definitive anti-subsidy duty on imports of coated fine paper originating in the People's Republic of China, OJ 2011 L 128/18, para. 354.

[46] Council Implementing Regulation (EU) No. 452/2011 of 6 May 2011 imposing a definitive anti-subsidy duty on imports of coated fine paper originating in the People's Republic of China, OJ 2011 L 128/18, para. 251.

between type of land and transaction, common demographic, linguistic and cultural features, the fact that both Chinese provinces in question had been designated top manufacturing provinces and, finally, the similarity of the GDP real growth rates in Taiwan and the two Chinese provinces.[47] Upon the objection of one Chinese producer that India constituted an in fact more suitable analogue country, the Commission stressed that the comprehensiveness of its analysis withstood alternative reasonings which relied on a more limited range of factors.[48]

4 WTO Law Compatibility of the EU Approach on the Use of Alternative Benchmarks

In the investigations that followed, the Commission took similar paths and continued patterns of argumentation it had commenced in *Coated Fine Paper (China)*. It has also become an established practice to explicitly refer to reasonings and results of previous investigations.[49]

Thereby, the EU has managed to build a yet small but highly effective AS practice. Reasonings are supported by seemingly well-founded arguments and objections are countered by plausible explanations.

The EU approach in the use of alternative benchmarks in AS law is, however, not immune to criticism. Whereas the Commission's argumentation proves one potential deduction from the facts that have been established, there are numerous alternative views that are equally persuasive. Against the backdrop of the recent challenge by China of EU and U.S. calculation methodologies in front of the WTO judiciary,[50] the question now poses itself whether or not a like challenge regarding the alternative benchmark methodologies in EU AS law would find them still in line with WTO law—or in breach of it.

---

[47] Council Implementing Regulation (EU) No. 452/2011 of 6 May 2011 imposing a definitive anti-subsidy duty on imports of coated fine paper originating in the People's Republic of China, OJ 2011 L 128/18, para. 356.

[48] Council Implementing Regulation (EU) No. 452/2011 of 6 May 2011 imposing a definitive anti-subsidy duty on imports of coated fine paper originating in the People's Republic of China, OJ 2011 L 128/18, para. 361.

[49] See e.g. Commission Implementing Regulation (EU) No 470/2014 of 13 May 2014 imposing a definitive anti-dumping duty and collecting definitively the provisional duty imposed on imports of solar glass originating in the People's Republic of China, OJ 2014 L 142/23, paras. 71 et seq.

[50] World Trade Organization, *US – Measures Related to Price Comparison Methodologies*, Request for Consultations by China, WT/DS515/1, 15 December 2016 and the correspondent *EU – Measures Related to Price Comparison Methodologies,* Request for Consultations by China, WT/DS516/1, 15 December 2016.

4.1   The Applicable Overall WTO Anti-Subsidy Legal Framework for China

Before a potential violation of WTO law can, however, be examined, a very different obstacle needs to be overcome: tracing the applicable WTO AS legal framework for China on the use of alternative benchmark methodologies.[51] The continuing establishment of the general alternative benchmark regime in WTO law by the Appellate Body has upset the relationship between the two distinct legal regimes that had been provided for in Article 14 ASCM for market economy situations on the one side and in Section 15(b) CAP for NMES on the other side. But with both provisions featuring different legal prerequisites, unravelling the entangled relationship is essential for assessing the WTO law compatibility of investigations against China.

Unlike the general relationship between the protocols of accession and the rest of the WTO agreements, which currently still remains unanswered, the relationship between general and country-specific alternative benchmark regime in AS law had per se been regarded as having been explicitly provided for in the protocols of accession themselves. According to the chapeau of Section 15 CAP,[52] the ASCM was to apply "consistent with the following" special provisions. As long as no alternative benchmark regime existed in general WTO AS law, i.e. until the *US – Softwood Lumber IV* decision in the year 2004, this meant the application of the general provisions in market economy situations and of the country-specific rules in NME situations. After the introduction of the general regime, the exclusivity of the special regimes became uncertain. Besides the question whether the general alternative benchmark regime was applicable to countries with special regimes at all, several options of applicability emerged. Due to the imprecise and ambiguous prerequisites of both regimes, however, it was not possible to give a clear answer as to which option prevailed. The application of the general alternative benchmark regime on China by the Appellate Body in *US – Anti-Dumping and Countervailing Duties (China)* at least solved the applicability question of the new general regime, but did not lead to further clarification as regards the mutual interaction between both regimes.

Taking together the possible interpretations of the wording of Section 15 CAP and the Appellate Body's jurisprudence in *US – Softwood Lumber IV* and *US – Anti-Dumping and Countervailing Duties (China)*, broadly speaking, three different applicability options remain. First, the prerequisites of both Article 14 ASCM and Section 15(b) CAP could be applied jointly in a two-tier test. The determination of an alternative benchmark would thus only be justified if e.g. both "market distortion by government predominance" and "special difficulties" were proven to exist. Second, the prerequisites of both regimes could be applied in a "merged" way. Here,

---

[51] For a more detailed account, see Mueller (2016), pp. 872 et seq.
[52] The same problematic issue exists regarding Viet Nam, see World Trade Organization, Report of the Working Party on the Accession of Viet Nam, WT/ACC/VNM/48, 27 October 2006, para. 255.

prerequisites with a like understanding are summarised and examined as one single prerequisite. Third and last, both regimes could be applied consecutively. Section 15(b) CAP would thus be applicable only if the prerequisites of the general regime of Article 14 ASCM are not met.

As this situation will probably remain so for the foreseeable future due to the lack of case practice forming the regime's yet indefinite legal prerequisites, the following brief compatibility analysis will take all options duly into account.

4.2 Compatibility "As Such"

Scrutinising WTO law compatibility "as such" in the light of the applicable overall WTO legal AS framework for China, the provision of Article 6(d)(ii) BASR proves problematic. The Appellate Body held that the adjustment of existing domestic prices and costs had priority to disregarding domestic values altogether.[53] The wording of Section 15(b) CAP also explicitly states such an order of priority. This is, however, not adequately reflected in the EU provision. Whereas Recital 2 of Regulation 1973/2002 still contained the order, the final regulation skipped it.

The practicability exception could prove a remedy, but only if attaching priority to a merged understanding of the prerequisites of Article 14 ASCM and Section 15(b) CAP and only if the appropriateness to disregard domestic prices and costs in Article 6(d)(ii) BASR could be understood to adequately reflect the practicability of adjustment in Section 15(b) CAP. For the remainder of cases, although there is no violation of written WTO law but only per se legally non-binding case law,[54] it seems likely that if once called to decide, the Appellate Body will stand with its own precedent and hold EU law to be in violation of the WTO legal framework.

4.3 Compatibility "As Applied"

A contravention of the EU approach against China "as applied" is, however, not so obviously detectable. At first glance, the Commission's reasoning appears solid and well-founded. But some arguments lose their coerciveness upon deeper scrutiny.

When establishing market distortion, the Commission often considers the mere ability of a government to influence the conditions on the market as positive proof

---

[53] Appellate Body Report, *United States – Final Countervailing Duty Determination with Respect to Certain Softwood Lumber from Canada*, WT/DS257/AB/R, adopted 17 February 2004, DSR 2003:VI, para. 106.

[54] On the legal effect of WTO DSB decisions, see Articles 3.2 and 19.2 of the Understanding on Rules and Procedures governing the Settlement of Disputes (DSU) as well as Articles IX:2 and X of the WTO Agreement. On the evolution of the Appellate Body's role regarding WTO law and the process of "judicialisation", see Steinberg (2004), pp. 255 et seq.; and Ferejohn (2002), pp. 41 et seq.

of distortion. If, for instance, the government acts as major shareholder and owns more than two-thirds of the banks, the Commission considers this sufficient to conclude on a market distortion and does consequently not examine whether or not the government does indeed uses its predominant position to distort competitive equivalence.[55]

The Appellate Body, however, has constantly stressed that the mere fact that a contribution originated from the government was not by itself sufficient to prove a distortive impact on the market.[56] The EU's reasoning in this regard does will hence likely be found in violation of WTO law.

Moreover, the EU has, in particular in investigations connected to the land market, repeatedly resorted to the difference of the market situations between China and Taiwan (which it later often chose as alternative third country) to make a positive finding of market distortion.[57] But for several reasons, the reference to Taiwan at this juncture seems out of place. An alternative benchmark may only be chosen after sufficient evidence for market distortion on the domestic market of a country has been gathered. In its argumentation, the Commission compared current conditions in China with the conditions in the (potential) third-country benchmark and rendered an affirmative finding of distortion of Chinese market conditions. But this means taking B to establish A—and consequently constitutes circular reasoning. That the surrogate price demonstrates the lack of market conditions in the country investigated is evident, considering the diligent examination that is required to establish it. Hence, this part of the Commission's reasoning is not a valid argument.

Furthermore, in selecting the alternative benchmark in cases of loan subsidies, the Commission frequently relied on Bloomberg ratings.[58] Whereas the choice does per se not appear unreasonable, it lacks a deeper convincing justification. Upon the objection of one Chinese producer, which claimed it had received a more favourable

---

[55] Council Implementing Regulation (EU) No 215/2013 of 11 March 2013 imposing a countervailing duty on imports of certain organic coated steel products originating in the People's Republic of China, OJ 2013 L 73/16, paras. 159 et seq.

[56] Appellate Body Report, *United States – Definitive Anti-Dumping and Countervailing Duties on Certain Products from China*, WT/DS379/AB/R, adopted 25 March 2011, DSR 2010:III, para. 443.

[57] See e.g. Council Implementing Regulation (EU) No 452/2011 of 6 May 2011 imposing a definitive anti-subsidy duty on imports of coated fine paper originating in the People's Republic of China, OJ 2011 L 128/18, para. 261; Council Implementing Regulation (EU) No 1239/2013 of 2 December 2013 imposing a definitive countervailing duty on imports of crystalline silicon photovoltaic modules and key components (i.e. cells) originating in or consigned from the People's Republic of China, OJ 2013 L 325/66, para. 371 et seq.; Commission Implementing Regulation (EU) No 1379/2014 of 16 December 2014 imposing a definitive countervailing duty on imports of certain filament glass fibre products originating in the People's Republic of China and amending Council Implementing Regulation (EU) No 248/2011 imposing a definitive anti-dumping duty on imports of certain continuous filament glass fibre products originating in the People's Republic of China, OJ 2014 L 367/22, para. 200.

[58] Council Implementing Regulation (EU) No 452/2011 of 6 May 2011 imposing a definitive anti-subsidy duty on imports of coated fine paper originating in the People's Republic of China, OJ 2011 L 128/18, para. 99.

rating from Moody's,[59] the Commission briskly set aside the objection by declaring the Moody rating being based on unfair governmental advantages and consequently rejected its employment as "fruit of the poisonous tree".[60] Arguably, however, the Bloomberg BB rating the Commission relied on as highest non-investment grade and "appropriate"[61] benchmark could also not properly reflect actual market conditions in China, which might be even worse due to "fruits of the poisonous tree" granted to other Chinese companies.

Selecting an alternative benchmark for the distorted land market in China, the Commission performed a nine-factor-analysis and concluded on Taiwan as appropriate benchmark. Although the number of factors promises a comprehensive analysis and reliable result, not all the factors convince. Physical proximity between China and Taiwan, for instance, bears no significance on its own. Rather, what aids in finding a comparable benchmark are the type of land and transaction. Also, strong common demographic, linguistic and cultural features do not permit a deduction regarding economic comparability. Moreover, the singularity of the Chinese culture would then almost without exception demand the application of Taiwanese benchmarks.

Although not convincing throughout, the reasoning of the Commission is not evidently inconsistent or even illegal. Whether a challenge of the extremely EU-favourable approach in front of the WTO judiciary will be successful is hard to predict. In the end, regarding the problematic issues that have been demonstrated, WTO law consistency will not depend so much on the final result but rather on the Commission's process of reasoning[62]—and on how much significance the Appellate Body will attach to the single elements in relation to the argumentation in its entirety.

5   WTO Law Compatibility of the Adoption of Country-Specific Accession Commitments in Anti-Subsidy Law

The EU is not the only jurisdiction with an AS case practice that draws heavily from the great amount of discretion investigating authority enjoy at the expense of countries investigated. Both Canada, the first user of AS law against a NME country—China—in 2004 and the U.S., the presently largest user of the AS instrument against

---

[59] Council Implementing Regulation (EU) No 452/2011 of 6 May 2011 imposing a definitive anti-subsidy duty on imports of coated fine paper originating in the People's Republic of China, OJ 2011 L 128/18, para. 326.

[60] Council Implementing Regulation (EU) No 452/2011 of 6 May 2011 imposing a definitive anti-subsidy duty on imports of coated fine paper originating in the People's Republic of China, OJ 2011 L 128/18, para. 326.

[61] Council Implementing Regulation (EU) No 452/2011 of 6 May 2011 imposing a definitive anti-subsidy duty on imports of coated fine paper originating in the People's Republic of China, OJ 2011 L 128/18, para. 99.

[62] Consentient Vermulst and Gatta (2012), p. 547.

NME countries, have developed similar regimes. Other major economies, like Australia and Japan, have followed.

Although their present AS practices puts these countries in comfortable positions, whether or not the recent evolution of the alternative benchmark regime for NME countries in WTO AS law still finds itself in accordance with the WTO legal framework is doubtful. Two issues in particular raise concerns. First, it is not sure whether WTO AS law actually permits an alternative benchmark regime for NME situations. This could contravene e.g. Articles 14, 19.3 and 19.4 ASCM and VI:3 GATT. Second, it is unclear whether the adoption of country-specific rules upon accession is allowed by WTO law. This refers to the legality of the Chinese and the Vietnamese special regimes—which shall now be subjected to closer scrutiny.

That countries accept specific commitments upon accession to the WTO is per se not unprecedented. Market access commitments, like tariff schedules, have always been tailored to the economic development status of the respective accession candidate.[63] Rule-based commitments have, however, previously amounted to merely adopting the existing uniform WTO law framework. Contrary to the legal patchwork of the *"GATT à la carte"*, WTO membership had been designed as a "single package of rights and obligations".[64,65] The country-specific AS provisions protrude this single package and create additional individual obligations of acceding countries (WTO-plus commitments) as well as additional rights of incumbent WTO members (WTO-minus commitments).[66]

5.1 Compatibility with Article XII WTO Agreement

Besides a potential violation of the WTO founding principle of non-discrimination (Article I:1 GATT), which has been brushed aside by the now notorious "entry fee theory" of the panel in *China – Raw Materials*,[67] validly introducing country-specific rules commitments upon accession has always been considered firmly grounded in Article XII WTO Agreement. As only provision regulating the accession procedure,[68] it stipulates that any state or separate customs union may accede

---

[63] Grynberg et al. (2002), p. 5; Qin (2003), p. 485.

[64] Appellate Body Reports, *China – Measures Related to the Exportation of Rare Earths, Tungsten, and Molybdenum,* WT/DS431/AB/R, WT/DS432/AB/R, WT/DS433/AB/R, adopted 29 August 2014, DSR 2014:III-V-VI, para. 5.62.

[65] Jackson (1997), p. 47.

[66] Qin (2003), pp. 488 and 490.

[67] Panel Reports, *China – Measures Related to the Exportation of Various Raw Materials,* WT/DS394/R, WT/DS395/R, WT/DS398/R, 22 February 2012, para. 7.112. For heavy criticism, see only Qin (2015), pp. 440 et seq.

[68] Cattaneo O and Primo Braga CA, Everything You Always Wanted to Know about WTO Accession (But Were Afraid to Ask). World Bank, Policy Research Working Paper 5116, November 2009, http://documents.worldbank.org/curated/en/440471468331183983/pdf/WPS5116.pdf   (last accessed 14 March 2018), pp. 12 et seq.; Nguyen (2008), pp. 246 et seq.; Grynberg et al. (2002), p. 4.

to the WTO Agreement "on terms to be agreed" between it and the WTO (Article XII:1 WTO Agreement). Lacking details, it confers to the negotiating parties a great amount of discretion as regards the kind of accession commitments. Thus, Article XII WTO Agreement has been named the "loophole in the system",[69] which legalised the adoption of country-specific rules commitments.

But taking a closer look at the provision, especially its context, its rationale and its historic genesis,[70] yields a different conclusion.

According to Article XI WTO Agreement, which regulates the prerequisites for original membership in the WTO, the former GATT members had to fulfil two conditions for WTO membership: they had to accept the uniform rules of conduct of the WTO and to agree on schedules of tariff and non-tariff commitments that were to be annexed to the GATT and the GATS. There are no indications that at the time of the conclusion of the Marrakesh Agreement, the original members intended a distinction between original and acceded WTO members—to the contrary, the Ministerial Decision on the Acceptance of and Accession to the Agreement Establishing the World Trade Organization[71] expressly stated coequality between incumbent and acceded members.[72]

Moreover, the WTO lacks the procedural framework for the unlimited integration of country-specific rules. According to Article II GATT and Article XX GATS, the schedules of tariff and non-tariff commitments of the members are to be integrated into the respective agreements as annexes and constitute integral parts of these agreements (Article II:7 GATT and Article XX:3 GATS). This confers to the schedules a defined legal rank in the WTO legal hierarchy. The WTO agreements only leave room for temporary country-specific deviations from the general framework to ease the integration of the acceding countries.[73] They do not contain any rules for the integration of new permanent country-specific commitments.[74] Rather, it is the accession protocols themselves, like the CAP in Section 1.2, that state that they *"shall be an integral part of the WTO Agreement."* This method of integration

---

[69] Qin (2015), p. 389.

[70] According to Articles 31 and 32 of the Vienna Convention on the Law of Treaties (VCLT), wording, context and rationale of a provision shall priorly be consulted for the purpose of interpreting a provision. As supplementary means, the preparatory work of the treaty and the circumstances of its conclusion may also be considered.

[71] World Trade Organization, Ministerial Decision, Agreement Establishing the WTO: acceptance of and accession to the agreement, 15 April 1994.

[72] Charnovitz S, Mapping the law of WTO accession. GWU Law School Public Law Research Paper No. 237, https://scholarship.law.gwu.edu/cgi/viewcontent.cgi?article=1430&context=faculty_publications (last accessed 30 April 2018), pp. 55 et seq.; Qin JY, Mind the gap. Navigating between the WTO Agreement and its accession protocols. Wayne State University Law School Legal Studies Research Paper Series No. 2016-05, 2 February 2016, https://papers.ssrn.com/sol3/papers.cfm?abstract_id=2727031 (last accessed 30 April 2018), p. 12.

[73] E.g. Articles 27 and 29 ASCM; Qin JY, Mind the gap. Navigating between the WTO Agreement and its accession protocols. Wayne State University Law School Legal Studies Research Paper Series No. 2016-05, 2 February 2016, https://papers.ssrn.com/sol3/papers.cfm?abstract_id=2727031 (last accessed 30 April 2018), p. 12.

[74] Qin (2015), pp. 400 et seq.

is, however, highly dubious. Usually, in international law, it is the treaty itself that provides for an integration procedure, not the accession agreement.[75] Moreover, making accession protocols an "integral part of the WTO Agreement" does not attach to their provisions any definite legal rank, without which their status in the WTO legal hemisphere ultimately remains unclear.

The rationale behind accession agreements also casts doubts on WTO law legality of the alternative benchmark regimes. Accession agreements constitute amendments of the original treaty in that they extend its application to the candidate country.[76] Sometimes, accession situations permit a wider scope of amendment. Certain jurisdictions explicitly allow for necessary formal treaty amendments that closely relate to the accession process. Article 49 TEU, which allows for "*adjustments to the Treaties on which the Union is founded, which such admission entails*" constitutes an example here. Although the scope of adjustment is subject to some discussion, it is majorly deemed to exclude substantive alterations, which are still to be performed under the formal treaty amendment procedure.[77] Anyway, as regards accession to the WTO, such an extensive interpretation is out of the question. Article XII WTO Agreement does not even include any additional rule-making competences. Furthermore, the WTO possesses a rigorous regime on treaty amendments in Article X WTO Agreement, which makes apparent that the negotiating parties of the Uruguay Round envisioned that treaty amendments other than the accession itself were to fall under Article X and not Article XII WTO Agreement.[78] Thus, the principle pacta sunt servanda applies[79]—which sets the adoption of a permanent alternative benchmark regime in AS law as treaty amendment outside the WTO's legal boundaries.

These findings of non-compatibility are supported by a look into the GATT era. At first glance, GATT history of country-specific rule-making upon accession seems to indicate that rules commitments upon accession which derogate from the general WTO legal framework were in fact accepted. When starting in 1967, Poland, Romania and Hungary subsequently entered the WTO, they did so only after agreeing on certain country-specific NMES provisions.[80] The rules included a special safeguards provision and confirmed the use of alternative benchmark methodologies for the calculation of anti-dumping duties. They were deemed necessary because all three countries constituted state economies, so that their economic systems sometimes rendered standard GATT rules inapplicable.

As Article XXXIII GATT 1947 corresponds to Article XII WTO Agreement, it could be concluded that country-specific rules commitments are thus also allowed

---

[75] E.g. the aforementioned Articles II:7 GATT and XX:3 GATS.

[76] Ehlermann and Ehring (2005a), p. 57.

[77] De Witte (2012), p. 125; Tatham (2009), p. 260.

[78] Charnovitz S, Mapping the law of WTO accession. GWU Law School Public Law Research Paper No. 237, https://scholarship.law.gwu.edu/cgi/viewcontent.cgi?article=1430&context=faculty_publications (last accessed 30 April 2018), p. 59.

[79] Pauwelyn (2003), p. 38.

[80] Polouektov (2002), pp. 9 et seq; Qin (2015), pp. 383 et seq.

under the WTO. But this view does not sufficiently consider the fundamental difference between the GATT and the WTO legal regime. Whereas the GATT had merely
been rule-oriented, the WTO has been created as a rule-based system. WTO law
thus inheres a much stronger degree of legal bindingness.[81] In consequence, accession agreements outside the scope of Article XXXIII GATT 1947 were possible
under the GATT, but are no longer admitted under the WTO Agreement. Moreover,
the commitments of the three former Soviet countries were much more moderate
than the commitments China agreed on.[82] Even if the commitments had been
adopted legally under Article XXXIII GATT 1947, this bears no significance with
regard to WTO law compliance of the country-specific alternative benchmark
regimes in the modern accession protocols. Unless justified, country-specific rule-
making upon accession thus contravenes Article XII:1 WTO Agreement.

5.2 Justifying the Violation of Article XII WTO Agreement?

WTO law, in its anti-subsidy law and its general framework, as well as general
international law permit limited exceptions from existing binding treaty
obligations.

In WTO law, Articles 27 and 29 ASCM allow developing countries the use of
certain export subsidies to aid their transformation into a market economy. The
provisions offer a way to legally deviate from the general rule-based regime and
thus seem to constitute solid bases for the alternative benchmark regimes in AS
law.[83] Both Articles have, however, expired by today.[84]

The accession commitments could also constitute reservations on part of the
acceding country. According to Article 2(1)(d) VCLT, the term reservation is understood as *"a unilateral statement, however phrased or named, made by a State, when
signing, ratifying, accepting, approving or acceding to a treaty, whereby it purports
to exclude or to modify the legal effect of certain provisions of the treaty in their
application to that State."* Although under the GATT, some of the obligations acceding members took on were indeed regarded as reservations,[85] WTO law strictly prohibits reservations to the WTO Agreement itself and only allows them with regard
to the annexed agreements as far as these agreements provide for this possibility
(Article XVI:5 WTO Agreement). No such exceptions exist for AS law.

The country-specific alternative benchmark regimes are furthermore not justified
as waivers. Principally, Article IX:3 WTO Agreement allows the Ministerial
Conference to waive obligations of the WTO Agreement or the multilateral

---

[81] Hilf (2001), p. 114.

[82] Qin (2015), pp. 383 et seq.

[83] Appellate Body Report, *Brazil – Export Financing Programme for Aircraft*, WT/DS46/AB/R,
adopted 20 August 1999, DSR 1999:I, para. 6.47, fn. 49.

[84] See Article 31 ASCM.

[85] Qin (2015), p. 401.

agreements upon request of a member if three quarters of the members agree. Such waivers are, however, mandatorily temporary (Article IX:4 WTO Agreement)— whereas the alternative benchmark regimes are permanent.

The accession commitments do also not meet the necessary requirements for a formal treaty amendment. Unlike general international law, WTO law comprises a rigorous regime on amendments. According to Article X:1 WTO Agreement, an amendment to the WTO Agreement or one of the multilateral agreements in Annex 1 shall preferentially be conducted through unanimous consent of the Ministerial Conference and then be accepted by all members, which usually involves ratification. If unanimity is not reached, a two-thirds majority in the Ministerial Conference shall suffice to pass the proposal on to the members for acceptance. The amendment of certain provisions, like Article I:1 GATT, requires acceptance by all members (Article XVI:2 WTO Agreement). Amendments of the WTO Agreement and the multilateral agreements in Annexes 1 A and C, which alter rights and obligations of the members, are binding upon a majority of two-thirds of the members, but only on those members which have actually accepted the respective amendments (Article XVI:3 WTO Agreement). Then, each following accepting member shall be bound immediately upon consent. If rights and obligations are not changed, the two-third majority of the members instantly binds all members (Article XVI:4 WTO Agreement).

The main setback in that the accession commitments could be regarded as amendments in the sense of Article X WTO Agreement is the lack of procedural equivalence of amendment and accession procedure.[86] With Article XII:2 WTO Agreement permitting the approval of accession terms by the Ministerial Conference upon a two-third majority of all WTO members, this does not suffice to match the respective majority requirements of Article X WTO Agreement because the accession commitments affect rights and obligations of the members. In practice, the issue will probably not pose much of an obstacle because accession decisions are mostly adopted unanimously.[87] But the formal legal prerequisites differ precludes by itself the coequality of proceedings.[88] In addition, accession protocols are not necessarily approved by the Ministerial Conference but by the General Council.[89] In consequence, not all WTO members decide on the accession. Moreover, only the parliament of the acceding member is required to ratify the accession package.[90]

---

[86] Charnovitz S, Mapping the law of WTO accession. GWU Law School Public Law Research Paper No. 237, https://scholarship.law.gwu.edu/cgi/viewcontent.cgi?article=1430&context=faculty_publications (last accessed 30 April 2018), p. 47.

[87] In the case of China, for instance, the accession terms were approved unanimously by all of the then 142 WTO members, see World Trade Organization, WTO Ministerial Conference approves China's accession, 10 November 2001, https://www.wto.org/english/news_e/pres01_e/pr252_e.htm (last accessed 30 April 2018).

[88] Charnovitz S, Mapping the law of WTO accession. GWU Law School Public Law Research Paper No. 237, https://scholarship.law.gwu.edu/cgi/viewcontent.cgi?article=1430&context=faculty_publications (last accessed 30 April 2018), p. 59.

[89] See https://www.wto.org/english/thewto_e/acc_e/acces_e.htm (last accessed 30 April 2018).

[90] See https://www.wto.org/english/thewto_e/acc_e/acces_e.htm (last accessed 30 April 2018).

The country-specific alternative benchmark regimes are thus not justified under Article X WTO Agreement.

In consequence, this also does not justify the alternative benchmark regimes as authoritative interpretations. Authoritative interpretations are a special feature of WTO law that derive legally-binding obligations from already existent legal rules.[91] But as any authoritative interpretation must not "undermine the amendment provisions" of Article X WTO Agreement, a lack of procedural equivalence again prevents compliance.

With WTO law not providing for a justification, the view wanders to general international law. With subsequent agreement and subsequent practice, two promising options seem to present themselves.

General international law provides several possibilities for the subsequent agreement of a treaty. Article 59 VCLT, for instance, regulates the implicit termination or suspension of a treaty through the conclusion of a subsequent treaty. Article 41 VCLT deals with "partial" or "relative" treaty modification by an agreement only consented to by some of the original contracting parties.[92]

Principally, the subsequent agreement must be concluded between the parties that also formed part of the original treaty. As regards accession commitments, this proves problematic. Accession protocols formally constitute bilateral agreements between the WTO itself and the acceding member, so that in fact neither party is also party of the original agreement that is modified by the accession protocol, i.e. the WTO Agreement.[93]

This obstacle is increasingly commonly set aside by piercing the veil of the international organisation and referring to the members behind it as acting on its behalf.[94] Discussing the relationship between the Doha Ministerial Declaration and the TBT Agreement, the Appellate Body also adopted this approach and held that the Declaration issued by the Ministerial Conference constituted a subsequent agreement to the TBT Agreement in the sense of Article 31(3)(a) VCLT, which had in fact been concluded by the members.[95] Strictly speaking, however, the WTO members which act in their capacity as WTO organs cannot simply be equated with the WTO acting itself.[96] Furthermore, at the time of conclusion of the agreement, the acceding country is yet neither party of the WTO Agreement nor member of the WTO and hence in no way part of the original treaty.

In contrast, subsequent practice offers a more flexible approach and does not only consider treaty amendments between the original members, but also includes

---

[91] Luo (2010), p. 99; Ehlermann and Ehring (2005b), p. 811.

[92] Pauwelyn (2003), pp. 315 et seq. For a more detailed discussion on the designation of accession protocols as amendments, see Qin (2015), pp. 403 et seq.; Tyagi (2012), pp. 420 et seq.

[93] Pauwelyn (2003), pp. 44 et seq.; Qin (2015), p. 405.

[94] Qin (2015), p. 406.

[95] Appellate Body Report, *United States – Measures Affecting the Production and Sale of Clove Cigarettes*, WT/DS406/AB/R, adopted 24 April 2012, DSR 2012:I, para. 267; Pauwelyn (2003), p. 47.

[96] Pauwelyn (2003), p. 45.

changes of practice of the international organisation.[97] Subsequent practice can be employed to either establish the original understanding of a treaty provision, i.e. to interpret it, or to change its previous meaning, i.e. to modify it.[98] Subsequent practice was commonly referred to during the GATT era: the whole apparatus of GATT institutions and dispute settlement procedure ultimately goes back hereto.[99]

With respect to the WTO, the Appellate Body has also recognised this practice, but has for a long time permitted it only for the interpretation, not for the modification of a WTO agreement.[100] Thereby, the tribunal stayed in line with Article IX:2 WTO Agreement, from which derives that every treaty modification outside the formal amendment procedure is illegal because it diminishes the competence of the members to decide on the adoption of new substantive rules. In suit of the ICJ,[101] the WTO judiciary has by now, however, presumably also embraced a wider interpretation of subsequent practice. The Panel in *China – Raw Materials*, for instance, adopted the so-called "entry fee theory", according to which candidate countries have to accept all possible kinds of accession commitments as "price" for joining the WTO.[102] The Panel in *China – Publications and Audiovisual Products* explicitly recognised that China took on commitments upon accession that are stricter than the commitments of other members.[103] The tribunals had no qualms in accepting the country-specific rules as part of an newly evolving accession practice.[104]

---

[97] Qin (2015), p. 411; Arato (2013), p. 307.

[98] Murphy (2013), pp. 83 et seq.; Arato (2013), pp. 307 et seq.

[99] Qin JY (2016) Mind the gap. Navigating between the WTO Agreement and its accession protocols. Wayne State University Law School Legal Studies Research Paper Series No. 2016-05, 2 February 2016, https://papers.ssrn.com/sol3/papers.cfm?abstract_id=2727031 (last accessed 30 April 2018), pp. 14 et seq.; Qin (2015), pp. 407 et seq.

[100] Appellate Body Report, *European Communities – Customs Classification of Frozen Boneless Chicken Cuts*, WT/DS269/AB/R, WT/DS286/AB/R, adopted 27 September 2005, DSR 2005:V, para. 259; Arato (2013), p. 315; Murphy (2013), p. 85.

[101] The ICJ has recognised subsequent practice of the UN as organisation itself as sufficient for a modification of the UN Charter, which had been concluded by its members. See ICJ cases Namibia, Legal Consequences for States of the Continued Presence of South Africa in Namibia (South West Africa) notwithstanding Security Council Resolution 276 (1970), Advisory Opinion, ICJ Reports 1971, pp. 16 et seq. and Wall, Legal Consequences of the Construction of a Wall in the Occupied Palestinian Territory, Advisory Opinion, ICJ Reports 2004, pp. 136 et seq., as well as Appellate Body Report, *India – Patent Protection for Pharmaceutical and Agricultural Chemical Products*, WT/DS50/AB/R, adopted 16 January 1998, DSR 1997:V, paras. 45 et seq.; Qin (2015), pp. 408 et seq.

[102] Panel Reports, *China – Measures Related to the Exportation of Various Raw Materials*, WT/DS394/R / WT/DS395/R, WT/DS398/R, adopted 22 February 2012, para. 7.112; Qin (2015), pp. 439 et seq.

[103] Panel Report, *China – Measures Affecting Trading Rights and Distribution Services for Certain Publications and Audiovisual Entertainment Products*, WT/DS363/R, adopted 19 January 2010, para. VII.281.

[104] See Tyagi (2012), p. 415.

But also subsequent practice cannot justify the introduction of the country-specific alternative benchmark regimes.[105]

The adoption of the country-specific accession commitments does not meet the necessary prerequisites of subsequent practice. According to the Appellate Body, "*in order for 'practice' within the meaning of Article 31(3)(b) [VCLT] to be established: (i) there must be a common, consistent, discernible pattern of acts or pronouncements; and (ii) those acts or pronouncements must imply agreement on the interpretation of the relevant provision.*"[106] In this process, "*not each and every party must have engaged in a particular practice for it to qualify as a 'common' and 'concordant' practice. Nevertheless, practice by some, but not all parties is obviously not of the same order as practice by only one, or very few parties.*"[107] For the introduction of the alternative benchmark regimes, the WTO members would have needed to agree to modify the WTO Agreement in that amendments upon accession do not have to follow the formal procedure of Article X WTO Agreement. But the accession negotiations lack such a common understanding. Although e.g. China's accession was approved by consent of all members without exception,[108] this does not constitute the result of a common process of reasoning in the awareness of modifying the formal WTO amendment procedure. Whereas all the members voted in favour of China's accession, not all of the members took part in the long accession negotiations and actively designed the new country-specific provisions. In fact, the Working Party on the Accession of China counted 58 members of a total of then 119 WTO members upon its establishment in 1996 (49%).[109] This number amounted to 78 of then 142 members shortly before the accession process was finalised in 2001 (55%).[110] Thus, the integration of the alternative benchmark regime in AS law was initiated and carried through by only half of the WTO's members, which by all standards is not enough for the positive assumption of "a common [...] pattern"[111] for a substantial treaty modification.

---

[105] Dissenting Qin JY (2016) Mind the gap. Navigating between the WTO Agreement and its accession protocols. Wayne State University Law School Legal Studies Research Paper Series No. 2016-05, 2 February 2016, https://papers.ssrn.com/sol3/papers.cfm?abstract_id=2727031 (last accessed 30 April 2018), pp. 14 et seq.; and Qin (2015), pp. 407 et seq.

[106] Appellate Body Report, *United States – Measures Affecting the Cross-Border Supply of Gambling and Betting Services,* WT/DS285/AB/R, adopted 20 April 2005, DSR 2005:V, para. 192.

[107] Appellate Body Report, *European Communities – Customs Classification of Frozen Boneless Chicken Cuts,* WT/DS269/AB/R, WT/DS286/AB/R, adopted 27 September 2005, DSR 2005:V, para. 259.

[108] See World Trade Organization, WTO Ministerial Conference approves China's accession, 10 November 2001, https://www.wto.org/english/news_e/pres01_e/pr252_e.htm (last accessed 30 April 2018).

[109] World Trade Organization, Report of the Working Party on the Accession of China, WT/ACC/CHN/2, 2 April 1996.

[110] World Trade Organization, Report of the Working Party on the Accession of Chin, WT/ACC/CHN/2/Rev.11, 7 June 2001 and Corr.1, 22 June 2001.

[111] Appellate Body Report, *United States – Measures Affecting the Cross-Border Supply of Gambling and Betting Services,* WT/DS285/AB/R, 20 April 2005, DSR 2005:V, para. 192.

Conclusively, the attested violation of Article XII WTO Agreement cannot be justified by WTO law or general international law—so that the adoption of the country-specific alternative benchmark regimes in WTO AS law is illegal.

6 The Future of Alternative Benchmark Methodologies in Anti-Subsidy Law: The Missing Reform

The previous analysis has highlighted several aspects that clearly demonstrate that a reform of current AS law is unavoidable. The country-specific alternative benchmark regimes laid down in WTO accession protocols have been found to violate WTO law. They should therefore be abolished. Moreover, the present design of the generally applicable alternative benchmark regime in WTO AS law is also in dire need of improvement. Unclear legal prerequisites and regulatory lacunae have resulted in AS proceedings where national investigating authorities enjoy an enormous amount of discretion—which is then not subject to effective judicial control and hence easily misused. If these developments are allowed to continue, they will ultimately endanger the credibility of the WTO and as such its status as major organisation in international trade.[112] Action is hence recommended rather sooner than later.

At present, proposals for AS reform exist on both WTO and EU level.

6.1 The Doha Development Agenda

The current negotiations on reforming the WTO agreements, the Doha Development Agenda or Doha Round, started in November 2001.[113] AS law is expressly included in the agenda.[114]

The latest draft consolidated chair text of the ASCM dates from 2008 and comprises reform proposals for the benefit calculation in AS investigations.[115] Much already presents itself as familiar from current investigation practice and WTO Appellate Body jurisprudence. The 2008 draft proposals majorly address three

---

[112] Bronckers (1999), p. 555; Elsig (2007), p. 75; Qin JY, Judicial authority in WTO law: A commentary on the Appellate Body's decision in China – Rare Earths. Wayne State University Law School Legal Studies Research Paper Series No. 2014-11, 6 November 2014, https://papers.ssrn.com/sol3/papers.cfm?abstract_id=2529200 (last accessed 30 April 2018), pp. 12 et seq.

[113] World Trade Organization, Doha Ministerial Declaration, WT/MIN(01)/DEC/1, 20 November 2001.

[114] World Trade Organization, Doha Ministerial Declaration, WT/MIN(01)/DEC/1, 20 November 2001, para. 28.

[115] New Draft Consolidated Chair Texts of the AD and SCM Agreements, TN/RL/W/236, 19 December 2008, pp. 37, 53 et seq.

aspects. They introduce a definition of the term "benefit" in Article 1.1(b) ASCM, add long-term loss-incurring financing as new type of subsidy and stipulate an explicit alternative benchmark regime for NMES in Article 14(d) ASCM for cases of regulated prices.[116] In such situations, draft Article 14.1(d) ASCM allows for the use of either the export price in the country of provision or any market-determined out-of-country price as benchmarks for the benefit calculation.

Unfortunately, draft Article 14.1(d) ASCM falls short in addressing the legal changes that are truly needed. Apart from unclear legal prerequisites, after the Appellate Body has extended the alternative benchmark regime in NMES also to Article 14.1(b) ASCM in *US – Anti-Dumping and Countervailing Duties (China)*, draft Article 14.1 ASCM is unnecessarily limiting. This is likely to cause applicability problems in the future—which might once more induce the Appellate Body to extend the scope of the codified alternative benchmark regime and re-establish the present situation. Furthermore, the range of permitted alternative benchmark methodologies surprises. Constructed prices, which have been included in the alternative benchmark methodologies of both anti-subsidy and anti-dumping law from the very beginning, are no longer listed. Being a comparatively transparent and well documentable concept, its removal lacks a convincing reason. Making matters worse, the draft proposal promotes the use of out-of-country benchmarks, which have so far served as an open door for arbitrary treatment in the imposition of CVDs. With the reform proposal lacking restrictions or guidelines, the arbitrary potential of the present regime is likely to be preserved beyond the Doha Round. Moreover, the recommended abolition of the country-specific alternative benchmark regimes is no subject in the Doha Round at all.

Until today, however, the "big round" has not been making any significant progress.[117] Partial successes in the areas of trade facilitation, agriculture and the economic advancement of developing countries were achieved by the adoption of the Bali Package of 2013[118] and the subsequent Nairobi Package of 2015.[119] In the area of AS law, the last significant development in amending the general ASCM framework dates back to the year 2008. The 2011 Communication by the Chairman of the Negotiating Group on Rules acknowledged that since then, "there have been no significant signs of convergence."[120] After the "early harvest of some low hanging fruits"[121] in the Bali and Nairobi Declarations, the array of dissenting opinions

---

[116] New Draft Consolidated Chair Texts of the AD and SCM Agreements, TN/RL/W/236, 19 December 2008, p. 54.

[117] Coppens (2014), p. 37.

[118] World Trade Organization, Bali Ministerial Declaration, WT/MIN(13)/DEC, 11 December 2013.

[119] World Trade Organization, Nairobi Ministerial Declaration, WT/MIN(15)/DEC, 21 December 2015.

[120] World Trade Organization, Communication from the Chairman of the Negotiating Group on Rules, TN/RL/W/254, 21 April 2011, p. 1.

[121] Coppens (2014), p. 35.

that remains makes a timely, if any, conclusion of the Doha Round highly unlikely.[122]

6.2 Regulation (EU) 2017/2321

AS reform has also only recently been on the EU's agenda. On 9 November 2016, the Commission issued a proposal for reforming the EU trade defence instruments.[123] On 12 December 2017, Council and Parliament adopted Regulation (EU) 2017/2321.[124] Whereas the greater part of the regulation concentrates on AD reform, a minor AS reform is also included. Article 2 of the Regulation (EU) 2017/2321 addresses the situation that the actual magnitude of subsidisation is only discovered in the course of the investigation or even only after the investigation has been terminated. To be able to nevertheless counter the entire amount of unfair subsidisation through respective CVDs and not only the part which has been covered by the Notice of Initiation, the enhanced Article 10(7) BASR allows for additional consultations between the Commission and the country of origin or export concerned, after which the lately discovered amount may be included in the on-going investigation.

The reform of December 2017 proves an important step in enhancing the impact of the AS instrument. It is, however, not sufficient.

With the EU not having explicitly adopted country-specific alternative benchmark regimes in AS law—unlike in AD law—there is no need to reform in this respect. EU AS law does, however, suffer from the same substantive indeterminateness as its WTO law role model. Alas, the recent reform does not contain any measures for endowing the process of reasoning in an AS investigation with more transparency and legal security. Necessary additional guidelines for the exercise of discretion of the Commission as investigating authority are still lacking. Whereas Regulation (EU) 2017/2321 elaborately introduces a novel and comparatively detailed AD concept to counter potential WTO illegality of its current AD law after the expiry of the China-specific WTO dumping law in December 2016, the scope of the AS reform lastly disappoints.

---

[122] Consentient, Coppens (2014), p. 37.

[123] European Commission, Proposal for a Regulation of the European Parliament and of the Council amending Regulation (EU) 2016/1036 on protection against dumped imports from countries not members of the European Union and Regulation (EU) 2016/1037 on protection against subsidised imports from countries not members of the European Union, 9 November 2016, COM(2016) 721 final, http://eur-lex.europa.eu/legal-content/EN/TXT/?uri=COM:2016:0721:FIN (last accessed 30 April 2018).

[124] Regulation (EU) 2017/2321 of the European Parliament and of the Council of 12 December 2017 amending Regulation (EU) 2016/1036 on protection against dumped imports from countries not members of the European Union and Regulation (EU) 2016/1037 on protection against subsidised imports from countries not members of the European Union, http://eur-lex.europa.eu/legal-content/EN/TXT/?uri=celex:32017R2321 (last accessed 30 April 2018).

7 Conclusion and Future Prospects

In consideration of the foregoing, it seems unlikely that AS investigations against China, including the use of alternative benchmarks, will be the EU's "great leap forward" in trade defence. Practically, this stands to be concluded in the light of the recent reform of EU trade defence. By majorly amending its AD law to steal the thunder of those arguing for WTO illegality of the current EU AD law after the expiry of Section 15(a)(ii) CAP in Chinese WTO AD law in December 2016, the Commission has demonstrated that the AD instrument will also in the foreseeable future constitute the cornerstone of its trade defence practice. The "great leap forward" is sought in AD law reform. Against this backdrop, AS law rather seems to be kept as a powerful standby.

The AS instrument will be able to give this role sufficient substance. It presents itself as effective countermeasure in particular in cases of subsidy-induced dumping, which, with respect to China, constitute the greater part of EU dumping investigations. In relatively short time, the EU has developed a small but effective AS investigation practice. Previous cases have shown the ease of applying the alternative benchmark regime due to the convenience of reasoning once a line of argumentation with respect to certain subsidy schemes has been established.

But despite its practical effectiveness, the legal regime for the use of alternative benchmarks in EU AS law does not possess the necessary substantive aptness to constitute solid ground for fair and transparent investigations. Rather, as inspired by the obscure patchwork framework on WTO level, EU AS law on the use of alternative benchmark methodologies in NME situations is affected by lacunae and ambiguities, which has opened a discretionary space for investigating authorities that tempts decisions in favour of the national industries. By continuing the present approach in AS investigations against NME countries, the EU's alternative benchmark regime will probably have to face a challenge in front of the WTO judiciary—just like the current AD regime.[125] Ultimately, persisting arbitrariness will also contribute to endangering the leading role of the WTO in international trade.

Overall, much is still in disorder in EU trade defence as a whole. That the recent AD reform will appease critics and ensure WTO law compatibility of EU AD law is also far from certain. That China will challenge the new AD methodology in front of the WTO judiciary is, anyway, only too likely.

Almost 60 years ago, Mao's "great leap forward" caused a famine that cost the lives of over 15 million Chinese people and politically resulted in "four small steps back". The EU's quest for its "great leap forward" in trade defence will not have such drastic consequences. But to avoid having to go "four small steps back", and to ensure the continued protection of the EU industries, in the light of the looming challenges of both its AD and AS law, the EU would be well advised to critically

---

[125] See World Trade Organization, *EU – Measures Related to Price Comparison Methodologies*, Request for Consultations by China, WT/DS516/1, 15 December 2016.

question its current trade policy. Time has come to finally initiate reforms that go to the roots of the present problems and create a more reliable and sustainable legal environment for a successful future of EU trade defence.

References

Ahn D (2001) United States – definitive anti-dumping and countervailing duties on certain products from China. Am J Int Law 105(4):761–767

Arato J (2013) Treaty interpretation and constitutional transformation: informational change in international organizations. Yale J Int Law 38(2):289–351

Bronckers M (1999) Better rules for a new millennium: a warning against undemocratic developments in the WTO. J Int Econ Law 2(4):547–566

Coppens D (2014) WTO disciplines on subsidies and countervailing measures. Balancing policy space and legal constraints. Cambridge University Press, Cambridge

De Witte B (2012) Treaty revision procedures after Lisbon. In: Biondi A et al (eds) EU law after Lisbon. Oxford University Press, Oxford, pp 107–127

Ehlermann CD, Ehring L (2005a) The authoritative interpretation under Article IX:2 of the agreement establishing the World Trade Organization: current law, practice and possible improvements. J Int Econ Law 8(4):803–824

Ehlermann CD, Ehring L (2005b) Decision-making in the World Trade Organization: is the consensus practice of the World Trade Organization adequate for making, revising and Implementing rules on international trade? J Int Econ Law 8(1):51–75

Elsig M (2007) The World Trade Organization's legitimacy crisis: what does the beast look like? J World Trade 41(1):75–98

Ferejohn J (2002) Judicializing politics, politicizing law. Law Contemp Probl 65:41–68

Grieger G (2017) Protection from dumped and subsidised imports. Publications Office [of the EU], Luxembourg

Grynberg R et al (2002) Paying the price for joining the WTO: a comparative assessment of services sector commitments by WTO members and acceding countries. Commonwealth Secretariat, London

Hilf M (2001) Power, rules and principles – which orientation for WTO/GATT law? J Int Econ Law 4(1):111–130

Hoyt R (1988) Implementation and policy: problems in the application of countervailing duty laws to nonmarket economy countries. Univ Pa Law Rev 136(6):1647–1675

Jackson J (1997) The World Trading System. Law and policy of international economic relations. MIT Press, Cambridge

Kelly M (2014) Resolving the double remedy dispute. A critique of the WTO Appellate Body's decision in United States – definitive anti-dumping and countervailing duties on certain products from China. J Int Econ Law 17(1):1–27

Luo Y (2010) Anti-dumping in the WTO, the EU, and China: the rise of legalization in the trade regime and its consequences. Kluwer Law International, Alphen aan den Rijn

MacLean R (2012) Adored and despised in equal measure: an assessment of the EU's principle of market economy treatment in anti-dumping investigations against China. In: Herrmann C, Terhechte JP (eds) European yearbook of international economic law, vol 3. Springer, Berlin, pp 191–239

Mueller S (2016) Mapping the aftermath of accession – which is China's applicable World Trade Organization anti-subsidy law for the use of alternative benchmarks? J World Trade 50(5):867–884

Murphy S (2013) The relevance of subsequent agreement and subsequent practice for the interpretation of treaties. In: Nolte G (ed) Treaties and subsequent practice. Oxford University Press, Oxford, pp 82–94

Nguyen N (2008) WTO accession at any cost? Examining the use of WTO-plus and WTO-minus obligations for least-developed country applicants. Temple Int Comp Law J 22(1):243–277

Pauwelyn J (2003) Conflict of norms in public international law: how WTO law relates to other rules of international law. Cambridge University Press, Cambridge

Polouektov A (2002) Non-market economy issues in the WTO anti-dumping law and accession negotiations. J World Trade 36(1):1–37

Prusa T, Vermulst E (2013) United States – definitive anti-dumping and countervailing duties on certain products from China: passing the buck on pass-through. World Trade Rev 12(2):197–234

Qian W (2012) The dilemma of China as respondent to anti-subsidy proceedings – a study of the first EU anti-subsidy investigation against China. J World Trade 46(4):961–978

Qin JY (2003) "WTO-plus" obligations and their implications for the World Trade Organization legal system. J World Trade 37(3):483–522

Qin JY (2015) The conundrum of WTO accession protocols: in search of legality and legitimacy. Virginia J Int Law 55(2):369–450

Steinberg R (2004) Judicial lawmaking at the WTO: discursive, constitutional, and political Constraints. Am J Int Law 98(2):247–275

Tatham A (2009) Enlargement of the European Union. Kluwer Law International, Alphen aan den Rijn

Thorstensen V et al (2013) WTO – market and non-market economies: the hybrid case of China. Latin Am J Int Trade Law 1(2):765–798

Tyagi M (2012) Flesh on a legal fiction: early practice in the WTO on accession protocols. J Int Econ Law 15(2):391–441

Van Bael I, Bellis JF (2011) EU anti-dumping and other trade defence instruments. Kluwer Law International, Alphen aan den Rijn

Vermulst E, Gatta B (2012) Concurrent trade defence investigation in the EU, the EU's new anti-subsidy practice against China, and the future of both. World Trade Rev 11(3):527–553

Walder A (2015) China under Mao. Harvard University Press, Cambridge

Wu X (2011) Rethinking China's membership in the WTO. Chic J Int Law 10(2):227–270

Yalcin E, Felbermayr G, Sandkamp A (2016) New trade rules for China? Opportunities and threats for the EU. Requested by the European Parliament's Committee on International Trade. Publications Office [of the EU], Luxembourg

Part III
TDI in the Context of Special (Regional) Trading Relationships

What Role for TDIs Between the EU and the UK After Brexit: A Trade or Competition Solution to a Future Problem?

Anna Khalfaoui and Markus W. Gehring

Contents

The authors are indebted to the comments from BIICL and other colleagues. All mistakes are their own. Markus also wishes to thank the participants of the TDI Conference in March 2017 and especially his former employer, Cleary Gottlieb Steen and Hamilton LLP.

A. Khalfaoui
American Bar Association Rule of Law Initiative, Washington, DC, USA

M. W. Gehring (✉)
British Institute for International and Comparative Law (BIICL), London, UK

University of Cambridge, Cambridge, UK
e-mail: mwg24@cam.ac.uk

Abstract This article examines different options for trade defence that would be open to the United Kingdom (UK) once it leaves the European Union (EU). It focuses on the role of trade defence instruments (TDIs) in the UK's future trading future outside the bloc. If the UK leaves the EU without a deal, the country will be left to rely on WTO trading rules. The article looks at the UK's continued membership to the WTO and the many hurdles the UK is likely to face in the WTO after Brexit, in particular in issuing independent schedules for trade and services and identifying the UK's own commitments independent of those of the EU. The article highlights the importance of TDIs to ensure that the UK is in a position to protect its industries from unfair competition after Brexit. It reviews recent proposals to establish a new trade authority and to build up the UK's TDI capabilities. The article looks at trade defence options that would be available to the UK if it agreed to take part in a customs union with the EU, taking stock of the EU-Turkey customs union's mixed record. Finally, it highlights that a competition law Brexit solution would leave no room for an independent trade defence.

1 Introduction

The triggering of Article 50 TEU on 29 March 2017 marked the beginning of lengthy divorce proceedings between the European Union (EU) and the United Kingdom (UK). Close to a year later, at the time of writing, the precise arrangements by which the UK will withdraw from the EU and the details of the future partnership remain considerably unclear.[1] Sober observers are left to hope that the worst possible outcome, a "no-deal Brexit", will not become reality.[2] According to a "no-deal Brexit", the UK would leave the EU without any form of deal and resort to World Trade Organisation (WTO) trade rules.

Trading under WTO rules would dramatically alter the UK's position to trade disputes post-Brexit. The EU as a whole is the UK's largest trading partner: in 2016, UK exports to the EU were made up 43% of all UK exports and UK imports to the EU 54% of all imports.[3] Disputes are bound to arise. The UK will need to have a

---

[1] Peers and Barnard (2017), Chapter 27.

[2] Leaked Government analysis suggests the UK will be worse off outside the EU under every scenario surveyed (no-deal, free trade agreement, and single market access through membership of the European Economic Area) and worst off under a "no-deal" scenario according to which the UK economic growth would reduce by 8% over the next 15 years compare to current forecasts, see Nardelli A, This Leaked Government Brexit Analysis Says The UK Will Be Worse Off In Every Scenario. Buzzfeed, 29 January 2018, www.buzzfeed.com/albertonardelli/the-governments-own-brexit-analysis-says-the-uk-will-be?utm_term=.pnRRn8jAw#.pfNQJq50b (last accessed 30 April 2018).

[3] Ward M, Statistics on UK-EU Trade. House of Commons Library, Briefing Paper No 7851, 19 December 2017, http://researchbriefings.files.parliament.uk/documents/CBP-7851/CBP-7851.pdf (last accessed 30 April 2018), p. 4.

way of resolving disputes with the bloc and individual member states. Conversely, the UK, under an independent trade policy, will have to be ready to resolve disputes with third states. Journalist Ian Dunt provides us with a telling worst-case scenario for trade remedies post-Brexit:

> On 31 March 2019, Britain [in the WTO] argues that it is still a party to an EU arrangement preventing the sale of cheap Chinese steel in Europe. Once those floodgates open, the UK knows domestic steel will be unable to compete. China reacts furiously, demanding that Britain demonstrate domestic injury and unfair trade. But the UK doesn't have an investigating authority capable of undertaking trade remedy investigations. It cannot fight back because it doesn't have the regulatory infrastructure. Workers in factories like Port Talbot start to fear for their livelihoods.[4]

This article explores options for trade remedies and trade disputes for the UK after Brexit. In particular, it concentrates on the role of trade defence instruments (TDIs) in the UK's trading future outside of the EU and mechanisms for implementing these instruments post-Brexit. This article first reviews potential issues linked to the UK's continued membership to the WTO once it leaves the EU. It, then, outlines the importance of TDIs in any modern trade policy to ensure a country's industries continued are protected from unfair competition and the current EU approach to trade defence. Third, this article highlights issues of capacity in the UK's ability to impose TDIs in the post-Brexit era and reviews recent calls for the UK to set up a new, independent trade remedies body capable of enforcing such instruments. A fourth section looks at trade defence in the context of a customs unions taking as a case study the EU-Turkey customs union. A final section highlights that a competition solution would leave no room for a UK's post-Brexit trade defence.

2 The UK's Post-Brexit WTO Membership and Commitments

This section details the first hurdle facing the UK upon leaving the EU when it comes to international trade, namely the UK's membership to the WTO and its ability to determine its own commitments, independent of those of the EU. As will be seen, although the UK's continued membership to the WTO is not doubtful, there is considerable uncertainty around its issuance of its own schedules of commitments for trade and services and negotiating its own commitments.

---

[4]Dunt (2016).

2.1   The UK as a Founding Member of the WTO with No Independent Schedule

The UK, together with the EU, are founding members of the WTO, whose member-ship terms are closely connected. Article XI(1) of the Marrakesh Agreement estab-lishing the WTO provides that:

> The contracting parties to GATT 1947 as of the date of entry into force of this Agreement, and the European Communities, which accept this Agreement and the Multilateral Trade Agreements and for which Schedules of Concessions and Commitments are annexed to GATT 1994 and for which Schedules of Specific Commitments are annexed to GATS shall become original Members of the WTO.[5]

The UK ratified the 1947 General Agreement on Tariffs and Trade (GATT) on 1 January 1948.[6] Only the EU (known at the WTO as the European Communities until 2009) has valid schedules to the GATT 1994, the successor to the GATT 1947 governing trade in goods, and the General Agreement on Trade in Services (GATS). The European Union, hence, has a single set of tariffs and quotas applicable to other WTO member states along with common commitments pertaining to trade in services. The European Court of Justice, in Opinion 1/94, held that the WTO Agreement constituted a mixed agreement, as such the European Community and its Member States shared competence to conclude this agreement.[7] But such mixed membership is not visible in practice. The EU does not merely represent its Member States when it comes to the WTO, Article 3 TFEU clearly states that the EU has exclusive competence when it comes to common commercial policy. The European Commission negotiates on behalf of the whole of the EU and also initiates and handles any WTO complaints. Member states, in turn, are bound to support the common EU position.

Lord Lawson, former chancellor and Brexit-supporter, confidently asserted: "*[o]ur trade relations with the rest of the world remain unchanged.*"[8] The reality may, however, be more complicated.[9] A month before the referendum, in May 2016, Roberto Azevêdo, the Director-General of the WTO, warned:

> Pretty much all of the UK's trade [with the world] would somehow have to be negotiated… It is a very important decision for the British people. It is a sovereign decision and they will decide what they want to decide. But it is very important, particularly with regard to trade,

[5] Article XI, Marrakesh Agreement Establishing the World Trade Organization, 15 April 1994.
[6] See www.wto.org/english/thewto_e/gattmem_e.htm (last accessed 30 April 2018).
[7] CJEU, Opinion 1/94, *WTO Agreement,* ECLI:EU:C:1994:384.
[8] Lord Lawson, BBC Radio 4 interview, quoted in Gehring M, Brexit and EU-UK trade relations with third states. EU Law Analysis, 6 March 2016, http://eulawanalysis.blogspot.co.uk/2016/03/brexit-and-eu-uk-trade-relations-with.html (last accessed 30 April 2018).
[9] For a useful retrospective on declarations in the context of Brexit and the WTO, see Green D, Brexit and the issue of WTO schedules. The Financial Times, 28 February 2017, https://www.ft.com/content/42b59126-794c-3a0b-b19a-6d4b0a11c990 (last accessed 30 April 2018).

which is something very important for the British economy, that people have the facts and that they don't underestimate the challenges.[10]

Azevêdo stressed that the UK would not be able to simply "cut and paste" the EU terms of membership; instead, it would have to renegotiate brand new schedules, without the "institutional mechanism" to negotiate such deals or to deal with disputes.[11] By October 2016, the Director-General, in another interview, seemed ready to alleviate fears of a disruptive vacuum for UK businesses, stressing that:

> The UK is a member of the WTO today, it will continue to be a member tomorrow. There will be no discontinuity in membership… They have to renegotiate (their terms of membership) but that doesn't mean they are not members… Trade will not stop, it will continue and members negotiate the legal basis under which that trade is going to happen. But it doesn't mean that we'll have a vacuum or a disruption.[12]

Other commentators similarly highlighted that:

> Assuming the UK does not enter into a customs union with the EU after its withdrawal, it would no longer be part of the common [tariff] schedules. In this scenario, the UK must submit its own new schedules after the conclusion of an exit agreement with the EU if it is to remain a WTO member. These schedules need to be accepted by all other WTO members in consensus and certified following certain procedures, which might create difficulties.[13]

In other words, it is not yet entirely clear under which condition WTO trade will progress once the UK leaves the EU. The UK will continue to be a member of the WTO upon leaving the EU. According to Lorand Bartels, *"what will change with Brexit are not the UK's underlying rights and obligations, but rather the EU's exercise of these rights and assumption of responsibility for the performance of these obligations."*[14] The rights and obligations of the EU and its member states, according to the WTO Agreement, are identical. Piet Eeckhout argued that, pursuant to Article XI, the *"then EC Member States and the EC became full original WTO Members, each apparently bound by all obligations resulting from the WTO Agreement."*[15] The EU's membership, further, was not expressly limited by any list or declaration of competences or an indication in the Agreement itself of the obligations binding onto the EU or its member states, as may be common in the context of international organisations or agreements.[16] When the UK and the EU agreed a

---

[10] Donnan S, WTO warns on tortuous Brexit trade talks. The Financial Times, 25 May 2016, https://www.ft.com/content/745d0ea2-222d-11e6-9d4d-c11776a5124d (last accessed 30 April 2018).

[11] Elliott L, WTO chief says post-Brexit trade talks must start from scratch. The Guardian, 7 June 2016, https://www.theguardian.com/business/2016/jun/07/wto-chief-brexit-trade-talks-start-scratch-eu-referendum (last accessed 30 April 2018).

[12] Conway E, Brexit will not cause UK trade 'disruption'—WTO boss. Skynews, 26 October 2016, https://news.sky.com/story/brexit-will-not-cause-uk-trade-disruption-wto-boss-10632803   (last accessed 30 April 2018).

[13] Koutrakos (2016), p. 54.

[14] Bartels L, The UK's status in the WTO after Brexit. SSRN Paper, 22 September 2016, https://papers.ssrn.com/sol3/papers.cfm?abstract_id=2841747 (last accessed 30 April 2018), p. 2.

[15] Eeckhout (2006), p. 451.

[16] Eeckhout (2006), p. 451.

division of agricultural quotas last year, many heralded this as a major breakthrough, however some of the UK's closes allies, such as the U.S. and New Zealand strenuously objected.[17]

The conclusion that the UK WTO membership rights are identical to that of the EU and other WTO States is supported by the WTO jurisprudence in *EC and Certain Member States – Large Civil Aircraft* where the EU requested the removal of five member states as respondents, arguing that it was the "only proper respondent" in the dispute and that it took "full responsibility" for those states' actions.[18] The Panel held that *"[e]ach of these five is, in its own rights, a member of the WTO, with all the rights and obligations pertaining to such membership, including the obligation to respond to claims made against it by another WTO Member."*[19] The Panel went further, stressing that *"[w]hatever responsibility the [EU] bears for the actions of its member States does not diminish their rights and obligations as WTO Members, but is rather an internal matter concerning the relationship between the [EU] and its member States."*[20] The UK will continue to benefit from its pre-existing rights and obligations as a WTO member.

2.2　The Issuance of Independent Schedules of Commitment

The key issue is not the UK's continued membership to the WTO but the question of reissuing its own schedules of commitment for goods and services. The UK government has maintained that there will be no negotiations as it plans to re-issue the EU schedules with a name change and other minor editorial changes. The international trade secretary, Liam Fox, in a statement to the House of Commons and the House of Lords recalled that the UK is a founding member of the WTO, apparently dispelling doubts that the UK would no longer be a member.[21] He further stated:

> The UK's WTO commitments currently form part of the European Union's schedules. When we leave the EU we will need UK-specific schedules. In order to minimise disruption to global trade as we leave the EU, over the coming period the Government will prepare the

---

[17] Ungphakorn, P, The limits of 'possibility': Splitting the lamb-mutton quota for the UK and EU-27. Trade Beta Blog, 6 January 2017, https://tradebetablog.wordpress.com/2017/01/06/limits-of-possibility/ (last accessed 30 April 2018).

[18] Panel Report, *EC and Certain Member States – Large Civil Aircraft*, WT/DS316/R, adopted 30 June 2010, paras. 7.169–7.177.

[19] Panel Report, *EC and Certain Member States – Large Civil Aircraft*, WT/DS316/R, adopted 30 June 2010, para. 7.174.

[20] Panel Report, *EC and Certain Member States – Large Civil Aircraft*, WT/DS316/R, adopted 30 June 2010, para. 7.175.

[21] Written Statement by Dr Liam Fox, Secretary of State for International Trade and President of the Board of Trade, UK's commitments at the World Trade organisation, House of Commons, HCWS316, 5 December 2016, https://www.parliament.uk/business/publications/written-questions-answers-statements/written-statement/Commons/2016-12-05/HCWS316/ (last accessed 30 April 2018).

necessary draft schedules which replicate as far as possible our current obligations. The Government will undertake this process in dialogue with the WTO membership.[22]

The UK Permanent Representative to the UN and WTO in Geneva, Julian Braithwaite, similarly, in January 2017, stated that *"as a full member, the UK already has its own schedules. But at the moment these are shared with the other EU Member States."*[23] The Permanent Representative notes that the UK will have to submit new schedules as part of the normal WTO process, subject to none of the WTO's other 163 members objecting to them. To minimise such disruption, *"we plan to replicate our existing trade regime as far as possible in our new schedules."*[24]

The Bar Council has taken the position that new schedules could be given effect through three different procedures: certification under the decisions of 26 March 1980 (L/4962) for goods and 14 April 2000 (S/L/83) for services; renegotiation under Article XXVIII GATT for goods and Article XXI GATS for services; and supplementary negotiations through a bespoke procedure per Article XXVIIIbis GATT and/or Article IV WTO Agreement.[25] Any WTO member state would be entitled to block certification of new schedules and negotiations under a bespoke procedure would have to be negotiated with the EU and other WTO states by consensus. It would, hence, leave the UK vulnerable to the veto of any of the WTO member, as highlighted by the UK Permanent Representative to the UN and WTO.

The advantage of renegotiation under Articles XXVIII GATT and XXI GATS is that it is not adversarial and, hence, does not provide for the possibility of a veto. Article XXVIII is specifically concerned with the question of "Modification of Schedules" where a WTO member wants to modify or withdraw a concession including in a schedule. Article XVIII provides that in such negotiations, *"the contracting parties concerned shall endeavour to maintain a general level of reciprocal and mutually advantageous concessions not less favourable to trade than that provided for in this Agreement prior to such negotiations."*[26] Only WTO members with "initial negotiating rights", which have a "principal supplying interest" or determined

---

[22] Written Statement by Dr Liam Fox, Secretary of State for International Trade and President of the Board of Trade, UK's commitments at the World Trade organisation, House of Commons, HCWS316, 5 December 2016, https://www.parliament.uk/business/publications/written-questions-answers-statements/written-statement/Commons/2016-12-05/HCWS316/ (last accessed 30 April 2018).

[23] Braithwaite J, Ensuring a smooth transition in the WTO as we leave the EU. Foreign & Commonwealth Office Blog, 23 January 2017, https://blogs.fco.gov.uk/julianbraithwaite/2017/01/23/ensuring-a-smooth-transition-in-the-wto-as-we-leave-the-eu/ (last accessed 30 April 2018).

[24] Braithwaite J, Ensuring a smooth transition in the WTO as we leave the EU. Foreign & Commonwealth Office Blog, 23 January 2017, https://blogs.fco.gov.uk/julianbraithwaite/2017/01/23/ensuring-a-smooth-transition-in-the-wto-as-we-leave-the-eu/ (last accessed 30 April 2018).

[25] Bar Council Brexit Working Group, The UK's position in the WTO. The Brexit Papers, Paper 21, June 2017, https://www.barcouncil.org.uk/media/575749/brexit_paper_21_-_wto.pdf (last accessed 30 April 2018), pp. 3–5.

[26] WTO Agreement, Article XVIII(2).

by the requesting party to have a "substantial interest" are entitled to negotiate with the requesting member. Such countries could adjust their own schedules in retaliation or claim compensation where the changes lead to damage to their own trade interests. It is interesting to point that Article XXIV(6) GATT notes that the renegotiation procedure under Article XXVIII can be triggered upon the creation of a customs union or free trade area. No such article is provided in the context of the dissolution of a customs union or, more relevantly in the case of Brexit, in the case of a member leaving a customs union.

Bartels argues that the proper procedure to give effect to the UK's new schedules should be through a "rectification".[27] The 1980 Decision on Procedures for Modification and Rectification of Schedules of Tariff Concessions distinguish between "modifications" and other "changes".[28] Paragraph 1 of the Decision provides that *"[c]hanges in the authentic texts of Schedules annexed to the General Agreement which reflect modifications"* resulting from action, including under Article XVIII, shall be certified by certification. Conversely, paragraph 2 describes other "changes" as *"[c]hanges in the authentic texts of Schedules"* done through *"amendments or rearrangements which do not alter the scope of a concession are introduced in national customs tariffs in respect of bound items."* The parallel GATS Decision also contains this distinction between ordinary modification under Article XXI GATS and modifications *"which consist of new commitments, improvements to existing ones, or rectifications or changes of a purely technical character that do not alter the scope or the substance of the existing commitments."*[29]

Bartels' argument is that *"new schedules scheduled by newly autonomous WTO Members… should, in the first instance, be treated as changes in a schedule not amounting to a modification within the meaning of paragraph 1 of the 1980 Decision."*[30] This, he posits, is justified on the basis that newly independent states, under Article XXVI:5(c) GATT 1947, were granted GATT contracting party status, under the sponsorship of the former coloniser and WTO member.[31] The newly independent States fully inherited the rights and obligations previously applicable to that territory, including the schedules which were treated as other "changes", except when it included an increase in duties beyond the rate set. It should be highlighted

---

[27] Bartels L, The UK's status in the WTO after Brexit. SSRN Paper, 22 September 2016, https://papers.ssrn.com/sol3/papers.cfm?abstract_id=2841747 (last accessed 30 April 2018), pp. 13–18; Bartels L, Understanding the UK's position in the WTO after Brexit (Part II—The consequences). International Centre for Trade and Sustainable Development Opinion, 26 September 2016, https://www.ictsd.org/opinion/understanding-the-uk-0 (last accessed 30 April 2018).

[28] GATT Contracting Parties, Procedures for Modification and Rectification of Schedules of Tariff Concessions, Decision of 26 March 1980, L/4962.

[29] WTO Council for Trade in Services, Decision on Procedures for the Certification of Rectifications or Improvements to Schedules of Specific Commitments, adopted 14 April 2000, S/L/83, 18 April 2000.

[30] Bartels L, The UK's status in the WTO after Brexit. SSRN Paper, 22 September 2016, https://papers.ssrn.com/sol3/papers.cfm?abstract_id=2841747 (last accessed 30 April 2018), pp. 15–16.

[31] Bartels L, The UK's status in the WTO after Brexit. SSRN Paper, 22 September 2016, https://papers.ssrn.com/sol3/papers.cfm?abstract_id=2841747 (last accessed 30 April 2018), p. 16.

however that state succession is not the best analogy for the obligations of the UK after Brexit. Brexit is distinctly not a case of state succession and thus most of the rules established for state succession are not applicable, as will be further discussed below.

The clear advantage of submitting new UK GATT and GATS schedules for certification as other changes, explains Bartels, is that WTO have limited grounds on which to object.[32] Indeed, per paragraph 3 of the Decision, the draft with such changes shall be certified unless an objection is raised by a contracting party, within 3 months, on the ground that *"in the case of changes described in paragraph 2, the proposed rectification is not within the terms of that paragraph."* Bartels points that, even if other WTO member states do object, *"the legal effect of certification of evidentiary."*[33] If the UK's new schedules were rejected by another WTO state, it would be left to that state to commence dispute proceedings. This could lead to the real danger of a zombie WTO member state because valid tariff schedules are a condition of membership in the WTO.

Unfortunately, looming WTO disputes are a very real possibility. Many WTO member states are unhappy with the UK's handling of Brexit in the organisation and rejection of all negotiations. Any restriction of market access will come under scrutiny with possibly damaging disputes from multiple WTO Members.

2.3 State Succession Issues and Identifying the UK's Own Commitments

There are two crucial issues left to explore pertaining to the UK's rights and obligations as a WTO member post-Brexit, pertaining, first, to state succession and, second, to identifying the UK's own commitments. The EU GATS schedule opens by stating that *"[t]he specific commitments in this schedule apply only to the territories in which the Treaties establishing the European Communities are applied under the conditions laid down in these Treaties."*[34] This has important implications in light of the law of state succession. From a public international law standpoint, as has been argued elsewhere,[35] the UK may have little room to argue that such reference to territorial application should be deleted or to succeed in its own name to the WTO Government Procurement Agreement, dating back to 2014, and to which the EU

---

[32] Bartels L, The UK's status in the WTO after Brexit. SSRN Paper, 22 September 2016, https://papers.ssrn.com/sol3/papers.cfm?abstract_id=2841747 (last accessed 30 April 2018), p. 17.

[33] Bartels L, The UK's status in the WTO after Brexit. SSRN Paper, 22 September 2016, https://papers.ssrn.com/sol3/papers.cfm?abstract_id=2841747 (last accessed 30 April 2018), p. 18.

[34] World Trade Organization, European Communities and their Member States—Schedule of Specific Commitments, GATS/SC/31, 15 April 1994, p. 1.

[35] Gehring M, Brexit and EU-UK trade relations with third states. EU Law Analysis, 6 March 2016, http://eulawanalysis.blogspot.co.uk/2016/03/brexit-and-eu-uk-trade-relations-with.html   (last accessed 30 April 2018).

alone is the relevant party.[36] Bartels argues that this is a straightforward case of state succession.[37] A 1971 UN Secretariat study on the succession of states in respect of bilateral treaties looking specifically at the question of trade agreements concluded that *"in general the members of a union remain bound by the trade agreements of the union following its dissolution, at least if there is a clear continuity of the entity involved."*[38] This is, however, not a case of dissolution. The UK and the EU both enjoy international legal personality and the EU will continue to do so post-Brexit.

The reason why negotiations may still be necessary relates to the second issue, namely, identifying and, likely, negotiating the UK's own commitments as a WTO member in the post-Brexit era. The UK cannot honour its current obligations under the WTO independently of its membership in the EU and its participation in the EU single market.[39] WTO membership and its liberalisation commitments entail that all goods, once imported into the EU, are treated as EU goods upon clearing customs and can move freely within the entire EU. Negotiations is crucial when it comes to the EU-wide tariff rate quotas in which UK participates. Such quotas provide lower duties on limited quantities of goods imported into a country.[40] An example is the tariff rate quota for 280 tonnes of duty free lamb shared out among Argentina, Australia, Chile, New Zealand, Uruguay and nine other states.[41] The EU and the UK would have to agree on how to divide such a quota. Similarly, the EU and the UK would also have to decide quotas enabling the EU to export to third countries on preferential terms.[42] The UK and the EU would also have to agree on dividing the entitlement to domestic subsidies, in particular agricultural subsidies.[43]

The WTO does not provide any guidance on dividing shared quotas. Where negotiations do not bear fruit, the fall-back will be to rely on normal WTO rules and

---

[36] Agreement on Government Procurement with appendices, rectifications and modifications, concluded at Marrakesh on 15 April 1994 (1996) 1915 UNTS 103.

[37] Bartels L, The UK's status in the WTO after Brexit. SSRN Paper, 22 September 2016, https://papers.ssrn.com/sol3/papers.cfm?abstract_id=2841747 (last accessed 30 April 2018), pp. 18–21.

[38] UN Secretariat, Succession of States in respect of bilateral treaties: third study prepared by the Secretariat on trade agreements, UN Doc A/CN.4/243/Add.1, 24 March 1971, para. 182.

[39] Gehring M, Brexit and EU-UK trade relations with third states. EU Law Analysis, 6 March 2016, http://eulawanalysis.blogspot.co.uk/2016/03/brexit-and-eu-uk-trade-relations-with.html   (last accessed 30 April 2018).

[40] House of Lords, European Union Committee, Brexit: the options for trade, 5th report of session 2016-17,   https://publications.parliament.uk/pa/ld201617/ldselect/ldeucom/72/72.pdf   (last accessed 30 April 2018), para. 178.

[41] House of Lords, European Union Committee, Brexit: the options for trade, 5th report of session 2016-17,   https://publications.parliament.uk/pa/ld201617/ldselect/ldeucom/72/72.pdf   (last accessed 30 April 2018), para. 178.

[42] House of Lords, European Union Committee, Brexit: the options for trade, 5th report of session 2016-17,   https://publications.parliament.uk/pa/ld201617/ldselect/ldeucom/72/72.pdf   (last accessed 30 April 2018), para. 179.

[43] House of Lords, European Union Committee, Brexit: the options for trade, 5th report of session 2016-17,   https://publications.parliament.uk/pa/ld201617/ldselect/ldeucom/72/72.pdf   (last accessed 30 April 2018), para. 180.

its dispute resolution mechanism. The UK's proposed tariff quote could, per Article XIII(2) GATT, aim at a *"distribution of trade in such product approaching as closely as possible the shares which the various contracting parties might be expected to obtain in the absence of such restrictions."* It would be up for the EU in turn to access the UK quota for products it has a substantial interest to export to the UK.[44] The EU would be in a position to start dispute proceedings and claim compensation for the imposition of such tariffs, per the normal WTO rules.

Thankfully, it appears that negotiations are ongoing and that identifying the UK's own commitment will not be done through the WTO dispute resolution mechanism. Recent reports have highlighted that the UK and the EU have struck a preliminary agreement on dividing up the tariff-rate quotas governing the import of farm products into the EU.[45] Renegotiating tariff commitments has proven difficult, even for large trading nations, such as Russia and China. WTO states may try to extract special liberalisation commitments from the UK. This could be done through non-violation complaints, pursuant to Article XXIII(1)(b) of the GATT, which may be instigated even when there has been no breach of the Agreement, and where a WTO member could argue that the measures applied by the UK result in "nullification or impairment of a benefit". It is to be hoped that negotiations in the context of the GATS schedules, where further liberation pressure in the context of trade in services may be particularly likely, also bear fruits so as to avoid heavy reliance on the WTO dispute settlement mechanism.

3 On the Importance of TDIs and Their Widespread Use by the EU

The issue of TDIs to post-Brexit trade is crucial and, this article argues, trade defence should be tackled head-on as part of the preparations made by the UK to leave the EU. TDIs are lawful measures under WTO rules, by which WTO members can protect their own industries from unfair competition through anti-dumping duties and countervailing measures directed at subsidies. This section provides an overview of the scope of measures directed at dumping and subsidies and of their widespread use by the EU.

---

[44] Bartels L, Understanding the UK's position in the WTO after Brexit (Part II—The consequences). International Centre for Trade and Sustainable Development Opinion, 26 September 2016, https://www.ictsd.org/opinion/understanding-the-uk-0 (last accessed 30 April 2018).

[45] Beattie A and Brundsen J, UK and EU strike initial deal on WTO quotas in Brexit breakthrough. Financial Times, 3 October 2017, https://www.ft.com/content/e30185c6-a83d-11e7-ab55-27219df83c97 (last accessed 7 March 2018).

3.1 Anti-Dumping Measures

Dumping occurs in a situation where *"an exporting country sells its products in an importing country at a lower price than that at which the products are sold in the exporting country's home market."*[46] Such practice is prohibited as a form of unfair price discrimination, which is contrary to the level playing field in international trade, and thus may allow for retaliatory anti-dumping measures. Article VI GATT provides for the authorisation for anti-dumping duties, while the Agreement on Implementation of Article VI of GATT 1994, commonly referred to as the Anti-Dumping Agreement, elaborates on Article VI. A WTO Member must show the following factors in order to justify the imposition of anti-dumping duties: first, that dumping is occurring; second, that domestic industry producing a similar product in the importing country suffers material injury; and third, that there is a causal link between the two.[47] Rules of origin post-Brexit might also constitute an obstacle to applying anti-dumping rules as such rules allow customs authority to check for anti-dumping compliance.[48]

The first hurdle is establishing that dumping is in fact occurring. The Anti-Dumping Agreement establishes different methods to determine calculating the "normal value" and the "export price", the first being the product's appropriate price in the exporting country's market and the second that product's appropriate price in the importing country's market. Article 2 of the Anti-Dumping Agreement provides three different methods to calculate the normal value of a product. In most instances, this value will be determined by the price consumers pay for the product "in the ordinary course of trade" in that exporting country. Sales will be excluded from the calculation of normal value where: the sales were made below cost; over an extended period of time; in substantial quantities; and at prices not allowing for the recovery of costs within a reasonable time.[49] Sales may also be too insufficient to allow for a proper comparison of prices in the exporting and importing countries' markets. In such cases, two other methods of calculating the normal value of a product may be used. The first involves calculating the normal value of a product by reference to its price when that product, or a similar product, is exported to an "appropriate third country, provided that this price is representative."[50] The second involves determining a "constructed normal value", defined as the cost of production plus *"reasonable amount for administrative, selling and general costs and for profits."*[51]

---

[46] Gehring et al. (2007), p. 87.

[47] Gehring et al. (2007), p. 88.

[48] Holmes P and Jacob N, Certificates and rules of origin: the experience of UK firms. UK Trade Policy Observatory, Briefing Paper 15, 15 January 2018, http://blogs.sussex.ac.uk/uktpo/files/2018/01/BP15-CRoO.pdf (last accessed 30 April 2018), p. 2.

[49] Article 2.2.1 Anti-Dumping Agreement.

[50] Article 2.2 Anti-Dumping Agreement.

[51] Article 2.2. Anti-Dumping Agreement.

Calculating the "export price", by comparison, is simpler and generally merely involves the price at which the importer buys the product from the exporting country.[52] This basic determination may be put aside in favour of a "constructed export price" where there are reasons to believe that price may not be fair, for instance because the export is an internal company transfer or there are compensatory arrangements between exporter and importer.

A fair comparison of the normal value and the export must be made between prices at the same level of trade, typically upon leaving factory, and the price of sales made at the same time. This further requires taking into account a host of technical differences in conditions in terms of sale, tax, quantities and physical characteristics. This allows to measure the margin of dumping, which, essentially, constitutes the *"advantage in monetary terms that the dumped product has over domestic like product."*[53] This is in turn crucial to determine the amount of anti-dumping duty that may lawfully be imposed to counter this advantage. Calculating the dumping margin, generally, involves either a comparison of the weighted average normal value to a weighted average of comparable export prices or a comparison of the normal value and export price on a "transaction-to-transaction" basis. Typically, the margin will be calculated for each individual exporter but, where a large number of exporters and producers are concerned, margins may instead be calculated across a valid sample of a reasonable number of exporters and producers and then applied across the board.

The process to determine that material injury to a domestic injury has occurred is described in Article 3. It involves first determining exactly which domestic industries are concerned. A "like product" is defined, in Article 2.6 as a *"product which is identical, i.e., alike in all respects"* or alternatively a product which *"has characteristics closely resembling those of the product under consideration."* In exceptional cases, the injury requirement may be satisfied when the injury affects only a specific part of the domestic industry and not the whole of it. Each separate "regional industry" may be considered as a microcosm of the country's total domestic industry, in which case duties must be only imposed on imported products designed for the specific area, and, if impossible, where they cannot be limited to specific producers supplying the area, duties may be imposed without limitation.[54]

The Anti-Dumping Agreement recognises three types of injuries: material injury to a domestic industry; threat of material injury to a domestic industry; or material retardation of the establishment of a domestic industry. As pointed out by Article 3.4, the examination of the impact of the dumped imports require:

> [A]n evaluation of all relevant economic factors and indices having a bearing on the state of the industry, including actual and potential decline in sales, profits, output, market share, productivity, return on investments, or utilization of capacity; factors affecting domestic prices; the magnitude of the margin of dumping; actual and potential negative effects on cash flow, inventories, employment, wages, growth, ability to raise capital or investments.

---

[52] Gehring et al. (2007), p. 89.

[53] Gehring et al. (2007), p. 90.

[54] Gehring et al. (2007), p. 90.

Article 3.4 expressly adds that this list is not exhaustive and that no single factor or combination of factors will necessarily be determinative. The country alleging dumping to establish material injury must *"examine the volume of dumped imports, their effect on prices of like products in the domestic market and the impact of the dumping on domestic producers of like products, taking into account all relevant economic factors such as actual or potential decline in sales, profits, output or market share."*[55] Relevant factors to establish a threat of material injury include *"the rate of increase of dumped imports, the capacities of the exporters and the likelihood of the lower-priced products increasing demand for more imports."*[56] No further guidance is provided in the Agreement on what constitutes material retardation.

The last step for a complainant is to prove that dumping from the exporting country is the cause of the injury being suffered. Article 3.5 states that such a determination *"shall be based on an examination of all relevant evidence before the authorities."* This includes *"any known factors other than the dumped imports which at the same time are injuring the domestic industry,"* which could include: changes in demand or consumption patterns in the importing country market; trade-restrictive or competitive practices in the exporting or importing countries' industries; technology development; and the domestic industry's productivity.[57]

In terms of procedural requirements, an investigation on anti-dumping may be carried out by the government of any WTO member state *"upon a written application by or on behalf of the domestic industry"*[58] and when there is sufficient evidence warranting such an investigation. Further, the collective output of those domestic producers supporting the investigation must be greater than 25% of the total production of the like product of all domestic producers.[59] The Anti-Dumping Agreement specifies that the government authorities, after considering an application or during an investigation, shall stop the investigation if there is no sufficient evidence of dumping. Per Article 5.8, this includes situations where the margin of dumping is less than 2% of the export price or the volume of allegedly dumped imports from the exporting question is less than 3% of imports of the like product, unless several exporting countries representing less than 3% each together constitute more than 7% of the like product in the complaining country. Investigations are conducted in accordance with fixed procedures established by the Anti-Dumping Agreement.

---

[55] Gehring et al. (2007), p. 91.
[56] Gehring et al. (2007), p. 91.
[57] Gehring et al. (2007), p. 91.
[58] Article 5.1 Anti-Dumping Agreement.
[59] Article 5.4 Anti-Dumping Agreement.

3.2 Anti-Subsidies Measures

The second type of measures against unfair practice target the practice of government to support domestic producers by granting them financial incentives in the form of subsidies.[60] Such subsidies allow domestic producers to sell their goods in local and international markets at cheaper prices, which may hurt foreign producers and lead to trade distortion. The WTO Agreement on Subsidies and Countervailing Measures regulates the provision of subsidies and the use of countervailing measures to offset their effect.

The Agreement on Subsidies and Countervailing Measures defines a subsidy as a *"financial contribution by a government or any public body within the territory of a Member"* where: a government practice involves a direct transfer of funds (e.g. grant, loan) or a potential transfer of funds (e.g. loan guarantee); when a government revenue normally due is not collected (e.g. tax credit); when a government purchases goods or provides particular goods or services, other than in the context of general infrastructure; when a government directs a private body to undertake any of the above activities.[61] The financial contribution must confer a benefit for it to amount to a subsidy.[62] A WTO Panel has interpreted this to mean that the financial contribution must be *"provided on terms that are more advantageous than those that would have been available to the recipient on the market."*[63] A loan provided to an enterprise at an interest rate not better than that generally available to the marketplace constitutes a financial contribution to that enterprise but does not confer a benefit, and hence, is not a subsidy.[64]

The Agreement on Subsidies and Countervailing Measures only applies to subsidies which are "specific" in the meaning of Article 2. A subsidy is specific if it applies to particular enterprises or industries. It is not specific if there are objective criteria or conditions governing the eligibility for and the amount granted. These criteria must be neutral, non-discriminatory, economic in nature and horizontal in application. Further, eligibility must be automatic and the conditions strictly adhered to. A subsidy, which at first appeared non-specific, may still be specific when considering other factors, including: predominant use of a subsidy programme by certain enterprises, disproportionately large amounts awarded to certain enterprises and the granting authority's exercise of discretion in granting the subsidy.[65] Subsidies may also be specific if they are limited to enterprises in a particular geographic region.[66]

---

[60] Gehring et al. (2007), p. 77.

[61] Article 1.1. Agreement on Subsidies and Countervailing Measures.

[62] Gehring et al. (2007), p. 78.

[63] Panel Report, *Canada – Measures Affecting the Export of Civilian Aircraft*, WT/DS70/R, adopted 14 April 1999, para. 9.112.

[64] Gehring et al. (2007), p. 78.

[65] Article 2.1(c) Agreement on Subsidies and Countervailing Measures.

[66] Article 2.2 Agreement on Subsidies and Countervailing Measures.

The Agreement sets out a three-tier system for subsidies. Part II sets out "red light" subsidies which are prohibited outright. This includes subsidies tied to export performance, for instance by requiring a level of export earnings for the subsidy to be granted.[67] Subsidies contingent on the use of domestic, as opposed to imported, goods are also prohibited. Part II establishes a complaints procedure starting with consultations between the complaining member and the member alleged to be making use of prohibited subsidies. Failing this, the dispute is passed on the WTO's dispute resolution body under an expedited timeframe. Following the dispute resolution procedure, if the prohibited subsidy is not immediately removed, the complaining WTO member is granted the right to take countervailing measures to avoid the subsidy's effect.

The second "amber light" category, under Part III of the Agreement, concerns actionable subsidies which may or may not be permitted depending on whether it has "adverse effects" on other WTO members. Per Article 5, adverse effect includes situations a subsidy causes: injury to another member's domestic industry; nullification or impairment of benefits accruing directly or indirectly to other Members under the GATT, in particular the benefits of bound concessions; or serious prejudice to the interests of another Member. Serious prejudice may be found where one of the following effects can be shown: the subsidy displaces or impedes the imports of a like of product of another member into the market of the subsidising member; the subsidies displaces or impedes the exports of a like product from the complaining country to third country; there is significant price undercutting, price suppression, price depression or lost sales of another member's like product in that market; the subsidy increases the world market share of the subsidising state in a particular primary product or commodity compared its average share in the previous 3 years.[68] The complaints procedure is similar to that of prohibited subsidies. Consultation, first, should serve to *"clarify the facts of the situation and to arrive at a mutually agreed solution."*[69] Where no solution is found, a Panel is convened to resolve the dispute, also allowing for a possible appeal to the appellate body. Countervailing measures are authorised where a subsidy is found to result in adverse effects to the complaining member. Such measure must be *"commensurate with the degree and nature of the adverse effects determined to exist."*[70]

Non-actionable subsidies feature in the "green light" category: members are permitted to make use of them as they do not adversely affect international trade.[71] Any form of government assistance not classified as a subsidy falls outside the scope of the Agreement and is, hence, allowed. Any subsidy not classified are specific are also allowed. A WTO member may approach the Permanent Group of Experts, a panel of five independent experts established under the Agreement, to obtain a

---

[67] Gehring et al. (2007), p. 79.
[68] Article 6 Agreement on Subsidies and Countervailing Measures.
[69] Article 4 Agreement on Subsidies and Countervailing Measures.
[70] Article 7.9 Agreement on Subsidies and Countervailing Measures.
[71] Gehring et al. (2007), p. 80.

confidential advisory opinion on any subsidy proposed by the member or that is currently maintained.

As has been sketched out above, the major remedies against prohibited and actionable remedies are either the removal of the remedy or the imposition of a countervailing duty offsetting the benefit of the exporting country's subsidy on those goods.[72] Article VI GATT provides the authorisation for WTO members to impose countervailing duties, elaborated on in Part V of the Agreement on Subsidies and Countervailing Measures. A member which is considering imposing such duties must first receive a request from domestic industry to commence a formal investigation into the subsidy. The investigation must establish that: there is a subsidy; a domestic industry is being materially injured, threatened with material injury or the establishment of a domestic industry is being impeded; and the situation was caused by the subsidy in question. Again, the first step of the investigation must be holding consultations with interested parties. The determination of injury, the factors to consider as part of a formal investigation, and procedures for conducting such an investigation are detailed in Article 15 of the Agreement on Subsidies and Countervailing Measures. Article 19 deals with the process of imposing a countervailing duty.

Agriculture subsidies are treated differently under the Agreement on Subsidies and Countervailing Measures. The WTO Agreement on Agriculture sets out two types of domestic support subsidies. Green box measures are described under the agreement has having "no, or at least most minimal, trade-distorting effects." Accordingly, the measure must be provided through a publicly funded government programme not involving transfers from consumers; and must not have the effect of providing price support to producers.[73] Examples of such measures are included in Annex 2 to the Agreement on Agriculture: research, pest and disease control, training services, inspection services, some forms of marketing services and infrastructural services not including on-farm facilities. A much wider range of domestic support is hence permitted for agricultural goods than other goods.[74] Domestic agriculture support not falling into the green box are considered trade-distorting measures which form part of the amber box. Typically, these are measures supporting prices or directly linked to production quantities. Calculations in Article 1 and Annexes 3 and 4 of the Agreement on Subsidies and Countervailing Measures lay out the total value WTO Members have agreed to reduce progressively from their amber box measures. Blue box measures are the third category encompassing domestic support that would typically feature in the amber box upon conditions of limiting production to reduce the goods' trade-distorting effect. Finally, Article 9 of the Agreement on Subsidies and Countervailing Measures covers export subsidies, which can include: cost reduction measures, internal transport subsidies, and

---

[72] Gehring et al. (2007), p. 80.
[73] Gehring et al. (2007), p. 81.
[74] Gehring et al. (2007), p. 81.

subsidies on agricultural products to be included in other products made for export.[75] WTO Members have committed to reducing these export subsidies, by the amounts listing in their schedules of commitment.

3.3 The EU's Approach to TDIs

The EU's approach to TDIs, both when it comes to dumping and subsidies, closely mirrors the processes laid out by the WTO. Trade remedies is an EU competence: investigations, implementation and monitoring of TDIs are taken up by the European Commission on behalf of all EU Member States, including the UK.

Anti-dumping requests, within the EU, are carried out by the Commission, according to the Council Regulation 384/96 of 22 December 1995, which closely mirrors the provisions of the WTO's Anti-Dumping Agreement. Any EU company may make a request, either directly or through its government, to the Commission to begin an investigation into dumping allegedly committed by a non-EU Member State. The EU conducts such investigations on behalf of the affected producers and concerned Member State(s).

Just like in the case of anti-dumping measures, the EU closely mirrors the terms of the WTO's Agreement on Subsidies and Countervailing Measures in its subsidies regime. An EU complainant may apply to the Commission, directly or through its government to instigate an investigation into alleged subsidies of non-EU States. The investigation must show that a specific subsidy has been granted which causes material injury to an EU industry. Upon such a showing, the Commission may impose countervailing duties. Communication 98/C 394/04 sets out the Commission's methods for calculating subsidies and the resulting countervailing duties and its methods of conducting investigations.

The EU has made prolific use of TDIs to preserve a competitive environment for EU industries. By the close of 2017, the EU had 99 provisional and definitive anti-dumping measures and 13 provisional and definitive countervailing measures in force, or overall 112 measures.[76] 46 investigations, including into re-openings and cases where provisional measures had been imposed.[77] The number of anti-subsidy and anti-dumping measures in force in the EU is at a historical low: from 156 in 2004, to 126 in 2011.[78] In comparison, the United States had a total of 303 measures

---

[75] Gehring et al. (2007), p. 82.

[76] European Commission, Anti-dumping, anti-subsidy, safeguard statistics covering the 12 months of 2017, 6 February 2018, http://trade.ec.europa.eu/doclib/docs/2018/february/tradoc_156598.pdf (last accessed 30 April 2018), p. 2.

[77] European Commission, Anti-dumping, anti-subsidy, safeguard statistics covering the 12 months of 2017, 6 February 2018, http://trade.ec.europa.eu/doclib/docs/2018/february/tradoc_156598.pdf (last accessed 30 April 2018), p. 2.

[78] European Commission, Trade Defence Instruments, September 2012, http://trade.ec.europa.eu/doclib/docs/2012/september/tradoc_149906.pdf (last accessed 30 April 2018), p. 2.

in force in 2011.[79] Similarly, these has been a decrease in the percentage of EU imports affected by EU anti-dumping and anti-subsidy measures, with less than 0.5% of total EU imports affected.[80]

The EU has embarked on a large-scale project to modernise its trade defence. On 3 October 2017, negotiators of the European Parliament reached an agreement on a Commission's proposal to introduce a new anti-dumping methodology for calculating dumping margins.[81] On 5 December, the European Parliament and the Council agreed on the Commission's proposal, initially presented in 2013, to modernise the EU's TDIs.[82] At the time of writing, the new rules were expected to enter into force by the end of May 2018.[83] The reforms are expected to ensure faster and more efficient investigations, with provisional measures being imposed within 7–8 months as opposed to the current 9 months; provide for the imposition of higher duties in anti-subsidy cases and anti-dumping cases of imports produced raw materials and energy provided at an artificially low price; improved calculation of injury by taking into account the costs of necessary investments (such as infrastructure or R&D) and future expenses related to social and environmental standards to reflect the 'non-injurious price' (the price the industry should have charged in normal circumstances); higher social and environmental standards; and among other things better access by EU small and medium-sized companies to trade defence investigations by putting in place bespoke streamlined procedures.[84]

4 Building Up the UK's TDI Capabilities in the Post-Brexit Era

The previous section has highlighted the complexity and technicality of the procedures laid out by the WTO to ensure that a WTO member is in a position to protect itself from unfair competition through either anti-dumping or anti-subsidy measures. Today, such measures are taken by the EU, on behalf of the affected industries or member states, including the UK. In the post-Brexit era, it will be up to the UK

---

[79] European Commission, Trade Defence Instruments, September 2012, http://trade.ec.europa.eu/doclib/docs/2012/september/tradoc_149906.pdf (last accessed 30 April 2018), p. 2.

[80] European Commission, Trade Defence Instruments, September 2012, http://trade.ec.europa.eu/doclib/docs/2012/september/tradoc_149906.pdf (last accessed 30 April 2018), p. 2.

[81] European Commission, Commission welcomes agreement on new anti-dumping methodology, 3 October 2017, http://trade.ec.europa.eu/doclib/press/index.cfm?id=1735&title=Commission-welcomes-agreement-on-new-anti-dumping-methodology (last accessed 30 April 2018).

[82] European Commission, EU modernises its trade defence instruments, 23 January 2018, http://europa.eu/rapid/press-release_MEMO-18-396_en.htm (last accessed 30 April 2018).

[83] European Commission, EU modernises its trade defence instruments, 23 January 2018, http://europa.eu/rapid/press-release_MEMO-18-396_en.htm (last accessed 30 April 2018).

[84] European Commission, EU modernises its trade defence instruments, 23 January 2018, http://europa.eu/rapid/press-release_MEMO-18-396_en.htm (last accessed 30 April 2018).

to handle its own trade defence, which, as will be shown in this section, represents a considerable challenge.

4.1 Post-Brexit Trade Defence Uncertainty

In contrast to the calls from the UK Prime Minister and Secretary for International Trade that the UK should capitalise on Brexit to be a "global champion of free trade",[85] experts testifying before the House of Lords' European Union Committee were quick to stress that it was vital for the UK to consider its trade defence measures as it leaves the EU.[86] Professor Piet Eeckhout of University College London noted being:

> [U]ncertain what would happen, for example, with the current antidumping measures that the European Union applies to imports from other WTO members, which have been the consequence of an EU-wide investigation into dumping. Lots of those currently apply, particularly to China. Whether the United Kingdom could simply continue to apply those or would not apply them may also be an issue that comes up in defining the UK's WTO status.[87]

Richard Eglin, Senior Trade Policy Advisor of White & Case LLP, took the example of anti-dumping duties currently imposed by the EU on Chinese steel.[88] If such anti-dumping measures were simply taken over and imposed by the UK, China could "object vigorously" demanding that a new investigation be carried out to demonstrate domestic injury and unfair trade. Eglin added that *"one major issue is going to be re-establishing in the UK an investigating authority that is capable of undertaking trade remedy investigations and protecting the UK's interests in any trade remedy measures that are taken against the UK."*[89] This, he stressed, is a

---

[85] Elgot J, Theresa May sets out stall for UK's place in Trump's world. The Guardian, 14 November 2016, https://www.theguardian.com/politics/2016/nov/14/uk-must-become-global-leader-in-free-trade-theresa-may-brexit-vote-donald-trump-election (last accessed 30 April 2018).

[86] House of Lords, European Union Committee, Brexit: the options for trade, 5th report of session 2016–17, https://publications.parliament.uk/pa/ld201617/ldselect/ldeucom/72/72.pdf (last accessed 30 April 2018), paras. 195–196.

[87] The Select Committee on the European Union, External Affairs and Internal Market Sub-Committees, Corrected oral evidence: Brexit: future trade between the UK and the EU, 8 September 2016, http://data.parliament.uk/writtenevidence/committeeevidence.svc/evidencedocument/eu-external-affairs-subcommittee/brexit-future-trade-between-the-uk-and-the-eu/oral/37864.html (last accessed 30 April 2018), Question 1.

[88] The Select Committee on the European Union, External Affairs and Internal Market Sub-Committees, Corrected oral evidence: Brexit: future trade between the UK and the EU, 8 September 2016, http://data.parliament.uk/writtenevidence/committeeevidence.svc/evidencedocument/eu-external-affairs-subcommittee/brexit-future-trade-between-the-uk-and-the-eu/oral/37864.html (last accessed 30 April 2018), Question 2.

[89] The Select Committee on the European Union, External Affairs and Internal Market Sub-Committees, Corrected oral evidence: Brexit: future trade between the UK and the EU, 8 September 2016, http://data.parliament.uk/writtenevidence/committeeevidence.svc/evidencedocument/eu-

"capacity-building problem", "not a negotiating problem" as the UK will not have to agree with the rest of the WTO Member States. Nonetheless, an investigating authority has to be set up, in a highly specialised area of work, over a very short period of time. According to Eglin, getting that done in 2 years "*although it is not contentious it is probably the most difficult thing facing the UK at the moment.*"[90]

Lord Aberdare asked whether the UK had the skills and capacity necessary to put in place an investigating authority.[91] Eglin emphasised in response that an investigating authority for trade remedies is "specialised work" requiring "targeted capacity-building":

The UK will need trade negotiators, trade analysts and statisticians and trade diplomats with a general background, but there will also need to be expertise in certain areas: one is dispute settlement, another is intellectual property, and another is certain parts of services. Those are specialised areas. You tend to find that people specialise in those particular areas through their career. We will need to get up to speed rather quickly on that. Dispute settlement lawyers do not grow on trees. We have plenty of good lawyers, I am sure, but whoever is doing it will need to go back and will need to know the last 20 years of dispute settlement cases in the WTO, and you do not learn that overnight; you do not pick it up that quickly. There is probably a big capacity gap, because we have not been doing this for so many years. I am sure it can be made up – we are not short of clever people – but there will need to be some rather targeted capacity-building, particularly in the investigating authority for trade remedies.[92]

Recommendation 35 of the House of Lords European Union Committee Report stressed:

Whatever framework the Government adopts, it will also need to establish a domestic authority for trade remedy investigations, to replace the work currently undertaken by the Commission on behalf of EU Member States. This will require capacity-building in a specialised area of law. This may take a considerable time, and should therefore be an early priority in preparing for Brexit.[93]

---

external-affairs-subcommittee/brexit-future-trade-between-the-uk-and-the-eu/oral/37864.htm (last accessed 30 April 2018), Question 2.

[90] The Select Committee on the European Union, External Affairs and Internal Market Sub-Committees, Corrected oral evidence: Brexit: future trade between the UK and the EU, 8 September 2016, http://data.parliament.uk/writtenevidence/committeeevidence.svc/evidencedocument/eu-external-affairs-subcommittee/brexit-future-trade-between-the-uk-and-the-eu/oral/37864.html (last accessed 30 April 2018), Question 2.

[91] The Select Committee on the European Union, External Affairs and Internal Market Sub-Committees, Corrected oral evidence: Brexit: future trade between the UK and the EU, 8 September 2016, http://data.parliament.uk/writtenevidence/committeeevidence.svc/evidencedocument/eu-external-affairs-subcommittee/brexit-future-trade-between-the-uk-and-the-eu/oral/37864.html (last accessed 30 April 2018), Question 5.

[92] The Select Committee on the European Union, External Affairs and Internal Market Sub-Committees, Corrected oral evidence: Brexit: future trade between the UK and the EU, 8 September 2016, http://data.parliament.uk/writtenevidence/committeeevidence.svc/evidencedocument/eu-external-affairs-subcommittee/brexit-future-trade-between-the-uk-and-the-eu/oral/37864.html (last accessed 30 April 2018), Question 6.

[93] House of Lords, European Union Committee, Brexit: the options for trade, 5th report of session 2016–17, https://publications.parliament.uk/pa/ld201617/ldselect/ldeucom/72/72.pdf (last accessed 30 April 2018), p. 75.

The Government in its response merely noted, very succinctly, that *"[w]ork is in hand to develop an independent trade remedies framework for the UK, and includes the need to develop an investigative function by recruiting and training staff."*[94] The key question facing the UK when it comes to post-Brexit trade defence is indeed, as right pointed out by Eglin, a question of capacity. It is expected that the UK will establish the institutional and legislative capacity to act in accordance with WTO rules but that institutional capacity needs to be built up. The Department of International Trade has focused exclusively on trade negotiations and not on building up TDI capabilities. HM Revenue and Customs, the non-ministerial department of the UK Government responsible for the collection of taxes and payment of state support, works on trade statistics but has no concrete TDI capabilities. The Department for Business, Energy & Industrial Strategy assists in state aid investigations but is not currently equipped to replace the EU Commission to complete complex investigations into allegations of dumping and subsidies. The Competition and Markets Authority (CMA) has responsibility over competition law in the UK and consumer protection but no capacity to deal with trade distortion investigations.

4.2   Establishing an Independent Investigative Authority

Given the urgent need to build up the UK's capacity to tackle allegations of unfair competition and impose TDIs, reports in August 2017 through a job advert that the UK Government was setting up a new trade authority were welcome.[95] An advert on the Department for International Trade website stressed that *"[w]e need to develop the UK's approach to tackling allegations of unfair competition and build the capability and capacity to investigate complaints and enforce the rules."*[96] The "UK Trade Remedies Organisation" would be an arm's length body of the Department for International Trade, would have around 130 staff and be operational by October 2018. The advert notes that setting up "a fully functional and fit-for-purpose organisation" would be a "huge challenge" for the UK given the "challenging deadline" and a "changing and uncertain environment".

---

[94] Department for Exiting the European Union, Department for International Trade, Response to Brexit: the options for trade, 28 February 2017, https://www.parliament.uk/documents/lords-committees/eu-external-affairs-subcommittee/Future-trade-EU-UK-Government-Response-and-Annex%20A.pdf (last accessed 30 April 2018), p. 14.

[95] Mance H, Job advert reveals surprise plans for new trade authority. Financial Times, 2 August 2017, https://www.ft.com/content/78201a5e-77a2-11e7-a3e8-60495fe6ca71 (last accessed 30 April 2018).

[96] Mance H, Job advert reveals surprise plans for new trade authority. Financial Times, 2 August 2017, https://www.ft.com/content/78201a5e-77a2-11e7-a3e8-60495fe6ca71 (last accessed 30 April 2018).

The Government White Paper on "Preparing for our future UK trade policy", published in October 2017, provided more detail about the UK's post-Brexit approach to trade remedies and trade dispute.[97] The White Paper states that *"the UK's framework will be implemented by a new mechanism to investigate cases and propose measures that offer proportionate protections for our producers."*[98] As part of this, the Government would identify existing EU members "essential to UK business" which would be carried forward. The White Paper notes that by the time the UK leaves the EU, it will be ready to *"act independently to protect UK interests should our trading partners fail to meet their international obligations and to defend any disputes brought against the UK."*[99]

The White Paper notes that as the UK leaves the EU, *"we will need to put in place an independent UK trade remedy framework to be implemented by a new mechanism to investigate cases and propose measures"*[100] in compliance with WTO rules. The following principles are listed as key to the UK's future trade remedies framework. First, impartiality, by setting up a *"new arm's length body that will investigate trade remedies cases and make recommendations on the basis of clear economic criteria"*[101] operational by the time the UK leaves the EU; ensure investigations are transparent, objective and effective; and provide a route for interested parties to appeal.

Second, proportionality to ensure the UK's TDI framework is "used judiciously and proportionately". Decisions will be based on *"clear evidence, targeted at addressing the injury caused, and take into account the interests of domestic producers and regional impacts, as well as those of other interested parties, such as user industries and consumers."*[102] This will require applying an economic interest test as part of the trade remedies investigation prior to imposing any measures; applying a UK-specific threshold for initiating cases; determining a methodology for calculating injury.

---

[97] Department for International Trade, Policy paper: preparing for our future UK trade policy, 9 October 2017, https://www.gov.uk/government/publications/preparing-for-our-future-uk-trade-policy/preparing-for-our-future-uk-trade-policy#trade-remedies (last accessed 30 April 2018).

[98] Department for International Trade, Policy paper: preparing for our future UK trade policy, 9 October 2017, https://www.gov.uk/government/publications/preparing-for-our-future-uk-trade-policy/preparing-for-our-future-uk-trade-policy#trade-remedies (last accessed 30 April 2018).

[99] Department for International Trade, Policy paper: preparing for our future UK trade policy, 9 October 2017, https://www.gov.uk/government/publications/preparing-for-our-future-uk-trade-policy/preparing-for-our-future-uk-trade-policy#trade-remedies (last accessed 30 April 2018).

[100] Department for International Trade, Policy paper: preparing for our future UK trade policy, 9 October 2017, https://www.gov.uk/government/publications/preparing-for-our-future-uk-trade-policy/preparing-for-our-future-uk-trade-policy#trade-remedies (last accessed 30 April 2018).

[101] Department for International Trade, Policy paper: preparing for our future UK trade policy, 9 October 2017, https://www.gov.uk/government/publications/preparing-for-our-future-uk-trade-policy/preparing-for-our-future-uk-trade-policy#trade-remedies (last accessed 30 April 2018).

[102] Department for International Trade, Policy paper: preparing for our future UK trade policy, 9 October 2017, https://www.gov.uk/government/publications/preparing-for-our-future-uk-trade-policy/preparing-for-our-future-uk-trade-policy#trade-remedies (last accessed 30 April 2018).

Third, efficiency, to ensure cases are *"investigated swiftly and effectively, avoiding unnecessary burdens on complainants as well as the subjects of the complaint."*[103] This is to be achieved through applying provisional measures according to WTO rules; developing a "digital service" to support the investigations process and introducing measures to tackle attempts to circumvent TDIs.

Fourthly, transparency to make sure relevant information is accessible and there is accountability for decision-making, without creating an unreasonable burden on businesses taking part in the process.

The White Paper recognises that the key need of UK companies is *"certainty, continuity and as much notice as possible for any significant changes that might directly impact them."*[104] Further, it notes that if no action is taken to transition existing EU trade remedy measures, these will no longer apply to products arriving into the UK, which could have serious effects on certain UK industries. The White Paper states that as a result, *"we will seek to effectively continue the existing trade remedies measures which matter to UK business, and which meet WTO requirements around the level of domestic production."*[105] This, it is expected, will emerge from a call for evidence from the public.

As was pointed out elsewhere by George Peretz QC,[106] the White Paper leaves considerable room for uncertainty: who ultimately will investigate and take decisions? The White Paper stresses the need for an independent evaluation and yet says that that independent body will merely "make recommendations". The White Paper does not discuss the powers of the authority to investigate, for instance, their ability to constraint information. The role of the courts, implied in the reference to the right of appeal by interested parties, is also left unclear. Who will constitute an interested party and what remedies are referred to? Interestingly, Peretz also notes that the future relationship between the UK and the EU in the field of TDIs is not sketched out in the White Paper. There may be significant advantage to extensive cooperation between the UK and the EU in the field where the interests of the EU are closely aligned.

The UK Government has since, in November 2017, set out proposed provisions for the UK trade remedies regime in the Trade Bill[107] and the Taxation (Cross-border

---

[103] Department for International Trade, Policy paper: preparing for our future UK trade policy, 9 October 2017, https://www.gov.uk/government/publications/preparing-for-our-future-uk-trade-policy/preparing-for-our-future-uk-trade-policy#trade-remedies (last accessed 30 April 2018).

[104] Department for International Trade, Policy paper: preparing for our future UK trade policy, 9 October 2017, https://www.gov.uk/government/publications/preparing-for-our-future-uk-trade-policy/preparing-for-our-future-uk-trade-policy#trade-remedies (last accessed 30 April 2018).

[105] Department for International Trade, Policy paper: preparing for our future UK trade policy, 9 October 2017, https://www.gov.uk/government/publications/preparing-for-our-future-uk-trade-policy/preparing-for-our-future-uk-trade-policy#trade-remedies (last accessed 30 April 2018).

[106] Peretz G, Trade defence instruments: issues for the UK post-Brexit. UK Trade Forum, 10 October 2017, https://uktradeforum.net/2017/10/10/trade-defence-instruments-issues-for-the-united-kingdom-post-brexit/ (last accessed 30 April 2018).

[107] Trade Bill, see https://publications.parliament.uk/pa/bills/cbill/2017-2019/0122/18122.pdf (last accessed 30 April 2018)

Trade) Bill.[108] Schedule of the Taxation (Cross-border Trade) Bill sets out the framework of operation of the Trade Remedies Authority for "dumping of goods or foreign subsidies causing injury to UK industry." Peretz notes that "*[t]he regime set out in Schedule 4 resembles maps of Africa produced by early 19th century European explorers: while the outlines are clear, large areas are, in effect, marked as 'unknown lands' or 'here be dragons'.*"[109] While the determination of an injury and the maximum amount of duty is to be handled by the Trade Remedies Authorities, the final determination as to whether the imposition of a TDI is in the public interest is left to the Secretary of State. Paragraph 30 notes regulations "*may make provision for or in connection with... the review or appeal of decisions made by the TRA or the Secretary of State under provision made by or under this Schedule.*" This does not elaborate on the already barely sketched out procedures for Appeal of the White Paper as to which decisions should be subject to appeal and how the balance between the judiciary and the executive is to be drawn. Altogether, in Peretz's words:

> If, as now seems likely, the United Kingdom does leave the EU trade remedy system, there will be considerable and immediate calls on the TRA to take action in all sorts of sectors. A robust legal framework therefore needs to be in place well before it starts work. The framework in the two Bills is a start, but there is much work still to do.[110]

It should be recalled that despite trading currently under the same rules, similar calls upon EU authorities to impose trade defence measures might also be made from the rest of the EU once the UK starts to restructure its economy, perhaps with the help of loosening rules on state aid or competition.

5 Post-Brexit Trade Defence Options in a Customs Union: The EU-Turkey Case Study

The previous sections have discussed options for trade defence in the situation where the UK, upon leaving the EU, leaves the customs union and is left to rely solely on WTO rules. The option of the UK remaining in the customs union was put back on the table on 26 February 2018. Jeremy Corbyn, leader of the Labour Party, shifted the party's position to remain in a customs union with the EU upon the UK leaving the bloc.[111] The speech was not free of ambiguity, particularly concerning

---

[108] Taxation (Cross-border Trade) Bill, see https://publications.parliament.uk/pa/bills/cbill/2017-2019/0128/18128.pdf (last accessed 30 April 2018).

[109] Peretz G, Briefing paper: the government's proposed legislation for trade remedies. UK Trade Forum, 22 January 2018, https://uktradeforum.net/2018/01/22/418/#wto (last accessed 30 April 2018).

[110] Peretz G, Briefing paper: the government's proposed legislation for trade remedies. UK Trade Forum, 22 January 2018, https://uktradeforum.net/2018/01/22/418/#wto (last accessed 30 April 2018).

[111] Pickard J, Parker G and Hughes L, Pro-EU toy faction to join Labour on Brexit in threat to May. Financial Times, 26 February 2018, https://www.ft.com/content/44558030-1ae8-11e8-aaca-4574d7dabfb6 (last accessed 30 April 2018).

Mr. Corbyn's insistence that the UK should join "*a customs union*" (emphasis added) as distinct from "the" customs union with the EU. Nonetheless, for this article's purposes, it opens up new options for the UK's post-Brexit trade defence that warrant separate analysis. Turkey is the natural point of comparison as a country which, although not a Member State of the EU, is in a customs union with the bloc.

5.1 Trade Defence Modalities in the EU-Turkey Customs Union

Decision No. 1/95 of the EC-Turkey Association Council, adopted on 22 December 1995, lays out the details of the Association between the Turkey and the EU (then the European Economic Community).[112] The agreement excludes agriculture and services and removes all tariffs between the parties, while providing for external trade rules. As provided in Article 12 of the Decision: "*Turkey shall, in relation to countries which are not members of the Community, apply provisions and implementing measures which are substantially similar to those of the Community's commercial policy.*"

When it comes to trade remedies, "*very strikingly, anti-dumping is still possible between the EU and Turkey*", as was pointed out by Dr Peter Holmes, Reader in economics at the University of Sussex, in his evidence to the House of Lords' European Union Committee.[113] Duties on goods traded between Turkey and the bloc can still be imposed. This has also been stressed by André Sapir:

> As a result, the EU-Turkey customs union is in fact a hybrid between a genuine Customs Union and a [Free Trade Agreement (FTA)]. This is demonstrated by the fact that Turkey has adopted the EU's common external tariff for most, but not all, industrial products and only for some agricultural products; it applies additional customs duties for some textile products from countries outside the EU and the EU's FTA partners; it applies trade defence instruments, such as anti-dumping and countervailing duties, in a totally different manner (for different products and countries) than the EU; and it has not concluded FTAs with some EU FTA partners (including Mexico, South Africa and Ukraine).[114]

Decision No. 1/95 generally provides that state aid and competition law apply between the EU and Turkey but countervailing measures may be permitted in specific circumstances. Section III of the Decision deals with TDIs. Per Article 44 of

---

[112] Decision No 1/95 of the EC-Turkey association council on implementing the final phase of the Customs Union (96/142/EC), 22 December 1995.

[113] House of Lords, European Union Committee, Brexit: the options for trade, 5th report of session 2016–17, https://publications.parliament.uk/pa/ld201617/ldselect/ldeucom/72/72.pdf (last accessed 30 April 2018), para. 92.

[114] Sapir A, Should the UK pull out of the EU customs union?. Bruegel, 1 August 2016, http://bruegel.org/2016/08/should-the-uk-pull-out-of-the-eu-customs-union/ (last accessed 30 April 2018).

the Decision, Article 47 of the Additional Protocol, signed on 23 November 1970, to the Agreement establishing the Association between the European Economic Community and Turkey provides the modalities of implementation of TDIs between Turkey and the EU.[115]

The EU and Turkey may apply to the Council of Association to complain of the other party's dumping practices. The Council of Association upon a finding that there has been dumping may issue recommendations to the person or persons to put an end to those practiced.[116] The injured party may take protective measure, after first having notified the Council of Association, where: the Council of Association has not taken any decision within 3 months from the making of the application or despite the issue of recommendations the dumping practice continue.[117] Interim protective measures may be introduced if immediate action is necessary to ensure the interests of the injured party but must not be in force for longer than 3 months from the date of application.[118] The Council of Association may recommend that TDI measures be suspended pending the issue of a recommendation and may recommend the abolition or amendment of measures taken when despite the issue of recommendations the dumping practice continued.[119]

Article 44 of the Decision provides that any anti-dumping or countervailing measures shall be reviewed by the EU-Turkey Association Council upon the request of either party. The Association Council may suspend the applications of those TDIs *"provided that Turkey has implemented competition, State aid control and other relevant parts of the acquis communautaire"*[120] to ensure Turkey is providing against unfair competition in a comparable way to that the EU.

The consultation and decision-making procedures laid out in Section II Chapter V of the Decision do not apply to TDIs put in place by either party. The EU and Turkey instead *"shall endeavour, through exchange of information and consultation, to seek possibilities for coordinating their action when the circumstances and international obligations of both Parties allow."*[121] Per Article 46, where the EU or Turkey has put in force TDIs against the other party or with third countries, *"that Party may make imports of the products concerned from the territory of the other Party subject to the application of those measures."*

---

[115] Additional Protocol and Financial Protocol signed on 23 November 1970, annexed to the Agreement establishing the Association between the European Economic Community and Turkey and on measures to be taken for their entry into force.

[116] Article 47(1) Additional Protocol.

[117] Article 47(2) Additional Protocol.

[118] Article 47(2) Additional Protocol.

[119] Article 47(3) Additional Protocol.

[120] Article 44 Decision No 1/95 of the EC-Turkey Association Council on implementing the final phase of the Customs Union (96/142/EC), 22 December 1995.

[121] Article 45 Decision No. 1/95.

5.2 Lessons for UK's Trade Defence Options in a Customs Union

A 2014 evaluation from the World Bank of the EU-Turkey customs union draws a very mixed portrait of trade defence measures between the EU and Turkey. The study notes that "*a key source of concern [is] the use of Trade Defense Instruments (TDIs) by both parties.*"[122] The World Bank study reveals two important lessons of the EU-Turkey customs union for the UK's own trade defence post-Brexit options: first, TDIs ability to undermine bilateral trade and, second, problems linked to a lack of coordination.

First, the World Bank study shows that TDIs may drastically impede trade between the parties of a common union. Thus, it notes that, while the use of TDIs by the EU and Turkey has mostly not been intended to undermine bilateral trade, it can "*still create a policy environment of substantial uncertainty for their exporters.*"[123] 3% of Turkey's dumping investigations between 1995 and 2015 targeted exports from the EU. Conversely, 9% of the total number of products investigated by the EU over the same period were aimed at Turkey. Further, the study emphasised that recent use of TDIs between the two parties could significantly threaten bilateral trade.[124] Turkey's actual or proposed TDIs could affect up to 1 billion in annual imports from the EU, while the EU's proposed TDIs could affect nearly US$500 million in annual imports from Turkey. The study also highlighted that Turkey's application of TDIs had created divergent economic incentives across different EU Member States, with anti-dumping measures being applied selectively across different EU countries.[125] Given that the EU is the UK's largest trading partner, it is imperative that trade continue to be able to flow between the two entities, so as to little the potential heavy economic impact. The EU-Turkey case study illustrates that, where the UK officially embraces the customs union option, it is crucial that sufficient time be given during the negotiations between the UK and the EU to the question of trade defence.

---

[122] World Bank, Evaluation of the EU-Turkey customs union. Report No. 85830-TR, 28 March 2014, www.worldbank.org/content/dam/Worldbank/document/eca/turkey/tr-eu-customs-union-eng.pdf (last accessed 30 April 2018), p. ii.

[123] World Bank, Evaluation of the EU-Turkey customs union. Report No. 85830-TR, 28 March 2014, www.worldbank.org/content/dam/Worldbank/document/eca/turkey/tr-eu-customs-union-eng.pdf (last accessed 30 April 2018), para. 75.

[124] World Bank, Evaluation of the EU-Turkey customs union. Report No. 85830-TR, 28 March 2014, www.worldbank.org/content/dam/Worldbank/document/eca/turkey/tr-eu-customs-union-eng.pdf (last accessed 30 April 2018), para. 76.

[125] World Bank, Evaluation of the EU-Turkey customs union. Report No. 85830-TR, 28 March 2014, www.worldbank.org/content/dam/Worldbank/document/eca/turkey/tr-eu-customs-union-eng.pdf (last accessed 30 April 2018), para. 78.

Secondly, the World Bank study shows that the use of Tdis by the EU and Turkey has not been coordinated.[126] There is very little overlap in the product coverage of the parties' use of Tdis or against common trading partners. 15% of the 329 different products that Turkey investigated and the 336 products that the EU investigated were subject to investigations by both parties between 1995 and 2011. In less than 2% of each party's total investigation was the particular good investigated by both the Turkey and the EU in the same year. According to the study, *"[t]his suggests that the differential use of Tdis across Turkey and the EU may be related to each economy facing different shocks for which there is evidence that movements in the business cycle and real exchange rates may be important determinants of new TDI import restrictions."*[127] Post-Brexit, as was already said above, there would be significant advantage to cooperation between the EU and the UK when it comes to trade defence. The UK and the EU will likely continue to have closely aligned interests on particular trade practices in the post-Brexit era. This could avoid a duplication of efforts and wasted resources. This question should hence also be tackled appropriately in negotiations between the UK and the EU as the UK prepares itself to leave the bloc.

6 Post-Brexit Competition Law Option

There is a small possibility that the hard stance of the UK government to this date is only a negotiation position. If the UK were to accept all competition and state aid rules, this would, de facto, leave no room for the application of any TDI.

This would notably by the case if the UK changed its approach to eventually embrace continued permanent membership in the European Single Market. This would be the case if the UK struck an arrangement by which it would be a party to the European Economic Area (EEA) Agreement. This would require the UK to join the European Free Trade Association (EFTA) as membership to the EEA is open to Member States of the EU and EFTA.

In an EEA-type agreement between the UK and the EU, competition rules could continue to apply in many areas, although there could be important exclusions in the areas of agriculture and fisheries. The EU Commission has sole responsibility for mergers and acquisitions which could significantly reduce competition in the Single Market, as provided in Council Regulation No. 139/2004. The EFTA Surveillance Authority and the European Commission share other competition responsibilities, per Part IV of the Agreement on the European Economic Area which deals with

---

[126] World Bank, Evaluation of the EU-Turkey customs union. Report No. 85830-TR, 28 March 2014, www.worldbank.org/content/dam/Worldbank/document/eca/turkey/tr-eu-customs-union-eng.pdf (last accessed 30 April 2018), para. 74.

[127] World Bank, Evaluation of the EU-Turkey customs union. Report No. 85830-TR, 28 March 2014, www.worldbank.org/content/dam/Worldbank/document/eca/turkey/tr-eu-customs-union-eng.pdf (last accessed 30 April 2018), para. 74.

competition.[128] While EU Member States are subject to the European Commission's review of state aid, the EFTA Surveillance Authority, per Article 62 of the Agreement, would be responsible for state aid enforcement, in the context of the UK if it were to become an EFTA state.[129] Such decisions are subject to the determination of the EFTA Court.

7 Conclusion

This article has reviewed various trade defence options between the EU and the UK after Brexit. This analysis has shown that the imposition of trade defence measures is certainly on the horizon in EU-UK relations without a deal. In the event that the UK leaves the EU without any form of agreement, the UK will be left to trade with the bloc on the basis of WTO rules. WTO rules will also be the basis of trade between the UK and any third State, in the absence of any comprehensive free trade agreement.

While the UK will continue to be a member of the WTO upon its departure from the EU, the question of how the UK will be able to reissue the currently existing EU schedules of commitment under its own name is much more complex. New schedules can be given effect through a variety of procedures, renegotiation or rectification in particular could partly shield the UK from the risk of a veto from any other WTO Member State. Negotiations in any case will be necessary to identify the UK's own commitments, independent of those of the EU. Reports of preliminary breakthrough in ongoing negotiations about dividing up the UK and the EU's tariff-rate quotas are hence particularly welcome.

This article has argued that the question of TDI is crucial and should not be overlooked as the UK makes its preparations to leave the EU. Anti-dumping measures and countervailing measures against subsidised goods are vital tools to ensure that the UK's own industries are protected from unfair competition in the post-Brexit era. While the UK as an EU Member State has so far relied on the sole competence and expertise of the European Commission when it comes to TDIs, the UK will be left to handle its own trade defence.

The only way to avoid the imposition of trade defence measures would be either full participation of the UK in the single market or at least an acceptance of all state aid and competition rules, probably including ultimately the jurisdiction of the Court of Justice. This latter element might not be acceptable to the UK government, which then makes TDIs in UK-EU relations unavoidable post-Brexit.

---

[128] Decision of the Council and the Commission of 13 December 1993 on the conclusion of the Protocol adjusting the Agreement on the European Economic Area between the European Communities, their Member States and the Republic of Austria, the Republic of Finland, the Republic of Iceland, the Principality of Liechtenstein, the Kingdom of Norway and the Kingdom of Sweden.
[129] Article 62 EEA Agreement.

While many in the UK argue for creative thinking on the topic, it is clear that the UK government prepares for a robust legal and institutional framework to impose TDI measures unilaterally post-Brexit. Only an agreement between the UK and the EU could prevent such imposition. An agreed solution would also make the enjoyment of WTO Membership for the UK much easier, as it would eradicate the considerable uncertainty about the terms of UK WTO Membership. There is an urgent need for the UK to build up its TDI capacity to prepare for the post-Brexit era. At present, while recent proposals for the UK government about setting up a Trade Remedies Authority are encouraging, they leave considerable room for uncertainty.

References

Dunt I (2016) Brexit: what the hell happens now? Canbury Press, Kingston

Eeckhout P (2006) The EU and its Member States in the WTO – issues of responsibility. In: Bartels L, Ortino F (eds) Regional trade agreements and the WTO legal system. Oxford University Press, New York, pp 450–464

Gehring M, Hepburn J, Segger J (2007) World trade law in practice. Globe Business Publishing, London

Koutrakos P (2016) Brexit and international treaty-making – editorial. Eur Law Rev 1:2–3

Peers S, Barnard C (2017) European Union law. Oxford University Press, Oxford

EU Trade Defence Instruments and Free Trade Agreements: Is Past Experience an Indication for the Future? Implications for Brexit?

Till Müller-Ibold

Contents

The views expressed by the author are his personal views. He is grateful for the input and support received from his colleagues Fynn Dewald and Marie-Astrid Dossche. Nevertheless, responsibility for errors or omission rests with the author alone.

T. Müller-Ibold (✉)
Cleary Gottlieb Steen & Hamilton LLP, Brussels, Belgium
e-mail: tmuelleribold@cgsh.com

© Springer International Publishing AG, part of Springer Nature 2018   191
M. Bungenberg et al. (eds.), *The Future of Trade Defence Instruments*,
European Yearbook of International Economic Law,
https://doi.org/10.1007/978-3-319-95306-9_9

Abstract This article considers the question of whether the European Union's regional trade agreements (RTA, free trade areas or customs unions) can provide for limitations to the use of anti-dumping and countervailing measures (TDIs). It finds, first, that the selective application of such measures is possible vis-à-vis WTO Members, provided that the RTA addresses the underlying causes for the difficulties created by dumping or subsidisation. Second, the practice of the European Union has been to rarely agree on the elimination of anti-dumping and countervailing measures. Such elimination required that market access, competition and the State aid (subsidisation) rules were fully aligned with those applicable in the Union and an effective independent enforcement mechanism was in place. Anti-dumping and countervailing measures have been subjected to certain (mainly procedural) restrictions, if market access, competition and State aid rules were largely harmonised (but not always fully aligned) and if there was some (but not sufficiently independent and effective) enforcement mechanism. It concludes that, to the extent history is a guide, there is a significant risk that once the UK is no longer a Member State, TDIs will reappear in the bilateral relationship unless (1) the full substantive alignment of the rules is maintained and (2) an enforcement mechanism for such rules can be found, which will be considered sufficiently "effective" and independent from the UK.

1   Introduction

The European Union (EU or Union) has concluded a significant number of bilateral or multilateral agreements, aimed at facilitating free trade between the parties. At the same time, the Union is an important "user" of trade defence instruments (TDI). For purposes of this article, we will only consider anti-dumping measures and anti-subsidy measures (countervailing duties) as TDI measures. Safeguards follow significantly different patterns and have a different economic logic.

Agreements aimed at liberalising trade usually are concluded as Regional Trade Agreements (RTA). RTA are Free Trade Agreements (FTA), aimed at eliminating customs duties and other trade restrictions as regards products (and services) originating in the territory of the parties, or Customs Unions (CU), which create a single customs territory, in which goods that are in free circulation can freely move. The reason that only FTA and CU are used lies in the WTO Agreements, which authorise a deviation from the "Most-Favoured Nation" (MFN) obligation in particular as regards these two types of RTA (Article XXIV GATT 1994).

This article considers the question of whether RTAs can provide for limitations to the use of TDIs (anti-dumping and countervailing measures) and under which circumstances the Union has agreed to such limitations. The analysis considers four main questions:

1. The analytical framework: Why are TDIs imposed and can RTA better deal with the issues in question than TDI?
2. WTO compliance: Is it legally possible (or even legally required) to eliminate the use of TDIs amongst the parties to an RTA under WTO rules (in particular in light of the MFN obligation and other non-discrimination rules)?
3. The EU's practice: What has the practice of the European Union been as regards the elimination (or limitation) of anti-dumping and countervailing measures on the basis of mutual market access commitments in Customs Unions and Free Trade areas?
4. Conclusion: What pattern can be identified in the approach of the European Union in this regard and can that pattern provide guidance for the Brexit process that is presently unfolding?

2 Analytical Framework

This chapter explains the basic concept of dumping and subsidisation, the economic and policy conditions for these practices and the reasons why countries take action against them. It also explains why anti-dumping and countervailing duties are relatively crude countermeasures and that more targeted measures with respect to the root cause of dumping and subsidisation or the policy considerations that lead to TDI measures can, in principle, be agreed upon in RTAs.

2.1 Rationale and Preconditions for Dumping Practices

Dumping is, by definition,[1] characterised by selling the same (or a very similar, "like") product at a higher price domestically than for export. It is, in other words, a form of price discrimination in international trade.[2] Such behaviour can be rational for exporters in essentially two cases. First, exporters may be forced by their

---

[1] See, inter alia, Agreement on Implementation of Article VI of the General Agreement on Tariffs and Trade 1994 (Anti-dumping Agreement or ADA), Article 2.1: "*For the purpose of this Agreement, a product is to be considered as being dumped, i.e. introduced into the commerce of another country at less than its normal value, if the export price of the product exported from one country to another is less than the comparable price, in the ordinary course of trade, for the like product when destined for consumption in the exporting country.*" See also Article 1(2) of Regulation (EU) 2016/1036, OJ 2016 L 176/21 (Basic Anti-Dumping Regulation or BADR).

[2] Müller et al. (2009), p. 5; Jessen (2012), pp. 263 et seq.

government to engage in such practices, for example, to overcome an imbalance of trade and the resulting shortage of foreign currencies. These are relatively rare cases, because they are typically economically harmful to both the exporter and the country of export, at least in the medium to long term.

Second, and more importantly, dumping can be economically rational for exporters when they are able to sustainably price in a discriminatory manner, without being constrained by a risk of arbitrage, i.e. the risk of exported goods being returned to the country of origin. If, for example, domestic prices and sales volumes are high enough to cover the full fixed costs of the entire production and the variable costs for products sold domestically, it would be sufficient to sell the production destined for export at or above variable (or at least marginal) costs to still improve the overall profitability of the undertaking in question, even if these sales are made below full costs. This will typically also help the "dumping" producer to reduce overall costs through economies of scale and/or scope. In the longer term, and assuming that producers in third countries targeted by the split pricing cannot sustain sales below full cost over a longer period of time, the "dumping" producer may even eliminate competition and then (later) enjoy supra-competitive rents in the affected export markets.

Yet, dumping without market segregation is unlikely to occur. The reason is that dumping will not work, if the lower priced exports can easily be returned to the country of origin and the resulting sales price can be transferred out of the country of origin. In such a case, with some price adjustment for transportation costs and arbitrage, the exported products would compete with the domestic sales of the producer in the exporting country, thus nullifying any benefit the producer may have sought. In addition, if similar goods are produced in other countries and can easily reach the home market of the producer, for example after having been displaced by its lower priced exports, they will undermine any potential benefit of such dumping, essentially in the same way as a return of the products exported at a lower price would.

A key requirement for dumping therefore is an effective market segregation.[3] Such segregation (or asymmetry in market access)[4] can have different causes. First, private action may restrain (re-)entry of products into the country of origin. Some "private" entry barriers can (in rare cases) result from unobjectionable consumer preferences, but they may also be induced by unilateral conduct of undertakings with significant market power (abuses of dominance, Article 102 EU Treaty), result from anti-competitive agreements between local competitors (e.g. boycott agreements) or result from indirect government action (government marketing campaigns benefitting domestic products (such as the famous "Buy Irish" campaign of the Irish government in the late 70s)).[5]

---

[3] See Baule (2017), paras. 76 et seq.

[4] Müller et al. (2009), p. 5; Giannakopoulos (2006), p. 3; Baule (2017), paras. 76 et seq.

[5] Under EU law, such state action is incompatible with the free movement rules (e.g. Article 34 TFEU, see CJEU, case C-249/81, *Commission v Ireland*, ECLI:EU:C:1982:402).

Second, market segregation and asymmetry in market access can result from state action.[6] The State may decide to protect its home market through customs measures (high duty rates used to be common), but recently non-tariff barriers (such as regulatory restrictions and obscure product standards) or simply delay and lots of red-tape have become the more common avenues for discouraging or even preventing effective market access by third country producers.[7]

The effect of dumping in the country to which products are exported is that prices are lower than they would have been absent such practices and based on undistorted market forces.

2.2 Rationale for Subsidisation

Subsidisation is a very different animal. Subsidisation occurs when the State interferes with markets by providing an economic benefit to one or more economic operators, on terms which that operator could not obtain on the market, in circumstances where such measure might distort competition.[8] This is typically an expression of public policy objectives, which are pursued by a given country or region in favour of one or several undertakings, "horizontal objectives" (support for research and development, education, employment of disadvantaged workers, etc.) or regional development objectives. This selective state support improves the beneficiaries' bottom line and thus typically affects competition.

Export prices for goods where the producer has benefitted from such benefits tend to be lower than they would have been absent such support, because the subsidies reduce, in effect, the costs of goods sold. In this respect, the outcome resembles the effect of dumping practices, namely that goods reach third countries at prices lower than what market forces alone would have led to.

---

[6] Müller et al. (2009), p. 7 suggest that dumping is typically a result of mercantilist government intervention.

[7] A well-known example from within the EU is the French decision in 1982 to require, just before then popular Japanese videorecorders for the Christmas holiday season were to be shipped to France, that all such VCRs needed to clear customs in the small and understaffed customs office of Poitiers, a small town in the middle of France. This virtually stopped all such imports. See, inter alia, Lewis P, The latest battle of Poitiers. The New York Times, 14 January 1983, http://www.nytimes.com/1983/01/14/business/the-latest-battle-of-poitiers.html (last accessed 30 April 2018).

[8] For a definition of the term *subsidy*, see Articles 1 and 2 of the WTO Agreement on Subsidies and Countervailing Measures (ASCM). The EU definition of "State aid" in Article 107(1) TFEU is very similar (but not identical), see, for greater detail, European Commission, Commission Notice on the notion of State aid as referred to in Article 107(1) of the Treaty on the Functioning of the European Union, OJ 2016 C 262/1.

2.3 Rationale for Combatting Dumping and Subsidisation

The rationale for combatting dumping and subsidisation is predominately one of economic policy. The rationale differs, however, between dumping and subsidisation.

2.3.1 Combatting Dumping

From an economic perspective, dumping results in a resource and welfare transfer from the country of origin to the country of destination, where consumers benefit from lower prices. Hence, prima facie, the effects may well be considered positive and desirable. Increased competitive pressure may also be viewed positively. Moreover, economists point towards the fact that it is in most instances unlikely that foreign and dumping producers are able to change course from any predatory pricing position without losing considerable market shares.[9] As Gabriel Felbermayr pointed out in the course of this conference, there is little economic evidence that dumping will typically lead to undesirable welfare effects.[10]

Nevertheless, asymmetric market access is a concern from the perspective of economic policy and for more general political reasons. Often it is difficult to identify the exact reasons for the asymmetry and even more difficult to combat their root cause.

As regards asymmetries caused by State interference, the root cause is often linked to sovereign decisions by trading partners. The EU cannot force them to change their policies (except those that are incompatible with WTO rules) and such policies may not be immediately apparent. For example, large trading partners of the European Union, such as India and China, are viewed as having both the economic potential and, at times, the political will to limit market access for third countries while expecting market access for their products. EU anti-dumping measures are then one instrument to combat such asymmetry, if the asymmetry leads to price discrimination and if the price discrimination leads to injurious effects in the Union.

Moreover, asymmetric market access can result from private behaviour. This behaviour may include anti-competitive agreements and concerted practices (e.g. an exclusivity agreement of the dominant domestic producer with distributors for such products in the country of origin) or exclusionary practices, which may amount to an abuse of market power by a dominant producer. Again, the underlying practices may not be immediately apparent or easy to detect, in particular if the relevant activities are conducted in third countries, where violation of EU competition rules

---

[9] Müller et al. (2009), p. 6.

[10] Gabriel Felbermayr, Economic Rationale and Relevance of TDIs, Global Trends and Empirical Evidence, Conference on "The Future of Trade Defence Instruments: Global Policy Trends and Legal Challenges", Brussels, 30–31 March 2017 and the critique of the traditional economic approach by Müller et al. (2009) pp. 7 et seq. For further reference on the discussion of the economic and policy justification for anti-dumping measures, see also Baule (2017), para. 77; Jessen (2012), p. 264 with reference to Trebilcock and Howse (2005), pp. 250–260 and other articles.

(e.g. under Article 101 and 102 TFEU) are difficult to pursue, in light of the territorial limitations of the Commission's investigative and enforcement powers. The often quoted concern that the "dumping" producer practices predatory pricing with the intent to monopolise the market may not have been proven very often,[11] but the EU's underlying policy objective of avoiding market segregation covers a much broader range of private actor anti-competitive behaviour than predatory pricing.[12]

In sum, market segregation is a prerequisite for effective dumping practices. Such market segregation is considered a problem, but it is often difficult to identify and combat the root cause for such segregation. Therefore, the existence of dumping practices is an indicator of such segregation and by combatting the dumping practices the Union is acting against specific effects of such segregation on its domestic industry.

It is also for this reason that the GATT 1947[13] and today the WTO rules (including the GATT 1994[14] and the Anti-Dumping Agreement[15]) permit anti-dumping measures. However, the WTO rules do not make all price discrimination and not all forms of dumping illegal. Rather they provide for a more balanced approach: anti-dumping measures are permissible if, and only if, the dumping causes injurious effects for a domestic industry.[16]

However, the Union uses an imperfect tool, which does not directly deal with the root cause of the market access asymmetry but tries to soothe the symptoms by limiting certain harmful effects on the domestic industry. In the absence of other effective mechanisms, this tool is in many cases the only tool available.

---

[11] Müller et al. (2009), p. 7.

[12] Müller et al. (2009), p. 7.

[13] General Agreement on Tariffs and Trade (GATT 1947), Article VI:1 and 2: *"The contracting parties recognize that dumping, by which products of one country are introduced into the commerce of another country at less than the normal value of the products, is to be condemned if it causes or threatens material injury to an established industry in the territory of a contracting party or materially retards the establishment of a domestic industry". (...) "In order to offset or prevent dumping, a contracting party may levy on any dumped product an anti-dumping duty not greater in amount than the margin of dumping in respect of such product."*

[14] The General Agreement on Tariffs and Trade 1994 (GATT 1994) incorporates Article VI of the GATT 1947 by reference.

[15] See Part I, Article 1 ADA (Principles): *"An anti-dumping measure shall be applied only under the circumstances provided for in Article VI of GATT 1994 and pursuant to investigations initiated(1) and conducted in accordance with the provisions of this Agreement."*

[16] Article VI:6 GATT 1947 and GATT 1994: *"No contracting party shall levy any anti-dumping (...) duty on the importation of any product of the territory of another contracting party unless it determines that the effect of the dumping (...) is such as to cause or threaten material injury to an established domestic industry (...)."*

2.3.2   Combatting Subsidisation

The reason for combatting subsidisation are generally policy reasons. Subsidies granted in the country of origin that benefit certain products and that lead to a reduction of prices in the country to which they are exported will lead to a transfer of economic resources from the country of origin to the country of destination. In economic terms, that is generally a benefit for the economy of the country of destination.

However, the effect of such resource transfer may not always be welcome. The country of destination may have other policy priorities and may thus find subsidies objectionable that favour conflicting policy objectives, but that have nevertheless an effect in the country of destination. Moreover, the distortion of competition, which is inherently a consequence of subsidisation, is a basis for legitimate concerns of the country of destination.

This logic is also the basis for the basic WTO rules, laid down in Article VI GATT 1947 and 1994 as implemented in more detail in the WTO Agreement on Subsidies and Countervailing Measures (ASCM).[17] The ASCM defines the concept of a "subsidy" (Articles 1 and 2 ASCM) and distinguishes certain "prohibited" types of subsidies (such as export subsidies)[18] from merely "actionable" subsidies (those which cause adverse effects in the country of destination).[19] A WTO member can adopt countervailing measures (typically a countervailing duty equal to the amount of the subsidy embodied in an imported product) with respect to imported products that benefitted from such subsidies.[20]

A third group of essentially authorised forms of public support (e.g. subsidies for research and development, etc.; "non-actionable subsidies") was originally identified in Article 8 ASCM, but these rules expired after 5 years (pursuant to Article 31 ASCM), because WTO Members could not agree (based on diverging policy objectives(!)) to prolong or reformulate the green light package.[21]

Countervailing measures aim at siphoning off the subsidy value represented in each unit of product brought to the country of destination. Often, subsidies indirectly contained in downstream products are not captured. In addition, the WTO rules do not make all forms of subsidisation illegal. Rather they provide for a more limited approach: countervailing measures are permissible if, and only if, subsidisation causes injurious effects for a domestic industry.[22]

---

[17] Agreement on Subsidies and Countervailing Measures (ASCM).
[18] Part II, Articles 3 and 4 ASCM (Prohibited Subsidies).
[19] Part III, Articles 5–7 ASCM (Actionable Subsidies).
[20] Article 7 ASCM.
[21] See ASCM Overview, Note 1, https://www.wto.org/english/tratop_e/scm_e/subs_e.htm (last accessed 30 April 2018).
[22] Article VI:6 GATT 1947 and GATT 1994: *"No contracting party shall levy any (…) countervailing duty on the importation of any product of the territory of another contracting party unless it determines that the effect of (…) the subsidization is such as to cause or threaten material injury to an established domestic industry (…)."*

In sum, countervailing measures are again a fairly crude measure, in that they deal with limited economic effects of the subsidisation and they do not confront directly the policy divergence, which is the reason for the country of destination taking countervailing measures.

2.4 Combatting the Underlying Root Cause

The main objective in establishing RTAs is to increase the level of trade liberalisation. One of the central propositions of this article is that RTAs (Customs Unions and Free Trade Agreements) can address the concerns that lead countries to combat dumping practices and subsidisation, by means which are more directly aimed at the concerns and root causes, in a more trade enhancing manner and not through the relatively crude approach that is inherent to the imposition of anti-dumping or countervailing measures.

As outlined above, dumping practices presuppose the presence of an asymmetric market access, which can be largely avoided in the framework of an RTA. Market access and the free movement of goods can be ensured by a combination of measures.

- *State induced* limitations can be countered. First, customs duties and all charges having an equivalent effect can be abolished, which is a typical feature of RTA and a requirement under the WTO rules for their lawful existence. Second, non-tariff barriers can be eliminated (or at least significantly reduced), inter alia through harmonisation of norms and products requirements and specifications. Third, other forms of State intervention in the market (and including through "soft" measures, such as the "Buy Irish" campaign) can be declared illegal. And fourth, the free movement of capital (including as regards the purchase price for goods sold) can be guaranteed.
- Limitations on market access resulting from *private action* aimed at market segregation can be countered by application of competition rules, in particular by application of harmonised competition rules relating to cartels, concerted practices and abuse of market power.

As regards subsidisation, parties to an RTA can align their subsidisation policies. A minimum harmonisation had been temporarily possible at the WTO level,[23] but policy differences re-emerged and policy harmonisation ended after 5 years. However, such policy alignment is easier in the context of RTA, with a smaller number of players and, often, a higher level of similarity in economic conditions.

Against this analytical background, we now proceed to the analysis of the question of whether is it necessary, impermissible or simply permissible under WTO rules to replace anti-dumping and countervailing measures as regards RTA partner

---

[23] Article 8 and 31 ASCM.

countries with market access, competition and subsidisation rules in RTAs, while retaining anti-dumping and countervailing measures vis-à-vis all other WTO Members, that did not enter into such agreements. Thereafter, we turn to an analysis of the actual practice of the EU in its RTAs with other countries.

3   Can (or Must) TDI Be Eliminated Between Members of a Customs Union or Free Trade Area?

Is the elimination of Trade Defence Instruments in the framework of Customs Unions or Free Trade Agreements, which invariably relate to some, but not all WTO Members, consistent with WTO law?

International trading relations are marked by an ever-growing number of preferential trade agreements. The key objective of the parties to such agreements is to mutually improve market access and to remove remaining trade restrictions through a more preferential treatment than the treatment granted to third countries. Such preferential trade agreements, while requiring justification as diverging from the basic MFN principle,[24] are clearly contemplated in WTO law, as is apparent from the exceptions set out in Article XXIV of the GATT 1994 in relation to regional trade agreements (RTAs).[25]

At first blush, the preferential treatment that lies at the core of these agreements conflicts with one of the central principles of the WTO system: the "elimination of discriminatory treatment in international commerce".[26] This objective is provided for in a number of provisions and with varying degrees of flexibility.

The most well-known, and strictest, of such requirements is the Most-Favoured-Nation (MFN) treatment obligation under Article I:1 GATT, which requires that *"customs duties and charges of any kind (…), and with respect to all rules and formalities in connection with importation and exportation, (…) any advantage, favour, privilege or immunity granted by any contracting party to any product originating in or destined for any other country shall be accorded immediately and unconditionally to the like product originating in or destined for the territories of all other*

---

[24] See Alavi (2012), p. 408.

[25] It is important to note that recent practice has shown that preferential trade agreements (the more generic term) tend to become "cross-regional". An example of such an agreement would the EU-South Korea Free Trade Agreement. However, as scholars as well as the WTO Secretariat continue to use the term "regional trade agreements", this article will also continue to use this term. See Van den Bossche and Zdouc (2013), pp. 671–672. See also Gobbi Estrella and Horlick (2006), pp. 109–110. See also Lockhart and Mitchell (2005), p. 3.

[26] Marrakesh Agreement Establishing the World Trade Organization; the third Recital of the Preamble reads: *"Being desirous of contributing to these objectives by entering into reciprocal and mutually advantageous arrangements directed to the substantial reduction of tariffs and other barriers to trade and **to the elimination of discriminatory treatment in international trade relations**."* (emphasis added).

contracting parties."[27] Article I:1 goes beyond a mere prohibition of discrimination between WTO Members, because non-discrimination obligations require treating similar situations in a similar manner but to also treat dissimilar situations in a dissimilar manner, while Article I:1 disregards all potential dissimilarities, except for the likeness of the product in question.

Therefore, the WTO rules allowing WTO Members to depart from MFN treatment, when they establish customs unions or free trade areas, are of particular importance provided they fulfil specific conditions. These exceptions are set out in Article XXIV of the General Agreement on Tariffs and Trade (GATT 1994) (and Article V of the General Agreement on Trade in Services (GATS)).[28]

Section 3.1, below, will examine the general purpose and nature of this provision. Section 3.2 will address the question of whether the application of TDIs[29] vis-à-vis third countries only is permissible under Article XXIV of the GATT 1994. Section 3.3 will consider whether the non-discrimination obligations in the WTO Agreements implementing Article VI GATT or any general principle of non-discrimination would limit the ability of the parties to an RTA to agree on an elimination or limitation of the use of TDI between them.

3.1   The Rationale Behind the Exceptions for RTAs

The GATT 1994 expressly permits preferential treatment among the members of a customs union (CU)[30] or free trade area (FTA) (including the granting of preferences in interim agreements leading to a customs union or FTA).[31]

---

[27] See Article I:1 of the General Agreement on Tariffs and Trade (GATT 1994). For services, see Article II of the General Agreement on Trade in Services (GATS). See also Lockhart and Mitchell (2005), p. 3; Van den Bossche and Zdouc (2013), p. 306.

[28] Developing countries entering into regional trade agreements covering trade in goods with other developing countries may also avail themselves of the exception provided by the Enabling Clause. See Appellate Body Report, *Peru – Additional duty on imports of certain agricultural products*, WT/DS457/AB/R, adopted 20 July 2015, DSR 2015:III, fn. 300.

[29] These are the measures as set out under Article VI of the GATT 1994 (anti-dumping and countervailing measures), but not Article XIX (safeguard measures), which are not addressed in this article.

[30] Alavi (2012), p. 407: "*Customs unions are those agreements whose parties agree upon a common external tariff on imported goods from non-parties. In free trade agreements, parties maintain their individual external tariff rates on imported goods, but reduce or remove them among themselves. Interim agreements are those agreements which operate with a long transitional period before they are finalised either as a customs union or as a free trade agreement.*"

[31] This is confirmed by the language of paragraph 5 of this provision stating: "*the provisions of this Agreement shall not prevent, as between the territories of contracting parties, the formation of a customs union or of a free-trade area or the adoption of an interim agreement.*" See Appellate Body Report, *Turkey – Restrictions on Imports of Textile and Clothing Products*, WT/DS34/AB/R, adopted 22 October 1999, DSR 1999:V, para. 45. See also Lockhart and Mitchell (2005), p. 4.

This exception is based on the acknowledgement by the contracting parties of the positive effects of an increase in trade liberalisation through closer economic integration, even if it only affects a subset of WTO Members.[32] Importantly, Article XXIV:4 adds that *"the purpose of a customs union or of a free-trade area should be to facilitate trade between the constituent territories and not to raise barriers to the trade of other contracting parties with such territories."*[33] The Appellate Body (AB) clarified that this paragraph contains *"purposive, and not operative, language"* and that the other relevant paragraphs of Article XXIV must be *"interpreted in the light of the purpose."*[34]

Hence, the goal of Article XXIV of the GATT 1994 is to ensure that the RTAs are aimed at increasing the economic integration among its contracting members, without creating trade restrictive effect vis-à-vis third countries.[35]

3.2 The Substantive Conditions Under Article XXIV of the GATT 1994 and the Elimination of Intra-Regional Trade Defence Instruments

In *Turkey – Textiles*, the AB set out two conditions that have to be met under Article XXIV in order to justify a deviation from the MFN principle in Article I:1 of the GATT 1994: (1) the measure must be adopted upon formation of a CU or FTA that fully meets the requirements of Article XXIV and (2) the formation of this CU or FTA would be prevented if this measure were not allowed.[36] Importantly, the AB has never assessed the consistency of a specific CU or FTA with the conditions under Article XXIV of the GATT 1994.[37]

---

[32] It must be noted that there is still an ongoing discussion regarding the question of whether RTAs can be a stepping stone for more trade liberalisation on a multilateral level. See Van den Bossche and Zdouc (2013), p. 674.

[33] Article XXIV:4 of the GATT 1994. The Understanding on Article XXIV explicitly reaffirms this purpose.

[34] Appellate Body Report, *Turkey – Restrictions on Imports of Textile and Clothing Products*, WT/DS34/AB/R, adopted 22 October 1999, DSR 1999:V, para. 57 and Lockhart and Mitchell (2005), p. 5.

[35] Olsen et al. (2012), p. 82.

[36] Appellate Body Report, *Turkey – Restrictions on Imports of Textile and Clothing Products*, WT/DS34/AB/R, adopted 22 October 1999, DSR 1999:V, para. 58. This dispute concerned a CU, but the conditions are presumably also applicable to FTAs. See Lockhart and Mitchell (2005), pp. 6–8. These conditions have been criticised by scholars, e.g. by Lockhart and Mitchell (2005), pp. 5–8; and Pauwelyn (2004).

[37] This was done once by the Panel, in *US – Line Pipe*, see Panel Report, *United States – Definitive Safeguard Measures on Imports of Circular Welded Carbon Quality Line Pipe from Korea*, WT/DS202/R, adopted 29 October 2001. See Van den Bossche and Zdouc (2013), p. 680.

Under the first prong of this test, the CU or FTA must meet the requirements of Article XXIV of the GATT 1994. The relevant parts of the definitions of a CU and FTA read as follows:

> For the purposes of this Agreement: (a) A customs union shall be understood to mean the substitution of a single customs territory for two or more customs territories, so that (i) duties and other restrictive regulations of commerce (except, where necessary, those permitted under Articles XI, XII, XIII, XIV, XV and XX) are eliminated with respect to substantially all the trade between the constituent territories of the union (...)

> (b) A free-trade area shall be understood to mean a group of two or more customs territories in which the duties and other restrictive regulations of commerce (except, where necessary, those permitted under Articles XI, XII, XIII, XIV, XV and XX) are eliminated on substantially all the trade between the constituent territories in products originating in such territories (...).[38]

Hence, Article XXIV imposes the elimination of "duties and other restrictive regulations of commerce" (ORRC), without defining these terms. In addition, the provisions of the GATT 1994 regarding anti-dumping and countervailing measures (Article VI of the GATT 1994) and other trade remedy measures such as safeguard measures (Article XIX of the GATT 1994) have been left out of the exceptions list "(except, where necessary, those permitted under Articles XI, XII, XIII, XIV, XV and XX)".[39]

These observations raise the following questions: (1) whether trade remedy measures should be considered duties or ORCCs and (2) if the answer to the first question is positive, whether the exceptions list is illustrative or exhaustive.[40] Given the lack of guidance by the AB, the answers to most of these questions are the subject of discussions among WTO Members and scholars.

3.2.1 Are TDI Measures Duties and Other Restrictive Regulations of Commerce in the Sense of Article XXIV of the GATT 1994?

Article XXIV:8(a)(i) and (b) refers to the elimination of duties and ORRC with respect to *the trade between the contracting parties*. This indicates that the terms "duties or ORRC" encompass, and are limited to, regulations that restrict the cross-border movement of goods between the RTA parties. This interpretation is also in line with the language of the Understanding on Article XXIV of the GATT 1994, which refers to the "elimination *between the constituent territories* of duties and other restrictive regulations of commerce."[41]

As to the question of whether trade remedy measures fall within the scope of the terms "duties and ORRC", N. Lockhart and A.D. Mitchell have observed that "*anti-*

---

[38] Article XXIV:8(a)(i) and (b) of the GATT 1994.
[39] Lockhart and Mitchell (2005), p. 14.
[40] Gobbi Estrella and Horlick (2006), p. 111.
[41] Gobbi Estrella and Horlick (2006), p. 119 (emphasis added).

dumping and countervailing duties are described as "duties" in Articles II and VI of GATT 1994, as well as in the Anti-Dumping Agreement and the SCM Agreement. These "duties" are imposed, in addition to ordinary customs duties, on the importation of products.[42] *Moreover, the very purpose of these duties is to restrict imports of specific products."*[43] This suggests that trade remedy measures fall within the scope of the term "duties or ORRC".[44]

However, both Article VI and Article XXIV of the GATT 1994 provide exceptions to the MFN obligation. It can therefore be argued, with equal force, that because the right of WTO Members to impose anti-dumping and countervailing measures is governed by a specific rule (Article VI), that such rule, as a lex specialis, should govern the question of when such duties can be imposed. That Article VI is not mentioned in the list of exceptions in Article XXIV would not be relevant, because of the lex specialis character of Article VI. This interpretation has the benefit of being consistent with the practice of WTO Members, because anti-dumping and countervailing measures have quite regularly been adopted between Members of RTAs.[45]

In addition, and even if one would assume that TDI measures fall within the scope of the term "duties and other restrictive regulations of commerce", such conclusion would not lead to the further conclusion that all trade remedy measures are prohibited *per se* within CUs and FTAs.[46] Importantly, Article XXIV indicates that these should be eliminated on *substantially* all trade.[47] The AB clarified this point as follows:

> It is clear, though, that "substantially all the trade" is not the same as all the trade, and also that "substantially all the trade" is something considerably more than merely some of the trade. We note also that the terms of sub-paragraph 8(a)(i) provide that members of a customs union may maintain, where necessary, in their internal trade, certain restrictive regulations of commerce that are otherwise permitted under Articles XI through XV and under Article XX of the GATT 1994. Thus, we agree with the Panel that the terms of sub-paragraph 8(a)(i) offer "some flexibility" to the constituent members of a customs union when liberalizing their internal trade in accordance with this sub-paragraph. Yet we caution that the degree of "flexibility" that sub-paragraph 8(a)(i) allows is limited by the requirement that

---

[42] However, Gobbi Estrella and Horlick argue *"that trade remedies are not comprehended within the meaning of "duties" in Article XXIV:8, taking into account the text of the French and Spanish versions of the GATT, which indicate that the term "duties" in this provision refers to customs duties only. Nonetheless, the authors conclude that trade remedies are encompassed within the meaning of "other restrictive regulations of commerce" in Article XXIV:8."* Gobbi Estrella and Horlick (2006), pp. 114 and 120–121.

[43] Lockhart and Mitchell (2005), pp. 14–15.

[44] Lockhart and Mitchell (2005), p. 15.

[45] The examples outlined in Sects. 4 and 5 of this article are indicative of such practice.

[46] For more details on the alleged mandatory nature of the elimination of TDIs, see Gobbi Estrella and Horlick (2006), pp. 114 et seq.

[47] This point is also the subject of discussions. See for example Gobbi Estrella and Horlick (2006), p. 136 and further.

"duties and other restrictive regulations of commerce" be "eliminated with respect to substantially all" internal trade.[48]

Hence, the GATT offers a certain degree of flexibility and allows WTO Members to liberalise "less than "all" the trade".[49]

3.2.2 Is the Exceptions List in Article XXIV of the GATT 1994 Illustrative or Exhaustive?

As to the second question, the AB in *Turkey – Textiles* held that sub-paragraph 8(a)(i) of Article XXIV "***requires** the constituent members of a customs union to eliminate 'duties and other restrictive regulations of commerce' with respect to 'substantially all the trade' between them.*"[50] As set out above, it added that "*the terms of subparagraph 8(a)(i) provide that members of a customs union may maintain, where necessary, in their internal trade, **certain** restrictive regulations of commerce that are otherwise permitted under Articles XI through XV and under Article XX of the GATT 1994.*"[51] Hence, this paragraph highlights the *optional* character of the exceptions list of measures that Members may continue to apply in an RTA.[52]

Scholars have debated whether the exceptions list is illustrative or exhaustive. If it were illustrative, other duties or ORRC not mentioned in this list would also be permitted.[53] Based on the language of the provision, however, this list constitutes an exception to the general obligation to eliminate duties and ORCCs, which implies that it should be considered to be an exhaustive enumeration. In addition, the AB seems to endorse this interpretation, as it described this list as "***certain** restrictive regulations of commerce that are otherwise permitted under Articles XI through XV and under Article XX of the GATT 1994.*"[54]

In sum, only if one assumes that TDIs are "duties and ORRC" and are applied to a large part of all intra-regional trade, could one argue that the liberalised part of the intra-regional trade no longer covers "substantially all trade",[55] as a result of TDI measures being imposed. Only then could an RTA become incompatible with WTO requirements, unless the use of TDIs is reduced. By contrast, if Article VI of the

---

[48] Appellate Body Reports, *Turkey – Restrictions on Imports of Textile and Clothing Products*, WT/DS34/AB/R, adopted 22 October 1999, DSR 1999:V, para. 48.

[49] Gobbi Estrella and Horlick (2006), p. 140.

[50] Appellate Body Reports, *Turkey – Restrictions on Imports of Textile and Clothing Products*, WT/DS34/AB/R, adopted 22 October 1999, DSR 1999:V, para 48.

[51] Appellate Body Reports, *Turkey – Restrictions on Imports of Textile and Clothing Products*, WT/DS34/AB/R, adopted 22 October 1999, DSR 1999:V, para 48 (emphasis added).

[52] Gobbi Estrella and Horlick (2006), p. 113.

[53] Lockhart and Mitchell (2005), p. 15.

[54] Appellate Body Reports, *Turkey – Restrictions on Imports of Textile and Clothing Products*, WT/DS34/AB/R, adopted 22 October 1999, DSR 1999:V, para 48; Gobbi Estrella and Horlick (2006), p. 142 (emphasis added).

[55] Pauwelyn (2004), p. 127.

GATT 1994 is viewed as a lex specialis (both as regards Article I:1 and Article XXIV), the use of TDIs will not be subject to an MFN requirement, for as long as the substantive conditions under Article VI (and its implementing agreements) are being complied with.

3.3 Limitations Resulting from General Non-Discrimination Obligations Under the GATT Generally and the Implementing Agreement on Article VI in Particular

Non-discrimination is a fundamental principle of the multilateral trading system and is recognised in the Preamble to the WTO Agreement as a key instrument to achieve the objectives of the WTO.[56] WTO members express their desire to eliminate discriminatory treatment in international trading relations. And while non-discrimination in the WTO is specifically embodied by two principles, the most favoured nation (MFN) treatment obligation and the national treatment obligation, there is a broader non-discrimination requirement as regards the use of TDIs.

Article 9.2 of the WTO Anti-Dumping Agreement (ADA)[57] and Article 19.3 of the WTO Agreement on Subsidies and Countervailing Measures (ASCM)[58] specifically require the non-discriminatory application of anti-dumping and countervailing measures. Article 9.2 ADA provides: *"When an anti-dumping duty is imposed in respect of any product, such anti-dumping duty shall be collected in the appropriate amounts in each case, on a non-discriminatory basis on imports of such product from all sources found to be dumped and causing injury (...)."* Similarly, Article 19.3 ASCM provides: *"When a countervailing duty is imposed in respect of any product, such countervailing duty shall be levied, in the appropriate amounts in each case, on a non-discriminatory basis on imports of such product from all sources found to be subsidized and causing injury."*

On the basis of a literal interpretation, both rules apply only once the existence of dumping (or subsidisation) and injury have been established in the framework of a properly initiated proceeding. These rules are thus arguably not directly applicable to the question of whether the instrument will not be used and investigations will never be initiated as between the partners of an RTA. However, both rules (coupled

---

[56] Marrakesh Agreement Establishing the World Trade Organization; the third recital of the preamble reads: *"Being desirous of contributing to these objectives by entering into reciprocal and mutually advantageous arrangements directed to the substantial reduction of tariffs and other barriers to trade and **to the elimination of discriminatory treatment in international trade relations**."* (emphasis added).

[57] Agreement on Implementation of Article VI of the General Agreement on Tariffs and Trade 1994.

[58] Agreement on Subsidies and Countervailing Measures.

with the preamble and the two principles) are indicative of a more general non-discrimination requirement in the WTO framework.

That non-discrimination principle, in line with non-specific non-discrimination rules generally, would require matters to be treated in the same manner if they are alike but to be treated differently if they are different.[59] In the author's view, if within an RTA parties to such agreement have agreed to ensure (1) free movement of goods and capital, (2) common competition rules, (3) common State aid rules and (4) the related enforcement mechanisms for the underlying substantive rules to combat the root cause for concerns about injurious dumping and subsidisation, then that is a material difference that allows the parties of an RTA to be differentiated from other third countries in the application of AD and CVD rules.

Hence, the elimination of TDIs between the EU Member States and between the European Union and third countries in the framework of an RTA such as the EEA Agreement, would be justified by objective differences.

That result would also be consistent with the reason why RTAs are permissible under the WTO rules. The AB underscored, in *Peru – Agricultural Products*, that the goal of Article XXIV of the GATT 1994 is "to facilitate trade" between the constituent members. It added that *"these references in paragraph 4 [of Article XXIV of the GATT 1994] to facilitating trade and closer integration are not consistent with an interpretation of Article XXIV as a broad defence for measures in FTAs that roll back on Members' rights and obligations under the WTO covered agreements."*[60] The elimination of the restrictive effect of TDI measures, however, does not "roll back on Members' rights and obligations", but rather results in a higher level of liberalisation among the contracting parties.[61] In addition, although such measures may indirectly raise barriers against third countries, they do not constitute an *"increase in barriers to trade with third parties which did not exist on beforehand."*[62] Hence, this practice is in line with the purpose of CUs and FTAs as set out in Article XXIV:4 of the GATT 1994.[63]

---

[59] See *Matadeen v Pointu*, Privy Council (UK), Judgment of 18 February 1998, 1 AC 98, 109, www.bailii.org/uk/cases/UKPC/1998/9.html (last accessed 30 April 2018): "... *treating like cases alike and unlike cases differently is a general axiom of rational behaviour.*" There are many similar statements of senior courts throughout the world.

[60] Panel Report, *Peru – Additional duty on imports of certain agricultural products*, WT/DS457/AB/R, adopted 20 July 2015, para. 5.116.

[61] This dispute concerned additional duties imposed by Peru on imports of certain agricultural products.

[62] Pauwelyn (2004), p. 137.

[63] Pauwelyn (2004), p. 137.

3.4   Conclusion

Even though every WTO Member is today also a Member of at least one RTA,[64] the exact interpretation of the relevant exceptions to the MFN rules, such as Articles VI and XXIV of the GATT 1994 remain disputed.[65] Nevertheless, the better arguments suggest that neither the MFN obligation nor broader non-discrimination rules require or prevent parties to an RTA to eliminate recourse to anti-dumping and countervailing measures as between the Members of such an RTA. The Parties may, in the exercise of their discretion choose to do so, in particular, if the RTA provides for mechanisms that counter more directly the root cause of dumping and subsidisation.

4   The EU's Customs Unions

The following two sections analyse the limitations on the imposition of trade defence measures in the framework of the Union's Customs Unions (Sect. 4) and Free Trade Agreements (Sect. 5) and links such limitations to the level of effective protections against the underlying root causes.

4.1   The European Union Itself

The European Union is itself a customs union. No trade defence measures can be imposed as regards trade between Member States. Specifically, anti-dumping and countervailing duties are prohibited as a result of Article 28(1) TFEU: *"The Union shall comprise a customs union which shall (…) involve the prohibition between Member States of customs duties on imports and exports and of all charges having equivalent effect."* Other, non-tariff, measures would be inconsistent with Article 26 TFEU and could not be justified on the basis of Article 27 TFEU.

That was not always true. Originally, anti-dumping measures of sorts could be imposed on trade between Member States. At the time, Article 91(1) of the E(E)C Treaty provided for the possibility of the Commission authorising anti-dumping measures between Member States until the end of the transitional period on 31 December 1969.[66] However, the provision was never used. In the advent of the

---

[64] Van den Bossche and Zdouc (2013), p. 674.
[65] Lockhart and Mitchell (2005), p. 23.
[66] Article 91 EEC Treaty (and EC Treaty prior to the Amsterdam revision) was interestingly placed in Chapter 1 of Part III of the Treaty, entitled "Competition Rules" and was located between the rules applicable to undertakings (Section 1) and those primarily directed towards state action (State aid rules, Section 3), suggesting that dumping was considered something in between. (Ex-)Article 91 EC read as follows: *"If, during the transitional period, the Commission, on application by a*

completion of the internal market and well after the end of the transitional period, ex-Article 91 EC was repealed by the Treaty of Amsterdam.

By contrast, there never was a treaty rule that would have permitted the imposition of countervailing duties, because State aid rules (prohibiting subsidies, except those granted with the approval of the Commission) provide for an entirely different mechanism to ensure that subsidies can only be granted based on consistent policy objectives throughout the Union.

This underscores why no trade defence measures can be taken as between Member States: The European Union has adopted internal rules that deal with the root causes for dumping and subsidisation and, specifically, with the reasons why countries resort to trade defence measures.

As between the Member States, EU rules prohibit the segregation of markets, be it by state or private action. Market segregation resulting from state interference is prohibited by Article 26 TFEU and the internal market legislation.[67] The prohibition extends to "soft" measures such as marketing campaigns for national products.[68] The Commission has the power to enforce compliance with such rules against the Member States, if necessary, by court action in the European Court of Justice.[69] Member States have no possibility to prevent such court action or to prevent or avoid a judgment. Non-compliance with judgments can lead to the imposition of significant periodic penalty payments against the Member State in question.[70]

Competition rules limit the ability of private actors to segregate markets. As outlined above, the rationale for the adoption of countervailing measures is based on differences in the policy objectives for subsidisation. The EU avoids clashes over such policy objectives, because State aid policies are decided at the level of the Union by the Commission and typically implemented throughout the Union in a uniform manner.[71] Hence, the EU addresses the root causes for combatting dumping and subsidisation.

Member State or by any other interested party, finds that dumping is being practised within the common market, it shall address recommendations to the person or persons with whom such practices originate for the purpose of putting an end to them. Should the practices continue, the Commission shall authorise the injured Member State to take protective measures, the conditions and details of which the Commission shall determine."

[67] Article 26 TFEU provides: *"1. The Union shall adopt measures with the aim of establishing or ensuring the functioning of the internal market, in accordance with the relevant provisions of the Treaties. 2. The internal market shall comprise an area without internal frontiers in which the free movement of goods, persons, services and capital is ensured in accordance with the provisions of the Treaties."* An overview of the (vast) internal market legislation can be found at https://ec. europa.eu/growth/single-market_en (last accessed 30 April 2018) and http://eur-lex.europa.eu/ summary/chapter/internal_market.html?root_default=SUM_1_CODED%3D24 (last accessed 30 April 2018).

[68] CJEU, Case 249/81, *Commission v Ireland*, ECLI:EU:C:1982:402.

[69] See Article 258 TFEU.

[70] Article 260 TFEU.

[71] Article 107 and the implementing legislation adopted based on Article 109 TFEU (a collection of the relevant rules can be found at: http://ec.europa.eu/competition/state_aid/legislation/legislation. html (last accessed 30 April 2018), including European Commission, Commission Regulation

Importantly, the Union also provides for enforcement mechanisms that ensure implementation of the rules. The European Commission can take effective action against private actors and the Member States, if they fail to comply with EU rules. Based on competition laws, inconsistent market segregation measures will be null and void[72] (or voidable) and companies can be fined for illicit conduct.[73] The Commission can also order the recovery of subsidies that are granted without regard to EU State aid rules[74] and Member States can be forced, if necessary, through action taken in the European Courts[75] to comply with State aid rules and with rules prohibiting market segregation (based on the rules on the free movement of goods, services, capital and people).

In sum, the European Union does not need Trade Defence Instruments as regards trade between Member States, because it offers an effective protection against the root causes for combatting dumping and subsidisation.

4.2   The Customs Union with Turkey

The Union has also established a customs union with Turkey.

The original agreements with Turkey date back to the 1963 Ankara Agreement.[76] That agreement envisaged a gradual establishment of a customs union (by going through a preparatory, transitional and final stage) and alignment of the respective economic policies.[77] An Association Council was set up, which is entitled to adopt decisions to implement the Ankara Agreement and to resolve disputes between the parties.[78] The Association Council can only act by common accord, i.e. both the EU

(EU) No 651/2014 of 17 June 2014, declaring certain categories of aid compatible with the internal market in application of Articles 107 and 108 of the Treaty).

[72] Article 101(2) TFEU provides: *"Any agreements or decisions prohibited pursuant to this Article shall be automatically void."*

[73] See Council Regulation (EC) No 1/2003 of 16 December 2002 on the implementation of the rules on competition laid down in Articles 81 and 82 of the Treaty, OJ 2003 L 001, p. 1, as amended.

[74] Article 108 TFEU and implementing legislation, in particular, Council Regulation (EU) 2015/1589, OJ 2015 L 248/9 (Procedural Regulation).

[75] Article 108(2)(2) TFEU allows the Commission to directly commence enforcement actions against a Member State in the European Court of Justice, if the Member State does not properly implement certain State aid decisions, in particular, recovery orders. The procedure avoids the more cumbersome process of "normal" infringement proceedings against Member States, based on Article 258 TFEU.

[76] Agreement establishing an Association between the European Economic Community and Turkey (Ankara Agreement), OJ 1964 L 3687/64, pp. 3687–3697.

[77] Ankara Agreement, Article 4 and 6.

[78] Ankara Agreement, Article 25.

and Turkey must agree (so that each party has effectively a veto power as regards decisions taken by the Association Council).[79]

The Ankara Agreement was revisited in 1995, which led to the Association Council Decision 1/95 on the final phase of the Customs Union.[80] The customs union is limited to goods other than agricultural products. Turkey and the EU agreed to reciprocally remove any obstacles to the free movement of industrial goods between them.[81] Decision 1/95 provides, in particular, that:

• Turkey must, in relation to countries that are not EU Member States, align itself on the Common Customs Tariff (Article 13), implement the Unions common commercial policy rules (Article 12) and adopt provisions similar to the Community customs code (Article 28);
• Import or export customs duties and charges having equivalent effect must be wholly abolished between the Union and Turkey (Article 4);
• Quantitative restrictions on imports and exports as well as all measures having equivalent effect are prohibited between the Union and Turkey (Article 5 and 6); and
• Turkey must incorporate into its internal legal order the Community instruments relating to the removal of technical barriers to trade (Article 8).

The rules against technical barriers to trade are subject to minor exceptions, inter alia linked to public morality, public policy or public security; the protection of health and life of humans, animals or plants; the protection of national treasures possessing artistic, historic or archaeological value; or the protection of industrial and commercial property. Such prohibitions or restrictions must not, however, constitute a means of arbitrary discrimination or a disguised restriction on trade between the Parties (Article 7).

The policy alignment is further enhanced by an obligation by Turkey to adopt the Unions competition rules, including, in particular, those relating to undertakings and State aid. Specifically, "*all agreements between undertakings, and concerted practices which have as their object or effect the prevention, restriction or distortion of competition*" are prohibited and void (Article 32). A similar rule applies to "*any abuse by one or more undertakings of a dominant position in the territories of the Community and/or of Turkey*" (Article 33).

State aid is subject to the same substantive limitations that apply within the EU (Article 34). Moreover, Article 35 provides that "*[a]ny practices contrary to Articles 32, 33 and 34 shall be assessed on the basis of criteria arising from the application of the rules of Articles 85 [now 101], 86 [now 102] and 92 [now 107] of the EC Treaty [now TFEU] and its secondary legislation.*"

Hence, in substance, the objective was to establish full and unrestricted market access for industrial goods. However, the Customs Union does not provide for

---

[79] Ankara Agreement, Article 23(3).

[80] Council, Decision No 1/95 of the EC-Turkey Association Council of 22 December 1995 on implementing the final phase of the Customs Union, OJ 1996 L 35/1.

[81] See also Van Bael and Bellis (2011), pp. 28 et seq.

unrestricted market access in all areas: agriculture (to which bilateral trade concessions apply), services and public procurement rules are not harmonised in the same way.

Moreover and importantly, there is no alignment on enforcement aspects. Each party is, of course, required to fully implement the substantive rules. But in case of Turkey, there is no independent authority charged with ensuring the full application of the substantive rules and no supranational court (other than national Turkish courts) to adjudicate on disputes over the proper interpretation of the substantive law. In case of dispute, there is also no "external" dispute settlement procedure: the matter is referred to the Association Council, in which both sides are represented and who decides by unanimous vote, so that each side retains full veto powers.[82] Procedural rules for the application of competition and State aid rules should have been adopted within 2 years of Decision 1/95 (Article 37), but were not adopted.

For purposes of the present analysis, it is interesting to note the consequences that the parties attached to the absence of independent enforcement rules. Article 38 provides that if either party *"considers that a particular practice is incompatible with the terms of Articles 32, 33 or 34 [and in the absence of implementing rules], if such practice causes or threatens to cause serious prejudice to the interest of the other Party or material injury to its domestic industry, it may take appropriate measures after consultation within the Joint Customs Union Committee. (...) In the case of practices incompatible with Article 34, such appropriate measures may, where the General Agreement on Tariffs and Trade applies thereto, only be adopted in conformity"* with applicable WTO rules.

In addition, Article 44 provides that *"the Association Council shall review (...) the principle of application of trade defence instruments other than safeguard by one Party in its relations with the other. During any such review, the Association Council may decide to suspend the application of these instruments provided that Turkey has implemented competition, State aid control and other relevant parts of the acquis communautaire which are related to the internal market and ensured their effective enforcement, so providing a guarantee against unfair competition comparable to that existing inside the internal market."*[83]

It is apparent from Article 38 and 44 of Decision 1/95 that the EU was willing to consider quite far ranging concessions on trade defence measures, if and to the extent Turkey would be bound by procedural rules and effective enforcement provisions, aimed at ensuring that no market segregation could occur and that the policy considerations for the granting of subsidies were fully respected. It is apparent from these rules that effective enforcement of the underlying substantive rules was of tantamount importance to the EU.

---

[82] See Article 23 and 25 Ankara Agreement. See also, Alkan U, The Modernization of Turkey's Customs Union with the European Union: Reasons and Possible Outcomes. College of Europe, EU Diplomacy Papers 9/2017, https://www.coleurope.eu/news/eu-diplomacy-paper-9/2017 (last accessed 30 April 2018), p. 12.

[83] Article 44 of Decision 1/95, see also Van Bael and Bellis (2011), pp. 29 et seq.

In sum, the Agreements establishing a customs union with Turkey provide for a broad commitment to ensure the free movement of goods and to prevent market segregation and asymmetrical access to the market for industrial goods. Turkey undertook to align its competition and State aid rules to those of the Union.

Nevertheless, in the absence of binding procedural rules and a system of independent effective enforcement, the Union was not willing to renounce the use of TDIs. The Union only accepted some procedural limitations: that any anti-dumping action should, in principle, be subject to prior consultation of the Association Council[84] and that the Union would *"give on a case to case basis, where appropriate, a clear preference to price undertakings rather than duties in order to conclude anti-dumping cases where injury is found."*[85] The actual practice confirms the essence of the rules outlined above. The Union maintains a number of trade defence measures that are applicable to exports from Turkey.[86]

5 The Union's Free Trade Agreements

5.1 The European Economic Area

The Agreement establishing the European Economic Area (EEA) was signed on 2 May 1992 and entered into force on 1 January 1994.[87] A free trade area between the EU and the then-remaining EFTA Countries (other than Switzerland) was established. The agreement goes far beyond establishing a traditional free trade area, as it provides for a wide ranging convergence on all policies related to the internal market, with certain exceptions for agricultural and fishery products. Since its conclusion, a number of former EFTA countries became full Member States of the Union, so that only three non-EU Member States remain parties in addition to the EU: Iceland, Lichtenstein and Norway (referred to as the "EFTA-States" in the Agreement, even though Switzerland, that remains in the EFTA, has decided not to join the EEA).

---

[84] Article 44 of Decision 1/95.

[85] Article 44 of Decision 1/95; Statement by the Community on Article 44 (published at the end of the agreement).

[86] For example: Council Implementing Regulation (EU) No 78/2013 of 17 January 2013, imposing a definitive anti-dumping duty and collecting definitely the provisional duty imposed on imports of certain tube and pipe fittings of iron or steel originating in Russia and Turkey, OJ 2013 L 27/1.

[87] Agreement on the European Economic Area, OJ 1994 L 1/3, Article 129. The entry into force for Liechtenstein was delayed until 1 January 1995, as a result of certain amendments to the Customs Union between Liechtenstein and Switzerland, that became necessary after Switzerland decided not to join the EEA, see Decision of the EEA Council No 1/95 of 10 March 1995 on the entry into force of the Agreement on the European Economic Area for the Principality of Liechtenstein, OJ 1995 L 86/58.

The EEA Agreement provides the three countries with unrestricted access to the EU's single market in return for them adopting the EU's internal market related legislation, including any subsequent modification adopted after the signature of the EEA-Agreement.[88] Hence, the full internal market legislation applies throughout the EEA, which includes, in particular, the four freedoms (free movement of goods, capital, persons and services). Customs duties on imports or exports, any charges or measures having equivalent effect are prohibited between the EU and the EFTA States as regards the products originating in these countries.[89] Discriminatory internal taxation is prohibited and the simplification of border controls and administrative requirements is envisaged.[90]

Similarly, the entire competition law framework (including Articles 101, 102, 106–109 TFEU) applies *mutatis mutandis* in the EEA. This includes merger control and other implementing rules. This also applies to State aid control.[91] The entire acquis in this regard is reflected in EEA rules, which are regularly updated to reflect subsequent amendments of EU rules (and the EFTA States are consulted in the preparation of such subsequent EU rules). Enforcement powers are vested, as regards cases arising in the EU, in the European Commission, but as regards cases arising in the EFTA States, in the EFTA-Surveillance Authority (ESA),[92] which is an independent supra-national body set up by the EEA Agreement and the three EFTA States, which has enforcement powers equivalent to those of the European Commission.

The EEA implementation by ESA and the EFTA States is subject to the judicial control of the EFTA Court (Article 108(2) EEA), which has jurisdiction over direct actions against ESA and the behaviour of EFTA States, much in the same way as the Union courts (General Court and ECJ) have jurisdiction to hear cases against the EU institutions and the Member States under Article 263 TFEU. The EFTA Court has also jurisdiction to adjudicate on preliminary ruling requests by national courts in the EFTA States, in essentially the same way as the ECJ under Article 267 TFEU. Both the ECJ and the EFTA Court must take the ECJ case law that existed at the time of signature into account when rendering judgments. In addition, the entire EEA Agreement is based on *"the objective of the Contracting Parties to arrive at, and maintain, a uniform interpretation and application of this Agreement and those provisions of Community legislation which are substantially reproduced in this Agreement."*[93]

---

[88] Article 80 EEA.
[89] Part II and Part III of the EEA.
[90] Article 21 and 30 EEA.
[91] Article 61–64 EEA.
[92] Article 108 EEA.
[93] Recital 15 of the Preamble to the EEA Agreement, see also Article 105 et seq. EEA. The importance of this principle was underlined by the EU's General Court in GC, case T-115/94, *Opel Austria v Commission*, ECLI:EU:T:1997:3, paras. 104 et seq.

If, in spite of the elaborate rules aimed at ensuring uniform interpretation of the rules, a dispute arises between the parties to the EEA Agreement, there is, as regards the interpretation of the rules, a traditional dispute settlement procedure in the EEA Joint Committee provided for, which aims at a consensual resolution of disputes and allows for unilateral measures, if no consensus can be reached (Article 111 et seq. EEA). Special dispute resolution procedures are also provided in case of a State aid related dispute between the Commission and the EFTA Surveillance authority. Again, if no consensual resolution is possible, either of the agencies can adopt pro-portional measures to offset the resulting distortion.[94]

As a consequence of the high degree of legislative harmonisation and institu-tional alignment,[95] Article 26 provides that "*anti-dumping measures, countervailing duties and measures against illicit commercial practices attributable to third countries shall not be applied in relations between the Contracting Parties, (...).*" The scope of application of Article 26 is limited by (1) Article 8(2) EEA, which provides that Article 26 only applies to goods "originating" in the EEA and (2) Protocol 13 to the EEA which provides for an exception for the sectors not fully covered by the acquis under the EEA Agreement (i.e. fisheries and agriculture).[96] As a result, in practice, the Union has adopted and maintained anti-dumping measures only as regards Norwegian salmon and rainbow trout,[97] which fall within the fisher-ies exception.

In sum, the EEA agreement ensures a particularly high degree of harmonisation as regards the three key areas of substantive law: (1) market access through free movement rules and the prohibition of discriminatory treatment, (2) competition rules as regards private behaviour and (3) state intervention (State aid rules). In addition, effective enforcement is provided for through the establishment of an independent supranational authority (ESA) and an independent supranational court (reducing the risk that a single EFTA country could influence the stance taken by ESA or the court), coupled with an express commitment to the uniform interpreta-tion of the substantive rules. The combination of the substantive rules aimed at preventing asymmetrical market access with the effective enforcement infrastruc-ture was a sufficient basis for accepting to forego (in most cases) the possibility of adopting trade defence measures. This is in spite of the fact that if differences arise between the Union institutions on the one hand, and the ESA and the EFTA Court on the other, the dispute resolution process requires the adoption of a unanimous decision in the EEA Joint Committee.

---

[94] Article 64 EEA.

[95] The considerations that led the Union to accept the non-applicability of the TDI measures are described by Van Bael and Bellis (2011), pp. 25 et seq.

[96] Article 26 EEA with Protocol 13 to the EEA Agreement (OJ 1994 L 1/175).

[97] See, e.g. (1) Council Regulation (EC) No 319/2009 of 16 April 2009 clarifying the scope of the definitive anti-dumping duties imposed by Regulation (EC) No 85/2006 on imports of farmed salmon originating in Norway, OJ 2009 L 101/1 and (2) Council Regulation (EC) No 437/2004 of 8 March 2004 imposing a definitive anti-dumping duty (...) on imports of large rainbow trout originating in Norway and the Faeroe Islands, OJ 2004 L 72/23.

5.2   EC-Switzerland Free Trade Agreement of 1972

The Union concluded an early set of multiple Free Trade Agreements with various then EFTA countries in 1972. All but one of these early FTAs were superseded by the EEA Agreement or by EFTA States joining the Union as a Member State. But Switzerland decided not to join the EEA (let alone the EU), as a result of referenda in Switzerland. EU trading relations with Switzerland are therefore still based on the 1972 Free Trade Agreement, which provides for the main rules ensuring (1) the free movement of goods, as well as for (2) competition and (3) State aid rules. Other parts of the EU acquis were implemented, as regards Switzerland, by a series of bilateral agreements, in particular seven agreements concluded in 1999 (including on the avoidance of technical barriers to trade and public procurement rules) and further agreements concluded in 2004 and 2011. Overall, more than 100 bilateral agreements currently exist between the EU and Switzerland.

As regards the free movement of goods, the free trade agreement of 1972 is considered the cornerstone of EU-Swiss trade relations.[98] The free trade agreement of 1972 set out in Article 3 that no new custom duties can be introduced and that then existing customs duties were progressively abolished.[99] This also applied to any measures having an equivalent effect.[100] Similarly, no quantitative restrictions on imports or measures having an equivalent effect could be maintained. The free movement of capital was also ensured, subject to certain transitional arrangements,[101] but payments related to trade in goods had to be free of all restrictions (Article 19).

Article 23 of the 1972 FTA requires the adoption of competition rules. Any agreements between undertakings, decisions by associations of undertakings and concerted practices that have as their object or effect the prevention, restriction or distortion of competition as regards the production of trade in goods are declared incompatible with the FTA by Article 23(1)(i) FTA insofar as they could affect trade between the Union and Switzerland. Article 23(1)(ii) FTA also declares any abuse of a dominant position incompatible with the Agreement. Finally, Article 23(1)(iii) FTA declares any public aid which distorts or threatens to distort competition incompatible with the FTA.

Interestingly, the provisions mirror the prohibitions in Article 101, 102 and 107 TFEU, but they do not expressly provide for exceptions, they do not mandate a specific authority to deal with such cases and they do not provide for express powers to authorise (or declare illegal) certain of such actions. The Union, in a declaration annexed to the Final Act,[102] took the view that the provisions of Article 23 FTA should be interpreted according to the criteria applicable in the application of what

---

[98] See http://ec.europa.eu/trade/policy/countries-and-regions/countries/switzerland/ (last accessed 30 April 2018).

[99] EC-Switzerland Free Trade Agreement, OJ 1972, L 300/189, Article 3.

[100] EC-Switzerland Free Trade Agreement, Article 6.

[101] EC Switzerland Free Trade Agreement, Article 4.

[102] See Final Act, OJ 1972 L 300/280, Declaration with respect to Article 23.

is today Article 101, 102, 106 and 107 TFEU (but this remained a unilateral declaration of the Union). The similarity of the provisions in the FTA with corresponding provisions in the TFEU nevertheless suggests that the provisions are meant to be interpreted in a broadly similar fashion, albeit by taking into account the structural differences between the FTA and EU law.[103]

The FTA does not provide for any specific enforcement powers vested in an independent body or authority. A joint committee is tasked with exercising oversight and coordination functions.[104] This forum is—as the EC-Turkey Association Council—characterised by its bilateral composition and the requirement to adopt decisions or recommendations only by mutual consent, i.e. subject to veto by either party.[105] Nevertheless, the joint committee is competent to consider concerns about dumping or distortive subsidies. For this purpose, an obligatory consultation procedure was established, which requires the party concerned to refer issues of concern to the Association Council and to then wait a certain period, before imposing "appropriate measures".[106] But each party is free to proceed after the lapse of the waiting period.

In fact, Article 25 FTA provides that if one of the contracting parties finds that dumping is taking place, that party may take countermeasures in accordance with the GATT rules (Article VI GATT). Article 27(3) FTA permits, in case one party finds that Article 23 has not been complied with, including as regards State aid, that the aggrieved party may take appropriate measures and, in particular, withdraw tariff concessions granted under the FTA. In fact, the Union adopted, in parallel to concluding the FTA with Switzerland, the procedural rules[107] for adopting the measures[108] envisaged by the FTA.

Trade defence measures have never been imposed by the Union against Switzerland. Nevertheless, the Union did use its trade defence powers (albeit rarely) against other EFTA States under the parallel FTA's that had been concluded in 1972.[109]

---

[103] See, as regards the interpretation of Article 23, Judgment of the Court of First Instance of 22 January 1997, GC, case T-115/97, *Opel Austria v Commission*, ECLI:EU:T:1997:3, outlining the differences in approach of the parties and some guidance of the Court (the case was decided on other grounds).

[104] Final Act, Article 29.

[105] Final Act, Article 30.

[106] Final Act, Articles 24–27.

[107] Regulation (EEC) No 2841/72 of the Council of 19 December 1972 on the safeguard measures provided for in the Agreement between the European Economic Community and the Swiss Confederation, OJ 1972 L 300/284.

[108] The term "safeguard" measure in this context is not a reference to the GATT terminology and the term "safeguard measures" as used in the WTO context.

[109] The best know examples related to Austrian subsidies in favour of Grundig, Chrysler and General Motors, to which the Union objected just prior to the entry into force of the EEA Agreement. Grundig and Chrysler accepted to return most of the State aid, General Motors' refusal led to the General Court's decision in GC, Case T-115/94, *Opel Austria v Commission*, ECLI:EU:T:1997:3, which annulled the Union's countermeasures.

5.3   *Europe Agreements: The Example of Poland*

During the 1990s, the European Community entered into a number of association agreements with central and Eastern Europe, including Hungary, the Czech Republic, Slovakia, Bulgaria, Romania and Poland, which are commonly referred to as "Europe Agreements". Those treaties aimed at establishing free trade between the parties, but were, in no small measure, also aimed at preparing the future accession of these countries to the Union. To that end, they provided for a classical free trade area coupled with a detailed arrangement for approximating economic conditions, mainly by ensuring a progressively increasing level of market liberalisation and the free movement of goods, services, capital and people. The structure and implementation of these Europe Agreements was very similar among each of the various Agreements.[110] Below, the Europe Agreement with Poland is analysed as an example for all the Europe Agreements.[111]

The Europe Agreement with Poland established, first and foremost, a Free Trade Area with full mutual market access (with a 10-year transitional period, Article 7), in which customs duties were abolished (after a 7-year period, Article 10). For this purpose, any customs duties or quotas on imports and exports between the parties, as well as any measures having equivalent effect, were abolished.[112] Special rules existed as regards certain sectors: agricultural products (Article 18 et seq.), fisheries (Article 22 et seq.) and coal and steel products (Protocol 2 on ECSC products).

The Europe Agreement prohibited the introduction of any new custom duties or measures having an equivalent effect (except, in very limited circumstances by Poland during the first 5 years to protect infant industries).[113] Similarly, no quantitative restrictions on imports or measures having an equivalent effect could be maintained. Discrimination through internal fiscal measures was also prohibited (Article 26). As regards technical requirements for products, to the extent not covered by the prohibition of measures having an equivalent effect to customs duties, the Agreement provided that Poland will use its best endeavours to ensure that its future legislation would comply with EU law (Article 68 et seq.).

The Agreement also provided for the free movement of capital; in particular when transactions underlying the payments concern movements of goods, services or persons between the Parties which have been liberalised pursuant to the Agreement (Article 59 et seq.).

---

[110]See, e.g. Teasdale A, Europe Agreement. The Penguin Companion to European Union, 1 October 2012, https://penguincompaniontoeu.com/additional_entries/europe-agreements/ (last accessed 30 April 2018).

[111]Europe Agreement establishing an association between the European Communities and their Member States, of the one part, and the Republic of Poland, of the other part (Europe Agreement Poland), OJ 1993 L 348/2, formally concluded for the Union by Decision 93/743/EC of the Council and the Commission of 13 December 1993, OJ 1993 L 348/1. Entry into force: 1 February 1994.

[112]Article 9 Europe Agreement Poland.

[113]Article 25 and 28 Europe Agreement Poland.

With respect to competition and State aid rules, Article 63 follows the pattern of the Free Trade agreement with Switzerland and provides that any practices described in Articles 101(1), 102, or 107(1) TFEU is incompatible with the proper functioning of the Europe Agreement, insofar as such practices may affect trade between the Community and Poland.[114] The Europe Agreement requires, as part of the Agreement (and not "just" a unilateral declaration on the part of the Union), that any practices in this respect shall be assessed on the basis of criteria established under EU competition law.[115] To ensure continued alignment between EU rules and those applicable in Poland, the Europe Agreement envisaged the adoption of implementing rules through Decisions of the Association Council.[116] Such a decision was first adopted as regards the less contentious issues surrounding the application of the competition rules applicable to undertakings.[117] It took considerably longer to also agree on an Association Council Decision implementing the State aid rules[118] and reinforcing transparency and providing detailed information about single cases, if requested.[119] Both decisions ensured an even closer approximation of the rules Poland was required to implement with those applicable in the Union and identified authorities to conduct the proceedings that are envisaged by the substantive rules. The Union insisted, at the time, that these authorities had to have a high level of independence from the State.

The implementation of the Europe Agreement is subject to the oversight of an Association Council (Article 102 et seq.). The Association Council is, inter alia, responsible for the settling of disputes. It decides by consensus. However, if no consensus can be reached, each party may refer disputes to arbitration. Each party may nominate one arbitrator, the third arbitrator must be nominated by the Association Council (Article 105). The arbitrators decide by majority vote. However, since the parties have to appoint the third arbitrator, each party has the possibility to prevent the arbitration from happening.

In spite of the market access rules, and of the far reaching harmonisation of the competition and State aid rules, Article 29 provides that "*if one of the Parties finds that dumping is taking place in trade with the other Party within the meaning of Article VI of the General Agreement on Tariffs and Trade, it may take appropriate*

---

[114] Article 63(1) Europe Agreement Poland; the Agreement and certain of its Protocols provided for modifications, in particular, as regards agricultural and ECSC products.

[115] Article 63(2) Europe Agreement Poland.

[116] Article 6(3) Europe Agreement Poland.

[117] Decision No 1/96 of the Association Council between the [EU and Poland] of 16 July 1996 adopting the implementing rules necessary for the application of Article 63(1)(i), (1)(ii) and (2) of the Europe Agreement (…) and the rules implementing Article 8(1)(i), (1)(ii) and (2) of Protocol 2 on ECSC products to that Agreement; OJ 1996 L 208/24.

[118] Decision No 3/2001 of the EU-Poland Association Council of 23 May 2001 adopting the implementing rules for the application of the provisions on State aid referred to in Article 63(1)(iii) and (2) pursuant to Article 63(3) of the Europe Agreement (…), and in Article 8(1)(iii) and (2) of Protocol 2 on European Coal and Steel Community (ECSC) products to that Agreement (2001/615/EC), OJ 2001 L 215/39.

[119] Article 63(4)(b) Europe Agreement Poland.

measures against this practice in accordance with the Agreement relating to the application of Article VI of the General Agreement on Tariffs and Trade, with related internal legislation and with the conditions and procedures laid down in Article 33." Article 33(3)(b) provides that "*the Association Council shall be informed of the dumping case as soon as the authorities of the importing Party have initiated an investigation. When no end has been put to the dumping or no other satisfactory solution has been reached within 30 days of the matter being referred to the Association Council, the importing Party may adopt the appropriate measures.*" Hence, the Union and Poland retained the right to resort to anti-dumping proceedings, the only additional procedural safeguard is the consultation of the Association Council, which is only required after a formal anti-dumping investigation has already been initiated. Anti-dumping proceedings were, in fact, directed against Poland after the Europe Agreement had come into force.[120]

As regards State aid, Article 8 of the Decision provides that differences in opinion in State aid matters should first be resolved as between the European Commission and the Polish State aid monitoring authority. If that was not possible, it should be referred to the Association Council. But Article 8(3) further states that any such procedures are "without prejudice" to the ability of each party, to resort to trade defence measures (in accordance with Article 63(6) of the Europe Agreement (which permits countervailing measures taken in conformity with the WTO rules)), albeit only as a matter of last resort. No such measures were in fact taken in the State aid context.[121]

5.4 Stabilisation and Association Agreement with Serbia

One of the more recent EU Free Trade Agreements preparing for a possible future EU membership is the Stabilisation and Association Agreement (SAA) with Serbia of 2008, which entered into force in September 2013.[122] However, the parts that fell

---

[120] See e.g. Council Regulation (EC) No 1697/2002 imposing definitive anti-dumping duties on imports of certain welded tubes and pipes, of iron or non-alloy steel originating in the Czech Republic, Poland, Thailand, Turkey and the Ukraine, OJ 2002 L 259/8. There are, of course, no such duties since Poland joined the Union as a Member State.

[121] The absence of countervailing measures is probably due to the fact that the accession treaty of Poland to the EU provided for a mechanism by which the Commission could unilaterally take measures (and in a way retroactively) against much of the State aid granted while the Europe Agreement was in force, to the extent such aid still had an effect after the accession (and provided the Commission had not authorised such aid before).

[122] Stabilisation and Association Agreement between the European Communities and their Member States of the one part, and the Republic of Serbia, of the other part of 29 April 2008 (Association Agreement EU-Serbia), OJ 2013 L 278/16, adopted by the Union by Council and Commission Decision 2013/490/EU of 22 July 2013 on the conclusion of the Stabilisation and Association Agreement [with Serbia], OJ 2013 L 278/16, as amended (consolidated version: http://eur-lex. europa.eu/search.html?qid=1518638668739&text=2013A9018&scope=EURLEX&type=quick& lang=en (last accessed 30 April 2018)).

within the exclusive competence of the European Union were reflected in an Interim Agreement, which entered into force already on 1 February 2010.[123] The SAA established, first and foremost, a Free Trade Area with full mutual market access (within a 6 year transitional period, Article 18), in which customs duties on exports and imports, quantitative restrictions and measures having an equivalent effect were abolished. The Union abolished all duties on industrial goods originating in Serbia (Article 20, 22), Serbia abolished them for most industrial products originating in the Union (Article 21, 22 and Annex I). Special rules existed as regards certain sectors: for agricultural products (Article 24 et seq.) and fish and fisheries (Article 29 et seq.).

The SAA prohibits the introduction of any new custom duties or measures having an equivalent effect (Article 36). Similarly, no quantitative restrictions on imports or measures having an equivalent effect can be introduced or made more restrictive (Article 36). Discrimination through internal fiscal measures was also prohibited (Article 37). As regards technical requirements for products, to the extent not covered by the prohibition of measures having an equivalent effect to customs duties, the Agreement provides that Serbia recognises the importance of the approximation of the existing legislation in Serbia to that of the Community and of its effective implementation. Serbia endeavoured to ensure that its existing laws and future legislation would be gradually made compatible with the Community acquis. Approximation had, at an early stage, to focus on fundamental elements of, in particular, the Internal Market acquis (Article 72).

The Agreement also provides for the free movement of capital; in particular when transactions underlying the payments concern commercial transactions or the provision of services in which a resident of one of the Parties is participating (Article 62, 63 et seq.).

With respect to competition and State aid rules, Article 73 follows the pattern of the Europe Agreements and provides that any practices described in Articles 101(1), 102, 106 or 107(1) TFEU are incompatible with the proper functioning of the Europe Agreement, in so far as such practices may affect trade between the Community and Serbia. The Europe agreement requires, as part of the Agreement (Article 73(2) SAA) that any practices in this respect shall be assessed on the basis of criteria established under EU competition law.[124] Serbia is required to set up authorities competent to enforce the substantive rules. The SAA provides that these authorities have to have a high level of operational independence from the State (Article 73(3) and (4)).

---

[123] Interim Agreement on trade and trade-related matters between the European Community, of the one part, and the Republic of Serbia, of the other part, of 29 April 2008 (Interim Agreement), OJ 2010 L 28/2, adopted by the Union through Council Decision 2010/36/EC concerning the signing and conclusion of the Interim Agreement [with Serbia], OJ 2010 L 28/1.

[124] Interim Agreement, Article 73(2), with some specific modifications as regards State aid to the steel industry (Article 37(8)) and to the competition rules and State as regards agricultural products (Article 37(9)).

The implementation of the Europe Agreement is subject to the oversight of a Stabilisation and Association Council (SAC, Article 11, 119 et seq.). The SAC is, inter alia, responsible for the settling of disputes. It decides by consensus. However, if no consensus can be reached, each party may refer a limited number of disputes to arbitration, not including the competition and State aid rules (see Article 2 of Protocol 7 to the SAA).

In spite of the market access rules, and of the far reaching harmonisation of the Competition and State aid rules, Article 29 provides, that *"if one of the Parties finds that dumping and/or countervailable subsidisation is taking place in trade with the other Party, that Party may take appropriate measures against this practice in accordance with the WTO Agreement on Implementation of Article VI of the GATT 1994 or the WTO Agreement on Subsidies and Countervailing Measures and the respective related internal legislation."* Hence, the Union and Serbia retain the right to resort to anti-dumping proceedings. And anti-dumping proceedings were, in fact, directed against Serbia, after the SAA Agreement had come into force, but ultimately did not lead to the imposition of measures.[125]

5.5   EuroMed Agreements: The Example of Israel

Towards the end of the 1990s, the European Community began to conclude a number of additional association and free trade agreements with trading partners located around the Mediterranean Sea. This includes the "EuroMed" agreements with Algeria, Egypt, Israel, Jordan, Lebanon, Morocco, Palestine and Tunisia. A similar agreement with Syria was initialised in 2008 but has not been signed or ratified and no agreement has been reached with Libya; efforts as regards the latter two countries are presently suspended.[126] The agreement with Turkey is also part of the EuroMed partnership approach, but is structured quite differently (see above Sect. 4.2).

The EuroMed agreements aim to establish free trade between the parties and were modelled, to a significant extent, on the Europe Agreements, but in contrast to them did not intend to prepare for the future accession of these countries to the Union. They provide for a classical free trade area (not limited to goods, but also extending to services and capital, and to a much lesser extent to the free movement of people) coupled with a detailed arrangement for a progressively increasing level

---

[125] Commission Implementing Regulation (EU) 2017/1795 imposing a definitive anti-dumping duty on imports of certain hot-rolled flat products of iron, non-alloy or other alloy steel originating in Brazil, Iran, Russia and Ukraine and terminating the investigation on imports of certain hot-rolled flat products of iron, non-alloy or other alloy steel originating in Serbia, OJ 2017 L 258/24.

[126] See overview prepared by the European Commission, http://ec.europa.eu/trade/policy/countries-and-regions/regions/euro-mediterranean-partnership/ (last accessed 30 April 2018).

of market liberalisation. The structure and essential content of these EuroMed Agreements is very similar as between each of the various Agreements.[127] The analysis below is based (by way of example) on the EuroMed agreement with Israel,[128] which entered into force on 1 June 2000.[129] The Agreement established, first, a free trade area in which all customs duties (on originating products) on imports and exports are prohibited (Article 8, as regards industrial products, the liberalisation of agricultural products is much more limited). Second, quantitative restrictions on imports and exports as well as all measures having equivalent effect are prohibited between the Community and Israel (Article 16 and 17), as well as direct or indirect fiscal discrimination of imports (Article 19). The EuroMed agreement also ensures the free circulation of capital.[130]

With respect to competition and State aid rules, Article 36 follows the pattern of the Europe Agreements and provides that any practices described in Articles 101(1), 102 or 107(1) TFEU are incompatible with the proper functioning of the Europe Agreement, insofar as such practices may affect trade between the Community and Israel.[131] Similar to the FTA with Switzerland, but in contrast to the Europe Agreements, there is (only) a unilateral declaration by the Union (of which Israel "took note") that any practices in this respect shall be assessed on the basis of criteria established under EU competition law.[132] To ensure continued alignment between EU rules and those applicable in Israel, the EuroMed Agreement envisaged the adoption of implementing rules within 3 years, through Decisions of the Association Council.[133] Such rules have not been adopted. Similar to the Europe Agreements, Article 36(3) imposes transparency obligations as regards State aid so that parties have the right to request information from the other as regards State aid granted, aid schemes and, upon request, individual aid cases.[134]

The implementation of the Israel EuroMed Agreement is subject to the oversight of an Association Council (Article 67 et seq.). The Association Council is, inter alia, responsible for the settling of disputes (Article 75). It decides by consensus. However, if no consensus can be reached, each party may refer disputes to arbitration. Each

---

[127] See European Commission, Euro-Med Association Agreements, Implementation Guide, Relex F, 30 July 2004, http://www.eeas.europa.eu/archives/docs/euromed/docs/asso_agree_guide_en. pdf (last accessed 30 April 2018).

[128] Euro-Mediterranean Agreement establishing an association between the European Communities and their Member States, of the one part, and the State of Israel, of the other part, signed on 20 November 1995, OJ 2000 L 147/3. The Agreement was adopted by the Union through Decision of the Council and the Commission of 19 April 2000 on the conclusion of the Euro-Mediterranean Agreement with Israel (2000/384/EC, ECSC), OJ 2000, L 147/1.

[129] See Notice, OJ 2000 L 147/172.

[130] Euro-Mediterranean Agreement with Israel, Article 31.

[131] Euro-Mediterranean Agreement with Israel, Article 36(1). The Agreement and certain of its Protocols provided for modifications, in particular, as regards agricultural and ECSC products.

[132] Declaration by the European Community relating to Article 36, annexed to the Final Act, OJ 2000 L 147/171.

[133] Euro-Mediterranean Agreement with Israel, Article 36(2).

[134] Euro-Mediterranean Agreement with Israel, Article 36(4).

party may nominate one arbitrator, the third arbitrator must be nominated by the Association Council (Article 75(4)(2)). The arbitrators decide by majority vote. However, since the parties have to appoint the third arbitrator, each party has the possibility to prevent the arbitration from happening.

In spite of the market access rules, and of the agreement on Competition and State aid rules, Article 22 provides, that *"if one of the Parties finds that dumping is taking place in trade with the other Party within the meaning of Article VI of the General Agreement on Tariffs and Trade, it may take appropriate measures against this practice in accordance with the Agreement on implementation of Article VI of the GATT and with its relevant internal legislation under the conditions and in accordance with the procedures laid down in Article 25."* Article 25(3)(a) provides that *"the Association Council shall be informed of the dumping case as soon as the authorities of the importing Party have initiated an investigation. If no end has been put to the dumping or no other satisfactory solution has been reached within 30 days of the notification being made, the importing Party may adopt the appropriate measures."* Hence, the Union and Israel retain the right to resort to anti-dumping proceedings; the only additional procedural safeguard is the consultation of the Association Council, which is only required after a formal anti-dumping investigation has already been initiated. Anti-dumping proceedings were, in fact, directed against Israel after the EuroMed Agreement had come into force.[135]

As regards to countervailing measures, the EuroMed Agreement provides in Article 36(2), that in the absence of an Association Council implementing decision *"the provisions of the Agreement on interpretation and application of Articles VI, XVI and XXIII of the GATT shall be applied as the rules for the implementation of [the State aid rule in Article 36 (1) iii]."*[136] Hence, the Union and Israel retain the right to adopt countervailing measures, in accordance with WTO rules.

5.6 Free Trade Agreement with Singapore

The EU-Singapore Free Trade Agreement (EUSFTA) was one of the first new comprehensive trade agreements the EU has agreed with a South-East Asian Country.[137] The Agreement has gained special notoriety as a result of a dispute between EU

---

[135] Anti-dumping measures were limited to anti-circumvention measures, see Council Regulation (EC) No 1975/2004 of 15 November 2004 extending the definitive anti-dumping duty imposed by Regulation No 1676/2001 on imports of polyethylene terephthalate (PET) film originating, inter alia, in India to imports of polyethylene terephthalate film consigned from Brazil and from Israel, whether declared as originating in Brazil or Israel or not, OJ 2004 L 342/1.

[136] Interestingly, this reference in the agreement is to the pre-Uruguay round GATT Agreement on interpretation and application of Articles VI, XVI and XXIII and not to the WTO Agreement on Subsidies and Countervailing Measures presumably, because the latter agreement had not entered into force at the time the Israel EuroMed Agreement was signed.

[137] The provisional text of the agreement (as of May 2015) can be found at http://trade.ec.europa.eu/doclib/press/index.cfm?id=961 (last accessed 30 April 2018).

Member States and the European Commission, over the attribution of competences to conclude the agreement. Following the European Court of Justice's Opinion 2/15,[138] the full agreement will be formally concluded as a mixed agreement, but the Union competences have been effectively consolidated and strengthened.[139]

The agreement provides for the freedom to import and export goods.[140] The agreement covers a broad range of matters, including provisions on market access and national treatment as regards to the import of goods and the progressive reduction or elimination of customs duties over a short period of time and the prohibition of new or increased charges or customs duties (standstill obligation) (Chapter 2). The EUSFTA also provides for the elimination of technical barriers to trade (Chapter 4) and other measures for customs and trade facilitation (Chapter 6). The free movement of capital is mentioned, Parties agree to authorise any payments and transfers on the current account of the balance-of-payments between the Parties.[141] Nevertheless, in other market access contexts, the agreement also simply reaffirms the Parties commitments under the WTO rules.[142]

The Agreement reaffirms the commitment to the application and effective enforcement of competition rules. Specific substantive rules mirror the provisions in Articles 101 and 102 TFEU and include a statement on merger control.[143] The Parties retain their competence to enforce and further develop their competition laws.[144]

By contrast, the rules on subsidisation essentially repeat and further implement the WTO rules, in particular Article VI GATT 1994 and the ASCM, clarifying, however, that these rules apply to goods and services.[145] The WTO rules on prohibited subsidies are reinforced[146] and mandatory dispute settlement is provided for prohibited subsidies (but specifically excluded as regards the competition rules for undertakings or other forms of State aid or subsidisation).[147]

Institutional oversight over the implementation of the agreement should be exercised by the established Trade Committee, which however, has limited powers to amend the EUSFTA. Decisions require a unanimous vote.

The Parties agreed on relatively stringent rules for State-to-State Arbitration (Chapter 15), which is available for all substantive rules of the agreement, except those explicitly excluded, such as the competition and State aid rules.

---

[138] ECJ, Opinion C-2/15, *Free Trade Agreement with Singapore*, ECLI:EU:C:2017:376; the Court issued a press release outlining the essence of the (long) opinions, see https://curia.europa.eu/jcms/upload/docs/application/pdf/2017-05/cp170052en.pdf (last accessed 30 April 2018).

[139] See, inter alia, Müller-Ibold T, German Report on Topic III for FIDE 2018, forthcoming.

[140] Article 2 EUSFTA.

[141] Article 17.7 EUSFTA.

[142] Article 2.9–2.12 EUSFTA.

[143] Article 12.1 EUSFTA.

[144] Article 12.2 EUSFTA.

[145] Article 12.7 EUSFTA.

[146] Article 12.7 EUSFTA.

[147] Article 12.14 EUSFTA.

The parties reaffirm the respective rights to resort to anti-dumping and counter-vailing duty proceedings. However, the agreement provides for a limited strengthening of the WTO rules by requiring both sides to apply the lesser duty rule in anti-dumping proceedings and to provide more information earlier in the process, compared to WTO rules.[148] In recent times, Singapore has not often been the object of TDI measures imposed by the Union (a countervailing measure was imposed against biodiesel consigned from Canada and Singapore in 2010).[149]

5.7 Comprehensive Economic and Trade Agreement with Canada – CETA

The President of the European Commission, Jean-Claude Juncker, referred to the new Comprehensive Economic and Trade Agreement (CETA)[150] with Canada as an agreement that *"encapsulates what the EU wants its trade policy to be in reference to, among other things, an instrument for growth, a harness of globalization and a tool to shape global trade rules."*[151] CETA (the provisions falling within the scope of competences of the Union) entered provisionally into force on 21 September 2017.[152]

CETA establishes a Free Trade Area between Canada and the Union. Trade in goods is progressively liberalised (Article 2.1) and full market access is to be granted in particular as regards industrial products. Customs duties on exports are abolished, no new duties and charges may be introduced (standstill) and existing duties on imports are being eliminated, phased-out or reduced according to tariff elimination schedules.[153] Market access is facilitated through national treatment obligations for

---

[148] Article 3.2 EUSFTA.

[149] Initiation of investigation concerning the possible circumvention of countervailing measures imposed by Council Regulation (EC) No 598/2009 on imports of biodiesel originating in the U.S. by imports of biodiesel consigned from Canada and Singapore (August 2010).

[150] Comprehensive Economic and Trade Agreement (CETA) between Canada, of the one part, and the European Union and its Member States, of the other part, OJ 2017, L 11/23.

[151] European Commission, EU-Canada trade agreement enters into force, 20 September 2017, http://trade.ec.europa.eu/doclib/press/index.cfm?id=1723 (accessed 30 April 2018).

[152] See Council Decision (EU) 2017/38 of 28 October 2016 on the provisional application of the Comprehensive Economic and Trade Agreement (CETA) OJ 2017 L 11/1080 and Notice concerning the provisional application of the Comprehensive Economic and Trade Agreement (CETA), OJ 2017 L 238/9.

[153] Article 2.4, 2.6, 2.7 CETA with Annex 2-A.

goods (consistent with Article III GATT 1994),[154] the reduction of technical barriers to trade (consistent with WTO rules and the WTO TBT Agreement) [155] and the improvement of customs procedures. [156]

With respect to competition law rules applicable to undertakings, Parties agree in Chapter 17 on the importance of free and undistorted competition in their trade relations (Article 17.2) and agree to prohibit anti-competitive conduct and to cooperate in competition matters based on a pre-existing cooperation agreement between the EC and the Canadian Government from 1999.[157] Nevertheless, there is no attempt to substantively harmonise such rules.

As regards the issue of State aid, the parties reaffirm in Chapter 7, the application of the WTO rules, agree on a definition of subsidies that is consistent with the WTO rules (in particular Article 1 and 2 ASCM) coupled with some additional commitment to information exchange and transparency. There is no attempt made to harmonise the substantive conditions under which subsidies can be granted.

A CETA Joint Committee was established to supervise and facilitate the implementation of the agreement and to function as a forum to find appropriate solutions or settle disputes arising out or in connection with the agreement.[158] The Joint Committee decides by mutual consent (i.e. each party has an effective veto over any decisions). The agreement also provides for binding state-to-state dispute resolution through arbitration (Chapter 29), but such dispute resolution does not apply to competition and subsidisation matters under Chapters 7 or 17.

Rather, the parties reaffirm the respective rights to resort to anti-dumping and countervailing duty proceedings (Chapter 3). Nevertheless, the agreement aims at a rather limited strengthening of the WTO rules as between the parties, by requiring both sides to consider public interests and the possibility of applying the lesser duty rule in TDI proceedings.[159] In recent times, Canada has not often been the object of TDI measures imposed by the Union (the last decision involving trade defence measures concerned biodiesel originating in the United States and consigned from Canada in 2011).[160]

---

[154] Article 2.3 CETA.

[155] Chapter 4 (and 5, on phytosanitary measures) CETA.

[156] Chapter 6 CETA.

[157] Chapter 17 CETA.

[158] Article 26.1. CETA.

[159] Article 3.3 CETA.

[160] Council Implementing Regulation (EU) No. 443/2011 extending the definitive countervailing duty imposed by Regulation (EC) No 598/2009 (...) to imports of biodiesel consigned from Canada, (...), and extending the definitive countervailing duty imposed by Regulation (EC) No 598/2009 to imports of biodiesel in a blend containing by weight 20% or less of biodiesel originating in the United States of America and terminating the investigation in respect of imports consigned from Singapore, OJ 2011 L 122/1.

6 Lessons To Be Learned: Is There an Identifiable Pattern?

The EU has engaged, over the past 60 years, in a number of different agreements aimed at improving and facilitating trade with non-Member States. At the same time, the Union has been one of the more important users of trade defence instruments, such as anti-dumping actions and countervailing measures.

In the framework of its trading relations, the Union has only rarely accepted limitations on the use of its trade defence instruments. Even in agreements establishing Free Trade Areas or Customs Unions, the Union has not generally accepted such restrictions. Cases in which such restrictions were accepted can be summarised and characterised as follows:

- The Union accepted not to resort to trade defence measures at all only in exceptional circumstances, where full market access and the free movement of, in particular, goods and capital was guaranteed, the Union's competition and State aid rules were fully applicable and, importantly, enforcement through independent authorities and courts was ensured. It is worth noting that so far the Union has only been willing to forgo the possibility of adopting trade defence measures if enforcement was guaranteed by supranational authorities and courts. This was the case for enforcement within the Union itself and within the EEA.
- The Union also accepted in some cases to resort to trade defence measures only after consultation with particular trading partners. The underlying free trade agreements (and the agreement on the customs union with Turkey) are characterised by an alignment of the substantive rules relating to market access, free movement of goods and capital, competition and State aid to the Union's substantive rules. However, the enforcement of the substantive rules based on the mechanisms set forth in the agreements was not considered equivalent of the Union itself, in particular, in terms of independence from a particular country and its government. Exceptionally, possibly as a result of the few recent cases where TDI measures had to be adopted, such procedural benefits are also provided for in the EUSFTA with Singapore.
- There is a suggestion, in Article 44 of Decision 1/95 of the Association Council with Turkey,[161] that "*the Association Council may decide to suspend the application of these instruments provided that Turkey has implemented competition, State aid control and other relevant parts of the acquis communautaire which are related to the internal market and ensured their effective enforcement*" (emphasis added). Only then might a further decision be taken to do away with trade defence measures in the EU/Turkey relations. Given today's environment, it appears unlikely that this statement will be acted upon any time soon.
- In free trade agreements aimed at establishing an association with the Union (but not future membership in the Union), there are often far reaching market access commitments and there is agreement on principles of competition rules, but less

---

[161] See above, Sect. 4.2.

of an alignment as regards State aid policy, a lesser degree of commitment to fully adopt EU internal competition policy and less stringent enforcement and dispute settlement obligations. In these cases, the Union has not accepted to forego its right to resort to TDIs, at most it agreed to inform and consult with the other party on the need to resort to such TDI measures.

• In other free trade agreements with third countries, in particular, those neither aimed at future membership in, nor towards an association with the Union, even broad market access commitments as regards trade in goods, elimination of tariff and non-tariff barriers and reinforcement of competition law principles have not led to the elimination or any significant restriction of the right to resort to anti-dumping measures. Other than limited procedural commitments (and an attempt to agree on the equivalent of the lesser duty rule (which the Union applies any-way)), there is no substantive limitation in such agreements. Moreover, there is generally little alignment on State aid policy, so that no restriction on the use of countervailing measures is agreed. If anything, the parties reaffirm their commitment to follow the WTO rules if and when they resort to TDIs.

In sum, the Union's right to resort to TDI measures is typically maintained in the framework of the RTAs. The Union has concluded with third countries. The only exception relates to the relationship as between the EU Member States themselves and the Union with the EEA members (as regards industrial products), which are characterised by a particularly high level of economic integration, substantive rule harmonisation and an enforcement through supra-national institutions and courts, which is both mandatory and not subject to influence by individual countries.

In a broader group of agreements, the EU accepted procedural limitations on the use of TDI measures, by agreeing to consultations, either prior to the initiation of investigation procedures or (more common) concurrent with or after such initiation. The Union's differentiated approach to the elimination/limitation of its right to resort to TDIs is consistent with WTO rules. The MFN treatment requirement under Article I GATT does not apply to such a differentiation.

7 Implications for Brexit

The United Kingdom has announced its desire to leave the European Union and has triggered the process for leaving provided for in Article 50 TEU on 29 March 2017.[162] Therefore, the United Kingdom presently is a Member State and will (likely) remain a Member State until 29 March 2019. During that time, no TDI can be adopted between the UK and the other EU Member States.

---

[162] See Council, Statement by the European Council (Art. 50) on the UK notification, 29 March 2017, http://www.consilium.europa.eu/en/press/press-releases/2017/03/29/euco-50-statement-uk-notification/ (last accessed 30 April 2018) and the formal notice submitted by the UK Government to the Council of 29 March 2017, http://www.consilium.europa.eu/media/24079/070329_uk_letter_tusk_art50.pdf (last accessed 30 April 2018).

In connection with the possible interim arrangements for Brexit, there is one element that distinguishes the UK from all other third countries so far: at the point of departure, the free movement of goods, free movement of capital, competition and State aid rules will be perfectly aligned. However, the UK Government has indicated that it is not willing to accept existing enforcement mechanisms. The jurisdiction of the Commission and the EU courts in Luxembourg is viewed as a red line.[163] Nevertheless, it appears from more recent statements that for an interim period, the UK might be willing to accept that such enforcement mechanisms will continue to apply. If that is true, and based on the example of the EEA Agreement, it is conceivable that the EU and the UK would also agree not to apply TDI during such interim period.

However, as regards to a longer term free trade agreement, the UK has not indicated a clear willingness to accept the continued jurisdiction of the Commission and the EU courts or the creation of any alternative structure that would be independent of the UK, even though some press reports seem to suggest an increased flexibility[164] (but also the risk of a Brexiteer backlash). Given the practice so far, it would seem difficult to imagine that the EU would accept to waive the application of TDI in such circumstances. Only the language of the Decision of the EU-Turkey Association Council decision might suggest otherwise; it could be read as an indication that a sufficiently independent enforcement mechanism for the substantive rules within the UK might be enough to limit the application of TDIs, even in the framework of such future FTA, assuming that the alignment on substance would remain.

However, Members of the UK Government have been understood to suggest possible modifications as regards the substantive rules. One particular suggestion related to possible (tax) incentives to keep business interested in coming to or staying in the UK.[165] Such new rules may be a first step away from common State aid

---

[163] See, inter alia, Newton Dunn T, EU can't lay down law: Defiant Theresa may unveils plans for a joint-run panel to settle post-Brexit rows and won't let EU courts dictate rules. The Sun, 22 August 2017, https://www.thesun.co.uk/news/4299962/theresa-may-eu-court-joint-post-brexit-panel/ (last accessed 30 April 2018); see also a more nuanced policy paper released by the UK Government, Policy Paper: Enforcement and dispute resolution – a future partnership paper, 23 August 2017, https://www.gov.uk/government/publications/enforcement-and-dispute-resolution-a-future-partnership-paper (last accessed 30 April 2018).

[164] See, e.g., Ross T, May Proposes Blurring Her Brexit Red Line on ECJ. Bloomberg, 23 February 2017, https://www.bloomberg.com/news/articles/2018-02-23/may-is-said-to-propose-blurring-her-brexit-red-line-on-ecj (last accessed 30 April 2018).

[165] Nissan, a Japanese automaker, agreed to build a new car at its plant in Sunderland, England, after receiving assurances, not publicly specified, from the government that the company would be protected from any negative impact from Brexit, see Wallace T, Nissan row as government denies 'secret deal' to support Sunderland factory post-Brexit. The Telegraph, 27 October 2016, https://www.telegraph.co.uk/business/2016/10/27/nissan-to-build-new-cars-in-sunderland-as-it-rejects-brexit-doub/ (last accessed 30 April 2018) and The New York Times, How 'Brexit' Could Change Business in Britain. The New York Times, updated 18 September 2017, https://www.nytimes.com/interactive/2016/business/international/brexit-uk-what-happens-business.html (last accessed 30 April 2018).

(or subsidisation) rules. If such plans would materialise, it would be hard to see why the EU would waive one effective remedy against such an approach taken by the UK.

If history is a guide, there is a significant risk that once the UK is no longer a Member State, TDIs will reappear in the bilateral relationship unless (1) the full substantive alignment of the rules is maintained and (2) an enforcement mechanism for such rules can be found, which will be considered sufficiently "effective" by the EU without infringing the UK's strengthened sense of sovereignty.

References

Alavi A (2012) Regional trade agreements. In: Oslen BE, Steinicke M, Sorensen KE (eds) WTO law from a European perspective. Wolters Kluwer, Alphen aan den Rijn, pp 407–422

Baule S (2017) 70. Verordnung (EG) Nr. 1225/2009 des Rates über den Schutz gegen gedumpte Einfuhren aus nicht zur Europäischen Gemeinschaft gehörenden Ländern. In: Krenzler H, Herrmann C, Niestedt M (eds) EU-Außenwirtschafts- und Zollrecht. Beck, München

Giannakopoulos T (2006) A concise guide to the EU anti-dumping/anti-subsidies procedures. Wolters Kluwer, Alphen aan den Rijn

Gobbi Estrella T, Horlick GN (2006) Mandatory abolition of anti-dumping, countervailing duties and safeguards in customs unions and free trade areas constituted between WTO members: re-visiting a long-standing discussion in light of the Appellate Body's Turkey – textiles ruling. In: Bartels L, Ortino F (eds) Regional trade agreements and the WTO legal system. Oxford University Press, New York, pp 109–148

Jessen PW (2012) Anti-dumping. In: Oslen BE, Steinicke M, Sorensen KE (eds) WTO law from a European perspective. Wolters Kluwer, Alphen aan den Rijn, pp 181–226

Lockhart N, Mitchell AD (2005) Regional trade agreements under GATT 1994: an exception and its limits. In: Mitchell AD (ed) Challenges and prospects for the WTO. Cameron May Ltd, London, pp 217–251

Müller W, Khan N, Scharf T (2009) EC and WTO anti-dumping law – a handbook, 2nd edn. Oxford University Press, Oxford

Müller-Ibold T, FIDE (2018) Thema III – Die externe Dimension der EU-Politiken. Deutschland, Landesbericht

Olsen BE, Steinicke M, Sorensen KE (2012) The WTO and the EU. In: Oslen BE, Steinicke M, Sorensen KE (eds) WTO law from a European perspective. Wolters Kluwer, Alphen aan den Rijn, pp 79–112

Pauwelyn J (2004) The puzzle of WTO safeguards and regional trade agreements. J Int Econ Law 7(1):109–142

Trebilcock MJ, Howse R (2005) The regulation of international trade. Routledge, New York

Van Bael I, Bellis JF (2011) EU anti-dumping and other trade defence instruments. Wolters Kluwer, Alphen aan den Rijn

Van den Bossche P, Zdouc W (2013) The law and policy of the World Trade Organization: text, cases and materials. Cambridge University Press, Cambridge

Trade Defense Instruments: The Leading Edge of U.S. Trade Policy

Bruce Malashevich and Mark Love

Contents

B. Malashevich (✉) · M. Love
Economic Consulting Services, LLC, Washington, DC, USA
e-mail: bruce.malashevich@economic-consulting.com; mark.love@economic-consulting.com

© Springer International Publishing AG, part of Springer Nature 2018   233
M. Bungenberg et al. (eds.), *The Future of Trade Defence Instruments*,
European Yearbook of International Economic Law,
https://doi.org/10.1007/978-3-319-95306-9_10

Abstract On 1 March 2017, the Office of the U.S. Trade Representative released the 2017 National Trade Policy Agenda of the President of the United States. The introductory chapter stated in part: *"In 2016, voters in both major parties called for a fundamental change in direction of U.S. trade policy. The American people grew frustrated with our prior trade policy not because they have ceased to believe in free trade and open markets, but because they did not all see clear benefits from international trade agreements..."* (Office of the U.S. Trade Representative, 2017 Trade Policy Agenda and 2016 Annual Report).

This chapter explores the profound changes in U.S. trade policy since the 2016 election and the key use of Trade Defense Instruments (TDIs) in setting a new direction for U.S. international trade relations. Also discussed are challenges to the long-standing bipartisan U.S. consensus for trade liberalization, as supported through multilateral trade negotiations (MTN). These challenges have also affected the international community, as witnessed by the lack of any successful new MTN round since the WTO came into force in 1995. None is seriously being entertained.

The chapter concludes with observations about current and future U.S. use of TDIs in trade disputes. With Mr. Trump as U.S. President, the era of MTN "rounds" is dead. Regional arrangements will likely have similarly reduced priority, with unilateral and bilateral actions taking center stage.

1   U.S. Trade Policy Undergoes a Profound Change in Direction

On 1 March 2017, the Office of the U.S. Trade Representative released the 2017 National Trade Policy Agenda of the President of the United States.[1] The introductory chapter summarized President Trump's trade policy objectives and priorities for the United States and the reasons therefor, stating in part:

> In 2016, voters in both major parties called for a fundamental change in direction of U.S. trade policy. The American people grew frustrated with our prior trade policy not because they have ceased to believe in free trade and open markets, but because they did not all see clear benefits from international trade agreements… The overarching purpose of our trade policy will be to expand trade in a way that is freer and fairer for all Americans. Every action we take with respect to trade will be designed to increase our economic growth, promote job creation in the United States, promote reciprocity with our trading partners, strengthen our manufacturing base and our ability to defend ourselves, and expand our agricultural and services industry exports. As a general matter, we believe that these goals can be best accomplished by focusing on bilateral negotiations rather than multilateral negotiations – and by renegotiating and revising trade agreements when our goals are not

---

[1] Office of the United States Trade Representative, 2017 Trade Policy Agenda and 2016 Annual Report of the President of the United States on the Trade Agreements Program, 1 March 2017, https://ustr.gov/about-us/policy-offices/press-office/reports-and-publications/2017/2017-trade-policy-agenda-and-2016 (last accessed 30 April 2018).

being met. Finally, we reject the notion that the United States should, for putative geopolitical advantage, turn a blind eye to unfair trade practices that disadvantage American workers, farmers, ranchers, and businesses in global markets.[2]

It cannot be overemphasized how profound a change this new direction sets for
U.S. trade policy. Since the end of World War II in 1945, there has existed a bipartisan consensus in the United States at the highest levels based on the assumption
that liberalizing trade is a good thing, best accomplished through multilateral trade
negotiations (MTN). The history of trade liberalization has proceeded apace in just
this way, first under the auspices of the General Agreement on Tariffs and Trade
(GATT), from 1948 through 1994, and then under the auspices of its successor
organization, the World Trade Organization (WTO), from 1995 until today.

Indications that fundamental economic and social trends may have contributed to
the recent seismic shift in U.S. trade policy are suggested from a comparison of the
track record of trade liberalization agreements that were reached during the 47 years
of the GATT to the track record under the WTO. From 1947 to 1994, the world's
countries that participated as members of the GATT initiated, negotiated and came
to final agreements in eight separate MTN Rounds. The last such GATT MTN
agreement was fashioned during the Uruguay Round (1986–1994). One result of the
Uruguay Round Agreement was the formation of the WTO.

In the 23 years since the WTO began, however, only one MTN Round has been
initiated—the Doha Development Agenda (Doha Round). But the Doha Round was
an abject failure. From initiation in 2001, the Doha Round bogged down through
years of contentious and, ultimately, unproductive negotiations. It was finally
viewed as hopelessly stalled by 2008. Thus, since GATT, there has been no new
MTN agreement.[3]

In fairness, the Doha Round's negotiating difficulties may be a consequence of
the dramatic progress that had been made in trade liberalization over the prior half
century. If so, this has perhaps left only the more difficult, complex issues whose
benefits are less obvious and whose costs in additional economic, social and political integration do not seem worth the effort.

Alternatively, the Doha Round experience may simply reflect an exhaustion of
interest in the MTN process. The world community may need more time to adjust
to the effects of decades of steady trade liberalization. The process of rejection by

---

[2] Office of the United States Trade Representative, 2017 Trade Policy Agenda and 2016 Annual
Report of the President of the United States on the Trade Agreements Program, 1 March 2017,
https://ustr.gov/about-us/policy-offices/press-office/reports-and-publications/2017/2017-trade-
policy-agenda-and-2016 (last accessed 30 April 2018), Chapter I, p. 1.
[3] The paralysis is evident as countries prepare for the 11th WTO conference in Argentina in
December 2017. Sixteen years have passed since the Doha round negotiating mandate was agreed
to at the 4th ministerial conference in Doha, Qatar in 2001. Yet today, WTO members are reportedly debating whether the Doha round mandate is even still in effect. See Fortnam B, U.S. role in
WTO talks unclear as others prepare for ministerial outcomes. Inside U.S. Trade, 4 August 2017,
pp. 15–16.

the United States of the long-standing direction of traditional trade policy could be a case in point.[4]

More generally, the intractability of disagreements between large blocks of countries over international trade issues indicates a lack of consensus over any acceptable course for "trade liberalization" for the time being. The consensus of the world community seems to be that world trade is sufficiently liberalized and a majority of the world community does not wish to go further at this time.

Notwithstanding the unprecedented turnabout in official U.S. Government trade policy, the authors do not anticipate a wholesale movement to unilateralism. It does appear that the Brussels conference was indeed prescient in its focus on the importance of Trade Defense Instruments (TDIs). There is strong evidence, on multiple fronts, that TDIs have taken a place at the tip of the spear in a more aggressive trade policy for the United States. Examples include: (1) self-initiation by the government of trade actions and investigations involving major industrial sectors, (2) the unprecedented use of trade negotiating authority to renegotiate existing trade agreements, (3) encouragement of use of industry petitions under existing, but neglected, statutes, and (4) executive actions to enhance the conduct and enforcement of antidumping and countervailing duty investigations and orders. The remainder of this paper will expand on the ways and means by which TDIs have become the preeminent tool in a more aggressive U.S. trade policy.

While most of the attention in the trade arena has focused on the policies and actions taken by the Trump administration, it must be noted that the new prominence of TDIs resulted in large part from antecedent action taken well before the current administration. We thus begin in the next section with a review of legislative action in the recent past that has set the stage and provided important means for enhancing the use of TDIs in current U.S. trade policy.[5]

2 The Contribution of Recent Changes in U.S. Trade Laws to the Enhancement of TDIs in Current U.S. Trade Policy

The emergence of the new U.S. trade posture was foreshadowed by a flurry of new trade laws passed and signed into law during the last 2 years of the Obama administration. Political changes resulting from the 2014 Congressional elections

---

[4]The beginning of the ongoing process of the rejection of the multilateral approach to trade negotiations was most clearly and publically demonstrated with the withdrawal of the U.S. from with the Trans-Pacific Partnership (TPP). The United States was the dominant presence in that multiyear negotiation among 12 Pacific Rim countries and it was the United States that rejected the agreement. The reader can find further insight and information on the process of TPP rejection in an article by the authors published in mid-2015. The article assessed the prospects for U.S. acceptance of a TPP agreement and presented specific predictions for the TTP's failure. See Malashevich and Love (2015).

[5]The authors note that they are not lawyers and do not practice law. Their observations are based on their experience and service as economic experts in hundreds of trade disputes over the past 40 years.

activated major trade-related legislative efforts in Congress in 2015 that led to the consideration of trade legislation that had been held in abeyance for years. The 2014 election also enabled Congress to actually pass all of the major pieces of trade legislation that were introduced.

President Obama was an advocate for much of this trade legislation. This support by the President was more in line with the traditional positions on trade of the Republican members of Congress and put the President in conflict with some of the Democratic leadership of the House and Senate. The irony is that the combination of the active support of President Obama and the increase in Republican seats in the House and Senate directly aided the passage of trade laws that, in turn, created the means now being used to implement the more aggressive U.S. trade policy that we see today. A review of the most important of these trade-related laws is in order to appreciate their importance in making TDIs the "tip of the spear" of the new direction in U.S. trade policy.

2.1   Trade Promotion Authority Renewal in 2015 and the Commencement of the Use of Renegotiating Authority

On 29 June 2015, President Obama signed into law the Bipartisan Congressional Trade Priorities and Accountability Act of 2015, more commonly known as "Trade Promotion Authority" or TPA.[6] The United States had been without such authority since the last version of the TPA law expired in 2007. Thus, Congress previously had kept from President Obama the authority that was necessary for a President to be able to enter into any international agreement that was negotiated. The 2015 passage of TPA opened the door once again to credible international trade negotiations and a President's ability actually to enter into international trade agreements.

Even more important for the succeeding Trump Administration, the TPA renewal also included the authority to renegotiate existing agreements. The new administration announced its intention to use this authority to enter into renegotiations, a process that already has begun with several current trade agreement partners.[7]

These renegotiations represent a sharp change in direction in U.S. trade policy. However, they came in response to long-standing criticism that had become increasingly prominent in trade agreement negotiations. Basically, the complaint was that the U.S. consistently refused to take any action when bilateral or multilateral

---

[6] Trade Priorities and Accountability Act, Pub. L. 114-26, 129 STAT 319, 29 June 2015.

[7] On 2 February 2017, President Trump announced the United States' intention to engage in negotiations related to NAFTA. Negotiations were initiated and are continuing. On 12 July 2017, USTR requested a meeting with Korea to discuss the KORUS Agreement (i.e. the bilateral free trade agreement between Korea and the United States). Negotiations on KORUS were initiated and are continuing.

agreements were seen as hurting the U.S. or not creating the benefits anticipated. A common argument cited large increases in the U.S. trade deficit that occurred after the U.S. entered into new free trade agreements (FTAs), such as when Mexico became a part of the North American Free Trade Agreement (NAFTA). The long-standing reluctance on the part of elected U.S. officials of both parties to take action had become a major cause of disillusionment with trade agreements.

While renegotiation of an established trade agreement may not be viewed as a traditional "Trade Defense Instrument," or TDI, the authors suggest that renegotiations represent a new and potentially effective form of TDI. The renegotiation process is intended to re-set the rules by which trade relations are conducted. As such, the renegotiation process could potentially and directly affect trade in a range of goods and services in ways comparable to the effect of traditional TDIs.

2.2   The Trade Preferences Extension Act of 2015 and Enhancements in Provisions Affecting the Outcome of U.S. Anti-Dumping and Countervailing Duty Investigations

The second major piece of legislation passed was the Trade Preferences Extension Act of 2015.[8] This legislation renewed several major U.S. trade preference programs, including the African Growth and Development Act, the Generalized System of Preferences and the decades-long program of trade adjustment assistance for workers affected by trade.

More to the point of TDI enhancement, there were also provisions in the Trade Preferences Extension Act that made changes in how the U.S. conducts its anti-dumping (AD) and countervailing duty (CVD) investigations. These changes had been long advocated by trade-impacted U.S. industries with the intent to remove what were viewed as procedural barriers to the effectiveness of these TDIs against unfair trade practices.

Certain of the modifications in the law made it easier for domestic industries to receive affirmative injury determinations in anti-dumping and countervailing duty investigations conducted by the U.S. International Trade Commission (ITC). These changes included the following[9]:

Section 503(a) (Effect of Profitability of Domestic Industries):

---

[8] The Trade Preferences Extension Act, Pub. L. 114-27, 129 STAT 362 entitled "An Act to extend the African Growth and Opportunity Act, the Generalized System of Preferences, the preferential duty treatment program for Haiti, and for other purposes," was signed into law on 29 June 2015.

[9] All of these changes affecting determinations of material injury or the threat thereof are contained in Section 503 of Title V of the Trade Preferences Extension Act of 2015 (Definition of Material Injury).

The ITC may not determine that there is no material injury or no threat of material injury merely because the industry in profitable or because the performance of the industry has recently improved.

Section 503(b) (Evaluation of Impact on Domestic Industry in Determination of Material Injury):

With respect to relevant economic factors which have a bearing on the state of an industry, the factor of profits was expanded to specifically include gross profits, operating profits, and net profits, and the factors of the ability to service debt and the return on assets were added.

Section 503(c) (Captive Production):

The definition of captive production was altered in a way that expanded the circumstances in which the ITC's injury determination can be based on an evaluation of conditions specifically in the merchant market.

These changes are believed to have had immediate effects. In a recent round of U.S. anti-dumping and countervailing duty investigations involving steel, the International Trade Commission unanimously determined in favor of the domestic industry that there was material injury in every case. Some analysts familiar with the facts of each case are of the opinion that the uniform determinations of material injury may have reflected the influence of these changes in the laws relating to injury determinations by the ITC.

Similar changes were made to the procedures governing the determinations by U.S Department of Commerce (Commerce Department) of the existence of dumping or subsidization and the margins thereof, in anti-dumping and countervailing duty investigations. As in the case of the changes affecting injury determinations by the ITC, these changes to the Commerce Department practice likewise resolved ongoing disputes over certain methodological issues. Generally, the changes in the law granted the Commerce Department greater discretion in how to conduct their analyses. In practice, application of this discretion tends to operate in favor of the U.S. domestic industry. The changes include the following[10]:

Section 502 (Consequences of Failure to Cooperate With a Request for Information in a Proceeding):

Among other things, the Commerce Department is given greater discretion in the choice of rates and margins used in adverse inference determinations and in the application of highest rate or margin, and has no obligation to make certain estimates or to address certain claims if an interested party is found to have failed to cooperate.

Section 504 (Particular Market Situation):

The definition of ordinary course of trade is modified and the Commerce Department is given greater flexibility to use alternative calculation methodologies to determine constructed value.

Section 505 (Distortion of Prices or Costs):

---

[10] All of these changes affecting determinations of anti-dumping and countervailing duty margins are contained in Sections 502 and 504–506 of Title V of the Trade Preferences Extension Act of 2015 (Improvements to Antidumping and Countervailing Duty Laws).

Among other things, further clarification is provided regarding reasonable grounds for the Commerce Department to believe that certain prices are less than the cost of production and greater discretion is given to disregard certain price or cost values.

Section 506 (Reduction in Burden on Department of Commerce by Reducing the Number of Voluntary Respondents):

Among other things, this Section expands the considerations that may apply to the number of voluntary respondents examined by the Commerce Department.

These new provisions have had a direct effect on the course and results of anti-dumping and countervailing duty investigations by the Commerce Department since their implementation. One notable example is the use of the "Particular Market Situation" provision of Section 504 in a recent administrative review of the anti-dumping order on Oil Country Tubular Goods from Korea. In that review, the application of Section 504 increased the anti-dumping margin of one of the respondents from 8.04% to 24.92%.[11] The change has been implemented in fact.

Since this final determination in Oil Country Tubular goods from Korea, Section 504 has been alleged and considered in other anti-dumping investigations as well. The growing application of Section 504 has significantly affected anti-dumping margins found in investigations involving market economies, which encompass virtually all anti-dumping investigations other than those involving China.[12] In essence, Section 504 opens up market economy cases to the use of alternative measures of costs of production and constructed value in a manner similar to those used in the non-market economy (NME) methodology that is applied in cases involving China. These direct legislative changes governing the conduct of AD/CVD investigations by the Commerce Department and the U.S. International Trade Commission are only one of multiple policy initiatives aimed specifically at intensifying the use and effectiveness of U.S. antidumping and countervailing duty (AD/CVD) laws. As discussed in subsequent sections, these additional initiatives include, but are not limited to, the following: (1) improved enforcement of AD/CVD orders under new anti-circumvention authority for U.S. Customs and Border Protection (CBP) (Sect. 2.3), (2) stricter conditions being applied to the conduct of AD/CVD investigations by the Commerce Department (Sect. 4.1), (3) intensification of participation by the Office of the United States Representative (USTR) in the WTO and other bilateral and plurilateral agreements (Sect. 4.2), and (4) other new enforcement directives through Executive Orders (Sect. 4.3).

---

[11] U.S. Department of Commerce, Certain Oil Country Tubular Goods from the Republic of Korea: Final Results of Antidumping Duty Administrative Review; 2014–2015, 82 FR 18105, 17 April 2017.

[12] China has long been considered a non-market economy, or NME, in the context of anti-dumping investigations. China's status as an NME is subject to transition to market economy status pursuant to commitments contained in China's accession protocol at the time of China's membership in the WTO in December 2001. That protocol was scheduled to expire in December 2016. China's status as a market economy for purposes of anti-dumping investigations is being challenged in a variety of ways by numerous countries, including the United States.

This focus on AD/CVD activity writ large has significantly increased the effect of these laws on U.S. trade. As of 30 September 2016, CBP reported enforcing 363 existing AD/CVD orders.[13] By March 2018, or 18 months later, the number of AD/CVD orders maintained by the U.S. Department of Commerce (Commerce Department) had risen to 424. During the period from 20 January 2017 through 13 March 2018, the Commerce Department had initiated 102 new AD/CVD investigations.[14]

2.3 The Trade Facilitation and Trade Enforcement Act of 2015 and Enhancements in Anti-Circumvention Enforcement by the U.S. Customs and Border Protection of Anti-Dumping and Countervailing Duty Orders

The Trade Facilitation and Trade Enforcement Act of 2015 (TFTEA) was the third piece of major trade legislation passed by Congress in 2015.[15] Title IV of this legislation, entitled the "Enforce and Protect Act of 2015" or EAPA, added new and significant TDI capability to the Customs and Border Protection (CBP) in its enforcement of anti-dumping and countervailing duty orders.

For years prior to this law, evasion of anti-dumping and countervailing duty orders had become an increasing problem. The amount of anti-dumping and countervailing duties that escaped collection because of a wide variety of fraudulent schemes is estimated to have run into billions of dollars.

Section 421 of EAPA provided a more rapid and transparent enforcement regime, including a well-defined, deadline-driven investigatory procedure to govern anti-evasion efforts. On 22 August 2016, CBP issued interim regulations for this new type of investigation.[16] By statue and regulation, Section 421 investigations can impose an onerous investigatory burden on affected foreign producers and importers. If evasion of an anti-dumping or countervailing duty order is determined to have occurred, CBP is authorized to apply a range of strict measures to collect unpaid duties and to assure full payment of duties on any future entries.

---

[13] Data as reported in the Antidumping and Countervailing Duty Enforcement Actions and Compliance Initiatives: Fiscal Year 2017, Report to Congress from U.S. Customs and Border Protection, 17 November 2017, p. iii.

[14] Data as reported in a Commerce Department press release (U.S. Department of Commerce Issues Affirmative Preliminary Antidumping Duty Determination on Uncoated Groundwood Paper from Canada), 13 March 2018, https://www.commerce.gov/news/press-releases/2018/03.us-department-commerce-issues-affirmative-preliminary-antidumping-duty (last accessed 18 March 2018).

[15] Trade Facilitation and Trade Enforcement Act, Pub. L. 114-125, 130 STAT 122 was signed into law by President Obama on 24 February 2016.

[16] Department of Homeland Security, Customs and Border Protection, and Department of the Treasury, Investigation of Claims of Evasion of Antidumping and Countervailing Duties, 81 FR 56477, 22 August 2016.

Since the commencement of the 421 authority in August 2016, CBP has initiated investigations involving six products covered by anti-dumping and/or countervailing duty orders on imports from China. One allegation submitted shortly after 421 investigations commenced was found not sufficient for initiation of an investigation.

For the allegations that led to the initiation of investigations, there were 16 separate importers named. Because CBP initiates separate investigations for each importer, there have been 16 separate investigations initiated in the first year of the 421 process.

Experience thus far with 421 shows that the investigations by CBP are intensive and rapid. In the case of investigations involving transshipments of product through third countries, on-site investigations are conducted of facilities located in foreign countries alleged to be the transshipment point. As of February 2018, CBP had conducted 10 foreign on-site verifications in Thailand, Malaysia, and Cambodia. CBP has undertaken domestic (i.e., U.S.) on-site verifications as well as cargo examinations at U.S. ports when such actions were appropriate to the allegations made and evidence related thereto.[17] All such on-site verifications and examinations supported allegations of circumvention.

CBP also undertakes extensive research of data available to it through its own resources, through the resources of other government agencies and from any other relevant sources. The interim measures that have been implemented in each case thus far are comprehensive and strict, with immediate effect on the level of imports under investigation.

The possible broader reach and effect of 421 investigations remain to be seen. This enforcement mechanism, by definition, applies directly only to trade that is subject to AD/CVD orders. While the volume of imports subject to such orders is in the billions of dollars,[18] this is nevertheless not a major portion of overall merchandise imports. Moreover, the 421 investigations conducted to date have involved imports entered under six separate AD orders. This is a relatively small portion of the 424 AD/CVD orders the Commerce Department currently maintains.

One factor that will affect future utilization of the 421 process is the content of the final regulations. Since 22 August 2016, CBP has operated with interim regulations. Comments submitted on the interim regulations have been critical of certain rules that inhibit transparency of the process and the ability of parties to participate. Other aspects of the rules are viewed as setting evidentiary requirements that are beyond the ability of most parties to meet. The final rules are expected to be implemented some time before the end of 2018. These final rules will have a bearing on the effectiveness of 421 on circumvention of AD/CVD orders.

---

[17] Information about on-site visits and cargo examinations is from U.S. Customs and Border Protection, Trade Facilitation and Trade Enforcement Act Accomplishments 2018, February 2018, https://www.cbp.gov/sites/default/files/assets/documents/2018-Mar/cbp-tftea-factsheet.pdf (last accessed 30 April 2018).

[18] CBP reports that imports subject to AD/CVD orders in the most recent annual period for which data are available reached $13.3 billion.

3 Expanded Use of Existing Trade Laws and Resurrection of Other Avenues of Import Relief

Outside of the trade laws passed and implemented in 2015–2016, there are numerous other statutory vehicles that allow for action in matters of international trade. Some of these vehicles had fallen into disuse because of a political environment generally opposed to what was considered undesirable protectionist trade policy. Threats of retaliation[19] by other countries also suppressed the use of some of these avenues of import relief. The Trump administration made a marked departure from that history. The following section identifies these existing legal import relief remedies and their current role in the expanded use of TDIs by the U.S.

3.1 Section 301 of the Trade Act of 1974

Perhaps the best example of a moribund trade statue has been Section 301 of the Trade Act of 1974. When enacted, Section 301 offered potential trade remedies to a wide range of potential policies or acts by foreign governments that burdened or restricted U.S. commerce. Many domestic interests availed themselves of this avenue of potential import relief.

Over time, however, the use of this provision of trade law declined. The decline was related to the complexity of the process and the difficulty of obtaining actual import relief from the sitting President. There were three main components of this difficulty.

First, there is the requirement for a political decision by the Executive Branch of the U.S. Government (ultimately, the President) for any trade action to be taken. Second, any affirmative decision by the Executive Branch must be based on investigations and advice provided by well-known trade-involved Executive Branch agencies. Input from members of Congress is also a major component of the decision-making process. Thus, there is always a lengthy, multi-step process involving substantial opportunities for presentation and argumentation of conflicting positions, as is the case with almost any proposed trade action.

Third, any unilateral 301 import relief action taken was subject to the additional consequence of retaliation by the affected foreign countries under international law. Such retaliation invariably involved increases by foreign countries in duties or other trade barriers on selected U.S. exported products. Push-back from particularly affected U.S. exporting interests often prevailed in preventing any trade action against imports. As a result, the use of Section 301 as an avenue for addressing

---

[19] In scholarly circles and official government communications, the correct term of art would be "compensatory measures". In the media and public discourse, the term "retaliation" is much more frequently found and reflects plain language. The authors use both terms interchangeably for present purposes.

international trade problems was increasingly discouraged. Sitting Presidents were generally either (1) philosophically not inclined to restrict trade, (2) not willing to accept the political burden of retaliatory action by foreign government against U.S. export interests, or (3) both.

Developments in an alternative internationally-sanctioned dispute-settlement process further pushed Section 301 into obsolescence. The WTO, created in 1995 as the successor organization to the GATT, established its own dispute settlement mechanism. This was in no small part designed to inhibit unilateral trade actions by individual countries. The United States, for its own reasons noted above, strongly promoted and readily adopted the WTO process as the arena to which all 301-type complaints were to be referred.[20]

In 2017, potential resurrection of the use of Section 301 was raised by the Trump Administration as part of its effort to address specifically the long-standing, widespread international problem of theft of intellectual property of U.S. companies. The prime target country under consideration is China, which has been among the world's most flagrant violators of laws intended to protect intellectual property. The extent of violations and the impunity with which China has engaged in the practice prompted serious consideration of a number of avenues available that might be effective in addressing the problem.

Prior legislative remedies, starting with those provided in the Trade Act of 1974, as well as actions by consecutive U.S. administrations and by international bodies, were unable to keep ahead of the ongoing problem of wide-spread violations of intellectual property protections. Enormous resources and attention have been applied to the problem by the United States through its constant review of the state of intellectual property protection and enforcement by U.S. trading partners. The annual "Super 301" reports by the Office of the U.S. Trade Representative chronicle the range of foreign country laws, policies, and practices that deny effective protection and enforcement of intellectual property protection, along with the efforts to address these problems.

Within this context, the administration released a Presidential Memorandum to USTR requesting a determination whether to initiate a Section 301 investigation of China. On 18 August 2017, USTR initiated such an investigation of China's acts, policies and practices related to technology transfer, intellectual property and innovation.[21] This marks the formal resurrection of Section 301 after a long period of disuse.

The 301 process in the United States provides 1 year to complete the investigation and to determine what remedial action to take. Owing to expeditious conduct of

---

[20] As noted in a recent article in the Wall Street Journal, U.S. administrations over the past two decades have decided to steer nearly all trade complaints through the WTO and have rarely touched Section 301. See Schlesinger J and Davis B, U.S. To Press China On Trade. The Wall Street Journal, 2 August 2017, Section A.

[21] Office of the United States Trade Representative, Initiation of Section 301 Investigation; Hearing; and Request for Public Comments: China's Acts, Policies, and Practices Related to Technology Transfer, Intellectual Property, and Innovation, 82 FR 40213, 24 August 2017.

the investigation, USTR reportedly completed its 301 report late in 2017. The remedy proposals contained in the report were vetted through the interagency trade policy review process.

One remedy option anticipated to be in the report was a tariff increase on a large basket of products imported from China. A tariff-like remedy was explicitly telegraphed in early 2018 by President Trump in a press interview, in which the President stated that the United States was considering a big fine as part of the probe of China's theft of intellectual property.[22]

These expectations proved correct with the announcement on 22 March 2018 that tariffs would indeed be imposed on a list of 1300 products. The list is focused on products incorporating technology that China is accused of forcefully taking from U.S. companies. Together, the products potentially subject to the tariff account for approximately $50 billion in U.S. imports from China. A list identifying the products will be published within 15 days of the announcement, and the tariff will go into effect within 60 days after a public comment period. In addition to tariffs, the 301 remedy will direct the Treasury Department to develop new restrictions to block Chinese companies from investing in certain high technology sectors of the U.S. economy.[23]

3.2 National Security Import Restrictions Under Section 232 of the Trade Expansion Act of 1962

Two National Security investigations under Section 232 of the Trade Expansion Act of 1962 were initiated early in 2017 involving two major industrial sectors. One sector was the steel industry and the other sector was the aluminum industry. These investigations are, as in the case of Section 301, clear examples of enhancements of the use of TDIs on two levels.

First, 232 National Security investigations had been unused for nearly two decades. The major reason for the disuse was that all investigations involving manufactured products resulted in no import relief being granted by the President. Thus, there has been no incentive for domestic industries to use that route to obtain a trade remedy. The new 232 investigations involving two prominent manufacturing sectors are a marked departure from long-term disuse.

Second, the two recent new 232 cases were specifically initiated by the U.S. Government, not a domestic industry. Since 232 investigations were first authorized in 1962, there had been no such self-initiations by the Executive Branch.

---

[22] Mason J, Exclusive: Trump considers big "fine" over China intellectual property theft. Reuters Business News, 17 January 2018, https://www.reuters.com/article/us-usa-trump-trade-exclusive/exclusive-trump-considers-big-fine-over-china-intellectual-property-theft-idUSKBN1F62SR (accessed 30 April 2018).

[23] Behsudi A, Trump strikes back at Chinese tech practices with new tariffs. Politico, 22 March 2018, https://www.politico.com/story/2018/03/22/trump-chinese-tech-practices-tariffs-428551 (accessed 30 April 2018).

Secretary of Commerce Wilbur Ross initiated the steel 232 investigation on 19 April 2017 and initiated the aluminum 232 investigation on 26 April 2017. The investigations were conducted on parallel schedules leading to a common conclusion, namely that steel and aluminum products, respectively, were being imported in such quantities and in such circumstances as to threaten to impair the national security of the United States. The investigations were concluded within the requisite 270 days allowed by statute. Secretary Ross transmitted the 232 reports on steel and aluminum to the President on 11 January 2018 and 19 January 2018, respectively.

The recommendation from the investigations to address the threat to national security was an adjustment to imports in the form of a tariff. Secretary Ross recommended a tariff of 7.7% for imports of aluminum products and a tariff of 24% for imports of steel. The Secretary also requested the authority to exclude from these tariffs any articles for which there is a lack of sufficient U.S. production capacity of comparable products or to exclude articles from the tariffs for specific national security-based considerations.

In the Presidential Proclamation issued several days after the completion of the investigations, the President modified the recommended adjustment to imports in several ways.[24] First, the tariff rate was increased to 10% for aluminum products and to 25% for steel. Second, imports of the covered products from Mexico and Canada were excluded from the tariff. Third, any country with which the United States has a security relationship was invited to discuss alternative ways to address the threat to the national security. In the case of Mexico and Canada, the tariff exemption that was provided to these two countries was linked with pre-existing ongoing discussions on trade matters. The date on which all covered imports of aluminum and steel would become subject to the 10% and 25% duty, respectively, was set as 23 March 2018.

In response to objections from affected foreign suppliers to the United States, additional modifications in the import relief program were made just as the 23 March 2018 date of imposition of tariffs arrived. The Trump Administration granted a temporary exemption from the tariffs to a large group of allies with which the U.S. has a security relationship. The countries/regions include, in addition to Canada and Mexico, the European Union, Australia, Argentina, Brazil and South Korea.[25] This tariff exemption is to last only until 1 May 2018, during which time countries may negotiate satisfactory alternative means to address the threat to the United States national security from current levels of steel and aluminum imports.

At the same time, however, the Trump Administration raised the possibility of putting in place an import quota on steel and aluminum imports from exempted countries in lieu of a tariff. The quota approach is being considered as a means of addressing the problem of transshipments of product to the United States through countries not covered by tariffs. The transshipment problem has long bedeviled

---

[24] The Presidential Proclamations for both steel and aluminum were issued on 8 March 2018.

[25] Tankersley J and Kitroff N, U.S. Exempts Some Allies From Tariffs, but May Opt for Quotas. New York Times, 22 March 2018, https://www.nytimes.com/2018/03/22/business/us-eu-tariffs-steel-aluminum.html (accessed 30 April 2018).

other efforts to address the import problem through measures such as anti-dumping and countervailing duties.

Beyond the immediate and crucial negotiations related to country exclusions, the 232 import adjustment program also developed procedures for requesting product-specific exclusions from the tariff program. These procedures were promulgated on 19 March 2018.[26] Product exclusion requests may be submitted only by individuals or organizations using steel or aluminum in business activities in the United States. Objections to a submitted exclusion request may be submitted by any individual or organization in the United States.

As demonstrated by the events since the 8 March 2018 Presidential Proclamations announcing the 232 import adjustment program, the steel and aluminum 232 investigations and proposed import relief have proved to be the most controversial of all of the TDIs used in the last several years. There are four reasons for this level of international controversy whose impact can be clearly understood.

First, these 232 actions encompass two large industrial sectors that are important not only to the United States but to every other developed economy in the world. Both of these industrial sectors also have a well-known history of struggle with import competition for which no satisfactory solution has yet been found. Second, the scope of the import remedy encompasses not only all steel and aluminum mill products, but also imports from all of the world's suppliers (except Canada and Mexico). Third, there is no set time limit on the import relief being provided under Section 232. As a result, these 232 import actions go beyond the limits of import relief remedies available from any other TDI, when all limits related to product scope, country coverage and allowed length of remedy are considered. Fourth, there is no explicit mechanism related to Article XXI GATT for compensation claims in response to a security-related trade action by another country. Nevertheless, trading partners adversely affected by the new tariffs, or the possible quota system, are preparing retaliatory measures within the WTO dispute settlement processes.

Press reports have detailed efforts of countries affected by the U.S. import relief action under Section 232 to seek compensation through the WTO. These compensation efforts have apparently raised difficult issues within the WTO dispute settlement process. The authors are not attorneys and cannot provide any legal analysis relevant to this issue. Details of the controversy can be found in an article on the 23 March 2018 of Inside U.S. Trade.[27]

How the 232 national security import relief program actually affects trade and trade relations remains to be seen.

---

[26] Department of Commerce, Bureau of Industry and Security, Requirements for Submissions Requesting Exclusions From the Remedies Instituted in Presidential Proclamations Adjusting Imports of Steel into the United States and Adjusting Imports of Aluminum into the United States, Interim final rule, 83 FR 12106, 19 March 2018.

[27] Caporal J, U.S., EU preview arguments in potential 232 showdown at WTO. Inside U.S. Trade, 23 March 2018, p. 11.

3.3   Section 337 of the Tariff Act of 1930

Another approach now finding new applications as a TDI is the long-standing provision Section 337 of U.S. trade law. For years, this statute has been intended for and used to address violations of intellectual property and other similar unfair acts such as theft of trade secrets.

Historically, almost all such cases involved patent violations. Now they extend considerably further. The recent action filed by U.S. Steel against the Chinese steel industry is a case in point. In what proved to be a wide-ranging legal effort, U.S. Steel claimed not only violations of trade secrets, but also more novel claims of antitrust violations and transshipments involving false designation of origin (FDO) claims. The claim of violation of trade secrets was withdrawn by U.S. Steel and the administrative judge essentially dismissed the other claims.

However, the U.S. International Trade Commission itself reversed the judge's initial findings on the FDO claim, determining that the complaint was sufficient to state a claim for FDO under 337. Subsequently, the judge made an initial determination (ID) of no FDO violation and the Commission determined not to review that ID. No new FDO claim has been made under 337.

3.4   Safeguard Actions Under Sections 201–204 of the Trade Act of 1974 (a.k.a. the "Escape Clause")

Another neglected trade defense instrument for the United States has been the Safeguard Action provided for in Sections 201–204 of the Trade Act of 1974. This U.S. trade remedy statute, often referred to as the "Escape Clause," was the U.S. embodiment of Article XIX of the GATT 1947 and today the GATT 1994 and Agreement on Safeguards. Article XIX was the major exception within the GATT Agreement to the prohibition on restrictions on trade. The provision permits temporary import restrictions to be applied in response to a "surge" in imports that cause serious injury to a domestic industry. Such temporary import restrictions were exempt from any retaliation by other countries for a limited period of time.

When Section 201 of the Trade Act of 1974 became effective in 1975, there was a flurry of new cases filed by U.S. industries before the U.S. International Trade Commission (ITC). In the first 5 years, 42 investigations were conducted by the ITC. More than half of the investigations resulted in an affirmative finding of serious injury or the threat thereof, with a number of industries ultimately receiving import relief.

However, the initial flurry of interest and use of Section 201 was relatively short-lived. There were three factors that combined to reduce the number of 201 investigations to zero by 2001. The first factor was the inherent difficulty of obtaining effective import relief through the 201 process. Such relief required not only an intensive investigation by the ITC to attain a positive determination of serious injury (or threat thereof) from imports, but also a political decision by the Executive Branch (again, involving ultimately a Presidential decision) to grant some type of effective import relief. Even in the heyday of 201 investigations, well less than half of industries that filed a 201 petition ever received any import relief. As the track record of Section 201 efforts became known, particularly the dependency of any import relief on the willingness of a given President to consider granting import restrictions, the use of Section 201 became more "selective."

The second factor that reduced the use of Section 201 was the impact of major improvements in the effectiveness of U.S. anti-dumping and countervailing duty investigations. These improvements came with the passage of the Trade Agreements Act of 1979, which completely overhauled the conduct of anti-dumping and countervailing duty investigations. Responsibility for the operation of anti-dumping and subsidy investigations was moved from the U.S. Department of the Treasury to the U.S. Department of Commerce. Through a combination of extensive changes in investigative procedures and the imposition of strict time limits, the effectiveness of these types of investigations was dramatically improved. The improvement in this TDI created an alternative to the Section 201 process that attracted the attention and energy of trade-impacted industries. Most important is that relief granted through this vehicle could not be overridden by the President.

The third and final factor was action taken at the international level through GATT and the WTO, in a manner similar to that which occurred with 301 investigations. Article XIX of the GATT 1994 was incorporated within Annex I of the WTO Agreement, with some modifications being made to the original GATT 1947 version. The modifications in the WTO agreement were in response to, among other things, certain trade restriction measures by some countries that were viewed as outside of the intent of permitted types of Article XIX import relief. Language put in the 1994 WTO preamble to the Agreement on Safeguards refers to "*the need to clarify and reinforce the disciplines of GATT 1994, and specifically those of its Article XIX (Emergency Action on Imports of Particular Products), to re-establish multilateral control over safeguards and eliminate measures that escape such control.*"[28]

The types of action causing concern were informal arrangements negotiated and agreed to by countries which were characterized as a "voluntary restraint agreements" or "orderly marketing agreements." Since these were technically not being "imposed" as unilateral import restraints by one country on another, these types of agreement were viewed as skirting the rules imposed specifically on restraints under Article XIX.

The tightened control and scrutiny after 1994 by the WTO over acceptable Article XIX relief further increased the political and procedural difficulty of obtaining import relief and then maintaining such relief in the face of legal challenges typically brought by interests opposed to any import relief. Just as occurred in the case of 301 investigations, there was a distinct unwillingness in the Executive

---

[28] World Trade Organization, Preamble to the Agreement on Safeguards as incorporated in Annex I of the Agreement Establishing the World Trade Organization, 15 April 1994.

Branch to engage in any 201-type import relief, regardless of the President or Party. This extinguished interest among domestic industries in pursuing this route to addressing trade problems.

In another marked departure from years of dormancy, 2017 saw two petitions filed for import relief under Section 201. The first investigation was initiated by the ITC on 17 May 2017 with respect to Crystalline Silicon Photovoltaic Cells (Inv. No. TA-201-75). The second investigation was initiated on 5 June 2017 with respect to Large Residential Washers (Inv. No. TA-201-76). These filings indicate that the more aggressive trade policy articulated by the current administration encouraged the use of Section 201 as a viable TDI available to U.S. industries.

However, it was not mere coincidence that this renewed use of Section 201 occurred with respect to large residential washers and solar panels. On the contrary, Section 201 was the only trade remedy option left to these industries that could effectively counter the particular trade patterns causing them injury. In both cases, the industries had sought relief against unfair trade practices. When these efforts successfully resulted in AD/CVD orders, the foreign producers avoided the AD/CVD duties by relocating production, in several steps, to other countries.

This pattern of country-by-country duty avoidance and continued use of unfair trade practices was more effectively addressed by global safeguard tariffs placed on imports for a multiyear period. For finished washers and parts, tariff-rate quotas were imposed for a 3-year period. For finished washers, a tariff of 20% is to apply to the first 1.2 million units and a 50% tariff will apply to any units above 1.2 million. These tariffs rates are for the first year and will decline modestly over the following 2 years. A certain quantity of parts may also enter with no additional duty. For solar cells and panels, a tariff-rate quota was also used, extending over 4 years. A quota up to 2.5 Gw of imported cells is excluded from the additional tariff, with all imports above the quota subject to an additional 30% tariff. The tariff is reduced modestly over the 4 years.[29]

It is too early to assess whether the experience of these Section 201 investigations will induce additional petitions. Given the number of industries that are competing with shifting country sources of unfairly-traded imports, additional investigations under Section 201 are probable, for at least as long as President Trump remains in office.

---

[29] For detailed information on the safeguard import relief program for each industry, see the Presidential Proclamation to Facilitate Positive Adjustment to Competition from Imports of Large Residential Washers and from Imports of Certain Crystalline Silicon Photovoltaic Cells, 23 January 2018, https://www.whitehouse.gov/presidential-actions/presidential-proclamation-facilitate-positive-adjustment-competition-imports-large-residential-washers/ (last accessed 30 April 2018) and https://www.whitehouse.gov/presidential-actions/presidential-proclamation-facilitate-positive-adjsutment-competition-imports-certain-crystalline-silicon-photovoltaic-cells/ (last accessed 30 April 2018).

3.5 International Emergency Economic Powers Act

The International Emergency Economic Powers Act is yet another venue through which certain serious trade problems might be addressed. In the context of intellectual property theft by China, use of this law was reportedly being considered by the administration's trade policy advisors.[30] This statute grants the president the authority to deal with *"an unusual and extraordinary threat with respect to which a national emergency has been declared."*[31] The limits of this law's potential applications are vague.

3.6 Tax Law Changes That Could Affect Trade

Major tax law changes were made in the United States by the passage in late 2017 of tax reform legislation (entitled "Tax Cuts and Jobs Act" or TCJA). In the long debates and many tax-change proposals considered in the lead-up to the final legislation, there were several ideas raised that would have made tax changes directly affecting trade. None of these proposals was incorporated in the final tax bill, but they indicate a unique type of potential TDI that was at least considered.

One such proposal was developed by Mr. Paul Ryan, the Speaker (leader) of the U.S. House of Representatives, that would have eliminated both the corporate deduction for the cost of imported products as part of the cost of sales and the tax on income from exports. The measure was dubbed a "border adjustment tax" which would, in effect, act as a reverse tariff that could seriously affect imports, as well as promote exports. This proposal was offered as a less disruptive trade-related tax measure than the direct border tax on imports of manufactured products promoted by President Trump. In the end, these measures explicitly affecting trade flows were not included.

Some provisions of the tax bill related to the new base erosion and anti-abuse tax (or BEAT) do make changes in the tax treatment of cross-border related party payments. However, further guidance about the operation of these provisions is required to determine what impact they may have on trade flows.

From the international trade perspective, it is the large reduction in the U.S. corporate income tax rate combined with the switch of the U.S. tax system to a territorial regime that are commonly expected to have the greatest impact on international trade flows. This impact is attributed to greater international competitiveness for U.S. companies from the tax rate reduction and simultaneous incentives for locating productive operations in the United States.

---

[30] Schlesinger J and Davis B, U.S. To Press China On Trade. The Wall Street Journal, 2 August 2017, Section A.

[31] International Emergency Economic Powers Act, Pub. L. 95-223, 91 STAT 1625, 29 December 1977, § 1701(2).

4   Executive Branch Authority Applied in Furtherance of a More Aggressive Trade Policy

The Executive Branch has significant authority to enhance the effectiveness of trade defense instruments and activities without resort to new legislation. This authority operates within what can be considered "bureaucratic discretion." Prime examples of the use of such discretion are found in the Executive Branch initiation of new investigations under long dormant sections of U.S. trade law, such as Section 301 of the Trade Act of 1974 and Section 232 of the Trade Expansion Act of 1962. Other examples include the initiation of negotiations to alter existing trade agreements with several countries.

We highlight in this section selected applications of bureaucratic discretion that are having a significant impact on trade enforcement in important, but perhaps more subtle, ways.

4.1   Stricter Conditions Applied to Standard Practices in the Conduct of Anti-Dumping and Countervailing Duty Investigations

With the prominence of anti-dumping and countervailing duty enforcement in current U.S. trade policy, the application of bureaucratic discretion is especially notable in this area. During 2017, there have been changes in long-standing practices governing the conduct of AD/CVD investigations by the U.S. Department of Commerce. In general, these changes in practice have granted less time and flexibility to interested parties in their efforts to participate in investigations. Some changes have caused procedural and informational requirements for acceptable responses to become more demanding. Other changes have altered methodological approaches to the measurement and calculation of dumping margins.

Overall, the changes in practice governing investigations are viewed as falling more heavily on respondents in investigations. This is in part because the purpose of the investigations is primarily to obtain information from respondent interested parties. Thus, some changes in practice will affect respondents disproportionately. The impact of some changes, such as those related to time deadlines, may fall equally on all parties.

Below we provide a list of some of these changes in practice over the last year:

1. Changes Related to Reduced Time Limits for Providing Information and Argument:

   • The amount of time allowed for submissions of information in response to Commerce Department questionnaires in general has been reduced.

- In particular, the amount of time that used to be typically granted to parties for extensions of deadlines for submission of information has been reduced severely (e.g. 10-day extension requests denied and reduced instead to 4-day extensions).
- The Commerce Department for the first time started to decline to extend the preliminary determination or the final determination in some cases. This is an unprecedented development, given that such extensions have always been granted in the past.
- There are more cases of extension requests being rejected initially and then subsequently being granted, thus reducing the effective amount of time of the extension.
- The general change toward granting shorter or no extensions in deadlines for extensions has caused domestic parties to increase the frequency of objections to any extension request.

2. Changes Related to Greater Frequency of Rejection by the Commerce Department of Submissions and Stricter Adherence to Standards of Responses to Questionnaire Responses and Other Submissions

- More scrutiny is being applied to bracketing of business proprietary information, requiring re-submission of properly bracketed document.
- More scrutiny is being applied to determine if ranging and otherwise summarizing business proprietary information are adequate.
- There is more rejection of submissions for inadequate responses to Commerce Department questionnaires (e.g. no response at all to a question, a partial response to only one part of a question, a response not relevant to the question asked).
- Submissions are being rejected and parties excluded from further participation in investigations because of untimely filing, requiring meetings with the agency and assurances of proper procedures to prevent any further untimely filings in the future.
- Submissions are being rejected for infractions of rules regarding the inclusion of certain comments or new information that were specifically to be excluded from the submission in a manner that would not under prior practice necessarily have resulted in rejection.

3. Changes Related to AD Margin Methodology

- In an increasing number of cases certain cost or price information is being required at levels of detail that are not reasonably maintained and available to any company and that are beyond levels of detail typically required in past cases (e.g. unique reporting of certain groups of sales by each possible detailed product type by separate invoice and by unique customer).
- Long-standing practice and precedent regarding the basis on which a sale and its terms are defined and determined is being reconsidered.

254 B. Malashevich and M. Love

- Long-standing precedents regarding costing of different categories of products in commonly-investigated industries have been changed with no prior announcement of consideration of change or opportunity to comment.
- The implementation and use of Section 504, as discussed at length in Sect. 2.2 of this paper, has made a significant difference with higher margins in the first case in which it was used.

Overall, the many changes in practice in the conduct of anti-dumping investigations have had a significant impact on participating parties, with a particularly greater burden being placed on respondents. Results of investigations also suggest that the dumping margins have been increased in some cases due to these changes in practice.

4.2 Intensification of Participation in the WTO and Other Bilateral and Plurilateral Agreements

There is a wide range of international negotiations constantly ongoing in trade policy implementation and enforcement. These negotiations command a large share of the resources and expertise of the Executive Branch agencies historically tasked with the conduct of U.S. trade policy, the most prominent of which is the Office of the United States Trade Representative (USTR). A full account and description of the countries, industries, issues, activities and accomplishments of the Executive Branch in international trade is provided every year in the Annual Report of the President of the United States on the Trade Agreements Program. This report, along with a companion paper on the President's Trade Policy Agenda, is prepared and released by USTR.

There has been an intention expressed by the Trump Administration to build upon the focus and functioning of the U.S. international trade policy apparatus to support ongoing efforts and negotiating goals. From what can be gleaned from the 2017 Trade Policy Agenda, an intensification of focus and activity will occur consistent with the increased trade enforcement activities discussed in the previous sections of this paper.

One high-priority target is a more aggressive defense of American sovereignty over matters of trade policy.[32] A specific part of this defense is active opposition to efforts by other countries to weaken the rights and benefits of, and/or increase the obligations under, trade agreements of which the United States is a member. This orientation of U.S. trade policy will invariably heighten U.S. involvement in dispute settlement activities at the WTO.

---

[32] Office of the United States Trade Representative, 2017 Trade Policy Agenda and 2016 Annual Report of the President of the United States on the Trade Agreements Program, 1 March 2017, https://ustr.gov/about-us/policy-offices/press-office/reports-and-publications/2017/2017-trade-policy-agenda-and-2016 (last accessed 30 April 2018), p. 2.

A prime example is the priority being assigned to the issue of the continuation of non-market economy (NME) status to China in Title VII AD/CVD trade remedy cases. In testimony before the Senate Finance Committee on 21 June 2017, U.S. Trade Representative Robert Lighthizer signaled that this dispute is *"without question the most serious litigation matter we have at the WTO right now. And I have made it very clear that a bad decision with respect to non-market economy status with China... would be cataclysmic for the WTO."*[33]

This same theme was reiterated by USTR in the July 2017 annual report to the Congress on U.S. trade enforcement priorities. The report states:

Our primary objective now is defending the ability of USDOC to apply appropriate anti-dumping and countervailing duties to combat distortions caused by China's non-market economy system and government subsidies that are injuring U.S. workers and industries.[34]

This suggests that there will be very active participation by the U.S. in the defense of U.S. interests within the context of international trade agreements.

4.3   New Trade Enforcement Initiatives Begun Through Executive Orders

Discretionary power has long been exercised by the Executive Branch through the use of Executive Orders. The Trump administration has utilized this vehicle to initiate actions by the agencies of the federal government in furtherance of international trade policies. Reflecting the administration's priorities, the first two trade-related Executive Orders involved (1) enhancing the collection and enforcement of anti-dumping and countervailing duties and trade law violations by Customs and Border Protection and (2) the conduct of an investigation and report by USTR and the Department of Commerce, supported by other trade-involved agencies, on significant U.S. trade deficits with other countries and the reason therefore.[35] These orders are intended, among other things, to focus the resources of the federal government on trade priorities and support implementation of policies and actions to improve trade enforcement and U.S. trade performance.

Subsequent Executive Orders were issued on other trade priorities. One addressed trade agreement violations and abuses by instituting performance reviews of all bilateral, plurilateral and multilateral agreements, reporting on violations found,

---

[33] Caporal J, Lighthizer: U.S. loss in China NME dispute would be "cataclysmic for WTO". Inside U.S. Trade, 23 June 2017, p. 20.

[34] Office of the U.S. Trade Representative, Report to the Committee on Finance of the Senate and the Committee on Ways and Means of the House of Representatives pursuant to Section 601 of the Trade Facilitation and Enforcement Act of 2015 on USTR Enforcement Priorities, July 2017, p. 2.

[35] Presidential Executive Order 13785—Establishing Enhanced Collection and Enforcement of Antidumping and Countervailing Duties and Violations of Trade and Customs Laws, 82 FR 16719, 31 March 2017 and Presidential Executive Order 13786—Omnibus Report on Significant Trade Deficits, 82 FR 16721, 31 March 2017.

and taking action to remedy violations and abuses. The other centered on "Buy American" and "Hire American" policies. This order reiterated and instituted monitoring of the implementation of and compliance with existing "Buy American" and "Hire American" legal and regulatory measures, including the impact of free trade agreements and the WTO agreement on government procurement and the operation of "Buy American" laws.[36]

5 Conclusion

This paper concludes with several summary observations about the current and future role of TDIs within the current direction of U.S. trade policy. At least so long as Mr. Trump is U.S. President, expanded use of TDIs will remain central to achieving U.S. goals, both broadly and in specific disputes. At the same time, the era of multilateral "rounds" of trade negotiations, originally under GATT and more recently under WTO auspices, is dead. The same probably is true with respect to regional arrangements, of which many have been reported to the WTO in recent years.

Within this broad policy approach, bilateral action will take center stage. Certain bilateral arrangements will have priority. Beyond the current focus on renegotiation of NAFTA and the free trade agreement with South Korea, there will be engagement with the United Kingdom following "Brexit". The theory behind the bilateral focus is that the U.S. has been sacrificing its considerable bargaining power by negotiating multilaterally; it is best off negotiating bilaterally in the context of so-called "game theory" as originally developed by John Nash while at Princeton University.

The heightened aggressiveness of U.S. trade policy will not lead to new TDI legislation for the foreseeable future. There is no such need, as amply demonstrated during the first year and one-half of the Trump Administration. There are many arrows already in the U.S. quiver within existing law.[37] In the eyes of the current Trump Administration, vigorous enforcement and application of existing law previously lacked political will in the White House.

---

[36] Presidential Executive Order 13796—Addressing Trade Agreement Violations and Abuses, 82 FR 20819, 29 April 2017 and Presidential Executive Order 13788—Buy American and Hire America, 82 FR 20821, 18 April 2017.

[37] See Annexes.

Annexes

Table 1a Most common actions in current use

Legal Actions Available in the United States for Use as Trade Defense Instruments Against Imports

Antidumping and Countervailing Duty Enforcement Measures			
"Title VII Investigations" Establishing AD/CVD Orders	**Anti-Circumvention Investigations**		
	Department of Commerce (Title VII)	**CBP**	**Section 421**
Intended Use: Addresses dumping and subsidization of imports into the U.S. and material injury caused thereby	*Intended Use:* Address the circumvention of existing AD/CVD orders under a variety of factual circumstances	*Intended Use:* Provides a means for the public to report to CBP any suspected violations of trade laws or regulations	*Intended Use:* Prevent the circumvention of existing AD/CVD orders
Relevant Law: Tariff Act of 1930	*Relevant Law:* Tariff Act of 1930	*Relevant Law:* Tariff Act of 1930	*Relevant Law:* Trade Facilitation and Enforcement Act of 2015
Possible End Result: Imposition of AD/CVD orders/duties on imports	*Possible End Result:* Expanding AD/CVD duties on additional products	*Possible End Result:* Penalties from twice the duties owed up to full value of imports	*Possible End Result:* Full recovery of unpaid duties on all unliquidated and liquidated entries to the full extent of CBP legal authority; live entry on all future imports & other measures
Presidential Involvement: None	*Presidential Involvement:* None	*Presidential Involvement:* None	*Presidential Involvement:* None
Historical Frequency and Current Usage: Most frequently used form of TDI	*Historical Frequency and Current Usage:* Rarely Used	*Historical Frequency and Current Usage:* Historically rarely used with limited success. Online "e-Allegations" system introduced in 2008, which increased frequency of use but not success rate	*Historical Frequency and Current Usage:* Recently created; investigation of 10 imports initiated in first year of operation

Source: Table created by the authors. Additional references: https://enforcement.trade.gov/regs/title7.pdf (last accessed 30 April 2018) for Title VII AD/CVD investigtions; https://enforcement.trade.gov/regs/title7.pdf (last accessed 30 April 2018) for Department of Commerce anti-circumvention investigations; https://www.law.cornell.edu/uscode/text/19/1592 (last accessed 30 April 2018) for CBP actions against AD/CVD evasion under Tariff Act of 1930 authority separate from the Enforce and Protect Act of 2015; https://www.congress.gov/114/plaws/publ125/PLAW-114publ125.pdf (last accessed 30 April 2018) for Section 421 investigations

Table 1b Most common actions in current use

Legal Actions Available in the United States for Use as Trade Defense Instruments Against Imports

Section 337: (Intellectual Property Violations & Other Unfair Trade Practices)	Whistleblower Investigations: (Federal False Claims Act)
Intended Use: Address violations of intellectual property, theft of trade secrets, and other similar unfair trade acts	*Intended Use:* Addresses whenever a party "concealed, avoided or decreased an obligation to pay or transmit money to the Government"
Relevant Law: Tariff Act of 1930	*Relevant Law:* Federal False Claims Act
Possible End Result: Exclusion from U.S. market	*Possible End Result:* Fines up to $11,000 per false claim and three times the actual damages to the government
Presidential Involvement: None	
Historical Frequency and Current Usage: Historically used for patent violations; recently broadened to include antitrust violations and false designation of origin	*Presidential Involvement:* None
	Historical Frequency and Current Usage: Infrequently applied to international trade customs violations; became more common following an amendment in 2009 that created ambiguity regarding the scope of the statute

Source: Table created by the authors. Additional references: https://www.law.cornell.edu/uscode/text/19/1337 (last accessed 30 April 2018) for Section 337 investigations; https://www.law.cornell.edu/uscode/text/31/3729 (last accessed 30 April 2018) for Whistleblower investigations

Table 2 Historically frequently used actions recently revived after a long period of disuse

Legal Actions Available in the United States for Use as Trade Defense Instruments Against Imports

Section 301: (Burden/Restriction on U.S. Commerce)	Section 201: (Global Safeguard)	Section 232: (National Security)
Intended Use: Impose trade sanctions on foreign countries that either violate trade agreements or engage in other unfair trade practices.	*Intended Use:* Addresses "surges" in imports that cause serious injury to a domestic industry	*Intended Use:* Addresses foreign threats to U.S. national security
Relevant Law: Trade Act of 1974	*Relevant Law:* Trade Act of 1974	*Relevant Law:* Trade Expansion Act of 1962
Possible End Result: Imposition of import duties or other restrictions on commerce	*Possible End Result:* Imposition of import restriction such as tariffs, quotas, tariff-rate quotas, or other negotiated agreements	*Possible End Result:* Various forms of "adjustment" to imports
Presidential Involvement: Presidential action required	*Presidential Involvement:* Presidential action required	*Presidential Involvement:* Presidential action required
Historical Frequency and Current Usage: Historically a common avenue of trade relief; unused for several decades before one case filed in 2017	*Historical Frequency and Current Usage:* Frequently used in the 1970s and early 1980s with sharp decline in usage thereafter; two new cases filed in 2017	*Historical Frequency and Current Usage:* Historically common but unused for nearly two decades; two cases were filed in 2017

Source: Table created by the authors. Additional references: https://legcounsel.house.gov/ Comps/93-618.pdf (last accessed 30 April 2018) for Section 301 investigations; https://legcounsel. house.gov/COMP/93-618.pdf (last accessed 30 April 2018) for Section 201 investigations; https:// www.law.cornell.edu/uscode/text/19/1862 (last accessed 30 April 2018) for Section 232 investigations

Table 3 Actions never or no longer used

Legal Actions Available in the United States for Use as Trade Defense Instruments Against Imports

Section 406	Tax Reform	Section 338: (Discrimination)	Section 122: (Balance of Payments)
Intended Use: Addresses "market disruptions" caused by imports from a Communist country (i.e. countries not receiving non-discriminatory tariff treatment, or MFN)	*Intended Use:* Amending the tax code to eliminate the corporate deduction of imported goods for U.S. income tax purposes	*Intended Use:* Addresses "discrimination" against U.S. commerce.	*Intended Use:* Addresses balance-of-payment deficits and disequilibrium, or potential significant dollar depreciation
Relevant Law: Trade Act of 1974	*Relevant Law:* N/A	*Relevant Law:* Tariff Act of 1930	*Relevant Law:* Trade Act of 1974
Possible End Result: Imposition of tariffs, quotas, or other restrictions as determined by the President	*Possible End Result:* Increased cost of imported materials bought by U.S. corporations	*Possible End Result:* New or additional duties up to 50% ad valorem and exclusion form U.S. market in some cases	*Possible End Result:* Imposition of import tariffs or quotas
Presidential Involvement: Presidential action required	*Presidential Involvement:* Presidential must sign legislation	*Presidential Involvement:* Presidential action required	*Presidential Involvement:* Presidential action required
Historical Frequency and Current Usage: Used from late 1970s into early 1990s, mostly against China; unused since 1993	*Historical Frequency and Current Usage:* Never been used	*Historical Frequency and Current Usage:* Unused since 1949	*Historical Frequency and Current Usage:* Never been used

Source: Table created by the authors. Additional references: https://legcounsel.house.gov/Comps/93-618.pdf (last accessed 30 April 2018) for Section 406 investigations; https://www.congress.gov/bill/115th-congress/house-bill/1/text (last accessed 30 April 2018) for Tax Reform; https://www.law.cornell.edu/cfr/text/19/159.42 (last accessed 30 April 2018) for Section 338 investigations; https://legalcounsel.house.gov/Comps/93-618.pdf (last accessed 30 April 2018) for Section 122 investigations

Reference

Malashevich B, Love M (2015) Political aspects of TTIP: the U.S. perspective. In: Dunin-Wasowicz M, Jarczewska A (eds) Transatlantyckie partnerstwo w dziedzinie handlu i inwestycji. Wydawnictwo Naukowe SCHOLAR, Warsaw, pp 123–134

Trade Defence Instruments and Switzerland: The Big Sleep

Matthias Oesch and Tobias Naef

Contents

Abstract Anti-dumping measures and countervailing duties are effective tools to combat trade practices which are considered unfair. Switzerland, however, has no track record of using these trade defence instruments. Since the coming into force of the WTO, no investigations have been initiated let alone measures imposed. The reasons for the abstinence of trade defence instruments in Switzerland are multifaceted. Central is Switzerland's approach to stick to an open trade regime and to refrain from pursuing an external trade policy which could be considered contentious by its trading partners. The Swiss industry is remarkably specialised and typically produces high-quality products which are less prone to take long lasting injurious blows from dumped or subsidised products as easily as industries abroad; moreover, Swiss consumers have a lower price sensibility than consumers abroad. The possibility to benefit from the use of trade defence instruments applied by the EU, i.e. to free-ride, might also play a role. Overall, it is decisive to observe that Switzerland has done well without taking recourse to trade defence instruments. At

M. Oesch (✉) · T. Naef
University of Zurich, Zurich, Switzerland
e-mail: matthias.oesch@rwi.uzh.ch; tobias.naef@rwi.uzh.ch

© Springer International Publishing AG, part of Springer Nature 2018   261
M. Bungenberg et al. (eds.), *The Future of Trade Defence Instruments*,
European Yearbook of International Economic Law,
https://doi.org/10.1007/978-3-319-95306-9_11

the same time, it might well be the case that there will be, in the near future, distress calls for the imposition of trade defence instruments against imported high-quality products also in this country. In particular, the prices of imports from emerging countries, such as China and India, are to be observed carefully. Against this background, it is conceivable that the Swiss government will have to reconsider its passive stance on the use of trade defence instruments in due course; the Swiss government is well advised to prepare the grounds for dealing with potential applications effectively and efficiently.

1 Introduction

Trade defence instruments, i.e. anti-dumping measures and countervailing duties, are effective tools to combat trade practices which are considered unfair. The basic rationale of trade defence instruments is to create a level playing field which has been distorted by practices like injurious dumping or the unlawful subsidisation of products. Anti-dumping measures aim at offsetting the negative effect of injurious dumping, i.e. when products are sold below their normal value. Countervailing duties are levied on imported products, whose manufacture, production or export has profited from prohibited or actionable subsidies, for the purpose of offsetting the subsidisation. The WTO Agreement on Implementation of Article VI of the GATT 1994 (AD Agreement) and the WTO Agreement on Subsidies and Countervailing Measures (SCM Agreement) lay down strict procedural and substantive rules which must be respected in imposing anti-dumping measures and countervailing duties. However, WTO members often take recourse to these instruments in an overhasty manner, knowing that it will then be up to the foreign companies and their countries to react and to challenge the legality of such instruments before their courts and the WTO Dispute Settlement Body (DSB). Moreover, as tariffs have been considerably lowered, or even abolished, over the last decades and non-tariff barriers to trade, such as technical regulations and standards, are more difficult to justify, the range of instruments on offer for domestic policy-makers to grant the domestic industry relief and to please domestic constituencies has gradually withered. Against this background, it is no surprise that trade defence instruments have moved centre stage as prime tools for the protection of domestic products and their producers on short notice.[1] The following figures are proof to the point: During the period of 1995–2016, the United States notified to the WTO 111 countervailing duties. The European Union (EU) imposed 37 countervailing duties. Other WTO members followed suit, such as Canada (28), Australia (12) and Mexico (11). The statistics are even more impressive with respect to anti-dumping measures. India ranks first, having imposed 609 anti-dumping measures during the

---

[1] See for these statistics www.wto.org (last accessed 30 April 2018) and link to anti-dumping and subsidies and countervailing measures; see also Matsushita et al. (2015), p. 301.

period of 1995–2016. The United States and the EU notified 395 and 314 anti-dumping measures, respectively. The Mercosur member states Brazil and Argentina imposed 241 anti-dumping measures each. Vice versa, China was the WTO member against which by far the most anti-dumping measures and countervailing duties were imposed (866, 74), followed by Korea (239, 12) and Taipei (194, 4). The United States (177, 8) and the EU (83, 12) were also often the targets of anti-dumping measures and countervailing duties.

By contrast, Switzerland has no track record of initiating and conducting anti-dumping or countervailing investigations within the meaning of the AD Agreement or the SCM Agreement. Under the GATT 1947, ad hoc and facilitated anti-dumping measures were taken occasionally against imports from non-market economies.[2] Since the coming into force of the WTO, no investigations have been initiated, let alone measures imposed.[3] Moreover, Switzerland notified to the WTO in 2009 that it has not established authorities competent to initiate and conduct investigations within the meaning of Article 16.5 of the AD Agreement and Article 25.12 of the SCM Agreement.[4] At the same occasion, Switzerland announced that it *"does not anticipate taking any anti-dumping [and countervailing] actions for the foreseeable future."*[5] These notifications are valid until further notice. At first glance, the notification to refrain from using trade defence instruments within the framework of the WTO seems somewhat unorthodox. And even though this notification is based on a format adopted by the WTO Committee on Anti-Dumping Practices and the WTO Committee on Subsidies and Countervailing Measures for members that have not established investigating authorities, and accordingly have never used any trade defence instruments,[6] it is remarkable and calls for an explanation why Switzerland does not, and for the foreseeable future will not, make use of trade defence instruments.

---

[2] Cottier and Oesch (2005), p. 1034.

[3] WTO Trade Policy Review Body, Report by the Secretariat on Switzerland and Liechtenstein, WT/TPR/S/355, 11 April 2017, para. 19, 3.50.

[4] WTO Committee on Anti-Dumping Practices, Notification of Switzerland under Articles 16.4 and 16.5 of the Agreement, G/ADP/N/193/CHE, 23 December 2009; WTO Committee on Subsidies and Countervailing Measures, Notification of Switzerland under Articles 25.11 and 25.12 of the Agreement, G/SCM/N/202/CHE, 23 December 2009.

[5] WTO Committee on Anti-Dumping Practices, Notification of Switzerland under Articles 16.4 and 16.5 of the Agreement, G/ADP/N/193/CHE, 23 December 2009; WTO Committee on Subsidies and Countervailing Measures, Notification of Switzerland under Articles 25.11 and 25.12 of the Agreement, G/SCM/N/202/CHE, 23 December 2009.

[6] WTO Committee on Anti-Dumping Practices, Format adopted by the Committee on 21 October 2009 on the Notification under Articles 16.4 and 16.5 of the Agreement, G/ADP/19, 3 November 2009; WTO Committee on Subsidies and Countervailing Measures, Format adopted by the Committee on 29 October 2009 on the Notification under Articles 25.11 and 25.12 of the Agreement, G/SCM/129, 29 October 2009. 46 WTO members submitted a similar notification to refrain from using anti-dumping measures; 39 WTO members submitted a similar notification to refrain from using countervailing duties. Switzerland and Liechtenstein are the only developed countries among those 34 WTO members which submitted both notifications.

This contribution recalls the legal framework based upon which it would be possible to impose trade defence instruments in Switzerland (Sect. 2). Thereafter, it discusses possible reasons for the abstinence of trade defence instruments in this country—the big sleep, so to speak (Sect. 3). An epilogue wraps up the contribution (Sect. 4).

2 Legal Framework

Swiss law only punctually lays down rules on the allocation of competences among the federal authorities and on the procedural and substantive requirements which must be observed when imposing trade defence instruments. Moreover, no formal mechanism exists to bring allegedly unfair trade practices of other countries and foreign companies to the attention of the government.

2.1 Legal Basis for the Imposition of Trade Defence Instruments

The Federal Act on External Economic Measures of 1982[7] and the Federal Act on Customs Tariffs of 1986[8] set out rules for the enactment of extraordinary measures in external economic matters. Article 1 of the Federal Act on External Economic Measures grants the Federal Council the competence to restrict the import and export of goods, trade in services and the movement of capital in extraordinary circumstances in general. Article 7 of the Federal Act on Customs Tariffs specifically deals with tariff measures[9]:

Article 7 **Extraordinary circumstances in foreign relations**

If, as a result of foreign measures or exceptional conditions abroad, Switzerland's foreign relations are influenced to such an extent that essential Swiss economic interests are prejudiced, the Federal Council may, for as long as the circumstances require, modify the relevant rates of duty, or, in the event of exemption from duty, introduce duties, or take other suitable measures.

Article 13 of the Federal Act on Customs Tariffs obliges the Federal Council to inform the Federal Assembly in its annual report after it has taken a measure pursuant to Article 7. The Federal Assembly then decides whether the measure should

---

[7] Federal Act on External Economic Measures of 25 June 1982, SR 946.201 [the "SR" is the official compilation of federal legislation in Switzerland; www.admin.ch (last accessed 30 April 2018) and link to Bundesrecht].

[8] Federal Act on Customs Tariffs of 9 October 1986, SR 632.10.

[9] Botschaft zu einem Bundesgesetz über aussenwirtschaftliche Massnahmen of 7 December 1981, BBl 1982 I 61, p. 70.

remain in force, be extended or modified. The involvement of the Federal Assembly is justified on the grounds that such measures might restrict economic freedom, which is guaranteed as a fundamental right pursuant to Article 27 of the Swiss Constitution,[10] to a considerable degree.

Article 7 of the Federal Act on Customs Tariffs provides the legal basis for the enactment of anti-dumping measures and countervailing duties in Switzerland.[11] Apart from this exceedingly open-textured provision, there are no laws specifically dealing with the imposition of anti-dumping measures or countervailing duties.[12] Switzerland deliberately refrained from introducing legislation to this effect in the aftermath of the Uruguay Round. Therefore, Switzerland has no legislation explicitly dealing with the procedural and substantive requirements relevant for the imposition of such measures, in stark contrast to, for instance, the EU and the United States which have in place elaborated legal frameworks on these matters.[13]

The lack of explicit legislation and practical cases means that various legal questions are left open. It is submitted that proper domestic legislation going beyond of what Article 7 of the Federal Act on Customs Tariffs regulates in Switzerland is not a cogent prerequisite for WTO members to impose anti-dumping measures or countervailing duties. Moreover, the fact that Switzerland has not notified to the WTO the competent authorities for initiating and conducting investigations does not hinder Switzerland to initiate and conduct an investigation either.[14] Of course, Switzerland would be obliged to duly notify its intention to initiate an investigation and, thereby, also to inform on the competent authority, which presumably is the State Secretariat for Economic Affairs (SECO).[15] Switzerland could inform the WTO upon the initiation of an investigation accordingly. The Federal Council takes the final decision to impose anti-dumping measures and countervailing duties, as explicitly provided for in Article 7 of the Federal Act on Customs Tariffs, insofar as

---

[10] Federal Constitution of the Swiss Confederation of 18 April 1999, SR 101.

[11] Weber (2007), p. 57; Diebold and Oesch (2008), p. 1538; Botschaft zu einem Bundesgesetz über aussenwirtschaftliche Massnahmen of 7 December 1981, BBl 1982 I 60, p. 70.

[12] Cottier and Oesch (2005), pp. 1007 and 1034.

[13] Regulation (EU) 2016/1036 on protection against dumped imports from countries not members of the European Union; Regulation (EU) 2016/1037 on protection against subsidised imports from countries not members of the European Union; also Regulation (EU) 2017/2321 amending these regulations; U.S. Tariff Act of 1930, 19 U.S.C. §§ 1671–1677n (2012).

[14] See for these notifications: WTO Committee on Anti-Dumping Practices, Notification under Articles 16.4 and 16.5 of the Agreement, G/ADP/N/193/CHE, 23 December 2009; WTO Committee on Subsidies and Countervailing Measures, Notification under Articles 25.11 and 25.12 of the Agreement, G/SCM/N/202/CHE, 23 December 2009.

[15] Cf. WTO Trade Policy Review Body, Report by the Secretariat on Switzerland and Liechtenstein, WT/TPR/S/355, 11 April 2017, para. 3.50. In two notifications of 1995, Switzerland informed the WTO that the Federal Office for External Economic Affairs, the predecessor office of SECO, was competent to initiate and conduct investigations pursuant to the AD Agreement and the SCM Agreement at the time; WTO Committee on Anti-Dumping Practices, Notification of Switzerland of Laws and Regulations under Article 18.5 of the Agreement, G/ADP/N/1/CHE/1, 4 May 1995; WTO Committee on Anti-Subsidy Practices, Notification of Switzerland of Laws and Regulations under Article 32.6 of the Agreement, G/SCM/N/1/CHE/1, 4 May 1995.

the requirements laid down in Article 7 of the Federal Act on Customs Tariffs are met and such action is deemed appropriate. It goes without saying that anti-dumping measures and countervailing duties can only be applied if the procedural and substantive requirements as provided for in the AD Agreement and the SCM Agreement are met. This holds true, in particular, for the due process provisions, including the obligation to conduct investigations in a transparent manner, to grant all interested parties the opportunity to defend their interests and to ensure that the investigating authorities adequately explain the basis for their determinations and that administrative actions can be challenged before an independent tribunal.[16] These WTO agreements provide for a comprehensive set of rules which are directly applicable domestically.[17]

2.2 Lack of Formal Procedures to Approach the Government

In Swiss law, no formal mechanism exists for private companies and business associations to bring allegedly unfair trade practices of other countries and foreign companies to the attention of the government. The Federal Act on External Economic Measures does not lay down a procedure for dealing with illicit commercial practices notified by affected companies or their industry, nor does any other act provide for such a mechanism. In particular, there is no legal entitlement on the part of private companies and business associations that the Swiss government investigate a complaint and take action, e.g. by imposing anti-dumping measures or countervailing duties or by requesting the WTO Dispute Settlement Body to establish a panel to examine the matter. Such complaints are dealt with informally under the government's broad discretionary powers in foreign affairs pursuant to Article 184 of the Swiss Constitution.[18]

In practice, private companies notify allegations and complaints as to unfair trade practices by other countries and foreign companies to SECO or another federal office which is deemed competent to deal therewith, such as the Federal Customs Administration, the Federal Institute for Intellectual Property and the

---

[16] See for these procedural requirements Van den Bossche and Zdouc (2017), pp. 737–749 and 847–855; administrative decisions, including the final decision to impose trade defence instruments, could arguably be challenged before the Swiss Federal Administrative Court; Diebold and Oesch (2008), p. 1541.

[17] Arpagaus (2007), p. 652, fn. 2245; Diebold and Oesch (2008), p. 1541; see also the response of Federal Councillor Flavio Cotti to a request to introduce anti-dumping measures against the import of wood in 1988, Amtl. Bull. NR 1988, p. 695. It must be noted, however, that the Swiss Federal Supreme Court has traditionally been reluctant to grant WTO law direct effect, based on similar rationales as those relied upon by the ECJ; Cottier and Oesch (2005), pp. 223–226.

[18] Cottier and Oesch (2005), p. 151.

Federal Office for Agriculture, through informal channels.[19] It then lies within the discretion of the government to take up the case and initiate steps to remedy the illicit practices through diplomatic means, by officially notifying the dispute to the WTO Dispute Settlement Body or by imposing anti-dumping measures or countervailing duties. The government decides on the basis of an assessment of the circumstances of the case at hand, taking into account not only the economic interests of the companies hit by the allegedly unfair trade practices but also the interests of other companies (which indeed might depend on cheap imports in order to process them) and the consumers as well as general foreign policy considerations, in short: "the interests of the whole country".[20] At least, it is submitted that the applicants have a right to be duly informed on the decision to take action or to refrain from doing so and to be provided with an adequate reasoning.[21] This setup reflects classic diplomatic protection by nation states as developed under general public international law. It is based on close and informal ties between the authorities and industry associations in Switzerland and, with respect to dispute resolution on the international plane, on long-standing preferences for diplomatic means rather than for contentious meetings before judges.[22] In fact, the system generally works well. The authorities are ready to support private operators and intervene by diplomatic means when they deem such action appropriate. Whereas Switzerland has not imposed anti-dumping measures or countervailing duties to date, it has at least occasionally initiated formal dispute settlement proceedings under the auspices of the WTO by notifying consultations to the Dispute Settlement Body.[23] All of these disputes were settled through mutually acceptable solutions, with one exception: the *US – Steel Safeguards* case could only be resolved upon the adoption of the Appellate Body report by the Dispute Settlement Body.[24]

---

[19] Cottier and Oesch (2005), p. 151; see also Article 5 of the Ordinance on the Organisation of the Federal Department of Economic Affairs, Education and Research of 14 June 1999, SR 172.216.1, according to which SECO is the centre of competence for external economic matters.

[20] Judgement of the Federal Supreme Court of 3 June 1955, *Schoenemann v Swiss Confederation*, BGE 81 I 159, p. 170 (own translation), with respect to interventions in favour of Swiss citizens abroad in general.

[21] Diebold and Oesch (2008), p. 1536.

[22] A notable exception was the intervention of Switzerland before the European Court of Justice in the so-called "airplane noise pollution dispute" concerning the conformity of the prohibition of flights over southern German territory during the night below a certain altitude imposed by Germany with the Agreement on Air Transport between Switzerland and the EU of 21 June 1999, SR 0.748.127.192.68; CJEU, Case C-547/10 P, *Swiss Confederation v Commission*, ECLI:EU:C:2013:139.

[23] Switzerland initiated three cases in 1997 (WT/DS94) and 1998 (WT/DS119, WT/DS133); moreover, it participated in several disputes as a third party [www.wto.org (last accessed 30 April 2018) and link to dispute settlement/disputes by members].

[24] Appellate Body Report, *United States – Definitive Safeguard Measures on Imports of Certain Steel Products*, WT/DS253/AB/R, adopted 10 November 2003, DSR 2003:III, and Panel Report, *United States – Definitive Safeguard Measures on Imports of Certain Steel Products*, WT/DS253/R, adopted 11 July 2003 (as modified by the former).

The Swiss tradition of sticking to the principle of classic diplomatic protection rather than to resolve disputes by taking recourse to dispute resolution by judges and unilateral counteractions contrasts to the law and practice developed in other legal systems of WTO members. Specific mechanisms exist, for instance, in the United States, the EU and China which allow private actors to bring alleged violations of international trade law to the attention of the authorities which then are obliged to examine the matter.[25] Section 301 of the US Trade Act introduced procedural rights of private operators as early as 1974.[26] The European Community followed suit in 1994 by setting up the Trade Barriers Regulation; moreover, the *EU market access database* informs on import conditions in third country markets in a transparent manner and ensures that operators can notify newly identified trade barriers efficiently and effectively.[27] China enacted the Investigation Rules of Foreign Trade Barriers in 2005.[28] It is within the discretion of the authorities also in these countries and entities as to whether they deem it necessary and to be in the interest of their country/entity to take action, i.e. to impose measures with a view to remove the injury or the adverse trade effects or to request the establishment of a WTO panel. In any case, the authorities are obliged to deal with the matter and to properly explain their action or inaction. It is no coincidence that these WTO members take recourse to trade defence instruments and to the WTO dispute settlement system remarkably frequently.

3   Reasons for the Big Sleep

The reasons for the abstinence of trade defence instruments in Switzerland are difficult to grasp. Official documents of the government do not shed light on the reasons for the big sleep. The same holds true for publications and statements of business representatives. It is submitted that the following five—partly overlapping—reasons are the relevant ones.

---

[25] In addition to these formal mechanisms, private operators and their lobby groups also continue, of course, to use informal channels to bring allegedly unfair trade practices to the attention of the authorities.

[26] Trade Act of 1974, § 301, 19 U.S.C. § 2411(a)(1) (2012); see for the procedures laid down by Section 301 Jackson et al. (2013), pp. 360–362.

[27] Trade Barriers Regulation (EU) No 2015/1843; International Trade Rules Enforcement Regulation (EU) No 654/2014; see for the procedures laid down by the Trade Barriers Regulation Van Bael and Bellis (2011), pp. 441–628 (for anti-dumping measures) and pp. 709–716 (for countervailing duties).

[28] The English translation is available on the website of the Ministry of Commerce of China, http://english.mofcom.gov.cn (last accessed 30 April 2018); Van den Bossche and Zdouc (2017), p. 184.

3.1 Open Trade Regime

Switzerland has a long tradition of maintaining an open trade regime, with the notable exception in agriculture where Switzerland continues to apply protective border measures (tariffs, quotas) and internal support measures (direct payments).[29] The policy to adhere to open borders in trade in industrial goods is not a means in itself. Rather, it is based on a deliberate choice to provide the internationally highly integrated Swiss economy with an ideal setup to prosper. The Swiss economy strongly depends on vivid and frictionless trading activities with other countries; it capitalises on the open trade regime for industrial products.[30] Against this background, it becomes obvious that the option to impose measures against unfair trading practices through trade defence instruments, safeguard measures and restrictions on the movement of capital has never been high on the agenda of policy makers in this country. A change of paradigm in this respect would send an unwelcomed signal to the trading community all over the globe. Arguably, the use of trade defence instruments by Switzerland would result in only marginal economic gains for the affected companies in Switzerland as the internal market in Switzerland is relatively small; in contrast, trade-restrictive measures applied by other trading partners against Swiss firms and products potentially have more damaging effects as access to much larger export markets is endangered and trade-related administrative procedures are unnecessarily complicated. Switzerland is doing well by taking recourse to trade defence instruments only in exceptional cases, if at all.

Moreover, economic studies suggest, based on strong circumstantial evidence, that the use of trade defence instruments can be linked to so-called "insurance policies" put in place by states when they agree to grand trade liberalisation projects, such as tariff reductions resulting from the GATT negotiation rounds, the trade reforms triggered by the creation of the European Single Market (with respect to the EU member states) and the accession of China to the WTO.[31] According to these studies, trade defence instruments constitute one of the elements by which the negative effects of trade liberalisation can be adjusted ex post.[32] In Switzerland, however,

---

[29] WTO Trade Policy Review Body, Report by the Secretariat on Switzerland and Liechtenstein, WT/TPR/S/355, 11 April 2017, para. 1.

[30] Cf. WTO Trade Policy Review, Report by the Secretariat on Switzerland and Liechtenstein, WT/TPR/S/13, 26 April 1996, p. xi.

[31] Bienen D, Ciuriak D and Picarello T (2012) Motives for using trade defense instruments in the European Union. BKP Development Trade and Development Discussion Paper No. 01/2012, March 2012, http://www.bkp-development.com/discussion-papers/BKP_DP_2012-01-Bienen-Ciuriak-Picarello-TDI-Motives.pdf (last accessed 30 April 2018), p. 39; see for further economic research in this area Mukunoki H (2017) Does trade liberalization promote antidumping protection? A theoretical analysis. RIETI Discussion Paper Series 17-E-031, March 2017, https://www.rieti.go.jp/jp/publications/dp/17e031.pdf (last accessed 30 April 2018); Bown and Crowley (2014); Feinberg and Reynolds (2007).

[32] Bienen D, Ciuriak D and Picarello T (2012) Motives for using trade defense instruments in the European Union. BKP Development Trade and Development Discussion Paper No. 01/2012,

trade defence instruments were never deemed necessary as "insurance policies" for the broader society. It has been argued that in this country social security policies developed alongside trade liberalisation projects and thus had an effect as "insurance policies" to mitigate the effects of an open trade regime.[33]

It is symptomatic that in Swiss law no formal mechanism exists for private companies and business associations to bring allegedly unfair trade practices of other countries and foreign companies to the attention of the government. The establishment of such a mechanism might be desirable from the perspective of individuals. At the same time, however, it might send out the unwelcomed signal that the authorities are well ready to initiate and conduct investigations which would contradict the official policy of restraint. Consequently, there have never been serious initiatives to formalise the process—according to the motto: Let sleeping dogs lie.

3.2 Cautious Approach in External Relations

Switzerland has traditionally applied, in external trade policy, a cautious approach with respect to actions which could be perceived as contentious by other trading partners. This cautious approach reflects the political maxim of neutrality, which has been a dominant instrument of Swiss external relations ever since the foundation of the modern Swiss federal state in 1848, and the deliberately applied passiveness in foreign relations which comes therewith. The fact that Switzerland has participated only once as complaining party in WTO panel and Appellate Body proceedings—and, then, in tandem with six other complaining parties, including the EU—is proof to the point.[34] The use of the WTO dispute settlement procedures might be considered, contrary to Article 3(10) of the Dispute Settlement Understanding (DSU), to be a "contentious act". The same argument holds arguably true with respect to the abstinence of trade defence instruments. The imposition of anti-dumping measures and countervailing duties might endanger, according to such an understanding, the good relations with the country whose products are targeted by such measures. Symptomatically, Switzerland has not only refrained from imposing trade defence instruments, but it has also refrained from adopting safeguard measures pursuant to Article XIX of the GATT 1994 and the Agreement on

---

March 2012, http://www.bkp-development.com/discussion-papers/BKP_DP_2012-01-Bienen-Ciuriak-Picarello-TDI-Motives.pdf (last accessed 30 April 2018), p. 39.
[33] Cottier and Naef (2014), pp. 185–187.
[34] See Appellate Body Report, *United States – Definitive Safeguard Measures on Imports of Certain Steel Products*, WT/DS253/AB/R, adopted 10 November 2003, DSR 2003:III, and Panel Report, *United States – Definitive Safeguard Measures on Imports of Certain Steel Products*, WT/DS253/R, adopted 11 July 2003 (as modified by the former).

Safeguards since the coming into force of the WTO.[35] These instruments are considered to be applied only as *ultima ratio*, if at all.

The reluctance to apply trade defence instruments seems to be particularly apparent vis-à-vis the EU. The EU is by far the most important trading partner of Switzerland.[36] Trade between Switzerland and the EU amounts to 1 billion Swiss Francs per day. 53% of Swiss exports go to the EU; 72% of the imports come from the EU. Most relevant are, of course, exports to and imports from the neighbouring countries Austria, France, Germany and Italy and, in particular, their regions with a common border with Switzerland. For instance, trade with Baden-Württemberg is almost as significant as trade with the United States. Switzerland and the EU are tied together by a tight network of bilateral treaties—some 20 main agreements and more than 100 secondary agreements—many of which need to be updated periodically. Consequently, there is a general perception in Switzerland that it does not behove to take measures by which trade is restricted (albeit on perfectly legitimate grounds) vis-à-vis the EU imprudently as such a move could derange the constructive atmosphere necessary for the maintenance and further development of smooth and frictionless bilateral relations.[37]

Several free trade agreements which Switzerland has concluded with trading partners all over the globe contain provisions explicitly mandating the parties to apply a cautious approach when referring to trade defence instruments. To name but a few, the Free Trade Agreement between Switzerland and Chile of 2003 obliges each party not to apply anti-dumping measures as provided for under the AD Agreement in relation to goods of the other party; it is recognised that the effective implementation of competition rules may address economic causes leading to dumping (Article 18).[38] The Free Trade Agreement between Switzerland and Canada of 2008 obliges the party which intends to initiate an investigation pursuant to the SCM Agreement to duly inform the other party whose goods would be subject to the investigation and to allow that party a period of 25 days for consultations with a view to finding a mutually acceptable solution (Article 17).[39] In contrast, the Free Trade Agreement between Switzerland and Mexico of 2000 obliges the party which intends to initiate an investigation pursuant to the SCM Agreement to grant the other party whose goods are allegedly being subsidised 2 days (*sic!*) to react with a view

---

[35] WTO Trade Policy Review Body, Report by the Secretariat on Switzerland and Liechtenstein, WT/TPR/S/355, 11 April 2017, para. 19, 3.50; exceptionally, in 1999, Switzerland notified the WTO the imposition of additional duties on swine meat, based on the special safeguard mechanism pursuant to Article 5 of the Agreement on Agriculture, see Cottier and Oesch (2005), p. 505.

[36] See for these figures https://www.eda.admin.ch/eda (last accessed 30 April 2018).

[37] Moreover, Article 27 of the Free Trade Agreement between Switzerland and the EEC of 22 July 1972 (SR 0.632.401) obliges the parties to supply the joint committee with all relevant information required for a thorough examination for the situation with a view to seeking a solution acceptable to the parties before a party imposes anti-dumping measures.

[38] Free Trade Agreement between the EFTA States and the Republic of Chile of 26 June 2003, SR 0.632.312.451.

[39] Free Trade Agreement between the EFTA States and Canada of 26 January 2008, SR 0.632.312.32.

to finding a mutually acceptable solution (Article 11).[40] With such "WTO-plus" provisions, Switzerland has deliberately tied its hands with respect to the use of trade defence instruments, of course on a reciprocal basis. It seems to be part of the negotiation strategy of Switzerland to convince free trade partners to make the use of trade defence instruments more cumbersome and thus to "export" its cautious approach to other countries.

Plausibly, the cautious approach which Switzerland adheres to in its external trade policy also applies to the emerging economies China and India, the two countries which have been most often the target of anti-dumping measures and countervailing duties by other WTO members over the last years. In 2013, Switzerland concluded a free trade agreement with China.[41] The agreement contains no "WTO-plus" provisions concerning anti-dumping measures and countervailing duties, with the subtle supplement that anti-dumping measures shall not be taken in an arbitrary or protectionist manner (Article 5.2) and that the party considering initiating an investigation to determine the existence, degree and effect of any alleged subsidy in the other party shall notify the other party and allow for a consultation with a view to finding a mutually acceptable solution in an amicable manner (Article 5.3). Switzerland is currently also negotiating a free trade agreement with India. Again, the frequent use of trade defence instruments against these countries by Switzerland arguably would result in only marginal economic gains for the affected companies in Switzerland; by contrast, restrictive trade policies by important trading partners such as China and India against Swiss firms and products could potentially severely affect the privileged trade relations that Switzerland maintains with China and intends to secure with India.

3.3 Structure of the Swiss Industry

The structure of the Swiss industry differs in various aspects from that of other WTO members which regularly take recourse to anti-dumping measures and countervailing duties. Products which are found to cause injury upon their importation into the EU and the United States, for instance, often do not reach the threshold of being found to cause injury to Swiss producers of like products.[42] In some cases, there are no Swiss producers of like products at all. In other cases, there are competing like products being produced in Switzerland; however, the impact of the dumped or subsidised imports does not reach the threshold for a determination of injury

---

[40] Free Trade Agreement between the EFTA States and the United Mexican States of 27 November 2000, SR 0.632.315.631.1.

[41] Free Trade Agreement between the Swiss Confederation and the People's Republic of China of 6 July 2013, SR 0.946.292.492.

[42] See Article 3 AD Agreement and Article 15 SCM Agreement for the requirement that the imposition of anti-dumping measures and countervailing duties requires a determination that the dumped or subsidised imports cause injury to the domestic industry.

because the competing Swiss products stand out for their quality and tradition and the producers do not need to drastically adjust their price policy.[43] Moreover, studies suggest that the label "Made in Switzerland" has a value on its own; Swiss products profit therefrom on the Swiss market and abroad.[44] Lastly, it is commonly held that Swiss consumers have a lower price sensibility than consumers abroad.[45] Thus, Swiss companies find themselves less often in a position in which market forces urge them to react instantaneously to cheaper imports than might be the case in other economies.

A side glance at anti-dumping measures and countervailing duties which the EU imposed over the last years seems to support this assumption.[46] Currently, the EU has in place several anti-dumping measures and countervailing duties directed against products which are not produced in Switzerland.[47] Some products against which the EU has taken action are also produced in Switzerland but only on a tiny scale.[48] In other cases, the Swiss industry does not seem to be injured (anymore) by the dumped products because of its specialisation and high-quality standards; bicycles and textile and clothing are examples to the point[49]:

– The EU imposed anti-dumping measures on imports of bicycles from China as early as in 1991. These measures have been applied until today, being the longest lasting anti-dumping measures currently in force in the EU. The EU extended them to bicycles from Indonesia, Malaysia, Sri Lanka and Tunisia in 2013 and to bicycles from Cambodia, Pakistan and the Philippines in 2014.[50] With these measures, the European bicycle industry has been granted ongoing relief against

---

[43] See for the main features of the Swiss economy—characterised by a large services sector but also possessing a strong, high-tech and export-oriented manufacturing base—WTO Trade Policy Review Body, Report by the Secretariat on Switzerland and Liechtenstein, WT/TPR/S/355, 11 April 2017, paras. 1.1 et seq.

[44] Müller (2015), para. 1, with further references.

[45] WTO Trade Policy Review Body, Report by the Secretariat on Switzerland and Liechtenstein, WT/TPR/S/355, 11 April 2017, para. 17.

[46] See for the sectoral distribution of anti-dumping measures and countervailing duties introduced by the EU www.wto.org (last accessed 30 April 2018) and link to trade topics, anti-dumping and www.wto.org (last accessed 30 April 2018) and link to trade topics, subsidies and countervailing measures; see for an overview on the current practice of the EU http://trade.ec.europa.eu/tdi (last accessed 30 April 2018).

[47] This holds true, for instance, for molybdenum wires; see the determination by the European Commission in European Commission, Proposal for a Council Regulation extending the definitive anti-dumping duty imposed by Regulation (EU) No 511/2010 on imports of certain molybdenum wires originating in the People's Republic of China to imports of certain molybdenum wires consigned from Malaysia, whether declared as originating in Malaysia or not, and terminating the investigation in respect of imports consigned from Switzerland, COM/2011/0867 final—2011/0422 (NLE), Explanatory Memorandum, Point 3.

[48] This holds true, for instance, for citrus fruits and rainbow trouts.

[49] Okoumé plywood, rebars, coated fine paper and aluminum foil are other examples.

[50] See for an overview on EU anti-dumping measures on bicycles http://trade.ec.europa.eu/tdi/case_history.cfm?init=1532 (last accessed 30 April 2018).

dumped imports. By contrast, Switzerland has never imposed anti-dumping measures against imported bicycles although the Swiss bicycle industry has also faced strong competition from Asia over the last 40 years. Some producers were even put out of the business. Irrespective of the abstinence of state action to protect the domestic industry, however, many Swiss bicycle producers have adjusted their business models to competition from abroad and have done well, mainly on the grounds of their policy to produce for consumers ready to purchase high-quality products. Imports from Asia do not substantially affect their successful course of business on the Swiss market.[51]

- The EU has a long history of protecting its textiles and clothing sector, dating back to the 1970s.[52] By 2005, however, the EU had to remove all quotas on textiles and clothing pursuant to the WTO Agreement on Textiles and Clothing (Article 9). Consequently, almost all product categories experienced a large increase in Chinese imports, as high as 500% and even more for some products.[53] After the application of safeguards, which were mutually agreed between the EU and China (2005–2007), and a follow-up joint surveillance system (2008),[54] the EU introduced anti-dumping measures on polyester yarn from China in 2009; these measures are still in force, set to expire in 2022.[55] By contrast, Switzerland has never protected its textiles and clothing sector beyond the use of tariffs.[56] Textiles and clothing are also covered by the free trade agreement between Switzerland and China. The Swiss textiles and clothing industry faced severe competition from Asia over the last 40 years and some producers were put out of the business. Driven by the necessary structural reforms, many Swiss textiles and clothing producers, however, are doing well today. Swiss textile industry is highly specialised, dependent on intellectual property protection (design) and focusing on specialties and luxury products.[57] Manufacturing is mechanised, whereby large parts of the production have been outsourced, having kept only the processes with the highest added value in Switzerland.[58]

---

[51] See for background information on the Swiss bicycle industry Brusa N, Der letzte Schweizer Velorahmen-Löter. Tagesanzeiger, 25 August 2014, https://www.tagesanzeiger.ch/wirtschaft/ unternehmen-und-konjunktur/Auf-den-Felgen/story/23460006 (last accessed 30 April 2018).

[52] See Eckhardt (2010), pp. 158 et seq., for a comprehensive account of EU protectionist textile and clothing trade policy.

[53] Eckhardt (2010), pp. 158 et seq. and 169.

[54] Eckhardt (2010), pp. 158 et seq. and 171–173.

[55] See for an overview on EU anti-dumping measures on polyester yarn www.trade.ec.europa.eu/ tdi/case_history.cfm?ref=com&init=1522 (last accessed 30 April 2018).

[56] Cottier and Oesch (2005), p. 748.

[57] Cottier and Oesch (2005), p. 748.

[58] See for background information on the Swiss textiles and clothing industry, Schmutz CG, Keine Angst vor chinesischer Billigware. Neue Zürcher Zeitung Online, 15 May 2014, https://www.nzz. ch/wirtschaft/keine-angst-vor-chinesischer-billigware-1.18302668 (last accessed 30 April 2018).

Overall, these examples imply that the Swiss industry has not been, generally speaking, prone to take long lasting injurious blows from dumped or subsidised products as easily as industries and products abroad. The resilience of the Swiss industry often lies in its capacity to adapt to competition by specialising the production; a process that is accelerated with the abstinence of public action to protect the domestic industry.

It is important to note that this situation might change in the future. In light of the ongoing development of high-tech industries in emerging economies, it might well be the case that there will be distress calls for the imposition of trade defence instruments against imported high-quality products also in Switzerland. Such imports could indeed cause injury to the Swiss industry which has been affected by dumped or subsidised products only marginally until now. Against this background, it is conceivable that the Swiss government will have to reconsider its passive stance on the use of trade defence instruments in due course.

3.4   Free Riding

The abstinence of trade defence instruments in Switzerland stands in stark contrast to the proactive use of such instruments by the EU. Legally, this is perfectly fine. Switzerland is not part of the EU. It pursues its own economic foreign policy and is not obliged to follow suit when the EU imposes anti-dumping measures and countervailing duties. At the same time, there are several scenarios where Switzerland benefits, directly or indirectly, when the EU imposes anti-dumping measures and countervailing duties against other countries and foreign companies. In such cases, Switzerland sits in the side-waggon and profits from the economic effects of the measures but does not engage in the formal decision-making process itself; it enjoys a free ride, so to speak.

With regard to subsidies, the EU regularly uses the two available tracks to remedy injurious effects, namely by challenging an unlawful subsidy directly before a WTO panel (multilateral track, *Track I*) or by offsetting the negative effects of a subsidy through the application of countervailing duties (unilateral track, *Track II*):

- If *Track I* is successful, the subsidy has to be withdrawn or its adverse effects have to be removed. In case the member concerned refuses to do so, the Dispute Settlement Body may authorise the EU to take appropriate countermeasures (Articles 4.10 and 7.9 SCM Agreement). WTO arbitration panel reports suggest that the purpose of such countermeasures is to induce compliance through the withdrawal of the unlawful subsidy.[59] Against this background, it becomes clear

---

[59] Decisions by the Arbitrators in *Canada – Measures Affecting the Export of Civilian Aircraft (Art. 22.6 – Canada)*, WT/DS222/ABR, adopted 17 February 2003, para. 3.59; *United States – Tax Treatment for "Foreign Sales Corporations" (Art. 22.6 – US)*, WT/DS108/AB/R, adopted 30 August 2002, para. 5.57; *Brazil – Export Financing Programme for Aircraft (Art. 22.6 – Brazil)*,

that Switzerland is indeed in position to profit as a free rider in such constellations, either from the withdrawal of the subsidy *eo ipso* or from the pressure on
the subsidising member to do so through the application of countermeasures by
the EU.
- If the EU chooses *Track II*, it has to initiate a formal investigation. With a preliminary affirmative determination of subsidisation and injury, the EU is in a
position to negotiate voluntary undertakings where either the subsidising member agrees to withdraw the subsidy or to take other measures offsetting its negative effects, or the exporting firms agree to revise their price policies so that the
injurious effect of the subsidy is eliminated (Article 18.1 SCM Agreement). If a
voluntary undertaking is put into place, Switzerland would again profit as a free
rider, particularly in case the subsidising member agrees to eliminate the subsidy
or to take other measures offsetting its negative effects. The proper implementation of a voluntary undertaking by the subsidising member would most likely
also offset the injurious effects on the Swiss economy. If the exporting firms
agree to revise their price policies, the consequences for the Swiss economy are
less obvious. The firms' new price policies might not automatically apply also to
products exported to Switzerland. At least, it is conceivable that Switzerland
would be able to negotiate the same outcome based on the terms granted to the
EU. Without a voluntary undertaking being negotiated, the EU might impose
countervailing duties. Contrary to countermeasures, such duties may not exceed
the amount of the subsidy.[60] Moreover, if the amount of the injury caused is less
than the amount of the subsidy, the definitive duties should preferably be limited
to the amount necessary to counteract the injury caused (the "lesser duty" rule).[61]
In such a case, Switzerland would profit as a free rider as long as the duties
imposed by the EU lead the member concerned to revise its subsidising policy
and this adjustment would also apply vis-à-vis Switzerland.

With regard to dumping, the notes on subsidies may largely be mirrored. A notable exception is, of course, the absence of a mechanism to challenge dumping practices directly before a WTO panel (multilateral track, *Track I*). The only means to
remedy injurious effects of dumped products are to negotiate a price undertaking
whereby the exporting firms agree to revise their price policies or cease to export the
products at dumped prices (Article 8 AD Agreement) or to impose anti-dumping
measures (unilateral track, *Track II*). If the EU accepts a price undertaking from the
exporting firms, Switzerland would again be able to profit as a free rider insofar as

---

WT/DS46/ABR, adopted 28 August 2000, para. 3.44; see Mitchell (2006), pp. 1003–1004; cf.
also, however, Decision by the Arbitrator, *United States – Subsidies on Upland Cotton (Art. 22.6 –
Brazil)*, WT/DS267/ABR/2, adopted 31 August 2009, para. 4.28, where the arbitrators were not
convinced that the term "countermeasures" necessarily connotes an intention to refer to retaliatory
action that goes beyond mere rebalancing of trade interests.
[60] Appellate Body Report, *United States – Definitive Anti-Dumping and Countervailing Duties on
Certain Products from China*, WT/DS379/AB/R, adopted 11 March 2011, DSR 2010:III, para.
554.
[61] Van den Bossche and Zdouc (2017), p. 858.

such price undertakings would also apply vis-à-vis Switzerland. If the EU imposes anti-dumping measures, Switzerland would profit as a free rider insofar as such measures lead the companies to adjust their price policies accordingly. Furthermore, there is yet another scenario where some form of free riding on the part of Swiss firms might take place. Insofar as the application of trade defence instruments by the EU affects prices in the EU but not in Switzerland, Swiss firms could buy subsidised or dumped products at a lower price than their European counterparts. Swiss firms could then process such products and sell the processed products, by virtue of the Free Trade Agreement between Switzerland and the EEC of 1972,[62] on the European market potentially at a lower price than their European counterparts can do. However, the EU could qualify such action as an illicit circumvention of EU trade defence interventions.[63] In 2011, Switzerland was subject of a formal investigation which was initiated by the European Commission in order to determine whether imports of molybdenum wire consigned from Switzerland amounted to a circumvention of anti-dumping measures imposed by the EU on Chinese products.[64] The Commission terminated the investigation with respect to Switzerland as no change in the pattern of trade between China, Switzerland and the EU could be established with regard to imports of molybdenum wire.[65] In constellations like this, it is often not clear at first sight whether such business practices of Swiss firms indeed constitute an illicit circumvention or whether they are lawful, to the detriment of legal security. Exemplarily, in 2016, a Swiss solar firm challenged two implementing regulations of the Commission extending definitive anti-dumping measures on photovoltaic modules based on crystalline silicon from China to Malaysia and Taiwan before the General Court of the EU.[66] The Swiss firm was unsure whether this extension also applied to exports of such modules from Taiwan to Switzerland where the Swiss firm further processed these modules and then

---

[62] Free Trade Agreement between Switzerland and the EEC of 22 July 1972, SR 0.632.401.

[63] See Brunschweiler and Troller (2014), para. 21, for a description of the potential for circumvention of EU trade defence interventions by Switzerland and China based on the Free Trade Agreement between Switzerland and China of 6 July 2013 (SR 0.946.292.492).

[64] Commission Regulation (EU) No 477/2011 of 17 May 2011 initiating an investigation concerning the possible circumvention of anti-dumping measures imposed by Council Implementing Regulation (EU) No 511/2010 on imports of certain molybdenum wires originating in the People's Republic of China by imports of certain molybdenum wires consigned from Malaysia and Switzerland, whether declared as originating in Malaysia and Switzerland or not, and making such imports subject to registration.

[65] Council Implementing Regulation (EU) No 14/2012 of 9 January 2012 extending the definitive anti-dumping duty imposed by Implementing Regulation (EU) No 511/2010 on imports of certain molybdenum wires originating in the People's Republic of China to imports of certain molybdenum wires consigned from Malaysia, whether declared as originating in Malaysia or not, and terminating the investigation in respect of imports consigned from Switzerland.

[66] GC, Case T-152/16, *Megasol Energie v Commission*, ECLI:EU:T:2017:446.

exported them to the EU. The General Court dismissed the claim as inadmissible.[67] In essence, cases like this boil down to determining whether the further processing of such imported products means that the product is considered of Swiss origin or not—which is often an art in itself.[68] Legal security can only be established by calling upon the EU courts to render an authoritative judgment *after* the EU has taken specific action against Swiss imports.

3.5   Lack of Expertise and Procedures in Domestic Legislation

The initiation and the conduct of an investigation leading to the imposition of anti-dumping measures and countervailing duties are complex. It requires enormous personnel resources. The civil servants need to possess the relevant knowledge and, ideally, experience in initiating and conducting investigations. Moreover, in many countries, the public authorities are routinely supported by external law firms and other specialists, e.g. in collecting economic data, conducting calculations and drafting legal and economic assessments. The United States (Department of Commerce, USDOC; International Trade Commission, USITC) and the EU (Directorate General for Trade, DG Trade) possess the relevant manpower and experience. Large teams deal with applications from companies and business associations to initiate and conduct investigations. Other WTO members which have also actively imposed anti-dumping measures and countervailing duties over the last two decades have followed suit in building up manpower and expertise.[69] Moreover, affected companies and their business associations actively contribute to the efforts made by the public authorities and the external specialists. These WTO members typically have mechanisms in place which allow private actors to bring alleged violations of international trade law to the attention of the authorities which then are obliged to examine the matter and to decide whether any action, such as anti-dumping measures or countervailing duties, shall be taken.[70]

In Switzerland, the State Secretariat for Economic Affairs (SECO) arguably is the authority in charge to deal with trade defence instruments. Due to the lack of any cases to date, it does not possess great expertise and experience in anti-dumping and

---

[67] The General Court denied a legitimate interest of the Swiss solar firm in the proceedings because the firm was, according to the General Court, looking for a declaratory judgment regarding a hypothetical situation, GC, Case T-152/16, *Megasol Energie v Commission*, ECLI:EU:T:2017:446, para. 23.

[68] See Bühlmann (2016), p. 20, concerning the difficulties of determining the origin of processed products according to the EU Customs Code in connection with potential circumventions of EU anti-dumping duties for Swiss online retailers.

[69] Cf. Thi Thu (2012), *passim*, for the limited management and investigation capacities in Vietnam, constituting, according to the author, a prime reason why a country such as Vietnam does not take recourse to trade defence instruments.

[70] Cf. supra Sect. 2.2.

countervailing matters.[71] Anyway, there is no doubt that SECO would be well positioned to catch up rapidly and indeed be ready to initiate and conduct an investigation if an application would be submitted. Realistically, SECO would probably need to outsource parts of an investigation to external specialists and thus to profit from their knowledge and expertise.[72] However, it is not to be taken as granted that the competent public bodies in the government will be ready to grant the necessary funding. In the *US – Steel Safeguards* case, SECO was not granted funding to mandate an external law firm.[73] Affected companies and business associations would possibly also need to contribute to the work undertaken by SECO and external specialists. Moreover, it might be helpful to coordinate an investigation with that undertaken by another WTO member, typically the EU, if such a parallel investigation makes sense, as has been the case in the *US – Steel Safeguards* dispute.[74]

Against this background, it becomes apparent that a more active attitude towards the use of anti-dumping measures and countervailing duties in Switzerland might also imply a change of paradigm with respect to the staffing policy in the government. It might be useful to build up expertise and experience in-house, with a view not to depend too much on external specialists. Moreover, it might be useful to reconsider the decision not to set up a formal mechanism by which affected Swiss firms and industries can approach the government and to request that it take appropriate measures.

4   Conclusion

The reasons for the abstinence of trade defence instruments in Switzerland are multifaceted. Each of the possible explanations discussed in this contribution adds to the picture. Central is Switzerland's approach to stick to an open trade regime and to refrain from pursuing an external trade policy which could be considered contentious by its trading partners. The Swiss industry is remarkably specialised and typically produces high-quality products which are less prone to take lasting injurious blows from dumped or subsidised products as easily as industries and products abroad. Swiss consumers have a lower price sensibility than consumers abroad and the label "Made in Switzerland" has a value on its own. The possibility to benefit from the use of trade defence instruments applied by the EU, i.e. to free-ride, might

---

[71] See for the presumed competence of SECO to initiate and conduct investigations supra Sect. 2.1.

[72] Luckily, Switzerland, as the host state of the WTO in Geneva, is in a position to swiftly acquire the relevant know-how from one of the many trade law firms, and other specialists, which are based, e.g., in Geneva.

[73] Diebold and Oesch (2008), p. 1536.

[74] Appellate Body Report, *United States – Definitive Safeguard Measures on Imports of Certain Steel Products*, WT/DS253/AB/R, adopted 10 November 2003, DSR 2003:III, and Panel Report, *United States – Definitive Safeguard Measures on Imports of Certain Steel Products*, WT/DS253/R, adopted 11 July 2003 (as modified by the former).

also play a role. Overall, it is decisive to observe that Switzerland has done well without taking recourse to trade defence instruments. Against this background, Switzerland is a good example that anti-dumping and countervailing duty legislation is not necessarily an essential part of external trade law.[75] Thus, the Swiss policy of refraining from taking recourse to trade defence instruments could arguably serve as a model for other economies which are similarly structured and are ready to apply a cautious approach towards the use of trade defence instruments.

However, trade defence instruments remain a useful tool to re-establish a level playing field *in exceptional cases*. It appears that to date Swiss companies and industries have not found themselves in a situation in which they would have urgently needed relief and such relief would have been considered to be in the public interest. This does not automatically mean that such a situation might never happen in Switzerland. It might well be the case that there will be, in the near future, distress calls for the imposition of trade defence instruments against imported high-quality products also in this country. In particular, the prices of products from emerging countries such as China and India, which are specialising their industries with remarkable speed and which are already today the targets of most anti-dumping measures and countervailing duties in place, are to be observed carefully. Against this background, it is conceivable that the Swiss government will have to reconsider its passive stance on the use of trade defence instruments in due course, and the Swiss government is well advised to prepare the grounds for dealing with potential applications effectively and efficiently.

References

Arpagaus R (2007) Zollrecht unter Einschluss der völkerrechtlichen Grundlagen im Rahmen der WTO, der WCO, der UNIECE, der EFTA und der Abkommen mit der EU. Helbing Lichtenhahn Verlag, Basel
Bown CP, Crowley MA (2014) Emerging economies, trade policy, and macroeconomic shocks. J Dev Econ 111:261–273
Brunschweiler A, Troller A (2014) Insight into the Swiss-Sino Free Trade Agreement – a path to new business opportunities. Jusletter 16. Juni 2014
Bühlmann L (2016) Zollrechtliche Aspekte im grenzüberschreitenden Online-Handel. Zollrevue Revue Douanière 1(1):17–25
Cottier T, Naef T (2014) Internationaler Handel und Soziale Sicherheit: Komplementarität und Herausforderung. In: Kunz PV, Weber J, Lienhard A, Fargnoli I, Kren Kostkiewicz J (eds) Berner Gedanken zum Recht – Festgabe zum Schweizerischen Juristentag 2014. Stämpfli Verlag, Bern, pp 179–195
Cottier T, Oesch M (2005) International trade regulation: law and policy in the WTO, the European Union and Switzerland. Cameron May, London
Diebold N, Oesch M (2008) Die Durchsetzung von WTO-Recht durch Schweizer Unternehmen. Aktuelle Juristische Praxis 17(12):1525–1552

---

[75] Cottier and Oesch (2005), p. 1034, with respect to the absence of anti-dumping legislation.

Eckhardt J (2010) The evolution of EU trade policy towards China: the case of textiles and clothing. In: Men J, Balducci G (eds) Prospects and challenges for EU-China relations in the 21st century – the partnership and cooperation agreement. Peter Lang, Brussels, pp 151–172

Feinberg RM, Reynolds KM (2007) Tariff liberalisation and increased administrative protection: is there a quid pro quo? World Econ 30(6):948–961

Jackson JH, Davey WJ, Sykes AO (2013) International economic relations: cases, materials and text. Thomson/West, St. Paul

Matsushita M, Schoenbaum TJ, Mavroidis PC, Hahn M (2015) The World Trade Organization: law, practice, and policy. Oxford University Press, Oxford

Mitchell AD (2006) Proportionality and remedies in WTO disputes. Eur J Int Law 17(5):985–1008

Müller N (2015) Swissness und die Veredelung im Ausland. Jusletter 9. März 2015

Thi Thu TL (2012) Trade defence instruments in Vietnam: reality and solutions. Global Trade Customs J 7(7/8):331–340

Van Bael I, Bellis JF (2011) EU anti-dumping and other trade defence instruments. Kluwer Law International, Alphen aan den Rijn

Van den Bossche P, Zdouc W (2017) The law and policy of the World Trade Organization: text, cases and materials. Cambridge University Press, Cambridge

Weber K (2007) Das Bundesgesetz über aussenwirtschaftliche Massnahmen. In: Cottier T, Oesch M (eds) Allgemeines Aussenwirtschafts- und Binnenmarktrecht. Helbing Lichtenhahn Verlag, Basel, pp 49–80

Anti-Dumping Laws and Implementation in China: A 16 Years Review After Accession to the WTO

Yusong Chen

Contents

Abstract   This article focuses on China's anti-dumping legal system and its implementation. After its accession to the WTO in 2001, China established its own trade remedy system in order to safeguard its own markets and industries. China now employs a single agency model in anti-dumping system and uses a prospective methodology for calculating and assessing anti-dumping duties. In using anti-dumping measures and also by implementing WTO rulings, China has continuously improved its practices and the investigation procedures are maturing. As China becomes one of the largest import markets in the world, the influence of China's anti-dumping system has significantly increased.

The views and opinions expressed in this article are those of the author only.

Y. Chen (✉)
Permanent Mission of China to the WTO, Geneva, Switzerland

© Springer International Publishing AG, part of Springer Nature 2018   283
M. Bungenberg et al. (eds.), *The Future of Trade Defence Instruments*,
European Yearbook of International Economic Law,
https://doi.org/10.1007/978-3-319-95306-9_12

1 Introduction

Dumping is a kind of international price discrimination reflecting the pricing practice of an exporting firm to charge a lower price for exported goods than it does for
the same goods sold domestically.[1] It has been a long history since the first anti-
dumping statute came into force in Canada in 1904.[2] However, for China, the anti-
dumping regime has not been established until 1990s, as a completely new
mechanism constructed under the policy of reform and opening up. Under the background of reform and opening up in the 1980s, China applied for the resumption of
its status in the GATT in 1986. This process continued after the establishment of the
World Trade Organization (WTO) in 1995. Upon its accession to the WTO at the
end of 2001, China conducted a comprehensive and substantial reduction of import
tariffs and non-tariff barriers and opened up its domestic market to WTO Members.
In the meantime, according to the WTO rules and drawing on the experience of
other WTO Members, China started to set up its own import anti-dumping investigation system.

2 China's Anti-Dumping Regime

2.1 General Feature

China has never enacted an anti-dumping or similar regime in its history. The establishment of a new anti-dumping system was an innovative government reform. At
the same time, China's administrative litigation and administrative procedural laws
are also in the process of constructing and developing.[3] Therefore, there is no mature
administrative procedure to learn from. Under such circumstances, in order to establish an effective anti-dumping system in line with the WTO rules within a short
period of time, it is necessary to draw on the experience of other WTO Members.
This initial stage is a process of "crossing the river by feeling the stones." China,
like many other WTO Members, uses a prospective methodology for calculating
and assessing anti-dumping duties. In this process, some problems are inevitable,
especially over-relying experience from other WTO Members and, in practice,
gradual adjustments are needed.

---

[1] See, Appellate Body Report, *United States – Final Anti-Dumping Measures on Stainless Steel
from Mexico,* WT/DS344/AB/R, adopted 30 April 2008, DSR 2008:I, fn. 208.
[2] See Ciuriak (2005).
[3] As a broader administrative law background of the anti-dumping legislation, China's first
Administrative Litigation Law was adopted by the National People's Congress in 1989 and came
into force on 1 October 1990. Since then, in the 1990s, China successively formulated the *State
Compensation Law,* the *Administrative Punishment Law* and the *Administrative Review Law.*
However, a uniform Administrative Procedure Law is still under drafting in China.

As for the institutional aspect, it could be seen that there exist two main institutional models of anti-dumping procedures over the world: the single agency model and the double agency model.[4] In 2002, the Ministry of Foreign Trade and Economic Cooperation (MOFTEC) established the Bureau of Fair Trade, an agency being responsible for responding to foreign trade remedy investigation cases and also to conduct dumping investigations against importation. At that time, the agency responsible for injury investigation is the Industrial Injury Investigation Bureau. In 2014, in order to better coordinate and streamline the procedures, the Bureau of Fair Trade and the Industrial Injury Investigation Bureau were merged into the Bureau of Trade Remedy Investigation. At present, in terms of the staffing, the Bureau of Trade Remedy Investigation is the number-one bureau inside the Ministry of Commerce (MOFCOM). This reflects the need both for implementing the anti-dumping investigation and for responding to the escalating trade conflicts.

2.2 Legal Framework

From a legislative point of view, China's legal framework of anti-dumping system consists of three level legislation, namely the *Foreign Trade Law*,[5] the *Anti-Dumping Regulations*[6] and a dozen of departmental Rules.[7]

First, with regard to laws, the *Foreign Trade Law of 1994* was the first and also the fundamental legislation in the area of international trade in China. Article 30 of the law stipulates that: "*Where a product is imported at a price lower than its normal value, thereby causing substantial damage or threat of substantial damage to the relevant domestic industries already established, or substantially retarding the establishment of relevant domestic industries, the State may take necessary measures to eliminate or reduce such damage or threat of damage or retardation.*" After China formally became a WTO Member, China conducted a comprehensive revision of the *Foreign Trade Law* in 2004. Chapter VIII of *Foreign Trade Law of 2004* provides for a series of trade remedies, of which Article 41 states: "*Where a product from other countries or regions is dumped into the domestic market at a price less than its normal value and under such conditions as to cause or threaten to cause material injury to the established domestic industries, or materially retards the establishment of domestic industries, the State may take anti-dumping measures to eliminate or mitigate such injury, threat of injury or retardation.*"

Second, with regard to administrative regulations, China's State Council promulgated the *Anti-dumping and Countervailing Regulations of China* on 25 March

---

[4] See, e.g. Reich (2003).

[5] Foreign Trade Law of the People's Republic of China, 12 May 1994, http://www.npc.gov.cn/wxzl/gongbao/2004-07/23/content_5335694.htm (last accessed 30 April 2018).

[6] Anti-Dumping Regulations of the People's Republic of China, 31 March 2004, http://www.mofcom.gov.cn/article/swfg/swfgbf/201101/20110107350758.shtml (last accessed 30 April 2018).

[7] Departmental rules, see http://trb.mofcom.gov.cn/article/bi/bj/ (last accessed 30 April 2018).

1997, making it the first administrative legislation on anti-dumping. On 26 November 2001, China's State Council issued Order No. 328, promulgating new *Anti-Dumping Regulations*. On 31 March 2004, the *Anti-Dumping Regulations* were further amended. The revisions mainly revise the Ministry of Foreign Trade and Economic Cooperation (MOFTEC) and the State Economic and Trade Commission (SETC) into Ministry of Commerce (MOFCOM) based on the institutional reform of the State Council in 2003. At the same time, some technical improvements were also introduced in those amendments.[8]

Thirdly, with regard to the departmental rules, the MOFTEC (now MOFCOM) formulated a series of departmental rules to implement the provisions of the Anti-Dumping Regulations during 2002–2003.[9] Those department rules covered essential aspects of China's anti-dumping regime, including, inter alia, initiation, sampling, questionnaire, disclosure of information, public hearing, on-the-spot verification, etc. All these Rules were formally notified to the WTO in accordance with the WTO Anti-Dumping Agreement.[10] To date, there has been no challenge under the WTO dispute settlement over those departmental rules so far.

In addition, in order to implement the Panel and Appellate Body's ruling in *China – GOES* (DS414),[11] MOFCOM promulgated the *Interim Rules Governing the Implementation of the World Trade Organization Trade Dispute Settlement Dispute* on 29 July 2013. There are eight articles in this Rule, but it provides a requisite domestic legal basis for revisiting the imposed anti-dumping measures so as to implement the WTO rulings and it also defines the range of measures that MOFCOM may take and the procedures to be followed.

---

[8] For instance, a new public interest provision was added in Article 37. Other improvements include issues on publication, deposit, termination of measures, etc.

[9] Those rules include *Provisional Rules on Initiation of Anti-dumping Investigations, Provisional Rules on Sampling in Anti-dumping Investigations, Provisional Rules Questionnaire in Anti-dumping Investigations, Provisional Rules on Disclosure of Information in Anti-dumping Investigations, Provisional Rules on Access to Non-Confidential Information in Anti-dumping Investigations, Provisional Rules on Public Hearing in Anti-dumping Investigations, Provisional Rules on On-the-spot Verification in Anti-Dumping Investigations, Provisional Rules on Price Undertakings in Anti-dumping Investigations, Provisional Rules on Interim Review of Dumping and Dumping Margin, Provisional Rules on New Shipper Review in Anti-dumping Investigations, Provisional Rules on Refund of Anti-dumping Duty, Provisional Rules on the Procedure of Adjustment to the Product Scope of Anti-dumping Investigation.* See, supra, Anti-Dumping Regulations of the People's Republic of China, 31 March 2004, http://www.mofcom.gov.cn/article/swfg/swfgbf/201101/20110107350758.shtml (last accessed 30 April 2018).

[10] Committee on Anti-Dumping Practices, Notification of Laws and Regulations under Articles 18.5 and 32.6 of the agreements, People's Republic Of China, G/ADP/N/1/CHN2/Suppl.1, 2, 4, 5, and 6.

[11] See, Appellate Body Report, *China – Countervailing and Anti-Dumping Duties on Grain Oriented Flat-Rolled Electrical Steel from the United States,* WT/DS414/AB/R, adopted 16 November 2012, DSR 2012:XII, p. 6251; Panel Report, *China – Countervailing and Anti-Dumping Duties on Grain Oriented Flat-Rolled Electrical Steel from the United States,* WT/DS414/R and Add.1, adopted 16 November 2012, upheld by Appellate Body Report WT/DS414/AB/R, DSR 2012:XII, p. 6369.

2.3 Judicial Review Rules

The WTO Agreements also clearly stipulate independent judicial review of administrative measures by Members. China's *Administrative Litigation Law*[12] also applies to anti-dumping measures. The Supreme Court of China also adopted certain rules concerning the judicial review of trade remedy measures in China in 2002. These rules are the *Rules of the Supreme People's Court on Certain Issues Concerning the Hearing of International Trade Administrative Cases*, the *Rules of the Supreme People's Court on Certain Issues Related to Application of Law in Hearings of Anti-dumping Administrative Cases* and the *Rules of the Supreme People's Court on Certain Issues Related to Application of Law in Hearings of Countervailing Administrative Cases*.[13] In a judicial review process, the Courts shall first and foremost following the requirements of the *Administrative Litigation Law*. At the same time, those rules from the Supreme Court provide more detailed guidelines for the Courts[14] in reviewing the cases.

According to the provisions of these judicial rules, China's Courts only conduct a limited judicial review over the anti-dumping measures taken by the MOFCOM, i.e., in the judicial review, a Court shall only make the legality examination of the accused anti-dumping measures, including whether the major evidence is true and adequate; whether the application of law is correct; whether there is any violation of legal procedures; whether there is any transgression of competence; whether there is any misuse of authority; whether the administrative punishment is obviously unjust; whether there is any failure to perform or delay in performing the legal duties.[15]

Another significant point in China's judicial review is that there is a clear deference to the multilateral trading rules, as it provides that, if there are two or more reasonable interpretations for a specific clause of the law or administrative regulations applied by a people's court in the hearing of an international trade administrative case and among which one interpretation is consistent with the relevant provisions of the international treaty that China concluded or entered into, such interpretation shall be chosen, with the exception of the clauses on which China claims reservation.[16]

---

[12] The People's Republic of China Administrative Procedure Law, 27 June 2017, http://www.npc.gov.cn/npc/xinwen/2017-06/29/content_2024894.htm (last accessed 30 April 2018).

[13] Supreme People's Court Provisions on Certain Issues Concerning the Trial of International Trade Administrative Cases, 1 October 2002, http://www.people.com.cn/GB/shehui/212/3572/3574/20020920/827588.html (last accessed 30 April 2018).

[14] As all the trade remedies in China are decided by the MOFCOM, the judicial review cases of trade remedies will be therefore handled solely by the Beijing Second Intermediate People's Court according to the geographical jurisdiction rule. The appeals will be submitted to the Beijing Higher People's Court.

[15] See Article 6 (Rules of the Supreme People's Court on Certain Issues Concerning the Hearing of International Trade Administrative Case).

[16] See Article 9 (Rules of the Supreme People's Court on Certain Issues Concerning the Hearing of International Trade Administrative Case).

3   Implementation of Anti-Dumping Laws in China

China opened its domestic market since joining the WTO. From 1978 to 2000, the average annual growth rate of China's imports was around 15%. From 2001 to 2010, the annual average annual growth rate was about 20%. China is now the largest trader in the world. In 2016, China imported US$1.32 trillion, making it the second largest importer in the world. In this regards, China has to the extent possible restraint on imposing anti-dumping measures. And anti-dumping measures in China have been at a relatively low level relative to their economies of scale.

In light of its huge import, China is a modest user of anti-dumping measures comparing with other major importers in the WTO (see Fig. 1). According to the notification database of the WTO, since 1 January 1995 to 31 December 2016, China initiated 234 anti-dumping investigation, 8 countervailing investigation and 2 safeguard investigation. China imposed 192 final anti-dumping measures, 6 countervailing measures and 2 safeguard measures during this period. However, during this period of time, 1217 anti-dumping investigations were initiated against imports from China and 866 final anti-dumping measures were imposed in the end of investigations.

For all those anti-dumping measures, the most frequent targets of China's anti-dumping measures are imports from the U.S. (36), Japan (35), Republic of Korea (29) and the EU (22). The products under investigation are mostly in the sector of Products of the Chemical or Allied Industries (98), Plastics and Articles Thereof, Rubber and Articles Thereof (36) and Base Metals and Articles Thereof (20).

As for judicial review of anti-dumping measures, China's MOFCOM as the investigation authority will defend the anti-dumping measures in an administrative

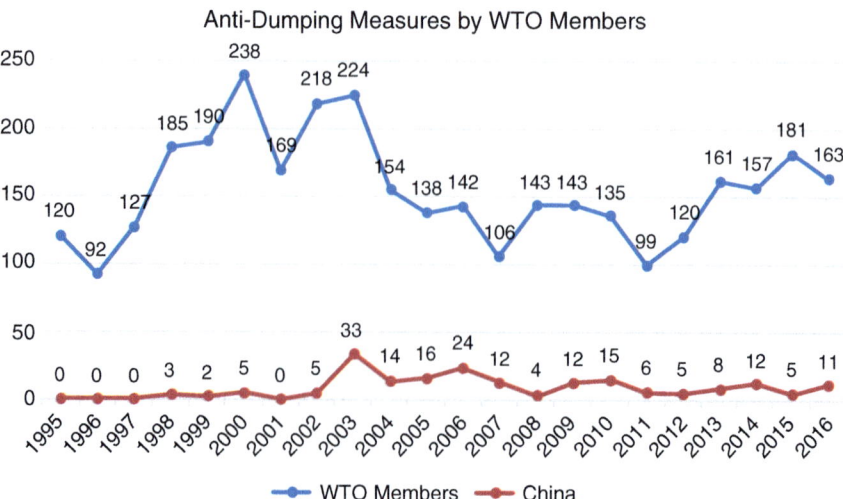

Fig. 1 Antidumping measures by WTO Members. Graph created by the author based on https://www.wto.org/english/tratop_e/adp_e/AD_MeasuresByRepMem.pdf (last accessed 30 April 2018)

litigation. Till now, administrative litigations against anti-dumping measures is very unusual in China. Just a few case examples could be found. For instance, in 2001, Russia's VIZ-Stal and Novolipetsk Steel filed an administrative litigation in Beijing Second Intermediate People's Court, requesting for cancelling the anti-dumping measures taken by the MOFCOM on the import-oriented silicon steel (oriented electrical steel) originating in Russia. The Beijing Second Intermediate People's Court accepted the case in accordance with the *Administrative Litigation Law*. Nevertheless, during the procedures, the plaintiffs, VIZ-Stal and Novolipetsk Steel, withdrew the claims in 2014, so there were no final rulings by the Court.[17]

It should also be mentioned that China has constructively participated in the multilateral negotiations on trade remedy rules and engaged in promoting the improvement of the WTO anti-dumping rules. Recently, in 2017, China tabled in the WTO rules negotiations proposals aimed at strengthening WTO disciplines on transparency and due process and also giving special consideration to small and medium-sized enterprises (SMEs) in trade remedy proceedings.[18] China has also on many occasions expressed its view on the opposition against trade protectionism.

4 WTO Cases Involving China's Anti-Dumping Measures

4.1 Overview

Under the WTO dispute settlement system, disputes over trade remedies account for the largest proportion of all the cases. As China established its own anti-dumping regime, it has been normal that dispute cases were raised against certain anti-dumping measures by China in the WTO (Table 1). The rulings of Panels and Appellate Body in those cases could be to some extent seen as a kind of test of China's anti-dumping investigations.

The first case is *China – Fasteners (EU).*[19] The consultation request under the WTO dispute settlement mechanism was made by the EU in May 2010, on the provisional anti-dumping duties taken by China on certain iron or steel fasteners from the EU. In its consultation request, the EU also claimed that Article 56 of China's

---

[17] See, the First Instance Ruling by Beijing Second Intermediate People's Court, *VIZ-Stal Ltd (VIZ) v Ministry of Commerce of the People's Republic of China*, Case (2011) No. 240, http://www. bjcourt.gov.cn/cpws/paperView.htm?id=100208506100&n=1 (last accessed 30 April 2018). The First Instance Ruling by Beijing Second Intermediate People's Court, *OJSC Nobolipetsk Stell (NLMK) v. Ministry of Commerce of the People's Republic of China*, Case (2011) No. 241, http:// www.bjcourt.gov.cn/cpws/paperView.htm?id=100208505861&n=2 (last accessed 30 April 2018).

[18] See, e.g., Negotiating Group on Rules, Proposal on trade remedies, Submission by China, TN/ RL/GEN/185, 24 April 2017.

[19] Request for Consultation, *China – Provisional Anti-Dumping Duties on Certain Iron and Steel Fasteners from the European Union*, WT/407/1, 12 May 2010.

Table 1 WTO cases involving China's anti-dumping measures

Title	Number	Complaint	Year
China – Provisional Anti-Dumping Duties on Certain Iron and Steel Fasteners from the European Union	407	EU	2010
China – Countervailing and Anti-Dumping Duties on Grain Oriented Flat-rolled Electrical Steel from the United States	414	US	2010
China – Definitive Anti-Dumping Duties on X-Ray Security Inspection Equipment from the European Union	425	EU	2011
China – Anti-Dumping and Countervailing Duty Measures on Broiler Products from the United States	427	US	2011
China – Anti-Dumping and Countervailing Duties on Certain Automobiles from the United States	440	US	2012
China – Measures Imposing Anti-Dumping Duties on High-Performance Stainless Steel Seamless Tubes (HP-SSST) from Japan and the European Union[a]	454/460	Japan/EU	2012/2013
China – Anti-Dumping Measures on Imports of Cellulose Pulp from Canada	483	Canada	2014

Table created by the author

[a]See, Panel Reports, *China – Measures Imposing Anti Dumping Duties on High-Performance Stainless Steel Seamless Tubes (HP SSST) from Japan* and *China – Measures Imposing Anti-Dumping Duties on High-Performance Stainless Steel Seamless Tubes from the European Union*, WT/DS454/R and Add.1, WT/DS460/R, Add.1 and Corr.1, adopted 28 October 2015, as modified by Appellate Body Reports, WT/DS454/AB/R and WT/DS460/AB/R; Appellate Body Reports, *China – Measures Imposing Anti-Dumping Duties on High-Performance Stainless Steel Seamless Tubes from Japan/China – Measures Imposing Anti-Dumping Duties on High-Performance Stainless Steel Seamless Tubes from the European Union*, WT/DS454/AB/R and Add.1/WT/DS460/AB/R and Add.1, adopted 28 October 2015, DSR 2015:IV and V

Anti-Dumping Regulations[20] was inconsistent with GATT 1994, the Anti-Dumping Agreement and the Dispute Settlement Understanding (DSU). This was the first time that a trade remedy measure of China was brought to the WTO dispute settlement system. However, after consultations between China and the EU on the measure, the EU did not further pursue the litigation process and China's provisional anti-dumping measures on fasteners eventually became a final ultimate anti-dumping measure.

The second case is *China – GOES*.[21] This dispute was initiated by the U.S. in September 2010, against China's countervailing and anti-dumping duties on grain

---

[20]Article 56 of China's Anti-Dumping Regulations provides that *"where a country or region discriminatorily imposes anti-dumping measures on the exports from the People's Republic of China, China may, on the basis of actual situations, take corresponding measures against that country or region."*

[21]See, Appellate Body Report, *China – Countervailing and Anti-Dumping Duties on Grain Oriented Flat-Rolled Electrical Steel from the United States*, WT/DS414/AB/R, adopted 16 November 2012, DSR 2012:XII, p. 6251; Panel Report, *China – Countervailing and Anti-Dumping Duties on Grain Oriented Flat-Rolled Electrical Steel from the United States*, WT/DS414/R and Add.1, adopted 16 November 2012, upheld by Appellate Body Report WT/DS414/AB/R, DSR 2012:XII, p. 6369.

oriented flat-rolled electrical steel from the U.S. This was a quite comprehensive dispute covering a range of issues in the anti-dumping and countervailing duty investigations. In its Panel Request, the U.S. alleged a number of deficiencies of China's anti-dumping and countervailing duty measures, including the initiation of the investigation, treatment of confidential information, notification and transparency, use of facts available, price effects analysis, causation analysis, all others rates, etc. The Panel Report upheld certain claims by the U.S., particularly transparency issues, like non-confidential summaries and also the price effects analysis. However, the Panel rejected U.S.'s request on publication of the calculations used to determine the dumping margins. China appealed the Panel's findings afterwards in relation to MOFCOM's price effects analysis and the related disclosure of underlying facts. The Appellate Body upheld most of the Panel's findings. Later on, the arbitrator under Article 21.3(c) DSU determined that the "reasonable period of time" for China to implement the recommendations and rulings in this dispute is 8 months and 15 days. In January 2014, the U.S. initiated a compliance procedure under Article 21.5 of the DSU. The compliance Panel ruled in July 2015 that MOFCOM erred in price effects analysis. However, the anti-dumping measure on GOES expired before the circulation of the compliance Panel Report.

China – GOES is the first substantive case involving China's anti-dumping measures and the proceedings went through nearly every step of WTO litigation procedures. In the following cases, including *China – X-Ray Equipment*,[22] *China – Broiler Products*,[23] *China – Automobiles*,[24] and *China – Cellulose Pulp*,[25] China chose not to appeal and withdraw the measures after the Panels' rulings.

4.2   Some Horizontal Issues

It could be seen from Table 2 that certain issues appeared repeatedly in WTO litigations involving China's anti-dumping investigations. In the following paragraphs, some examples are addressed.

---

[22] See, Panel Report, *China – Definitive Anti-Dumping Duties on X-Ray Security Inspection Equipment from the European Union*, WT/DS425/R and Add.1, adopted 24 April 2013, DSR 2013:III, p. 659.

[23] See, Panel Report, *China – Anti-Dumping and Countervailing Duty Measures on Broiler Products from the United States*, WT/DS427/R and Add.1, adopted 25 September 2013, DSR 2013:IV, p. 1041; Panel Report, *China – Anti-Dumping and Countervailing Duty Measures on Broiler Products from the United States – Recourse to Article 21.5 of the DSU by the United States*, WT/DS427/RW and Add.1, adopted 28 February 2018.

[24] See, Panel Report, *China – Anti-Dumping and Countervailing Duties on Certain Automobiles from the United States*, WT/DS440/R and Add.1, adopted 18 June 2014, DSR 2014:VII, p. 2655.

[25] See, Panel Report, *China – Anti-Dumping Measures on Imports of Cellulose Pulp from Canada*, WT/DS483/R and Add.1, adopted 22 May 2017.

Table 2 Issues in WTO cases involving China's anti-dumping measures

Short title	Major issues
China – Fasteners	Article 56 of the *Anti-Dumping Regulations*, provisional duties
China – GOES	Initiation, price effects analysis, non-confidential summary, public notice, use of facts available, causation analysis
China – X-Ray Equipment	Price effects analysis, state of the domestic industry, causation analysis, non-confidential summary, disclosure of essential facts, public notice
China – Broiler Products	Non-confidential summary, disclosure of essential facts, calculation the cost of production
China – Automobiles	Non-confidential summary, disclosure of essential facts, all others rate, domestic industry definition, price effects analysis, causation analysis
China – HP-SSST	Use of data, adjustment and fair comparison, price effects analysis, causation and non-attribution analysis, non-confidential summary, disclosure of essential facts, all others rate, application of provisional measures
China – Cellulose Pulp	Volume of the dumped imports, price effect analysis, causation and non-attribution analysis, impact of the dumped imports

Table and summaries created by the author

4.2.1 Due Process and Transparency

The issues of due process and transparency have been raised most frequently in WTO trade remedy disputes, and also in cases involving China. Particularly, in a number of cases raised by the U.S., alleged deficiencies of transparency had been the most significant claims. For instance, in *China – GOES*, the U.S. claims that China did not provide sufficient non-confidential summary with respect to confidential information. However, in subsequent investigations, China made substantial improvements on the procedure issues, which lead to much fewer claims on this aspect. On the other side, it should also be mentioned that in several dispute rulings, the Panel and Appellate Body have imposed very high standard of notification requirements by the investigation authority. Those requirements pushed the authority to improve its process.

4.2.2 Price Effects Analyses

Article 3.2 of the Anti-Dumping Agreement provides that the investigation authorities shall *consider* whether there has been a significant price undercutting by the dumped imports or whether the effect of such imports is otherwise to a significant degree depress prices or prevent price increase. This obligation has not been subject to the review of Panels or the Appellate Body before *China – GOES*. However, in *China – GOES, China – X-Ray Equipment, China – Broiler Products, China – Automobiles, China – HP-SSST* and *China – Cellulose Pulp,* Panels and the Appellate Body seemed to have levied various burdens on the investigation authorities, including conducting detailed comparisons and taking into account whether dumped imports have *explanatory force* for the occurrence of depression or suppression. Moreover, there seems still not to be a clear and objective standard for determining price undercutting, price suppression or depression in the price effects analysis.[26]

4.2.3 All Others Rate

The Anti-Dumping Agreement provides that, when the authorities have limited their examination on certain investigated exporters or producers, they also have to calculate and apply anti-dumping duties on other known and unknown exporters or producers, i.e. all others rate or residual rates. In *China – GOES, China – Broiler Products, China – Automobiles* and *China – HP-SSST*, Panels found that China acted inconsistently with Article 6.8 and Annex II of the Anti-Dumping Agreement in applying facts available as the "all others" rate for the unknown exporters. However, either the Anti-Dumping Agreement or previous Panels did not provide any guidance as to how investigating authorities may determine the "all others" rate. It seems that WTO Members could consider to negotiate a common understanding on how to calculate "all others" rate for *unknown* exporters without resorting to use facts available (Table 2).

Though Panels found deficiencies in these six cases, these are just a small portion of China's anti-dumping measures. In the most recent case, i.e. *China – Cellulose Pulp*, the Panel dismissed most of Canada's claims, finding instead that to a large degree, MOFCOM's final determination, including the injury and causation analyses, complied with the requirements of the Anti-Dumping Agreement. It could be seen that anti-dumping cases filed by WTO Members have pushed forward the improvement of China's anti-dumping system. On the other hand, in fact, certain legal standards adopted by the Panel and the Appellate Body are also seemed to be difficult to attain by many trade remedy investigation agencies. This may require future multilateral negotiations on anti-dumping rules within the WTO to further clarify and improve the current disciplines.

Though a number of cases with respect to China's anti-dumping measures were filed under the WTO dispute settlement mechanism, China also at the same time raised quite a few trade remedy cases against the U.S. and the EU, including, for example, *US – Anti-Dumping and Countervailing Duties,*[27] *EC – Fasteners,*[28] *US – Countervailing Measures,*[29] *US – Anti-Dumping Methodologies (China).*[30]

---

[26] See Qin and Vandenbussche (2016).

[27] Appellate Body Report, *United States – Definitive Anti-Dumping and Countervailing Duties on Certain Products from China*, WT/DS379/AB/R, adopted 11 March 2011, DSR 2010:III.

[28] Appellate Body Report, *European Communities – Definitive Anti-Dumping Measures on Certain Iron or Steel Fasteners from China*, WT/DS397/AB/R, adopted 15 July 2011, DSR 2011:II.

[29] Appellate Body Report, *United States – Countervailing Duty Measures on Certain Products from China*, WT/DS437/AB/R, adopted 18 December 2014, DSR 2014:VIII.

[30] Appellate Body Report, *United States – Certain Methodologies and their Application to Anti-Dumping Proceedings Involving China*, WT/DS471/AB/R/Add.1, adopted 11 May 2017, DSR 2016:VII.

5   Concluding Remarks

After China's accession to the WTO, it has been an important step to build an anti-dumping system in accordance with the WTO rules and in the light of the practices of other WTO Members while drastically opening up the market. Since then, China has progressively become a frequent but modest user of anti-dumping measures and effectively protected domestic industries and markets.

China has established a relatively mature anti-dumping investigation system. In WTO dispute cases involving China's anti-dumping measures, China has conscientiously implemented the rulings of the Panel and the Appellate Body and continuously improved the investigation techniques in subsequent cases. In recent years, anti-dumping measures taken by China have been significantly reduced and the quality of anti-dumping investigations of China is on the rise. With the growth of China's economy, China has become the second largest importer in the world. The influence of China's anti-dumping measures will further increase.

References

Ciuriak D (2005) Anti-dumping at 100 years and counting: a Canadian perspective. World Econ 28(5):641–649
Qin JY, Vandenbussche H (2016) China-GOES (Article 21.5): time to clarify the standard for price suppression and price depression in AD/CVD investigations. World Trade Rev 16(2):203–226
Reich A (2003) Institutional and substantive reform of the anti-dumping and subsidy agreements – lessons from the Israeli experience. J World Trade 37(6):1037–1061

The Latest on the Best? Reflections on Trade Defence Regulation in EU-Vietnam FTA

Julien Chaisse and Dini Sejko

Contents

Abstract Vietnam is increasingly participating in the global economic integration as part of its strategy in transition into a free market economy, and has recently concluded the negotiations with the European Union (EU) on the EU-Vietnam Free Trade Agreement (EVFTA). The EVFTA is the first Vietnam concluded FTA that specifies obligations with particular emphasis on trade defence instruments. This article analyses the international, as well as Vietnamese legal framework in light of the trade commitments under the EVFTA trade defence instruments. The article examines the situation in Vietnam with regard to compliance both in law and

J. Chaisse (✉)
Faculty of Law, Chinese University of Hong Kong, Ma Liu Shui, Hong Kong
e-mail: julien.chaisse@cuhk.edu.hk

D. Sejko
Faculty of Law, Chinese University of Hong Kong, Ma Liu Shui, Hong Kong

SovereigNet, The Fletcher Network for Sovereign Wealth and Global, The Fletcher School, Tufts University, Medford, MA, USA
e-mail: dinisejko@link.cuhk.edu.hk

© Springer International Publishing AG, part of Springer Nature 2018   295
M. Bungenberg et al. (eds.), *The Future of Trade Defence Instruments*,
European Yearbook of International Economic Law,
https://doi.org/10.1007/978-3-319-95306-9_13

practice with commitments in the aspects of anti-dumping, subsidies and safe-guards. This article further identifies the main gaps, including enforcement issues and provides relevant recommendations on the necessary legal steps and timeframes (new acts, amendments or repeal of existing legal texts) to promote the consistency of the Vietnamese legal system with the EVFTA obligations. The analysis also assesses the impact on the Vietnamese legal system of specific parts of the EVFTA. In totality, the EVFTA rules, reviewed in this article, do not contain highly demanding norms which would be expected to affect a great number of domestic rules. Rather, the EVFTA contains soft commitments with limited implementation issues which suggest and support reforms in Vietnam with regards to trade defence, and indirectly, state-owned enterprises and competition law.

1 Introduction

Safeguard measures or trade remedies are used against dumping or subsidised products as measures implemented in support of existing industries under duress. It is important for World Trade Organization (WTO) law to decide at what point would such domestic measures turn into disguised and unlawful protectionism for most jurisdictions in the world. However, over the last few years, a number of Free Trade Agreements (FTAs) have been negotiated, with the aim of adding and/or clarifying a number of trade rules, for instance, with respect to trade defence regulation.

This article provides a first analysis of the European Union (EU) approach with regards to trade defence regulation in the context of one of its latest FTAs concluded with Vietnam.[1] The Chapter on Trade Remedies is divided into three sections: (a) Anti-Dumping and Countervailing Duties, (b) Global Safeguard Measures, and (c) Bilateral Safeguard Clause. The Chapter aims at promoting transparency and procedure during the investigation and judgement of trade remedies, but does not affect the rights and obligations of the EU and Vietnam in their implementation of relevant WTO agreements. In addition, no Party shall have recourse to dispute settlement under this Agreement for any matter arising under this section.[2] In that sense, WTO law remains highly relevant and the role of the WTO Dispute Settlement Body is still pivotal.

---

[1] This article analyses the EVFTA trade defence chapter and uses the full text without amendment issued following Legal Scrubbing in Preparation of 3rd Round, EU comments at 25 October 2016 which is used in the preparation of the report. Currently, EU is negotiating FTAs with several partners in Asia and America. On 8 December 2017, the Parties communicated the conclusion of the EU-Japan Economic Partnership Agreement (EPA).

[2] Chapter 3, Article 5 EVFTA (Exclusion from Dispute Settlement) reads: *"The provisions of this Section shall not be subject to Chapter 15 (Dispute Settlement)."*

As part of the strategy to transit into a market economy, Vietnam is increasingly participating in global economic integration and recently Vietnam is negotiating[3] or has already signed[4] several FTAs and more importantly has concluded the negotiations with the EU for the EU-Vietnam Free Trade Agreement (EVFTA). On this basis, this article assumes the EVFTA, which final text was approved in June 2018 after a long stage of legal scrubbing and ratification is now expected only in early 2019.[5] The EVFTA is the first FTA[6] that specifies obligations in the field of trade defences that Vietnam has concluded.

The EVFTA represents a paramount treaty of the new generation of FTAs concluded by the European Union as it includes some paradigmatic features and drafting that probably the EU is going to repeat in other agreements. Consequently, the EVFTA incorporates provisions on state-owned enterprises (SOEs) that clarify the EU position on the regulation of SOEs, as an alternative approach to the TPP model. In addition, the EVFTA contains provisions on trade and sustainable development, where the parties commit themselves to uphold internationally recognised labour standards,[7] the promotion of decent work conditions and internationally recognised and agreed instruments on corporate social responsibility. The trade and sustainable development chapter also includes commitments on environmental matters. The EVFTA also includes specific norms on the positive use of subsidies and, so far, is the only EU bilateral agreement where the recognition of the importance of subsidies to pursue a public objective, defined as a *"general goal to deliver an outcome in the overall public benefit"*, foregoes—at least in the form of a general statement—the acknowledgment of their potential distortive effects on the functioning of the market and trade liberalisation.[8]

This article analyses the international and Vietnamese legal framework in light of the trade commitments under the chapter on trade defence of the EVFTA. Only

---

[3] Vietnam is participating in the negotiations of the Regional Comprehensive Economic Partnership that is expected to have a chapter on trade remedies and chapter on competition. See Joint Leaders' Statement on the Negotiations for the Regional Comprehensive Economic Partnership (RCEP), RCEP: A vehicle for economic integration and inclusive development, http://asean.org/storage/2017/11/RCEP-Summit_Leaders-Joint-Statement-FINAL1.pdf (last accessed 30 April 2018).

[4] Vietnam also signed the Trans Pacific Partnership (TPP) in February 2016. The treaty, which did not yet enter into force because the United States withdrew, contains a chapter on trade remedies, a chapter on competition and a chapter on state-owned enterprises and reflect a similar, yet competing regulatory approach to the one used in new FTAs negotiated by the EU. The TPP-name has changed to Comprehensive and Progressive Agreement for Trans-Pacific Partnership (CPTPP) and the other remaining 11 members (including Vietnam) will incorporate a great part of the TPP provisions. See New Zealand Foreign Affairs & Trade, CPTPP vs TPP, https://www.mfat.govt.nz/en/trade/free-trade-agreements/agreements-under-negotiation/cptpp-2/tpp-and-cptpp-the-differences-explained/#remaining (last accessed 30 April 2018).

[5] Nguyen Huong, EVFTA ratification expected early next year, Vietnam Economic News, 30 July 2018, http://ven.vn/evfta-ratification-expected-early-next-year-34025.html (accessed 2 August 2018).

[6] See New Zealand Foreign Affairs & Trade, CPTPP vs TPP, https://www.mfat.govt.nz/en/trade/free-trade-agreements/agreements-under-negotiation/cptpp-2/tpp-and-cptpp-the-differences-explained/#remaining (last accessed 30 April 2018).

[7] EVFTA Chapter 15, Trade and Sustainable development.

[8] Borlini and Dordi (2016), p. 575.

Article 11 (Conditions and Limitations) and Article 14 (Use of the English Language) are left aside as they are self-explanatory provisions. In this regard, the article places emphasis on the situation in Vietnam with respect to compliance both in law and in practice with commitments in the fields of anti-dumping, subsidies, and safeguards, including specific timeframes to promote the implementation of the EVFTA commitments. This article further identifies the main gaps, including the terms of enforcement and provides relevant recommendations on the necessary legal steps and timeframe (including new acts and amendments or repeal of existing legal texts), to promote the consistency of the Vietnamese legal system with the EVFTA obligations. The analysis will provide also an assessment of the impact of each part of the EVFTA on the Vietnamese legal system.

In totality, the rules of the EVFTA which are reviewed in this article do not contain highly demanding norms, which would be expected to affect a great number of domestic rules. Rather, the EVFTA seems to suggest and supports reforms in Vietnam with regards to trade defence (and indirectly, SOEs and competition law). The EVFTA contains rather soft commitments with limited implementation issues, which explains why the present article will look at and emphasise the status of the ongoing reforms in Vietnam.

2   Drivers to the EVFTA Trade Defence Provisions

Vietnam joined the WTO on 11 January 2007 and since accession, the Government has worked to withdraw export subsidies in many sectors, including agro-products. However, pursuant to the WTO Agreement on Agriculture, Vietnam can still use two forms of export subsidies, which are permitted for developing countries with a view to reducing the marketing cost for exported agro-products and internal transport cost for exported goods.[9] Previous to the WTO accession, the Vietnamese Government has used different types of subsidies in a broad range of economic sectors. Since 1998, the Vietnamese Government developed programmes to offer different forms of subsidies: interest rate subsidy, export bonuses, support to produce fruit and vegetables and other forms of payment support for enterprises exporting rice, pork and coffee, to offset their losses. The forms of agricultural export subsidies were offset directly from the state budget. The inception of Vietnam's WTO membership was also based on the commitment to stop maintaining all kinds of subsidy forms for agro-exports. Consequently, Vietnam has terminated the above-mentioned subsidies before or at the moment of accession.[10] Resources have been transferred to supporting activities for trade promotion.

---

[9]WTO Agreement on Agriculture, Article 9.4. During the implementation period, developing country Members shall not be required to undertake commitments in respect of the export subsidies listed in subparagraphs (d) and (e) of paragraph 1 above, provided that these are not applied in a manner that would circumvent reduction commitments.

[10]A small portion of the subsidies issued prior to the WTO accession were terminated within 5 years after Viet Nam's accession to the WTO, see World Trade Organization, Report of the Working

The Vietnam Development Bank (VDB) was established on 1 July 2006 following a decision[11] by the Prime Minister and has played an important role in subsidies. The VDB is mandated to provide export credits, investment credit guarantees and export guarantee projects.[12] The average outstanding for export support was as high as 16.15 trillion VND in 2010, while interest paid by the enterprises who had export credit loans was only 1000 billion VND. In addition, borrowers could benefit from a favourable interest rate of 4% if they had medium and long-term contracts of loans at the VDB.[13] As estimated by banks, the total lending support was over 97 trillion VND, of which the interest subsidy for export credits occupied more than 65 trillion VND. In fact, the Vietnamese Government and agencies have not conducted any export guarantee programs. Export credits are only guaranteed by the banks and there is no discrimination among Vietnamese banks, credit institutions or branches of foreign banks, as promulgated by Circular No. 28/2012/TT-NHNN dated 3 October 2012.[14] There is no discrimination either on activities of export credits guarantee and support.

In order to achieve the objectives set out in the national socio-economic development strategy and particularly to support the national industrialisation, modernisation, and orientation toward the market economy, the Government approved the "National Energy Development Strategy 2020, with 2050 vision."[15] The decision sets out the strategy for the development of the national energy sector in line with the trend of international integration, by utilising efficiently the energy sources, exploiting rationally and taking advantage of external resources, for which it is necessary to create an effective cooperation in the energy sector regionally and internationally, as well as develop the economy in an independent and self-reliant manner. The decision initiated the abolition of subsidies in energy production and consumption and adjustment of the electricity pricing to reach the long-term marginal cost of the power system. The National Energy Development Strategy and the successive amendments create a more efficient energy market with a greater attention towards renewable energy sources. The Vietnamese Government has put in place subsidies

---

Party on the Accession of Viet Nam, Draft Notification Pursuant to Article XVI:1 of the GATT 1994 and Article 25 of the Agreement on Subsidies and Countervailing Measures, WT/ACC/VNM/42, 27 October 2006.

[11] Prime Minister Decision establishing the Vietnam Development Bank, No. 108/2006/QD-TTg, 19 May 2006.

[12] The organisation and operations of the VDB have been updated on 3 September 2015 following Prime Decision on approval of the Charter on Organization and Operation of the Vietnam Development Bank, No. 1515/QD-TTg, 3 September 2015.

[13] State Bank of Vietnam Circular detailing the implementation of interest rate support for individuals and organizations acquiring medium and long term loans from Vietnam Development Bank, No. 18/2010/TT-NHNN, 16 September 2010, Article 3.

[14] State Bank of Vietnam Circular Providing on Bank Guarantee, No. 28/2012/TT-NHNN, 3 October 2012; see also WTO Trade Policy Review Body, Report by the Secretariat on Viet Nam, WT/TPR/S/287, 13 August 2013, p. 63.

[15] Prime Minister Decision approving the National Energy Development Strategy of Vietnam for the period up to 2020 with outlook to 2050, No. 1855/QD-Ttg, 27 December 2007.

for renewable energy projects that include: preferential corporate tax rates, exemption from import tax on equipment and materials, accelerated depreciation rates, export credits and land rate exemptions used for projects that comply with Clean Development Mechanism of the Kyoto Protocol.[16] According to the Vietnam Power Development Plan VII which was revised in 2016,[17] the total investment capital required by the energy sector for the period from 2016 to 2030 shall be approximately 3,206,652 billion VND (around US$148 billion).[18] The Plan considers the amendment and removal of these subsidies and the termination of the monopoly held by Vietnam Electric Group (EVN) in energy distribution to develop a power market conducive to fair competition.[19] These decisions have generated the requirement of developing an energy market of fair competition and promoting a generation of new, recycled, biological and nuclear energy, to meet demands of the country's socio-economic development. Moreover, it is also important to accelerate the removal of energy supports, and role of dominance and monopoly in the energy sector, with a view to realise social policies by controlling the energy price. The Revised National Power Development Master Plan enhances the equitisation process of the power sector's SOEs which are under the management of EVN, PVN and Vinacomin.[20] The plan aims also to attract more foreign direct investment (FDI) capital for the development of power projects.

The Vietnamese Government has traditionally been supportive to the fishery and aquaculture sectors and deployed several measures to maintain and bolster activities in the sectors, as it represents an important share of the GDP.[21] The Government Decision No. 289/TQ-TTg, issued in March 2008 to address higher fuel prices, provided temporary support to a number of sectors, including fuel subsidies for fishing vessels.[22] Total spending on the programme was 1600 billion VND. The

---

[16] See Asian Development Bank (2015) pp. 101–102.

[17] Prime Minister Decision on the Approval of the Revised National Power Development Master Plan for the 2011–2020 Period with the Vision to 2030, No. 428/QD-TTg, 18 March 2016.

[18] For the period from 2016 to 2020, around US$40 billion are required, of which 75% will be used for power generation development and 25% for power network development. The amount of US$108 billion is required for period from 2021 to 2030 with a similar distribution for power generation and network development respectively. See Deutsche Gesellschaft für Internationale Zusammenarbeit (GIZ) GmbH, Vietnam Power Development Plan for the period 2011–2020, Highlights of the PDP 7 revised, http://gizenergy.org.vn/media/app/media/legal%20documents/GIZ_PDP%207%20rev_Mar%202016_Highlights_IS.pdf (last accessed 30 April 2018).

[19] See Prime Minister Decision approving the National Energy Development Strategy of Vietnam for the period up to 2020 with outlook to 2050, No. 1855/QD-Ttg, 27 December 2007 and Prime Minister Decision on the Approval of the Revised National Power Development Master Plan for the 2011–2020 Period with the Vision to 2030, No. 428/QD-TTg, 18 March 2016.

[20] Prime Minister Decision on the Approval of the Revised National Power Development Master Plan for the 2011–2020 Period with the Vision to 2030, No. 428/QDTTg, 18 March 2016.

[21] In 2012, fisheries contributed about 4.2% to GDP (down from 10–11% in 1990s but up from 3.7% in 2009) and in 2011, it accounted for 3.2% of total employment. See WTO Trade Policy Review Body, Report by the Secretariat on Vietnam, WT/TPR/S/287, 13 August 2013, p. 103.

[22] Government Decision providing temporary support to a number of sectors, including fuel subsidies for fishing vessels, No. 289/TQ-TTg, March 2008.

Government took a more comprehensive approach as part of a greater policy that aimed at the organisation of information for preventing natural maritime disasters, including a project to build an information system on the management of marine fisheries.[23] The first phase of this project started in 2009 to provide fishers and management agencies with weather and oceanographic information. The second phase, initiated in 2010, introduced a GPS-based vessel position monitoring system and a ship-to-shore communication system. The total amount required for the first phase was 92.42 billion VND, of which 34.8 billion VND was from the state budget, and for the 2006–2010 phase of the programme for fisheries ports, landing sites and fish markets, the Ministry of Fisheries (now the Ministry of Agriculture and Rural Development) allocated 1498 billion VND.[24] Support measures in the fish and aquaculture sector are sensitive since products such as catfish and shrimp have often been subject to antidumping measures by importing countries.

Vietnam has provided various subsidies, mainly in the form of tax incentives, e.g. to encourage research and development, important infrastructure development, support for enterprises operating in education, training, and healthcare sectors, support for business development in the geographically disadvantaged areas through the VDB, financial and business development institutions. In spite of the tax incentives programs, trade promotion activities remain limited, therefore, the supporting level is still much lower than the demand of Vietnamese enterprises.

The Vietnamese trade defence regulatory framework was set up prior to the accession to WTO,[25] comprising various laws and the establishment of a competition authority. The Vietnam Competition Administration Department (VCAD) is the body in charge for the use of trade remedies instruments: anti-dumping, anti-subsidy, and safeguard measures. The VCAD was established under the Ministry of Industry and Trade (MOIT) and plays an important role.[26] In the case of the EVFTA, the VCAD negotiated the Competition Policy Chapter of the agreement, including the rules on subsidies.[27]

The Vietnamese Government has not made great use of trade defence instruments, but on the other hand Vietnamese products have been the subject of approximately 100 trade remedy cases in foreign countries. In some of these cases, Vietnam

---

[23] Prime Minister Decision Approving the Scheme on organization of communication in service of prevention and combat of natural disasters at sea, No. 137/2007/QD-TTg, 21 August 2007.

[24] See WTO Trade Policy Review Body, Report by the Secretariat on Vietnam, WT/TPR/S/287, 13 August 2013.

[25] See generally LE Thi Thuy Van and Sarah Y. Tong, Vietnam and Anti-Dumping: Regulations, Applications and Responses, (2009) EAI Working Paper N 146.

[26] The structure, function, task and authority of VCAD are stipulated in the Government Decree on functions, duties, powers and organizational structure of Vietnam Competition Administration Department, No. 06/2006/ND-CP, 9 January 2006 and the Trade Ministry Decision regarding the establishment and regulation of functions, tasks and powers of companies under the management of competition, No. 27/2006/QD-BTM, 28 August 2006.

[27] See Borlini and Dordi (2016), p. 583 when discussing injury to trade and impairment to competition.

has also responded and lodged WTO claims.[28] In the past 2 or 3 years, the trend has changed and Vietnam has started to be more active in the use of trade defence instruments. Vietnamese authorities have taken anti-dumping and safeguard actions in six cases so far.[29] In four of those cases, the targeted products/exporters are from the EU.[30]

Vietnam's greater participation in international trade and the negotiation of more FTAs has triggered a series of reforms of domestic regulations, i.e. in 2016, the National Assembly promulgated the Law on Export and Import Duties 2016, which came into force in September 2016. The new law integrates the regulation for anti-dumping, countervailing and safeguard measures under one umbrella.[31]

3 Dumping and Subsidies Regulation

Article 1, Section 1 of the Trade Remedies Chapter of the EVFTA affirms the Parties' rights and obligations arising from Article VI of the GATT 1994, the WTO Agreement on Implementation of Article VI of the GATT 1994 and from the WTO Agreement on Subsidies and Countervailing Measures.[32] The EU and Vietnam, recognising that *anti-dumping and countervailing measures* can be abused to obstruct trade, agreed that trade remedies should be used in full compliance with the relevant WTO requirements, should be based on a fair and transparent system and that careful consideration should be given to the interests of the Party against whom such measure is to be imposed. In the EVFTA, both Parties agree to strengthen procedural fairness and transparency in the application of anti-dumping and countervailing duties.

---

[28] See, for instance, Panel Report, *United States – Anti-dumping Measures on Certain Shrimp from Viet Nam*, WT/DS404/R, adopted 1 February 2010.

[29] Tuan D, New legislation strengthens Vietnam's trade remedy rules: finance ministry, 11 October 2016 https://e.vnexpress.net/news/business/new-legislation-strengthens-vietnam-s-trade-remedy-rules-finance-ministry-3481478.html (last accessed 30 April 2018).

[30] Data available on European Commission, Actions against exports form the EU, Viet Nam, All products All instruments Any year, http://trade.ec.europa.eu/actions-against-eu-exporters/cases/index.cfm?scoun=VN&sprod=all&sinst=all&sinit=all&scinv=all&sstat=all&smeas=all&search=ok&c_order=stat&c_order_dir=Up (last accessed 30 April 2018).

[31] The Law on Export and Import Duties, No. 107/2016/QH13, 6 April 2016, repeals the old legislation, the Law on Export and Import Duties, No. 45/2005/QH11, 14 June 2005.

[32] Chapter 3, Article 1 EVFTA (General Provisions) reads: "*(1) The Parties affirm their rights and obligations under Article VI of GATT 1994, the Anti-Dumping Agreement, and the SCM Agreement. The Parties, recognising that anti-dumping and countervailing measures can be abused to obstruct trade, agree that: (2) trade remedies should be used in full compliance with the relevant WTO requirements and should be based on a fair and transparent system; and when a Party considers imposing such measures, careful consideration should be given to the interests of the other Party. For the purposes of this Section, origin shall be determined in accordance with Article 1 of the Agreement on Rules of Origin.*"

3.1   Transparency

Article 2, Section 1 of the Trade Remedies in the EVFTA provides for transparency. Accordingly, the EU and Vietnam agreed that trade remedies should be used in full compliance with the relevant WTO requirements and should be based on a fair and transparent system.[33] Both Parties shall ensure, immediately after any imposition of provisional measures and in any case before final determination is made, a full and meaningful disclosure of all essential facts and considerations which form the basis for the decision to apply measures. This is without prejudice to Article 6.5 of the WTO Agreement on Implementation of Article VI of GATT 1994[34] and Article 12.4 of the WTO Agreement on Subsidies and Countervailing Measures.[35] Disclosures shall be made in writing and allow interested parties sufficient time to make their comments.[36]

Vietnamese domestic law was already amended to comply with WTO requirements. Point a, Clause 2, Article 71 of the draft Law on Foreign Trade Administration provides that relevant parties in a case shall be entitled to present information and comments related to the investigation to the investigating authorities. Also in Clause 5, Article 71 on the Notification Obligation of the Investigating Authority, it is regulated that:

• Upon the MOIT Minister's decision to conduct the investigation, the investigating authorities shall be responsible for notifying the Government of the country whose enterprises and parties are related to the case of these investigations;

---

[33] Chapter 3, Article 2 EVFTA (Transparency) reads: "*[w]ithout prejudice to Article 6.5 of the Anti-Dumping Agreement and Article 12.4 of the SCM Agreement, the Parties shall ensure, immediately after any imposition of provisional measures and in any case before final determination is made, full and meaningful disclosure to interested parties of all essential facts and considerations which form the basis for the decision to apply measures. Disclosures shall be made in writing and allow interested parties sufficient time to make their comments. Provided it does not unnecessarily delay the conduct of the investigation, interested parties shall be granted the possibility to be heard in order to express their views during trade remedies investigations.*"

[34] Agreement on Implementation of Article VI of the General Agreement on Tariffs and Trade 1994, Article 6.5: "*Any information which is by nature confidential (for example, because its disclosure would be of significant competitive advantage to a competitor or because its disclosure would have a significantly adverse effect upon a person supplying the information or upon a person from whom that person acquired the information), or which is provided on a confidential basis by parties to an investigation shall, upon good cause shown, be treated as such by the authorities. Such information shall not be disclosed without specific permission of the party submitting it.*"

[35] Agreement on Subsidies and Countervailing Measures, Article 12.4: "*Any information which is by nature confidential (for example, because its disclosure would be of significant competitive advantage to a competitor or because its disclosure would have a significantly adverse effect upon a person supplying the information or upon a person from whom the supplier acquired the information), or which is provided on a confidential basis by parties to an investigation shall, upon good cause shown, be treated as such by the authorities. Such information shall not be disclosed without specific permission of the party submitting it.*"

[36] Chapter 3, Article 2 EVFTA (Transparency).

• Investigating authorities shall be in charge of disclosing the investigation decisions, preliminary and final findings of the investigation and approve the price
  commitment as well as termination of the investigation, to relevant parties;
• Investigating authorities shall implement other notification obligations in compliance with international treaties signed by Vietnam or the international organisations that Vietnam has joined.

More specifically, notification obligation of the investigating authorities are provided as follows: all relevant parties of the case shall be notified by the appropriate
methods, the final conclusion and the primary basis leading to such conclusion:

(i) anti-dumping cases are provided at Point a, Clause 3, Article 84 of the draft
    Law[37];
(ii) anti-subsidy cases are regulated at Point a, Clause 3, Article 92 of the draft
    Law[38];
(iii) the application of safeguard measures is defined at Point a, Clause 2, Article 98
    of the draft Law.[39]

The Chapter grants to the interested parties the possibility to be heard in order to
express their views during trade remedies investigations if it does not unnecessarily
delay the conduct of the investigation.[40]

3.2 Consideration of Public Interest

As provided by Chapter 3, Article 3.2.2 of the EVFTA, Parties with relevant interests should have opportunities for justification with a view to presenting their opinions during the investigation process of trade remedies, if this does not cause any
unnecessary delay to the progress of investigation. The EVFTA provides an additional element to the anti-dumping test which is not required by the WTO rules. This
rule makes it possible to consider the overall economic interest of the EU and
Vietnam, including the domestic industry producing the product concerned,

---

[37] See also the combined application of National Assembly Standing Committee Ordinance on
Antidumping, No. 08/2004/L-CTN, 12 May 2004 and Government Decree Setting Forth Detailed
Regulations and Guidance for Implementing a Number of Provision of the Ordinance on
Antidumping of Imports into Vietnam, No. 90/2005/ND-CP, 11 July 2005.

[38] See also National Assembly Standing Committee Ordinance on Anti-Subsidy for Imports into
Vietnam, No. 22/2004/PL-UBTVQH11, 20 August 2004.

[39] See also the combined application of Government Decree detailing the implementation of the
Ordinance on Safeguards in the Import of Foreign Goods into Vietnam, No. 150/2003/Nd-Cp, 8
December 2003 and Order on the Promulgation of the Ordinance on Safeguards in the Import of
Foreign Goods into Vietnam, No. 12/2002/L-Ctn, 25 May 2002.

[40] Chapter 3, Article 3.2.2 EVFTA: "*Provided it does not unnecessarily delay the conduct of the
investigation, interested parties shall be granted the possibility to be heard in order to express their
views during trade remedies investigations.*"

importers, Community industries that use the imported products and will ultimately pay a higher price and where relevant the end consumer of the product.[41] The public interest test is a feature of the EU anti-dumping system that allows to balance the interests of exporters, importers, users and consumers in a given market[42] and affects the application of the lesser duty rule as analysed in the following section.

3.3   Lesser Duty Rule

When applying a provisional anti-dumping or countervailing measure or before issuing the final decision, the Party shall fully disclose the rationale for such measure, which allows relevant interested stakeholders to have the chance to make their consultation, justification and feedback.[43] During the investigation, if there is evidence for the investigating authorities to conclude that it is not in the public interest to apply such measures (public interest shall take into account the situation of the domestic industry, importers and their representative associations, representative users and representative consumer organisations), competent authorities shall consider not using such measures. Furthermore, should a Party decide to impose any anti-dumping or countervailing duty, that Party shall endeavour to ensure that the amount of such duty shall not exceed the margin of dumping or countervailable subsidy and it should be less than the margin if such lesser duty would be adequate to remove the injury to the domestic industry.

The "lesser duty rule" derives from the WTO law which suggest that the anti-dumping duty applied in case of dumping should be less than the margin if such lesser duty would be adequate to remove the injury to the domestic industry.[44] The EU is one of the supporters of the lesser duty rule approach. Recently, the EU has adapted her approach, to better address unfair competition from significant market distortions due to raw material pricing,[45] however, the EU remains a supporter of the lesser duty rule because of its effectiveness and includes the approach in its FTAs.

The EVFTA requires that both sides shall also endeavour to apply the lesser duty rule by which the amount of duty imposed on imports should not exceed the duty

---

[41] Chapter 3, Article 3.3 EVFTA: "... *In determining the public interest, the Party shall take into account the situation of the domestic industry, importers and their representative associations, representative users and representative consumer organisations, based on the relevant information provided to the investigating authorities.*"

[42] Wening (2005).

[43] Chapter 3, Article 4 EVFTA (Lesser Duty Rule): "*An anti-dumping or countervailing duty imposed by a Party shall not exceed the margin of dumping or countervailable subsidy, and the Party shall endeavour to ensure that the amount of this duty is less than that margin if such lesser duty would be adequate to remove the injury to the domestic industry.*"

[44] Agreement on Implementation of Article VI of the General Agreement on Tariffs and Trade 1994, Article 9.1.

[45] European Commission, EU modernises its trade defence instruments, 23 January 2018, http://europa.eu/rapid/press-release_MEMO-18-396_en.htm (last accessed 30 April 2018).

necessary to remove the injurious element of dumping,[46] and consider the interest of upstream and downstream industries as public interest test before imposing the duties.

4   Safeguards

Regarding *global safeguard measures*, basically, both Parties observe the principles defined in the WTO (namely Article XIX of GATT 1994, the WTO Agreement on Safeguards (SG Agreement) and Article 5 of the WTO Agreement on Agriculture).[47] Provisions on transparency and fairness in the procedures are similar to the ones on anti-dumping and countervailing measures. It is noted that the EVFTA does not allow any Party to apply both global safeguard and bilateral safeguard measures with respect to the same good at the same time.

4.1   Transparency

The Party initiating a global safeguard investigation or intending to impose global safeguard measures shall provide, at the request of the other Party and provided that it has a substantial interest, immediately, ad hoc written notification of all pertinent information leading to the initiation of a global safeguard investigation, and as the case may be, the proposal to impose the global safeguard measures, including the provisional findings.[48]

---

[46] See Appellate Body Report, *European Communities – Definitive Anti-Dumping Measures on Certain Iron or Steel Fasteners from China*, WT/DS397/AB/R, adopted 15 July 2011, WT/DS397/AB/R, para. 336: "*Article 9.2 states that anti-dumping duties "shall be collected in the appropriate amounts in each case" and that "authorities shall name the supplier or suppliers of the product concerned.*" It is thus clear from the wording of this provision, which uses the auxiliary verb "shall", that the collection in appropriate amounts of anti-dumping duties and the naming of the supplier are of a mandatory nature. The mandatory nature of the first and second sentences of Article 9.2 can be contrasted with the preference expressed in the second sentence of Article 9.1 for duties lesser than the margin of dumping, if lesser duties are adequate to remove the injury to the domestic industry. To express such a preference, Article 9.1 uses the expression "*it is desirable*".

[47] Chapter 3, Article 6 EVFTA (General Provisions) reads: "*(1) The Parties affirm their rights and obligations under Article XIX of GATT 1994, the Safeguards Agreement and Article 5 of the Agreement on Agriculture. (2) A Party shall not apply with respect to the same good at the same time: (a) a bilateral safeguard measure under Section C (Bilateral Safeguard Clause) of this Chapter; and (b) a measure under Article XIX of GATT 1994 and the Safeguards Agreement. (3) For the purposes of this Section, origin shall be determined in accordance with Article 1 of the Agreement on Rules of Origin.*"

[48] Chapter 3, Article 7 EVFTA (Transparency) reads: "*Notwithstanding Article 3.6 (General Provisions), the Party initiating a global safeguard investigation or intending to impose global safeguard measures shall provide, at the request of the other Party and provided that it has a sub-*

How are the necessary facts to be gathered and analysed, and the required conclusions to be reached? The WTO practice requires the conduct of an investigation, by authorities of the importing Member, on the basis of domestic procedures that have been published previously. These procedures in turn must comply with procedural requirements of the SG Agreement and the conclusions reached in the investigation must reflect the substantive requirements of that Agreement. Typically, an investigation will start on the basis of a request by a domestic industry.

The EVFTA requirement in Article 3.7 should be transposed into the domestic law of Vietnam, preferably in a Decree to amend the Decree detailing the Implementation of the Ordinance on Safeguards in the Import of Foreign Goods into Vietnam.[49]

4.2 Definitions

A WTO member may take a "safeguard" action in the sense of Article XIX of GATT 1994 and the SG Agreement (i.e. temporarily suspend multilateral concessions) to protect a specific domestic industry from an increase in imports of any product which is causing, or which is threatening to cause, serious injury to the industry.[50] Safeguard measures are inherently different from anti-dumping and anti-subsidy measures. Safeguard actions do not allege unfairness but merely posit that a nation needs time to adapt to rapidly changing competitive conditions.[51] Safeguard

---

stantial interest, immediately ad hoc written notification of all pertinent information leading to the initiation of a global safeguard investigation and, as the case may be, the proposal to impose the global safeguard measures, including on the provisional findings, where relevant. This is without prejudice to Article 3.2 of the Safeguards Agreement. When imposing global safeguard measures, the Parties shall endeavour to impose them in a way that least affects bilateral trade. For the purposes of paragraph 2, if a Party considers that the legal requirements for the imposition of definitive safeguard measures are met, it shall notify the other Party and give the possibility to hold bilateral consultations. If no satisfactory solution has been reached within 30 days of the notification, the Party may adopt the definitive global safeguard measures. The possibility to hold consultations should be offered to the other Party in order to exchange views on the information referred to in paragraph 1."

[49] See the combined application of Government Decree detailing the Implementation of the Ordinance on Safeguards in the Import of Foreign Goods into Vietnam, No. 150/2003/Nd-Cp, 8 December 2003 and Order on the Promulgation of the Ordinance on Safeguards in the Import of Foreign Goods into Vietnam, No. 12/2002/L-Ctn, 7 June 2002.

[50] Chapter 3, Article 9 EVFTA (Definitions) reads: *"For the purposes of this Section: (a) "domestic industry" shall be understood in accordance with subparagraph 1(c) of Article 4 of the Safeguards Agreement. To that end, subparagraph 1(c) of Article 4 of the Safeguards Agreement is incorporated into and made part of this Agreement, mutatis mutandis; (b) "serious injury" and "threat of serious injury" shall be understood in accordance with subparagraphs 1(a) and 1(b) of Article 4 of the Safeguards Agreement. To that end, subparagraphs 1(a) and 1(b) of Article 4 of the Safeguards Agreement are incorporated into and made part of this Agreement, mutatis mutandis; (c) "transition period" means a period of 10 years from the entry into force of this Agreement."*

[51] Barfield (2005), p. 731.

measures were always available under the GATT Article XIX. However, prior to the entry into force of the SG Agreement, Article XIX-safeguards were relatively under-utilised, with many governments preferring to protect their industries through "grey area" measures, because there were no clear multilateral rules on safeguard measures. In particular, there was no requirement to pay compensation to affected trading partners, as was the rule for Article XIX measures. Grey area measures include "voluntary" export restraint arrangements, minimum pricing arrangements and other sorts of measures. These were frequently employed on products subject to chronic trade frictions, such as cars, steel and semiconductors. The WTO SG Agreement broke new grounds in prohibiting "grey area" measures and setting time limits ("sunset clause") on all safeguard actions.

4.3   Application of a Bilateral Safeguard Measure

The concept of "serious injury" is central to the use of safeguard measures[52] and is generally understood to mean something more severe than the "material injury" required for imposition of an anti-dumping or countervailing measure. The SG Agreement defines serious injury as a significant overall impairment in the position of the domestic industry. It defines a threat of serious injury as "an injury that is imminent" and requires that a determination of a threat of serious injury, "*be based on facts, and not merely on allegation, conjecture or remote possibility.*"[53] To make a finding of serious injury or threat thereof, the investigating authority must conduct a detailed examination of all relevant indicators pertaining to the state of the domestic industry (such as production, sales, employment, capacity utilisation and financial performance). The examination should cover a sufficiently long period for the investigating authority to be able to discern trends in the data. The end of the examined period must be recent in order to fulfil the requirement of a present or imminent and have the basis to apply a safeguard measure.

The "domestic industry" is defined as the domestic producers of products that are like, or directly in competition with, the imported product in question. Given that, for purposes of safeguards, the domestic industry is not limited to producers only of "like" products, but also can encompass producers of products that are directly in competition with the imported products, the admissible competitive effects for the application of a safeguard measure can be broader than those for application of an anti-dumping or countervailing measure. For purposes of the injury and causation analysis, the domestic industry can be defined as the producers as a whole, of the like products in direct competition or those producers collectively accounting for a major proportion of the total domestic production of those products.

---

[52] De Kok (2016).
[53] Agreement on Safeguards, Article 4.1(b).

The EVFTA also has provisions in the Bilateral Safeguard section, which entitles Vietnam or the EU to adopt safeguard measures during the transition period (namely the duration to liberalise trade relations between the Parties) of 10 years, if the imports surge, as the result of a reduction or elimination of a customs duty under this agreement, cause serious injury, or threat thereof, to the domestic industry.[54] This is a common mechanism in the FTAs and is considered as a "safety valve" to curb negative impacts on the domestic industry due to the trade liberalisation. The language of the provisions on the bilateral safeguard measures in the Agreement are prepared more strictly than the ones in the WTO SG Agreement, thus, limiting the abuse, ensuring transparency by allowing stakeholders to access necessary documents, at the same time, and have opportunities to be notified before the safeguard measure will be in force, as well as to conduct consultation after the measure takes effect. The safeguard measures should be adopted for a period of 2 years and, in necessary cases, they could be extended for 2 more years to prevent or overcome serious damage.

Vietnam legislation relating to safeguards includes the Ordinance on Safeguards approved in 2002[55] and a Government decree[56] that implements the ordinance establishing that the Ministry of Industry and Trade is competent authority in charge of safeguard investigations and the VCA may act on its behalf upon request by the Ministry.

The EVFTA also mentions Conditions and Limitations on the bilateral safeguard measures and specifies that the applying Party shall provide compensation through consultation. According to the provisions a safeguard investigation and the application of measures adopted shall follow the WTO rules.[57]

---

[54] Chapter 3, Article 10 EVFTA (Application of a Bilateral Safeguard Measure) reads: *"(1) If, as a result of the reduction or elimination of a customs duty under this Agreement, any good originating in the territory of a Party is being imported into the territory of the other Party in such increased quantities, in absolute terms or relative to domestic production, and under such conditions as to cause or threaten to cause serious injury to a domestic industry producing like or directly competitive goods, the importing Party may adopt measures provided for in paragraph 2 in accordance with the conditions and procedures laid down in this Section during the transition period only, except as otherwise provided for in subparagraph 5(c) of Article 3.11 (Conditions and Limitations). (2) The importing Party may impose a bilateral safeguard measure which: (a) suspends the further reduction of the rate of customs duty on the good concerned as provided for in Annex 2-A (Elimination of Customs Duties); or (b) increases the rate of customs duty on the good to a level which does not exceed the lesser of: (i) the most-favoured-nation applied rate of customs duty on the good in effect at the time the measure is taken; or (ii) the base rate of customs duty specified in the Schedules included in Annex 2-A (Elimination of Customs Duties) pursuant to Article 2.6 (Reduction or Elimination of Customs Duties on Imports)."*

[55] National Assembly Standing Committee Ordinance on Safeguards in Import of Foreign Goods into Vietnam, No. 42-2002-PL-UBTVQH10, 25 May 2002.

[56] Government Decree detailing the implementation of the ordinance on safeguards in the import of foreign goods into Vietnam, No. 150/2003/ND-CP, 8 December 2003.

[57] Chapter 3, Article 11.3 EVFTA.

4.4   Provisional Measures

EVFTA Article 12 allows for the application of a provisional safeguard measure, based on a preliminary determination that there is clear evidence that increased imports have caused or are threatening to cause serious injury.[58] Provisional measures are only allowed in critical circumstances, where a delay in applying a measure would cause harm that would be difficult to repair. Provisional measures can only take the form of tariff increases (that is, *not* quantitative restrictions or any other form) and any such increased tariffs are to be promptly refunded if the final determination of injury and causation is negative. Provisional measures can be in place for no more than 200 days and the period of application of any provisional measure has to be counted toward the total maximum duration of any ensuing definitive measure.

4.5   Compensation

Under the general rules of the GATT and as provided for in Article XIX, when a Member reduces or eliminates a negotiated concession, it must provide trade compensation to the exporting Members that would be affected, in order to preserve the overall balance of rights and obligations among Members.[59] Furthermore, where no

---

[58] Chapter 3, Article 12 EVFTA (Provisional Measures) reads: "*In critical circumstances where delay would cause damage that would be difficult to repair, a Party may apply a bilateral safeguard measure on a provisional basis pursuant to a preliminary determination that there is clear evidence that imports of an originating good from the other Party have increased as the result of the reduction or elimination of a customs duty under this Agreement, and that such imports cause serious injury, or threat thereof, to the domestic industry. The duration of any provisional measure shall not exceed 200 days, during which time the Party shall comply with the requirements of paragraphs 2 and 3 of Article 3.11 (Conditions and Limitations). The Party shall promptly refund any tariff increases if the investigation referred to in paragraph 2 of Article 3.11 (Conditions and Limitations) does not result in a finding that the requirements of paragraph 1 of Article 3.10 (Application of a Bilateral Safeguard Measure) are met. The duration of any provisional measure shall be counted as part of the period prescribed by subparagraph 5(b) of Article 3.11 (Conditions and Limitations).*"

[59] Chapter 3, Article 13 EVFTA (Compensation) reads: "*(1) A Party applying a bilateral safeguard measure shall consult with the other Party in order to mutually agree on appropriate trade-liberalising compensation in the form of concessions having substantially equivalent trade effects or equivalent to the value of the additional duties expected to result from the safeguard measure. The Party shall provide an opportunity for such consultations no later than 30 days after the application of the bilateral safeguard measure. (2) If the consultations under paragraph 1 do not result in an agreement on trade liberalising compensation within 30 days after the consultations begin, the Party whose goods are subject to the bilateral safeguard measure may suspend the application of concessions, with respect to originating goods of the Party applying the bilateral safeguard measure, which have trade effects substantially equivalent to the bilateral safeguard measure. The obligation to provide compensation, incumbent on the Party applying the bilateral safeguard measure, and the other Party's right to suspend concessions under this paragraph shall terminate on*

agreement can be reached on the level and other terms of compensation, the affected exporting Members have the right to take trade retaliatory measures, i.e. themselves to suspend "substantially equivalent concessions" in respect of the Member applying the safeguard measure, again with a view to preserving the overall balance of rights and obligations among Members. Thus, in principle, all safeguard measures should give rise to the obligation to pay compensation to and the right of retaliation by the affected exporters.

Experience under Article XIX of GATT 1947 proved, however, that the compensation/retaliation clause of Article XIX was a major reason for which the GATT Contracting Parties resorted to "grey area" measures in lieu of Article XIX safeguard measures.[60] In light of this experience, the Uruguay Round negotiators introduced provisions in the SG Agreement to soften Article XIX's compensation/retaliation provisions. In particular though, a Member proposing to apply a safeguard measure must, in every case, consult with the exporting Members that would be affected. In many cases, the right to retaliate cannot be exercised immediately by the exporting Members in the event that no agreement is reached on compensation. In particular, where the findings of increased imports is based on an absolute increase (i.e. it is not just relative to domestic production), the affected exporting Members cannot exercise their right to retaliate for the first 3 years of application of the measure.

5   Conclusion

This article examined existing legislation and procedures in Vietnam on trade defence measures, for compliance with the relevant three chapters of the EVFTA. Overall, the three chapters of the EVFTA which are reviewed in this article do not contain highly demanding norms which would be expected to affect a great number of domestic rules. Rather, the EVFTA seems to suggest and supports reforms in Vietnam with regard to SOEs, competition and trade defence. The EVFTA rules are rather soft commitments with limited implementation issues which explains that the present article emphasises the status of the ongoing reforms in Vietnam and the needs to carefully support and encourage it with specific actions. Vietnam has recently carried out important work in law and practice to better meet the requirements of the WTO.

The trade defence regulations in the EVFTA (and its necessary implementation by Vietnam) also reveals the importance of some related issues such as the regulation of SOEs and competition. Trade defence instruments, only address a portion of

---

the same date as the bilateral safeguard measure terminates. (3) The right of suspension referred to in paragraph 2 shall not be exercised for the first 24 months during which a bilateral safeguard measure is in effect, provided that the safeguard measure conforms to the provisions of this Agreement."
[60] See generally Piérola (2014).

potential market distortive effects. It would be insufficient to regulate trade defence instruments if, at the same time, SOEs remain uncontrolled in their operations and impact on competition were not addressed by the same FTA. This is precisely why the EVFTA is ground-breaking. Although the pure trade defence regulation is rather modest, it is combined to a number of rules that simultaneously address SOEs and competition in a more comprehensive manner.

SOEs' commitments and the Chapter on SOEs are new to Vietnam too. In WTO law, there is no specific regulation of the activities of SOEs.[61] In addition, only two FTAs to which Vietnam is part (through ASEAN) incorporate provisions on competition, namely ASEAN-Australia and New Zealand[62] and ASEAN-China.[63] However, these two FTAs do not reach the depth of EVFTA in terms of SOE and competition regulation. Therefore, the EVFTA represents a benchmark also for Vietnam with regard to the regulation of SOEs. There is a chapter on competition disciplines in few Vietnam FTAs. In these FTAs with investment chapters, the commitments made by Vietnam are based on the principles: (1) The Parties recognise the importance of the adoption of national competition legislation to ensure the benefits of trade liberalisation and not to be distorted by anti-competitive conducts/transactions, and (2) The Parties shall maintain competition legislation to effectively eliminate agreements, decisions, concerted practices and abuses by one or more enterprises of a dominant position, which have as their objective or effect the prevention, restriction or distortion of competition and control concentrations between enterprises which would significantly impede effective competition. The objective of the Competition Chapter in the EVFTA is to ensure fair competition framework in trade and investment relations between the Parties, diminish and eliminate anticompetitive conducts, with the view to promote economic efficiency and consumer welfare. Generally, the commitments in the Competition Chapter of the EVFTA are consistent with the existing provisions of Vietnam legislation.

This is the sum of all these innovations that makes the EVFTA a ground-breaking FTA which has the potential to become a benchmark for all future EU FTA negotiations, with regards to trade defence and related disciplines. The EVFTA ratification and adaptation process requires the full involvement of all stakeholders since it implies structural and irreversible changes to the Vietnamese institutional setting and socioeconomic model, and the setting-up of a new model of industrial relations inspired by internationally agreed and recognised standards.

---

[61] GATT Article XVII regulating state trading enterprises, see Chaisse (2016) and Chaisse and Matsushita (2013).

[62] The AANZFTA was signed on 27 February entered into force on 10 January 2010.

[63] The ASEAN-China FTA entered into force on 1 July 2007.

References

Asian Development Bank (2015) Renewable energy developments and potential in the greater Mekong subregion. Asian Development Bank, Metro Manila

Barfield C (2005) Anti-dumping reform: time to go back to basics. World Econ 28(5):719–737

Borlini L, Dordi C (2016) Deepening international systems of subsidy control: the (different) legal regimes of subsidies in the EU bilateral preferential trade agreements. Columbia J Eur Law 23(3):551–606

Chaisse J (2016) Untangling the triangle – issues for state-controlled entities in trade, investment and competition law. In: Chaisse J, Lin TY (eds) International economic law and governance – essays in honour of Mitsuo Matsushita. Oxford University Press, Oxford

Chaisse J, Matsushita M (2013) Maintaining the WTO's supremacy in the international trade order, A proposal to refine and revise the role of the Trade Policy Review Mechanism. J Int Econ Law 16(1):9–36

De Kok J (2016) The future of EU trade defence investigations against imports from China. J Int Econ Law 19(2):515–547

Le TTV, Tong SY (2009) Vietnam and antidumping: regulations, applications and responses. EAI working paper no. 146

Piérola F (2014) The challenge of safeguards in the WTO. Cambridge University Press, Cambridge

Wening H (2005) The European Community's anti-dumping system: salient features. J World Trade 39(4):787–794

WTO Trade Policy Review Body, Report by the Secretariat on Vietnam, WT/TPR/S/287, 13 August 2013

Printed by Printforce, the Netherlands